SCHUMANN

SCHUMANN

A SYMPOSIUM

edited by

GERALD ABRAHAM

GREENWOOD PRESS, PUBLISHERS
WESTPORT, CONNECTICUT

Library of Congress Cataloging in Publication Data
Abraham, Gerald Ernest Heal, 1904-
    Schumann : a symposium.

    Reprint of the 1952 ed. published by Oxford University
Press, London.
    CONTENTS: Reich, W. Schumann the man.--Dale, K. The
piano music.--Cooper, M. The songs.--Dickinson, A. E. F.
The chamber music. [etc.]
    1. Schumann, Robert Alexander, 1810-1856.
2. Composers--Germany--Biography.
[ML410.S4A6317 1977]   780'.92'4 [B]   77-8051
ISBN 0-8371-9050-9

Originally published in 1952 by Oxford University Press,
London, New York

This reprint has been authorized by Oxford University Press.

Reprinted in 1977 by Greenwood Press, Inc.

Library of Congress catalog card number   77-8051

ISBN 0-8371-9050-9

Printed in the United States of America

PREFACE

OF the familiar nineteenth-century masters, none has had more fresh light thrown on his life and work during the last twenty-five or thirty years than Robert Schumann. The statement may surprise English readers, who have perceived very little of that light and who are probably quite unaware of the backward state of Schumann studies in this country. Even Niecks, in the valuable biographical study published posthumously in 1925, confesses that he had used only the third edition of Wasielewski's basic book, although the much larger and more important fourth edition had appeared as early as 1906; the English translation of Wasielewski, too, is based on that 1880 edition. Similarly, the second (1904) edition of Gustav Jansen's *Briefe von Robert Schumann : Neue Folge* is considerably fuller than the first, from which the English translation (*The Life of Robert Schumann told in his Letters*) was made. Only the English version (1913) of Litzmann's big biography of Clara Schumann, with its quantities of fresh biographical material about Robert, helped to bring the English reader's knowledge of Schumann's life more up-to-date. It is characteristic that, while Eugenie Schumann's *Memoirs* have been translated, her *Lebensbild meines Vaters* has not.

The first comparatively modern study which deepened our knowledge and understanding of Schumann's music was Viktor Ernst Wolff's *Robert Schumanns Lieder in ersten und späteren Fassungen*, which appeared in 1914 and perhaps escaped much notice in this country on account of the war. Wolff studied and compared the original versions of the songs—that is to say, the fair copies of the original versions—but he did not have access to the sketches. The earliest Schumann sketches to be published in any quantity came out in 1924: the annotated facsimile of the complete *Album für die Jugend*. Three years later Professor Willibald Gurlitt read a paper comparing Schumann's sketches with Beethoven's at the Beethoven Centennial Congress in Vienna, but the first detailed information concerning Schumann's sketches (for his early piano works) and concerning the unpublished sets of variations, &c., was given in Wolfgang Gertler's *Robert Schumann in seinen frühen Klavierwerken* and Werner Schwarz's *Robert Schumann und die Variation* (1931 and 1932 respectively); a year or so later Karl Geiringer brought out the early four-hand *Polonaises* and six of the early set of songs, Op. II.

But all these publications were overshadowed in importance by the publications of Wolfgang Boetticher ten years later: the two big books described by Dr. Reich in the first chapter of the present volume and various shorter studies contributed to the periodical *Die Musik*. Boetticher had access not only to practically all Schumann's sketches for his compositions in every genre and to the manuscripts of unpublished works; he was also able to study a vast quantity of unpublished Schumann letters and diaries and other literary remains; his contribution to our knowledge of both Schumann's music and his intimate life is therefore enormous. It is not the least valuable feature of the present volume that it draws heavily, though of course by no means exhaustively, on these new sources of information and for the first time makes them available to the English reader.

Owing to the activities of the Royal Air Force, Boetticher's books are rather rare even in Germany—particularly the more important of them, the *Einführung in Persönlichkeit und Werk*—and I am deeply indebted to Dr. Eberhard Borsche, of Hildesheim, for his prolonged loan of a precious copy. I am also heavily indebted to Dr. Georg Eismann, Curator of the Robert-Schumann Museum at Zwickau, for the gift of materials and for much helpful information, and to Mr. Frank Walker and Mr. Hyatt King for assistance on a number of bibliographical points.

G. A.

Spring 1951.

CONTENTS

CHAPTER I

SCHUMANN THE MAN

By WILLI REICH

THE main traits of Schumann's personality have often been drawn for the English-reading public both in translations of his letters and other writings and in several good English biographies. As they are well known and as the most essential dates of his life are given in the Chronology on p. 300, it seems hardly necessary to repeat in a short 'biographical sketch' things that have often been said before. I have preferred therefore to put before the reader *new* biographical material, published in Germany during the war of 1939–45 but for the most part in such a small edition that it attracted insufficient attention even in the land of its origin, while to most people in the English-speaking countries it has probably remained completely unknown. This new material completes the picture of 'Schumann the man' in many essential respects and a selection of its most important points seems to me of greater value than a more or less original rearrangement of facts already well known.

The material I have used is drawn from two volumes published by Wolfgang Boetticher in Berlin in 1942. The first is entitled *Robert Schumann in seinen Schriften und Briefen*, a volume in the series 'Klassiker der Tonkunst in ihren Schriften und Briefen'—soon afterwards discontinued. Its 516 pages, richly illustrated, are addressed to the wider musical public and seek by a skilful mixture of generous quotations from Schumann's letters and writings, linked by Dr. Boetticher's brief commentaries, to give a comprehensive picture of Schumann's life and intellectual personality. The more formidable second volume, with its 688 pages, comparable in size and format with a volume of the *Encyclopedia Britannica*, conceals behind its modest title, *Robert Schumann: Einführung in Persönlichkeit und Werk*, a typical German doctorate-dissertation, overloaded with material and footnote references and written in an academic style calculated to defeat the ordinary reader. Dr. Boetticher's main object was to apply to Schumann's work recent theories of the expressive symbolism of music. His two hundred or so pages of fresh biographical material serve first and foremost as the basis of his aesthetic speculations. Moreover, his commentaries on this material, which hardly serve to make his book more readable, are written from the point of view of Nazi ideology and bristle with anti-Semitism. It is deeply regrettable that such a work—invaluable as a collection of materials—should have been officially published by the German 'Robert Schumann Gesellschaft' 'to commemorate the 130th anniversary of Schumann's birth'. A shortened and 'purified' edition of this gigantic work seems highly desirable.

Some idea of the riches on which Dr. Boetticher was able to draw, thanks to the co-operation of the Schumann Museum at Zwickau and other collections, may be gathered from the fact that he was able to use something like two hundred of Schumann's hitherto unpublished literary and musical papers, including more than twenty diaries from the period 1827–52, one hundred and seventy unknown letters from Robert to Clara, and similar documents of equal value.

Let us begin with the 'Oldest musical recollections' (probably written in 1828):

Free improvisation, many hours daily. 1823: fortunate conditions for educating myself extra-musically. Love for the open air, for nature. Love of travel. Longing for the distant. Relationship to literature. German language. Reading, the German classics. Memory. Strongest in free improvisation. Infectious fire of my performance. Complete lack of guidance perceptible. Morbid longing for music and piano-playing, if I had not played for a long time. Enthusiasm for Jean Paul. Acceptance of music generally in Jean Paul's sense as a consoler in lonely hours. Mozart, Haydn, Beethoven.—Complete lack of ear, technique in particular, theory.—Mozart's operas.—Italian music found no favour. Higher impressions 1827: taking up of the youth by his elders.

In another passage ('Materials for a *curriculum vitae*') we read:

Easter 1828: Night ecstasies. Constant free improvisation daily. Also literary fantasies in Jean Paul's manner.—Particular enthusiasm for Schubert, also Beethoven, Bach less.—*Letter to Franz Schubert* (not sent). —Beginnings of shallow virtuosity (Herz, Czerny).—On the other hand also appearance of Paganini.—My rejection of that school and frequent disputes with Wieck.

On the last page of a note-book entitled *Hottentottiana* occurs (probably in the year 1832) the following characterisation of a certain 'Sch.'—and we may take it with absolute certainty that by 'Sch.' he meant either himself or a character embodying himself in one of his writings:

Without defining the limits of human greatness, I would not count Sch. among the quite ordinary men. Talent for many things and not personal peculiarities mark him out from the mass.—His temperament (melancholic).—His [artistic] sense expresses itself as a gift for feeling rather than a gift for contemplating, therefore more subjective than objective in judgments and in production. The feeling stronger than the effort. His understanding less reflection than surrender of feelings, more theoretical than practical reason (?).—Power of imagination strong, not very active (contradicts itself), *needing external excitement*. *Memory* and power of recollection passable.—Acuteness; feeling for art. Not very witty. Man of feeling rather than understanding. More suited to artistic activity than to speculation—excellent at music and poetry—not musical genius.— His talent as musician and writer stands on same level—with perseverance. Jean Paul has exercised a great deal of influence on him—unusual literary knowledge of all branches of science—much knowledge of books— taste and understanding in his judgment—as *man*—characterised by: firmness of purpose, free-and-easiness, strength of mind, amiability, artistic talent, where he wishes to please, he pleases, sharp with the stronger, he is proud with the weaker, often teases them, but knows how to win them easily back again.—*He is not a genius*, to plunge into life is foreign to him, he spins his fancies all the more in quiet.—He is never embarrassed and knows how to adapt every situation to his personality.—Fine tact, Attic jest, unceremoniousness, apparent look of circumspection, ease in execution.—From intercourse with the finer world he draws *pride*.—He has no self-conceit.—The pleasant element in his judgment is not to be misunderstood.

He loves purely and holily, he has loved much, nobly and divinely. He knows he pleases girls. *To be the first* is innate in him.—Gives himself the appearance of not wishing to do things. The earth is no pleasure garden for him, rather a holy temple of Nature. He is religious without religion. He neither loves man nor fears destiny. . . .

The importance of diary-keeping to Schumann is shown by the following entry from the year 1828:

Thou good, good Hottentottiana, who mirrorest all the Good Fridays and all the Easters and Pentecosts of my soul—thou wilt dry many a tear that will want to flow.—*Thou art written for no man, only for me and my solitary, happy, deeply-felt evenings.* Whosoever reads thee, be he mild and humane like Jean Paul, there are all my happy tears faithfully represented, as faithfully and frankly as my whole heart stands open to the world and to all men. Ah, I have been often sad, absolutely downcast and crushed; then I flew to thee and my soul wept no more because it was able to speak.

As early as 1831 there appear in the diary the figures of Florestan and Eusebius who were to play so great a role in the later 'David Club' time and which there represented the two sides of Schumann's nature.[1] At first their conversations are more generally philosophical and mystical than musical in nature and clearly reveal their origin in the world of E. T. A. Hoffmann. Consider, for example, the following quotation:

Florestan considered men exercised great influence on each other; great (moral) minds must have it in their power to be able to sway any company to their own mood and to guide other minds.—Eusebius replied . . . he had often tried to think himself entirely into the being of some other man, whom perhaps he was sitting opposite without their looking at each other, and with all the power of his soul to branch himself out into the other . . . in many cases, however, he had not succeeded.

The 'battle for Clara' so dramatically depicted in the first volume of Berthold Litzmann's well-known *Clara Schumann* is in many respects depicted more forcibly by newly published letters. I give here a few specimens from letters which are specially characteristic of Schumann the man:

Leipzig, 7 October 1837: Today again I can think of nothing but you or your father, who is showing himself so harsh. Like you I keep springing from laughter to crying. What a fearful night, the last one. How my head burned, how my fancy led me from cliff to cliff from which I constantly threatened to fall. I reproach myself for my discontent. After all, I have the word of a noble and determined girl . . . I am weaker than I had thought. . . .

Leipzig, 11 October 1837: You should get a letter from me today. Some things in it must have hurt you, and so rather read it later . . . later when time has calmed us both. You have, in many of the things you have said, invited me to brood over myself.—Where am I to begin? If I still thought you knew me, accepted the whole man with his faults and what is good in me, I should still think you loved me.—And a *lie* they have told you about me, so small and vulgar that I can't answer you at all, decides you—to speak—just now, a day after you promised me everything, assured me everything.—It looks so cold, what I have written, and yet it is so. . . . Not long ago you said I should be better if I could stay alone, keep away from others,—but I can bury myself thoroughly, bury myself thoroughly in sorrow.—You are right: I don't *deserve* you, but you ought not on that account to hurt, to bewilder me about myself, to make a man, melancholy to the point of illness, who has already suffered so much about

[1] They were originally conceived as characters in a novel; see page 10.—*Ed.*

you, still more timid. Don't abandon me. I cling to you, if you yield, it's all over with me. . . .

A diary-entry shortly afterwards shows complete ease of mind:

14 October 1837: How Clara's letter divinely uplifted me to strength and work. *The new life begins.* . . .

In February 1838 we learn from letters and diaries something of the intense creative activity of this period.

12 February to Clara from Leipzig: I've made a concert on you—even if it didn't tell you this, this single heart's cry for you, since at the end you didn't find that your theme cropped up in all possible shapes (forgive me, the composer speaks).

On the same day in the diary:

Composed several little things nicely. Up to Saturday, the 17th, composed *Kinderscenen.* . . . 24 February: Composed the little thing *Träumerei.* . . . Sunday, 25 February: My girl makes me so happy. . . .

The following passage from a letter refers to the news given him by Clara that his former *fiancée*, Ernestine von Fricken, had married:

Vienna, 24 January 1839: Now I am exculpated in everything and quite free and belong to no one but her whom I love above all. Only don't leave me, stay true to me; *otherwise I shall make a deep cut in my life, to bring it to rest.* Forgive all the gloomy thoughts today, the bad dreams too come to me from God. . . .

The failure of his attempts to move to Vienna and publish his musical paper there led Schumann to think of settling in England. He writes of this project to Clara on 20 February 1839:

Have you the courage to go with me to *England*? Only don't be alarmed by rash questions, my Clara. If I could only talk over everything with you for an hour or so. . . . If I gave 3–4 lessons a day, I should still have plenty of time left for composition; I should then belong entirely to music again. I know it's hazardous but it is also certain that if we were industrious for four years we should be safe for all time. Perhaps through Bennett, who has great influence, I shall manage to get a teaching post at the Academy. . . . London would be the grandest thing that we could get hold of; and we should be in a centre of artistic activity. . . .

A terrible picture of Schumann's spiritual condition is given by the following letter to Clara:

Leipzig, 8 June 1839: Today I entered my twenty-ninth year, *perhaps already the greater half of my life lies behind me.* Anyhow I shall not grow very old, as I well know. My great emotions have raged in me and anxiety on your account has wasted me too. But it is you too who will bring me peace and healing. I am not sorrowful today. How could I be. Heaven has preserved me from want and blessed me with intellectual powers. Nothing is needed for my happiness but domestic peace, tranquillity and security. . . .

In July 1839 the battle with Friedrich Wieck reached its final stage; the following letter bears witness to the fearful excitement into which Schumann was thrown by the approach of the threatened lawsuit:

Leipzig, 7 July 1839: *Ah, Clara, the man will yet put me under the ground —You will see.* . . . I can write you little good about myself; I am constantly so unwell that I often fear I shan't live to hear the legal decision. If you are near me, I shall be quite well again. My head is often so heavy, I struggle to work industriously, to compose what lies in my powers—but can't tear myself out of my gloomy brooding. But you mustn't call me weak on that account, only unstrung—I myself don't know. . . . And forgive this flat and morbid letter, I feel so weak in my whole body— trembling, anxiety, fearful oppressions, hot tears. . . .

Schumann found his sole consolation in creative activity:

Leipzig, 12 February 1840: Dear Clara, I am very industrious at the piano; there you always appear to me most beautifully. Besides, I'm happy when I can compose and forget for hours at a time the wicked man who is poisoning my life. . . . When I wake up, I often ask myself: 'Did all this happen to *you*, then?' Then I fall back into melancholy again. Well: let's leave that and don't talk about it. . . .

After their meeting in April:

Leipzig, 2 May 1840: Your head is probably just like mine, full of all the great happiness we enjoyed together. . . . I am not yet tranquil. . . . And I have music in me, so that I'd like to sing the whole day. Above all, however, I want to write the songs down. . . .

And from immediately before the wedding (12 September 1840) date two moving letters, the first from Robert to Clara:

Leipzig, 29 August 1840: I have two things at heart that I must say to you before the eternal Yes, my Clara.—You said not long ago in jest: 'You know my . . . tendency to jealousy'. . . . But I know very well your reproach was aimed at me on account of Verhulst.—Now listen. . . . I know Verhulst really loves you. As many love you, whom I myself love on that account. But let me tell you frankly—it often seems to me that Verhulst often speaks of you too familiarly.—This disturbed me. Verhulst is not such a great artist that he can praise or blame you without ceremony, just as he likes. He must keep a certain distance; besides he is young and has done nothing to earn . . . a ten years' immortality. All this together with a vanity that has come over him since his concert and of which I've sometimes wanted to cure him for his own sake . . . all this has probably combined to make me behave stupidly when we have been together. My annoyance went no further than that; for I have always liked his . . . sound qualities and his straightforward nature. But now I don't want you to be afraid of the future and take me for an Othello at heart. . . . If there are others of whom I might be jealous in the future, name them to me, so that you shan't be too proud in your belief in my jealousy.

The other thing . . . we have several times had downright quarrels, and that was good. But when next day, or a few hours later, I've wanted to explain everything quietly to you, you have flared up again and so violently that I have often been frightened. Clärchen, you must get out of that habit: one can't keep going over old squabbles. . . .

And since I'm in the vein . . . here is a *third* plea before the wedding: I've told you what I'm afraid of in you; now tell me what you find wrong in me. I want to reform myself. . . .

To which Clara replied from Erfurt on 3 September:

Your third plea, my beloved Robert, I cannot grant. I cannot think of anything at all that I find wrong in you, but if I do I will tell you frankly as I have already done several times. And then I'd rather not do it in writing for I don't always find the right way of putting it. That sort of thing can always be said so much more gently than written— don't you think so, too? . . . If it absolutely must be *before* the wedding, let's have a really good squabble. . . . Otherwise enough of that! As for Verhulst, let's forget all about him. . . .

Schumann's views on music and musicians are already fairly well known from his published writings and his letters, but the new material gives us a good deal of further interesting information. First of all let me quote a few autobiographical notes and diary-entries from the period 1830–40 concerning Bach, Mozart, Beethoven, and Schubert:

In 1831 I at last began a regular course of composition under Heinrich Dorn, an extremely sagacious and gifted man. About this time, too, my first compositions appeared in print; they are too small and rhapsodic to make much fuss about. But the Toccata, Intermezzi Op. 4, show more serious effort. Most of the time I constantly occupied myself with Bach, under whose influence there came into existence the Impromptus, Op. 5, which may be regarded as nothing but a new form of varying.

1832: Let only Mozart and Bach always be your models in form, treatment, motives and artistic poise (*Kunstruhe*). . . . This giant (Bach) holds in his hand the magic wand with which he conjures up a thousand new thoughts.

1832: Johann Sebastian Bach has done everything completely; he was a man through and through.

About 1832 Schumann copied out a quotation from Miltitz for his collection of mottos: 'I believe that the more imagination an artist has, the more he is an artist; the more reflection, so much the less is he one'. Some fifteen years later (about 1846) Schumann added the words: 'Then Bach must have been a bad character!'

Schumann's early view of Beethoven is characterized by the opinion—shared by Arnold Schering in our own day—that Beethoven composed his instrumental works on the bases of secret literary programmes:

1832: I said to Wieck, men were accustomed to find in music either cheerfulness or pain (sadness), especially in the general sense. Conditions, passionate moments go uncomprehended, even despised, by the less finely cultured. I demonstrate this with Schubert and Beethoven.—Why should there be no operas without text; that would certainly be dramatic. There is plenty for you in *Shakespeare*!

1832: The more special a music is, the more individual pictures it spreads before the hearer, the more it embraces and the more lasting it will be for all times. Such special traits are particularly common to Beethoven and Franz Schubert. . . . Time and taste may take what direction they will, there will always be such men just as there will always be those who read Jean Paul.

1834 (in a letter of 29 April to Theodor Mundt): It is precisely from music that philosophers could learn that it is possible to say the profoundest things in the world while preserving the appearance of frivolous youthful levity; for that is just what music does when, pretending to be a playing child with a brim-full heart that it is almost ashamed to reveal to the wise and learned, it mischievously hides behind its tinkling musical figures . . . with wonderful sound-meanings which knock at every human heart with the quiet question 'Do you understand me?' but are by no means understood by everyone.

The following diary entry from the year 1831 is the result of experiences in the course of his study of theory:

Whosoever has a beautiful thought, let him not worry it and caress it till it is vulgar and profaned, as many composers (as Dorn) do who call this 'development'. But if you want to develop, make something out of previous commonplaces—only don't commit that mortal sin. There Beethoven, like Jean Paul, is a splendid ideal.

1832: Beethoven! Thou art no guide to the goal, but the goal itself!
1837: Beethoven's B flat Quartet, Op. 130, heard for the first time. Ultimate goal!

About 1846 the ripe master returned to Beethoven once again with the words:

Beethoven: that law which guides the unwilling with iron staff. . . . What thou dost, what pleases thee, is law!

Among the earliest utterances on Schubert are the following from the year 1829:

C major Phantasy sought here to combine a whole orchestra in two hands and the inspired beginning is a hymn of praise to the Divinity, one sees the angels pray, the Adagio is a mild reflection on life and lifts the veil from it. Then fugues thunder, a song of the infinity of man and of sounds. . . .

Schubert polonaises: downright thunderstorms with romantic rainbows. . . . An extremely characteristic trait of Schubert's polonaises, as of most of his other compositions, is that he never writes a word like 'dolce' at his most beautiful passages; he has that in common with Goethe who never writes 'touchingly', 'mournfully', &c., in any of his tragedies. The works in which many 'dolces', &c. occur, are decidedly *not*, just as Jean Paul says in his aesthetics that the comedies, &c., which, according to the play-bills make you 'die of laughter', are really enough to make you die of weeping.

A friend of Schumann's youth, Emil Flechsig, tells us in his *Recollections* (only now partially in print) of that early enthusiasm for Schubert:

For Schubert—then in 1828 first becoming known—he developed a raving passion and got hold of everything of his that was to be had. In the polonaises I had to accompany the bass (*sic*). . . . When Schubert died the next winter, he got into such a state at the first report of his death that I heard him sob the whole night long. . . .

The diary for the year 1831 gives us some interesting sidelights on Schumann's own early compositions:

Ask yourself now: What is the most beautiful idea? . . . Life! . . . Yet how minds delude themselves on the summit of the ideal, Robert!—

B

Can't you go on? Only write on! Without end, without line, without break, only on! . . . There are many talents, but depth is lacking, intellectual digestion. . . . A musical language of flowers was one of my earliest ideas. . . .
I've got the idea for the second set of *Papillons*, whose beginning has something of a monastic song about it, not to forget the moonrise. . . .

On the 'understanding' of music he notes:

The impression of a piece should not be doubtful.—If it is, the uneducated listener says: It pleases me or it doesn't please me. . . . And who expects of the hearer, when a piece is played to him for the first time, that he shall analyse it in mechanical or harmonic detail?—With the *Papillons* perhaps one could make an exception, since the change is too quick, the colours are too motley and the listener still has the previous page in his head while the player has already finished. This 'self-obliteration' of the *Papillons* may perhaps be open to criticism but is certainly not inartistic. . . . The need for frequent hearing of something, however, seems to me no flattery for the composer.

Among the rough notes occurs the following self-critical addendum to the first 'David Club' article, the famous review of Chopin's Opus 2 in 1831:

We were all very anxious to hear Meister Raro's judgment on Chopin, for he is often all too Sebastian Bachish toward young men and a born enemy of everything half-baked, dull, morbid, aesthetic. He understands how to cool down the spirit without jesting and converts the fire of passion into a holy, clear flame. In short he hurts us. Your joy over the work, he began yesterday, does not displease me. You know how little I can tolerate picturesque music in general. But in the first place Chopin can hardly help it, since he employs only the hand of his genius (and in praiseworthy fashion), and secondly this work is distinguished by yet other merits. . . .

The following words of Florestan's have been preserved from a lost 'David Club' article from the year 1831:

Finally the physical is so often the reflex of the psychic, although on the other hand I know very well and assert that rich natural surroundings influence the colour and development of the feeling for beauty, [which] is (like Mozart, Haydn, Beethoven, these high priests of beauty) born in beautiful lands.

It seems likely that this fragment belongs to a big 'David Club' novel long planned by Schumann, a project finally abandoned for musical composition and musical criticism.

These hitherto unknown utterances which I have reproduced here belong for the most part to the period of Schumann's youth; but they contain already the most essential germs from which his human personality was later to unfold so richly. In this sense, therefore, they may well be regarded as an essential contribution to the study of Schumann the man. But these interesting fragments seem to me important also in another sense. The relatively little that has even now been published gives us some idea of the wealth of autobiographical material still buried in the archives and makes it imperative that the whole material, in its original form without pseudo-scientific interpretation, should be made generally accessible as soon as possible. Then, and only then, will it be possible to draw a really authentic picture of 'Schumann the man'.

CHAPTER II

THE PIANO MUSIC

By KATHLEEN DALE

SCHUMANN started his musical career as a pianist, and though it was not long before he decided to become a composer rather than a performer, his youthful experience at the keyboard left traces upon his creative output all through his life. From his youth up he played the instrument so easily that when he turned to composition, he inevitably expressed his musical ideas most spontaneously in terms of the piano, and found it difficult to compose in any other medium. Moreover, the kind of music he played in his student days was to exercise a strong and lasting influence upon his style as a composer.

His boyhood and early youth coincided with a period during which the music of the classical era was being temporarily superseded by that of a less permanent type. Schumann played and rejoiced in Bach, Beethoven, and Schubert, but he also luxuriated for a time in the less worthy productions of such composers as Pleyel, Moscheles, Hummel, Ries, Marschner and Herz, and he acquired the kind of facile technique which enabled him to perform in public so brilliant a composition as Moscheles' *Alexander* Variations. For brilliant, rather than intellectual or expressive sets of variations were the order of the day; they were manufactured in quantities by Hummel, Czerny, Hünten, and their fellows, and it was not unnatural that the young Schumann should early turn his attention to the composition of works in variation-form. His innate good taste, however, prevented him from ever producing variations which were either superficial or merely decorative, and in due course he was to take an active part in restoring to the variation the honourable status it had enjoyed in the hands of Bach and Beethoven. How Schumann treated variation-form is historically of some moment. How his preoccupation with the writing of variations influenced his whole art of composition is a matter which is of sufficient interest to stimulate investigation, and which must form an essential prelude to the study of his style as a composer of piano music.

It may be said at the outset that the opus-numbers of Schumann's works do not always synchronize with the chronological order of their composition, and that they are frequently misleading. As his production for the piano is unusually diverse and extensive, its classification into periods and groups for discussion in these pages will be determined as much by the style and content of the works as by their dates of composition. Wherever possible, however, works will be referred to in chronological order within their own period or group.

Although Schumann's first and last works for the piano were sets of variations, he was admittedly a far less prolific writer of independent variations such as these, or even of single movements in variation-form within the framework of larger compositions, than were Haydn, Beethoven, or Brahms. The conception of variation in its widest sense, however, exerted a powerful influence upon his imagination, conditioning his use of musical material and even becoming a habit of mind. In his early published works alone, his tendencies in these directions may frequently be observed. Among the more obvious examples between the publication of the *Abegg* Variations, Op. 1, and of the much better known set, the *Études symphoniques*, Op. 13, there are the two collections of studies, Op. 3 and Op. 10, which are pianistic variants of some of Paganini's *Caprices* for solo violin, as well as the variations forming the slow movement of the F minor Sonata, Op. 14, based upon a theme by Clara Wieck, who also furnished the theme of the set of variations entitled *Impromptus*, Op. 5 which, even after they had been published, Schumann thought fit to 'vary' by issuing them in a second edition with a number of basic and superficial alterations. The *Papillons*, Op. 2, were originally conceived to some extent as variations, as will be seen later, and what is *Carnaval*, Op. 9, but an incomparably imaginative series of variations *sur quatre notes*? Further examples belonging to the same period and to later years will be mentioned in due course. Meanwhile, it is more profitable to discover the origins of Schumann's essays in this sphere of composition, a procedure which will entail a passing glance at his other attempts to achieve mastery and fluency in the art of writing for the piano.

While every musician knows that the set of *Abegg* Variations was Schumann's first *published* composition, only a minority is aware that this work was not his first for piano. Still fewer realize that it was not his first set of variations, and that even after he had made his first appearance in print in 1831, he continued to devote time and energy to the creation of other sets of variations which have remained in manuscript until the present day.

There actually exists in print a piano work of Schumann's earlier than his Op. 1. This is a set of *Eight Polonaises for four hands*, Op. III, composed in 1828 but not published till 1933 when Karl Geiringer edited it for the Universal Edition. The work possesses a double interest: firstly, in having been written more than a year before the *Abegg* Variations and thus being one of the earliest of Schumann's works now actually available in print; and, secondly, in furnishing an early example of his 'variation' habit of mind in that it contains a number of phrases which the composer subsequently introduced, either note for note or in modified form and in different contexts into the *Papillons*, Op. 2, which he did not start to compose until 1829. Comparison of the youthful *Polonaises* with the more mature *Papillons* demonstrates how great was the advance in the art of composition made by the young composer in the short period of time separating the two works.

Schumann's youthful sketch-books, which are five in number and which relate to the years 1829–33, and the composer's 'Project-Book' dating back to 1828 are all in the Schumann Museum at Zwickau, and other manuscripts covering the same period are in private ownership. Not one of these indispensable documents is available in facsimile, and by reason of their domicile in the temporarily remote fastnesses of Zwickau and Berlin respectively, they are virtually inaccessible to the English student today. They have, however, been exhaustively described and analysed in two admirable monographs by German scholars,[1] one of whom, Werner Schwarz, concentrates his attention almost exclusively upon the works in variation-form both printed and in manuscript, while the other, Wolfgang Gertler, who deals principally with Schumann's first-period works in general, refers mainly to such sketches as were subsequently utilized by the composer in his published works in *any* type of form. These two little volumes have been extensively drawn upon for relevant details in the ensuing pages.

It is generally maintained that Schumann's musical education was of a desultory character, so that his production in after years inevitably suffered from his lack of serious training. It is also well known that he resented the strict discipline necessary in the training of a composer, and that he was always impatient of restraint. The contents of the Zwickau sketch-books (hereafter referred to by Roman numerals) and the few manuscript pages covering the same period show, however, that he did at least make very determined efforts to

---

[1] See p. v.

form a personal style, and that he was unceasingly occupied with plans to widen his experience as a writer of piano music. For instance, he went to the length of making memory copies in piano score of such works as the andante of Beethoven's Fourth Symphony and the *Leonora* Overture No. 3, afterwards correcting them in red ink (Sk. IV). He wrote out the openings of some of Bach's fugues from Book I of the *Forty-Eight*, as though intending to acquire understanding of this type of composition, which he utilized to some extent in his earlier works, but which he did not essay in its purest form until he wrote the contrapuntal works of 1845. He drafted sketches for a piano-school (Sk. I), wrote piano studies and fingering exercises (V), and in addition to the exercises in harmony and counterpoint which he worked for his master, Heinrich Dorn, (Sk. IV and V) and which included a projected 'Prelude and Triple Fugue in the olden style', he undertook a number of enterprises in free composition during the years 1831–5 which saw the publication of his Opp. 1–5 and 7–10 (Op. 6 was not composed until 1837). These compositions are as follows: a Concerto in F (I), a Piano Quartet in C minor (III), and a *Capriccio* for piano duet (V), all of which the composer left unfinished. In addition, he made a large collection of sketches of varying lengths for Opp. 1, 2, 3, 4, 8, 9, 11, 12, and 124 (I, II, III, V), among which the most extensive relate to *Papillons*, Op. 2.

More relevant to our immediate purpose, however, are the unpublished works in variation-form. In this connexion, an entry in the Project Book reveals that the collection of *Eight Polonaises* already referred to was not the only piano work which Schumann completed in 1828, for mention is made of a set of 'Variations for Four Hands upon a Theme from Prince Louis Ferdinand's Piano Quintet in C minor' written in the same year. The manuscript of this composition, Schumann's very first work in variation-form, has never come to light, but that it existed is proved by an entry in the composer's diary to the effect that he played the piece, and the *Polonaises*, too, with a fellow student, Glock, on 7 December 1828. The disappearance of the manuscript is much to be regretted, for apart from its intrinsic interest, it might have supplied the first evidence of the influence of Louis Ferdinand's keyboard style upon that of Schumann —an influence which can be detected later, especially in the decorative figures of accompaniment in either hand, melismatic filigree and graceful cross-hand passages adorning such works as the *Fantasiestücke*, Op. 12, and the *Études symphoniques*, Op. 13 (Ex. 1). The loss

Ex.1

a) **Prince Louis Ferdinand:** *Piano Trio in E flat, Op. 3*

b) **Prince Louis Ferdinand:** *Piano Quintet*

is, however, mitigated by the preservation of several other sets of variations for piano solo, complete or fragmentary, as follows: four unfinished variations, with orchestral introduction, upon the theme of the famous *Rondeau à la clochette* from Paganini's B minor Concerto (1830) (V and III); Variations upon an Original Theme, Andante in G (1831, completed 4 January 1832) (Sk. III and a separate MS.); Variations upon Schubert's *Sehnsuchtswalzer* (1833) (manuscripts and Sk. V); a number of variations upon the allegretto of Beethoven's Seventh Symphony (1833) (manuscripts and Sk. IV), and three variations—the third incomplete—upon Chopin's Nocturne in G minor, Op. 15, No. 3 (1834–5) (manuscript).

Schumann's choice of themes is interesting in itself, for it shows where his musical preferences lay. He warmly admired Prince Louis Ferdinand, played his chamber-music during and after his own student days, saw to it that his works were performed at the Leipzig Conservatorium, and wrote of him as the 'romantic of the classical period,' and as one whose 'highly poetic nature was, with Schubert's, of great influence upon contemporary music'. His enthusiasm for Paganini dated from 1830 when he first heard him play at Frankfurt, and was still glowing in 1833, when he wrote the second set of *Paganini Études*, Op. 10. He valued two of his unfinished variations on the Paganini theme (Sk. III, p. 89) sufficiently to make use of them in his own Opp. 4 and 8. Schubert's works had appealed to him strongly since boyhood, when he had performed the sonatas, waltzes, Trio in E flat and the four-hand *Polonaises* which, according to his partner, Töpken, he played in an individual and inimitably expressive manner. When he was studying law at Heidelberg in 1829, Schumann wrote to Wieck that he had managed to edge in a Schubert waltz between Roman Law and the Pandects, and had often hummed the Trio in his dreams. His affection for the *Sehnsuchtswalzer*, which he described as a 'heartfelt theme', was shared by his circle of friends. One of them, Ludwig Schunke, wrote a set of Concert Variations, Op. 14, upon it, and among other musicians of the day, Czerny also made it the basis of four virtuosic variations to which he added an introduction and cadenza. Schumann's lively interest in Chopin which, however, declined in later years, had first been aroused in 1831 by the composer's Op. 2 Variations, and it was rekindled by the publication of the Nocturnes, Op. 15, in 1834, when he reviewed the last-named in the *Neue Zeitschrift für Musik*. He described the third Nocturne in G minor as pointing towards the future, and signalized his preference for it by using the first twenty-seven

bars as the basis for a set of variations which, unfortunately, he
never finished and which remained undiscovered until 1929. The
second variation[1] comprises eighteen bars, in the course of which
fragments of the first four bars of the melody are treated in imitation
(Ex. 2)—a procedure hardly surprising in a Schumann work contemporary with *Carnaval*. Schumann's admiration for Beethoven,
though possibly less generally admitted than his veneration for Bach,

Ex.2

must nevertheless have been profound, for not only were his variations upon the Allegretto of the Seventh Symphony the most extensive and noteworthy of the unpublished sets, but the eight-bar
theme (Ex. 3) of his own *Andante and Variations* in G was of
markedly Beethovenian character, recalling that of the Thirty-Two
Variations in C minor. Schwarz points out that this work of
Schumann's, which was composed between the *Abegg* Variations
(1830) and the *Impromptus*, Op. 5 (1833), has features in common
with Beethoven's Fantasia, Op. 77: enharmonic changes at the ends
of sections, legato melody with staccato chords in the 2/4 adagios of
both works and similar melodic formulæ of notes foreign to the key.
Other traces of the influence of Beethoven's works upon Schumann's
will be mentioned in due course.

Before looking more closely at the variations of 1833, however, we
must return to 1830 to survey their predecessor, the *Abegg* Variations
composed in July–August of that year; for although one set of the
many sketches for *Papillons* (1829–31) was worked out on a plan

[1] Printed complete by Boetticher (*Robert Schumann: Einführung in Persönlichkeit und Werk*, p. 588).

entitled 'Variationen', the work as a whole does not belong to the category of variations now being reviewed, and it will be considered later. The *Abegg* Variations present several interesting points beyond being a record of Schumann's first public entry into the lists as a composer, and it may be noted in passing that he evidently found their structural arrangement—four variations and an extended finale —a satisfactory one, for he adopted a similar plan, though on a

Ex.3 *Andante*

smaller scale, for the unpublished Andante in G in the following year. According to a note in the project-book, the published *Abegg* Variations comprise only half of those Schumann planned, some of them being discarded as too virtuosic. In addition to the several sketches preserved in Sk. I and II, a sheet of manuscript in the Zwickau Museum shows that he conceived the work originally for piano and orchestra: 'Variationen über Abegg, eigentlich für Orchester.' Among the sketches is one of an orchestral introduction which incidentally recalls that of Beethoven's Second Symphony; it is forty bars in length and the theme is allotted to a solo horn, pianissimo. Of the two sketches Schumann wrote for the cantabile section, one marked 'Adagio' contains the indication 'attacca tutti' after the pause before the final movement. Schumann had learned to play Chopin's *Là ci darem* Variations, Op. 2, during 1830, and it may have been his high opinion of this work which caused him to contemplate emulating it by writing an orchestral accompaniment to his own Op. 1. Schwarz draws attention to the likeness between the introduction of the *Abegg* Variations and that of Moscheles' *Alexander* Variations, again in the key of F, a work which may also have induced Schumann to consider the desirability of employing the orchestra himself.

A comparison of the *Abegg* with the *Là ci darem* Variations shows that though Chopin's work is far more effective from the purely pianistic standpoint, Schumann's is musically much more interesting. In the individual variations, especially during the opening bars, Chopin followed his theme more closely and wove a cumulatively brilliant texture around it. Schumann preferred to use his theme as a basis for new musical ideas which should imply its harmonic structure without unduly stressing the melodic line. None of his variations opens with a literal quotation of the notes of the theme. The piano writing throughout is unequal, but whereas the commonplace accompaniment to the first statement of the theme and some of the more facile passage-work later on may be reminiscent of Hummel (Ex. 4 *a*) and Moscheles (Ex. 4 *b*), just as the flowing triplets of Var. 3 are of Chopin's Var. 2, the second variation is a movement in

Ex.4

typical Schumannesque pianoforte style which makes its effect by the freshness, expressiveness and originality of its figuration, especially in the ingenious repeat of the first section where the left hand plays its opening melody above, instead of below the urgent pulsation of the right-hand part. Other features more typical of Schumann's later, highly individual style are already exemplified in this early work: frequent cross-rhythms, syncopations, and irregular accentuations, and the gradual releasing of the notes of a sustained chord, a better-known example of which last-named device occurs at the end of *Papillons*, and another in the introduction to the *Paganini Étude*, Op. 3, No. 3. A further characteristically Schumannesque trait, his life-long delight in enigmas, is manifested for the first time in these variations in the employment of musical letters as the nucleus of the theme, and in the intriguing dedication to an imaginary countess.

The next set of variations Schumann wrote, in 1833, was *Impromptus sur une Romance de Clara Wieck, composés pour le piano et dédiés à M. Frédéric Wieck*. He took the theme from the fourteen-year-old Clara Wieck's *Romance variée, dédiée à M. Robert Schumann*, Op. 3, utilizing only the melody, however, and writing a fresh bass in which the intervals of falling and rising fifths are noticeable features, as they are in many of Schumann's melodies. Moreover, it is the distinguished quality of the bass, even more than the interesting melodic outline which is responsible for the superiority of the *Impromptus* over the *Abegg* Variations. The statement in single notes of the sixteen-bar bass by the left hand before the theme is announced in full harmony by both hands recalls the finale of the *Eroica* Symphony and is further evidence of Schumann's response to Beethovenian influence. The bass is used prominently in several of the variations, and its opening bars form the powerful subject of the concluding five-part fugue, devices which, together with its final presentation, complete, as a melody in double octaves just before the closing bars, lend the whole work the character of a chaconne and endow it with a unity lacking in the *Abegg* set. Schumann published the first edition in 1833 and a second, revised version in 1850. The two editions are so discrepant as regards numbering that before any reference can be made to individual variations, the main divergencies must be tabulated. In the first edition, the theme, entitled 'Romanza', was marked as No. 1 and the succeeding variations numbered from 2–12. The eleventh, a free interlude with few references to the theme, was omitted from the second edition, and the original No. 4 replaced by a fresh variant. In the later edition, the theme, which is itself altered during the first four and last four bars, is printed without title or number, and the variations consequently run from 1–10, which numbering will be used in these pages.

Apart from the differences already mentioned, the other principal dissimilarities between the two editions are as follows: In Var. 1 the accents formerly placed upon the tied first beats of the bar throughout the piece have disappeared, Schumann evidently realizing that they served no practical purpose. Var. 2, which had been written in 6/8, preserves the original time-signature only in the lower stave while the right-hand part is written in 2/4; the left-hand part is set out in simpler notation though it is unchanged in substance. Var. 3 is a much clarified version of the former Var. 4, in which the closeness of the part-writing produced such extreme density in the lay-out as to make the piece as trying to the eye as it was awkward for the fingers. The original version is, however, a most revealing example of Schumann's early tendency to weave a compact polyphonic texture. In the first bar of Var. 5, the right-hand part is slightly delayed so that the left-hand note may sound alone in order to emphasize its thematic importance. Var. 6, which begins in A minor and ends in C major, differs in length and character from its predecessor in the first edition by the omission of a statement in the tonic major of the eight-bar opening theme which had preceded the da capo repeat. During these bars, the theme, banished from the later edition, had made a brief appearance in the tenor part. While the substance of Var. 7 remains almost unchanged, the notation of the right-hand part is simplified in the same way as in the left-hand of Var. 2. In the fugue, the opening of which is marked 'quasi satira', there are slight differences in the counter-subject during the first eight bars; two unnecessary bars of repeated chords are omitted from before the first stretto (at bar 75 counting from the beginning of the Finale), and the time-signature is changed from 6/8 to 2/4 for the last statement of the theme. The principal revision, however, occurs at the very end, for whereas the progress of the harmonized theme had originally been halted by a sudden fading out of the melodic line which left the lower parts to languish picturesquely as tied notes during the last five bars (Ex. 5), it is now carried to a logical conclusion which rounds off the whole work more definitely, albeit far less imaginatively. A sketch of this Finale may be found in Sk. IV where it is designated 'Fuge No. 3' among the contrapuntal studies of 1831–32; it also appears among the sketches for the finale of the youthful Symphony in G minor.

The Variations upon Schubert's *Sehnsuchtswalzer*, written in 1833, will be discussed later in connexion with *Carnaval*. Their contemporaries, the Variations on the Allegretto of Beethoven's Seventh Symphony will be analysed here, not only because they are next in chronological order, but because they form an important link between

Ex.5

the still immature *Impromptus*, Op. 5, just described and the masterly *Études symphoniques*, Op. 13, of 1834–6. Schumann had heard the Seventh Symphony twice during 1833 and the impression it made upon him was evidently very deep, for he threw himself into the writing of four sets of variations upon the sixteen-bar theme which follows the opening sustained chord of the Allegretto. According to Schwarz's minute documentation, these four sets are closely interrelated, some of the variations appearing in two or more of the collections, which are as follows: (*a*) Eleven variations in Sk. IV, all finished except Nos. 9 and 11, and originally intended for dedication to Clara; (*b*) A four-page manuscript entitled 'Sechs Etuden in Form freier Variationen über ein Beethovensches Thema', in which No. 3 is No. 9 of (*a*), now completed, and Nos. 4 and 5 are new, though some of the material of No. 5 had already appeared as bars 78–83 of the Andante in G of 1832, and this whole variation was to take ultimate form as *Leides Ahnung*, No. 2 of the *Albumblätter*, Op. 124; (*c*) a two-page manuscript upon which the title appears in French with a dedication to 'mon amie, Clara Wieck', and in which No. 4 is an amalgam of Nos. 2 and 4 of (*a*); (*d*) 'Sept Variations exercices', of which only No. 5, thirty-two bars in the form of a five-part *Choral* motet is really new, and in which No. 7 is another, completed version of the unfinished No. 9 of (*a*).

From a glance at the opening bars of more than a dozen of these variations it is immediately apparent that in writing them, Schumann was more interested in resolving the thematic material into a type of decorative texture suitable for pianoforte studies than he was in using it as a basis for the development of fresh musical ideas as was his wont in earlier sets of variations. Indeed, the alternative titles,

'Études' and 'Exercices' denote that this was his main objective,
just as it was to be in the *Études symphoniques*. Two of the Beethoven
variations from (*a*) in particular, are very closely related to movements in the later work: No. 5 (Ex. 6) which is constructed on the

Ex.6

very same principle as the sixth *Étude* of Op. 13, the persistent
syncopation of both these pieces also prefiguring that of *Paganini* in
Carnaval; and No. 8 (Ex. 7), which has a restless inner voice of

Ex.7

demisemiquavers similar to the outline of the third *Étude symphonique*.
The Beethoven Variations display Schumann's skill in inventing figuration to maintain a continuously flowing texture within the confines
of simple chord progressions (Ex. 8), as well as his predilection for

Ex.8

Var. IV

combining different metrical units (Ex. 9) both of which latter
examples foreshadow metrically complex pieces such as Nos. 2 and
10 of *Davidsbündler*, Op. 6, *Des Abends*, Op. 12, No. 1, the posth.
Var. 5 of Op. 13 and the discarded finale of the G minor Sonata,
Op. 22. The first Beethoven variation exhibits Schumann's employ-

ment of a filigree of unison octave demisemiquavers prefiguring the lay-out of *Praeludium*, Op. 99, No. 10, which he composed in 1839. The *Études symphoniques* in C sharp minor, Schumann's next set of published variations which, like the Beethoven set, partake of the

Ex.9

Var. XI

character of both variations and études, underwent even more processes of revision than did their published predecessors, the *Impromptus*, Op. 5. Moreover, Schumann went so far as to alter the theme itself. He told the composer, Baron von Fricken, that it was already too much like a variation and that it needed to be reduced to its simplest terms. He originally intended to issue the variations, composed in 1834–6, as 'Zwölf Davidsbündler Etuden', and then as 'Etuden im Orchester Character, von Florestan und Eusebius'; but when they eventually appeared in 1837, he deferred to his publisher's wish in having them printed under his own name. He revised and reissued them in 1852 as *Études en forme de variations*, omitting Nos. 2 and 9 and altering the Finale. After his death, the work was published yet again, in 1862, this time with the two variations reinstated. Finally, in 1893, five other variations which Schumann had rejected from both his own editions were printed by Brahms in the Supplementary Volume of Schumann's Complete Works, and they have subsequently been included in most of the standard performing editions of the work.

Far more interesting, however, than the record of this process of subtraction and addition, is the actual existence in manuscript of an entirely different arrangement for the work. This manuscript, known as the Berlin sketch, gives the 'Tema quasi marcia funebre' and eleven variations, some complete and others only partially sketched. Among them are the five variations later published by Brahms. The relationship of this manuscript to the definitive version is as follows:

Var. I corresponds to Var. IV of the Supplement, but is written in 12/8 time instead of 3/4, under which later time-signature four bars of variation are the equivalent of one bar of the theme. Var. II

c

is Var. III of the Supplement, though the dotted melody is placed in the bass instead of in the treble part.

Var. III is Var. VIII (*Étude X*) of the 1862 edition, the right-hand figure, however, being written as [musical notation] instead of as [musical notation].

Var. IV was never published. It is in 12/8 time (Ex. 10) and bears a close resemblance to one of the Beethoven Variations in (c).

Ex. 10

Var. V is Var. I of the Supplement.

Var. VI is *Étude V* of 1852, but owing to an alteration in the last two bars, it ends in C sharp minor instead of in E.

Var. VII is no more than a brief sketch of a rhythmic motive.

Var. VIII corresponds to the beginning of Var. V of the Supplement.

Var. IX is the sketch of a passage which indicates the rhythmical pattern of Var. II of 1862, just as Var. X determines its melodic outline.

For the 'Finale marcia', only the first bar of Var. I (1862) is sketched, and there is no sign of the exultant theme in D flat major of the definitive finale which was written a year or two later, after Sterndale Bennett's arrival in Leipzig. In a letter dated 28 November 1834, Schumann mentioned that he wished to work up the funeral march to a triumphal victory march and also to introduce some dramatic interest, but that he could not escape from the minor mode or find a satisfactory ending. The only other item in the Berlin sketch is the first bar of the melody of Var. II of the Supplement, which is marked 'sempre pedale'. In this manuscript the last two bars of the first half of the theme differ from the 1852 edition by being more decisive in effect (a masculine instead of a feminine ending), and in bar 2 a dotted figure occurs on the second beat, possibly in compliance with the rhythmical demands of the 'marcia funebre' theme. It was possibly this characteristic dotted beat which gave rise to the distinctive figure in Var. I.

In the *Études symphoniques*, Schumann attained the height of his powers as a writer of variations within the accepted meaning of the term. While maintaining close contact with the structural basis of the theme or with either its harmonic or melodic implications, he contrived to design a succession of pieces of markedly individual character, some of which are sufficiently independent to stand apart from their context. Among the purely technical devices utilized in varying the theme are the following: its employment as the bass or the tenor part in Var. 2; its treatment by canon in chords in Var. 3, by free canonic imitation in Var. 4, and its decoration by one persistent metrical figure in Var. 5. The theme is also structurally contracted or expanded in accordance with the precipitate or leisurely character of the relevant variation, and sometimes one brief fragment is used either as the basis of a free variation within the structural framework, as in the quasi fugato of Var. 8 and the polyphony of Var. 7, or as an integral figure in the working-out sections of the finale. Throughout the work there are strong contrasts in mood and in tempo, though not in actual rhythm, for the one variation with a triple time-signature, the presto *Étude IX* in 3/16, is grouped rhythmically into units of four bars and makes the impression of being in quadruple time in triplets. Some of the variations are in the relative major, one is in G sharp minor, and the finale, a long movement in hybrid sonata-rondo form, is in the enharmonic major, D flat, with episodes in A flat and G flat. Pianistically the work is an epitome of all the most brilliant features of Schumann's first-period style, and is one of his most difficult to perform owing to the rich and intricate texture, rapid chord-passages and wide stretches including several fearsome successions of tenths in the left-hand.

The 'Quasi variazioni' movement of the F minor Sonata, Op. 14, the last of Schumann's first-period works in variation-form, is of a very different kind from the foregoing. It is designed on an altogether smaller scale, befitting its position as a subsidiary portion of a complete work. The theme, an Andantino in F minor by Clara Wieck, is of unusual character both structurally and melodically, and calls for imaginative treatment to counteract its inherent monotony. The twenty-four bars are divided into three equal sections, in each of which a different four-bar phrase is stated twice in identical terms. In the first section the melody is harmonized entirely above a tonic pedal; in the second it is borne along by the lower voices under an upper mediant pedal. While both these sections remain in the tonic key, the third modulates and brings the theme to an inconclusive ending on the dominant. The plaintive melody, which opens with a descending scale of five notes followed by a falling octave, sets the ominous tone prevailing throughout the four variations. In this respect it illustrates Schumann's expressed opinion that the style of a set of variations should be in keeping with that of the theme. Without employing pianistic resources comparable with those he had lavished upon the *Études symphoniques*, Schumann subjected the unpropitious theme to undeniably original treatment, by rearranging the order and the harmonic structure of the sections so that every variation except the first ends in the tonic and each is of a different length; by enhancing the theme with an unbroken fabric of flowing triplets in the second variation; by disguising it with chromaticisms and syncopations in the third and treating it by diminution and sequential canonic imitation in the fourth. To the last-named he appended a brief coda in which reiterations of a dotted quaver figure intensify the 'marcia funebre' inferences of the theme. After finally alluding to the opening notes of the melody, augmented to semibreves in the depths of the keyboard, he closed the movement with six bars of solemnly repeated tonic chords diminuendo—a typically Schumannesque colour-effect as well as an evocation of the tonic-pedal section which opened the movement.

Schumann had already gained much experience in the composition of variations before he completed the two mature works just mentioned. Not only had he engaged in the writing of the several sets of variations upon definite themes; he had tried his hand at other, less restricted forms of the same activity. Among the works thus produced are the two sets of *Paganini Études*, Opp. 3 and 10, transcriptions of twelve of Paganini's *Caprices for solo violin*, Op. 1.[1] They display a remarkable combination of qualities in being translations of music from one instrumental medium to another, studies in technique and interpretation as well as advanced performing-pieces for pianists, exercises in harmony and counterpoint for the composer himself, and above all, well constructed movements in which technical resource is counterpoised by artistic expression. The first set is prefaced by a long and valuable introduction on the art of playing the piano, and by a number of well-fingered passages of many types, both of which features give the volume something of the character of a pianoforte-school. Perhaps Op. 3 may have been the final realization of the plan for a work of this nature which Schumann

---

[1] At the very end of his life (1853–4) Schumann turned again to these *Caprices* of Paganini's and wrote piano accompaniments for them.—*Ed.*

had conceived and noted in his sketch-book in earlier years. The arch-pedagogue Czerny thought the opus worthy of inclusion in his *Art moderne du doigter*, No. 10, where it figures under the title of 'Six Amusemens en forme d'Études pour le Pianoforte d'après les Caprices de Paganini, dédiés aux professeurs avec avant-propos et Exercices préparatifs par Robert Schumann'. To the second set, Schumann added an introduction of an entirely different type: a highly imaginative and perceptive essay which demonstrates his charm and skill as a writer no less than do the studies his fine musicianship.

He regarded his self-imposed task of transcription very seriously. During 1832 he wrote to Wieck that Op. 3 had been a Herculean labour, and to Dorn, that he had missed his help in deciding on the basses which were often doubtful, and that he had surmounted the difficulties only by keeping everything as simple as possible. To Rellstab he pleaded for the 'stepchild' which he had reared with care and pleasure, and which he intended to place before the critics as an example of what he could do in theory. He added, however, that he would rather write six studies of his own than arrange three more by anyone else. Yet, by the time he came to arrange the second set a year later, he had acquired greater confidence in his own powers, and consequently felt justified in treating the *Caprices* with rather greater freedom in order to secure them independence of their violinistic origin. The *Études* of Op. 10 accordingly substantiate his claim to have completely assimilated the thoughts of a composer greater than himself and to have re-expressed them in his own language.

The indirect outcome of Schumann's concentrated activities as a transcriber was his greatly increased facility in writing effectively for his own instrument, and the intensifying of his already imaginative manner of weaving interesting pianistic texture. Freed from the problems of original creation, he was able to bestow all his attention upon scanning the given material for the principal points of interest and then upon enhancing them without restriction. That under these circumstances he remained almost entirely faithful to the originals bespeaks his ingrained artistic integrity. A comparison of Schumann's transcriptions with Liszt's highly-coloured versions of one or two of the same pieces serves to emphasize this latter point. In his Op. 10, Schumann did allow himself a little latitude occasionally in revising Paganini's formal structure, for, as he told Rellstab, he found some of the *Caprices* by no means perfect in form and symmetry. He sometimes omitted a bar or two of ineffective passage-work, replacing it by either a repetition or a development of a previous phrase or section in order to secure greater unity and a more logical balance. He used a diversity of means in adapting these violin soli to the idiom of the keyboard. To single-line passage-work he would often add an upper or a lower part of notes of the same value running in alternate similar and contrary motion as if it were the reflection of the given part,[1] or he would lend the solo part a polyphonic tinge by sustaining the first notes of groups to form an independent middle part simulating the effect of the accentuation provided by the bowing of the original (Ex. 11). He often presented

Ex.11

a) Paganini: *Caprice, No.12*

b) Schumann: *Op.10, No.1*

phrases alternately in the right and left hands, inventing entirely new melodic or rhythmic accompanying figures to lend them point and interest (Ex. 12). He sometimes translated treble-stoppings into light arpeggios. A telling example of the effectiveness of this treatment occurs in the minor section of Op. 3, No. 2, where the discreet left hand arpeggi (Ex. 13 on p. 32) reproduce the original far more accurately in spirit than do Liszt's solid chords which give no sense of the impact caused by the violinist's drawing the bow across three strings at once. Schumann sometimes replaced trills by broken chords, a far more truly pianistic effect than the mere literal reproduction of an abundance of unaccompanied trills. Indeed, he showed great discrimination in refraining from attempting to transfer to the keyboard types of figuration not ordinarily suited to it. For instance,

---

[1] As in Op. 10, No. 6 (after Paganini's *Caprice* No. 3), bars 9 *et seq.* of the allegro, where the right hand plays the original violin part.

in his Op. 10, No. 2, he translated Paganini's fifty-two bars of tremolando accompaniment (seventy-two demisemiquavers in a bar) into successive sections of repeated triplet chords between a melodic treble and ornamental bass, and of two lower parts of semiquaver triplets divided between both hands supporting the melodic line of quavers in the upper voice. In Liszt's transcription of the same

Ex. 12

a) Paganini: *Caprice No.12*

b) Schumann: *Op. 10, No.1*

Caprice (Paganini's No. 6), his unbroken succession of tremolandi, though it may perhaps manifest Paganini's violinistic intentions the more scrupulously, is as exhausting to the pianist as it is monotonous to the listener—an effect Schumann was at pains to avoid, as he explicitly stated in his introduction. Schumann had an instinctive flair for devising organic presentations of the material. Never do the *Paganini Études* convey the impression of being manufactured accompaniments to unrelated solo-parts. They sound like original conceptions in which every strand of the texture is of equal importance.

The two sets of *Études* are of great interest and value in summing up Schumann's previous achievements in piano technique and in adumbrating some of the more brilliant features of his first-period style. Among those exemplified are the combination of dissimilar metrical or rhythmical units; frequent series of syncopations and of unaccountable accents on apparently unimportant beats; riotous chromaticisms and swift modulations, and ingenious polyphonic texture which looks rather more impressive on paper than it sounds

Ex. 13

a) Paganini: *Càprice No. 9*

b) Schumann: *Op. 3, No. 2*

c) Liszt: *Paganini Study, No. 5 (La Chasse)*

in actual performance. In only a few of the *Études* is there any sign of Schumann's sustained, chordal style. One of them, Op. 10, No. 6, opens and closes with a stately section of spread chords in which the top note of each is played by the crossing left hand in the César-Franckian manner. Schumann showed a fine ear for pianoforte colour by directing the player to let the left-hand second finger coincide with the right-hand fifth so that the two highest notes should sound together—an effect far more arresting than the continuous spread of the single notes. In his introductory paragraph to the maestoso No. 4, he mentions that at the time of arranging this *Étude*, the Funeral March of the *Eroica* Symphony was in his thoughts, and the majestic spirit of that movement seems to hover above it. The majority of the *Études* are energetic pieces in which the figuration is generally quick and restless. That of Op. 3, No. 1, for instance, resembles the hurrying semiquaver pattern of his *Novellette* in D, Op. 21, No. 2, and of the first movement of the G minor Sonata, Op. 22, which movement also derives something from the figuration of Op. 10, No. 5. Many of the extreme chromaticisms of Op. 10, Nos. 3 and 5 reappear in several movements of the *Davidsbündler-tänze*, the *Kreisleriana*, and other works of the same extremely individual type.

Two other, infinitely more important compositions, which stand on the outer circle of Schumann's first-period ventures in the art of variation, remain to be discussed in this section: *Papillons* (1829–31) and *Carnaval* (1834–5). The first-named is included at this point only by courtesy, as it were, for it is not in itself a set of variations even in the widest meaning of the term. Nevertheless, since one group of the original sketches for the work was designated 'Varia-tionen' (Sk. III, p. 88),[1] and since the whole of the material of which it is composed underwent so many 'variations' before it reached its final state, it is entitled to consideration in juxtaposition to *Carnaval*, especially in view of the similarity in planning between the two works, and of the composer's own description of the later opus as 'a higher kind of *Papillons*'. When he began to compose *Papillons*, Schumann was an eighteen-year-old law-student at Heidelberg, with no settled plans as to his future musical career. How little could he have imagined that his miniature Op. 2 was to be the prototype of the resplendent Op. 9 which, in due course, would carry his name round the whole world!

Gertler states that the version Schumann first projected was a set of *Sechs Walzer* (Sk. III, p. 119–130) which correspond to the published *Papillons* as follows:

Walzer 4=*Papillon* 6
„ 5= „ 7
„ 6= „ 1

'Walzer 3', which was never published, is described by Gertler as being very Schubertian in style, especially in the modulation to the sub-dominant in bar 4, but typically Schumannesque in the feminine ending at bar 6. The other, far more comprehensive plan (Sk. III, p. 88) entitled 'Variationen' is arranged thus:

[1] Boetticher (*Robert Schumann: Einführung*, p. 332, footnote 31) denies any connection between this group of sketches and *Papillons*, however.—*Ed.*

No. 1, D major 3/4	No. 6, F minor 3/4
2, B minor 2/4	7, D minor 3/4
3, B flat minor 3/4	8, D minor 3/4
4, F major 2/4	9, A major 3/8
5, E flat major 2/4	10, C minor 3/4

Gertler thinks that No. 10 may be identical with the unpublished Waltz in C major just mentioned, which ends in C minor (another Schubertian touch). In connection with this second list there are several additional sketches, which are detailed here because most of them later became integral parts of other Schumann compositions.

(1) A sketch to No. 3 (this time in B minor), which, with some omissions, became the introductory cadenza of the *Allegro*, Op. 8. This sketch—which Schwarz relates not to *Papillons* but to the Variations on a Paganini theme—also determines the R.H. part in the B major coda of the same work.

(2) A sixteen-bar sketch to No. 10 in D major (III, p. 37), later much altered melodically to become the 'Alternativo' of the *Intermezzo*, Op. 4, No. 6.

(3) Two sketches to No. 4 in F major, one of which was subsequently transformed into the *Scherzino* in F, No. 3 of the *Albumblätter*, Op. 124 and still retains reminiscences of the 'Grossvatertanz' to remind musicians of its origin.

(4) A so-called *Papillon* which was adapted in 1835 for use in *Carnaval*, but rejected from that work to find an ultimate niche as *Elfe*, Op. 124, No. 17.

(5) Two other sketches never published, one of which (III, p. 51) is reminiscent of the Allegretto of Schubert's Symphony in C, though Schumann did not yet know that work.

As Schumann made more sketches for Op. 2 than for any other of his works, his methods of sketching in general may be briefly reviewed before the *Papillons* sketches are surveyed in particular. Gertler points out how profoundly different in character were Schumann's sketches from those of Beethoven. The latter's were generally brief and pregnant, comprising only a few bars of melody such as would lend themselves to thematic development at any time. Schumann's were urgent ideas—often short passages of pianoforte texture—which, if not straightway fixed in writing, were irretrievably lost. Although he thought that music should be written down immediately upon conception, that the first conception was the most natural and the best, and that 'intellect might err, but feeling, never', he did not hesitate to conceive pieces more than once. He employed his sketches as aids to memory. Indeed, they were in the nature of a musical diary which recorded not only the ideas themselves but the dates and the moods which saw their birth. To mention only one instance: a few bars, later used in the finale of the *Fantasie*, Op. 17, bear the superscription, '30.11.36, dabei selig geschwärmt, als ich krank war'. The sketches fall into two groups: (*a*) short fragments subsequently abandoned, probably because Schumann could not recapture the mood which had engendered them; (*b*) whole pieces, or largely developed sections which were sometimes written out several times with slight alterations. The sketches relating to *Papillons* belong almost entirely to this second category.

Papillons as we know it today is a work so fresh and original in effect that it is difficult to realize that it was the fruit of such laborious mental exertion and of so many heart-searchings. Placing the manuscript of each separate piece beside its published counterpart and noting the divergencies between them, one can feel nothing but admiration for the composer who finally succeeded in creating this little work of art. For such it is, despite unabashed borrowings from earlier efforts (the *Polonaises* of 1828), and numerous alterations, obviously worked out at the keyboard since they are largely improvements in the texture such as would occur more readily to the fingers than to the mind's eye.

Limitations of space make it impossible to enumerate all the many revisions. Only the principal dissimilarities can be tabulated in the appended list. (The sketches are all to be found in Sk. III, except one, to No. 2, which is in Sk. I.)

The Introduction was originally longer, and showed the influence of Weber's *Invitation to the Dance*.

No. 1. This piece was written out several times. The L.H. part between bars 3–8 was of a more primitive, uniform type, like the accompaniment to the theme of the *Abegg* Variations.

No. 2. There are two sketches containing two-part writing for the R.H. The contrasting types of figuration in bars 5–12 were not noted until the second sketch.

No. 3. Two versions exist, showing the theme by canon in two and four parts, at different intervals and in different keys. (In Sk. V the theme of No. 1 appears in three-part canon at the third.)

No. 4. Awkward stretches, later removed, existed in both R.H. and L.H. parts.

No. 5. Bar 8 contains a masculine instead of the feminine ending which is much more characteristic of Schumann. The most interesting point in this movement, however, is its connexion with the trio of the seventh Polonaise, Op. III. Professor Gerald Abraham, the first to draw the attention of English readers[1] to the close relationship between the two works, describes this *Papillon* as little more than an improved transcription of the afore-mentioned trio. He particularly mentions the *Papillon's* prominent cantabile bass motive which had only been implied in the secondo part of the trio.

No. 6. The F major section was not included, nor was the A major portion very extensive. The D minor cadence was an octave higher.

No. 7. There are several sketches and many changes. The key was originally B flat minor; the unexpected diminished-seventh chord in bar 8 was the tonic without the third; the portion in A flat belonged to 'Walzer 3' and appeared in 3/4 time and in two different types of notation. Bars 9–16 formerly corresponded with 1–8, proceeding from D flat to B flat.

No. 8. The A flat added to the treble part of the last bar of the final version, and the seventh added to the dominant at that point are the only revisions in the piece itself worth mentioning. Of greater interest is the fact that it was formerly preceded by an Intermezzo consisting of the first 16 bars of No. 10, transposed into D flat (another reminiscence of the *Invitation to the Dance*).

No. 9. Originally a Waltz in 3/4 time, it underwent an electrifying metamorphosis into a prestissimo in 3/8.

No. 10. Its introduction having been detailed for use earlier in the series, the piece consisted only of the waltz section, which was partly in E major. The ending of this section evidently caused Schumann trouble, for the melody was formerly outlined as in Ex. 14. The coda, too, was altered. (At some later period Schumann made a version of this *Papillon* in B flat.)

Ex.14

No. 11. The sketch refers only to the middle section, for reasons which will shortly become apparent. The substance of this G major interlude was similar to that of its final version, but the texture was far less graceful and the pianistic lay-out considerably less subtle.

[1] *Monthly Musical Record*, July–August 1946.

For the first and last sections, Schumann simply turned back to the *Polonaises*, Op. III, to borrow such figures and phrases as could be combined to form a single movement of the same type. Professor Abraham revealed the nature of the loans: the first bar of the third polonaise was impounded for use as the introduction; that of the fourth was extracted to open the principal section; and the eight bars following the double-bar of the same polonaise were transferred bodily to a similar position in the *Papillon*! The finished piece is, however, sufficiently well fabricated to belie its makeshift origin.

No. 12. For the renowned finale there are three sketches, two of them omitting the opening section, and the third, the ending. In all of them the waltz is presented only in combination with the 'Grossvatertanz', and the one sketch (III, p. 52) which gives the ending as it was eventually printed, omits the six chimes of the clock which lend so romantic a touch to this typically Schumannesque coda. The manner in which the melody is partitioned into isolated wisps above the horn-call progressions in the L.H., and the cloudy effect of the whole passage suggest that Schumann may have unconsciously adopted ideas from Beethoven's *Righini* Variations, particularly Nos. 20 and 6 respectively, the similarities in the two works being intensified by the identity of key.

Schumann claimed that his inspiration in writing *Papillons* had come from Jean Paul's *Flegeljahre*, specifically from Chapter 63, entitled 'Larventanz' ('Masked Ball'). Although this can hardly be literally true, in view of the independent origin of some of the pieces as waltzes and polonaises, he attempted to bring the whole set into relationship with *Flegeljahre*. In his own copy of the book, Vol. 29 of Reimer's complete edition of 1827, he marked passages in Chapter 63, with numbers referring to the first ten *Papillons*. It should be explained that two brothers, Walt and Vult, the prototypes of Eusebius and Florestan, are both in love with Wina; they go to a fancy dress ball—Walt as Hope, Vult as a coachman—but exchange disguises half way through and Vult, pretending to be Walt, is able to win from Wina the admission of her love:

I. As he came out of the little room, he asked God that he might happily find it again; he felt like a hero, thirsting for fame, who goes forth to his first battle. . . .

II. Characteristically taking a wrong turn he first entered the punch-room, which he took for the dance-hall. . . . Wina was not to be seen, nor any sign of Vult. . . . At last, wishing to examine the anterooms, he reached the real resounding, burning hall full of excited figures . . . an aurora-borealis sky full of crossing, zigzag figures. . . .

III. What most of all attracted him and his astonishment was a giant boot that was sliding around, dressed in itself. . . .

IV. Hope quickly turned herself round, an unmasked shepherdess and a simple nun with a half-mask and a scented bunch of auriculas. . . .

V. Now he stood for a second alone by the tranquil maiden, and the half rose and lily of her face looked out from the half-mask as from the flower-sheath of a drooping bud. Like foreign spirits from two far cosmic nights they looked at each other behind the dark masks, like the stars in a solar eclipse, and each soul saw the other from a great distance.

VIII. As a youth touches the hand of a great and celebrated writer: so—like a butterfly's wing, like auricula-pollen—he lightly touched Wina's back and withdrew as far as possible in order to look at her life-breathing face. If there is a harvest-dance that is the harvest, if there is a catherine-wheel of loving rapture: Walt the coachman had both. . . .

VII. He threw his mask away and a curious hot desert-aridity or dry fever-heat broke through his gestures and words. If you have ever felt love for your brother, he began with dry voice and took the wreath off and undid the female costume,—if the fulfilment of one of his dearest wishes is anything to you, and if it is not indifferent to your joys whether he has the least or the greatest, in short if you will listen to one of his most earnest entreaties:

IX. To that I can only answer you: Joyfully.—'Then be quick', replied Vult without thinking.

VI. Your waltzes up to now—don't be annoyed—have traversed the room as good mimic imitations, partly horizontal—of the coachman, partly perpendicular—of the miner.

X. As Walt entered, it seemed to him that everyone noticed his exchange of disguise; some women noticed that Hope now had fair hair behind the flowers instead of as before, and Walt's step was shorter and more feminine, as became Hope. But he soon forgot himself and the hall and everything else as the coachman Vult without ado placed Wina at the head of the 'English dance' and now to her astonishment sketched out a dance with her and, like some painters, at the same time painted with the foot—only with bigger strokes.

Towards the very end of the dance, in the hurried hand-reachings, the crossings, the runnings up and down, Vult allowed ever more confused sounds to escape him—only the breath of speech—only stray butterflies blown to sea from a far-off island. To Wina it sounded like a curious lark's-song on a summer night.

It will be observed that there are no references to No. 11, the polonaise-pastiche, or to No. 12, with the 'Grossvatertanz' and the clock striking. This seems to confirm Julius Knorr's statement[1] that the two last numbers were composed later. Schumann's first copy of *Papillons* also bears on the first page as a (never published) motto, the closing words of *Flegeljahre*: 'Hark, from the distance Walt listened in rapture to the fleeing notes; for he did not realize that his brother was fleeing with them'.

Schumann's unbounded enthusiasm for Jean Paul may well have led him to assimilate other features of this classic of the romantic era. Was it the title of Chapter 14, 'Kinderball', which suggested his own set of piano duets, Op. 130 bearing that name, and the reference in Chapter 20 to the musical letters of a surname (Harnisch) which gave him the idea of coining the A B E G G theme and later, the A S C H motto? Did the occurrence of the word 'Papillote' in Chapter 63 prompt his adoption of that epithet for one of his sketches (the andantino of Op. 22), and the description of the fight between the orchestral players and their instruments in Chapter 26 quicken his sense of the picturesque and whimsical in musical portrayal? And was it the following paragraph from the 'Larventanz' which formed the general background of his thought when he was composing *Carnaval*—the masquerade incarnate in musical sounds? 'A masked ball', writes Jean Paul, 'is perhaps the most perfect medium through which poetry can interpret life. In the same way that the poet conceives all conditions and seasons as being of equal worth, all outer phenomena as mere trappings, but all inner qualities as air and sound, the human being seeks in the masked ball to poetise both his very self and life as a whole. In the masquerade, everything is rounded into a buoyant, happy circle which is set in well-ordered motion as if in obedience to the laws of prosody. It moves, to wit, in the sphere of music—the region of the spiritual, as the mask is the region of the physical.'

Like *Papillons*, though in lesser degree, *Carnaval* was the product of a lengthy and selective process of thought. The work did not begin simply as *Carnaval*, but as a set of variations on Schubert's *Sehnsuchtswalzer*, for which purpose Schumann drafted as many as three sets of sketches. From among these, however, he preserved only the one single variation which eventually took shape as the opening twenty-four bars of *Préambule*. The three manuscripts, belonging to the Vietinghoff-Scheel (private) Collection in Berlin, are entitled:

[1] J. Knorr, *Führer auf dem Felde der Klavierliteratur*, Leipzig, 1861.

(1) *Sehnsuchtswalzer Variationen;*

(2) *Scènes mignonnes;*

(3) *Scènes musicales sur un thème connu de Fr. Schubert.*

The last-named manuscript bears a dedication to Henriette Voigt, later the dedicatee of the G minor Sonata. The opus-number 10 is appended, which seems to suggest that Schumann intended to complete and publish the work. He early rejected this idea, however, and transferred the opus-number to his second set of *Paganini Études* published in 1835. In so doing, he even replaced the arabic by a roman numeral, explaining his adoption of this symbol of the unknown quantity in a delightfully fanciful paragraph of the introduction to his new Op. X, the whole of which was subsequently printed in his *Collected Writings.*

Schwarz gives the following particulars of the three MSS.: In Nos. 2 and 3 the first piece of No. 1 is preceded by an almost literal version of the now well-known 24-bars opening of *Préambule.* In these bars Schumann does not follow the Schubert theme strictly, but alludes to two of its distinctive chord-progressions, bars 9–10 and 11–14 of each work being in close correspondence either harmonically or enharmonically. The majority of the sketched variations do, however, follow the theme, while remaining typically Schumann-esque in points of pianoforte texture and variation-technique such as the use of chromaticisms, syncopations and triplet figures; the division of the melody between the R.H. and L.H. parts and its concealment in chords, and the invention of new melodic and rhythmic figures. The individual variations are not as fully completed as are the *Beethoven* Variations of the same period, but many of them had reached the stage of acquiring titles, such as *Intermezzo, Burla* and *Ritornello.* In *Carnaval* itself, *Reconnaissance* is the only piece which maintained any essential connection with the *Sehnsuchts-walzer,* and Schumann made no further use of this theme till 1842 when he referred once more to its harmonic basis in the Andante quasi variazioni of his String Quartet, Op. 41, No. 2. The fundamental 'theme' of *Carnaval* is the four-note motto ASCH which denotes both the birth-place in Bohemia of his inamorata at that time, Ernestine von Fricken, and the musical letters in his own name. Every one of the *Carnaval* pieces except *Préambule* and *Paganini* is based upon these four notes, which are arranged in a succession of patterns melodically and rhythmically so diverse as to exclude any sense of monotony, though subtle enough to impart a feeling of

coherence to the whole series. Even these eighteen 'variations' did
not exhaust all the latent possibilities in the motto, for Schumann
contrived to produce five additional pieces which he withdrew from
Carnaval and held in reserve for later publication.

One of these, a *Walzer* which breathes the spirit of *Carnaval* so
strongly as to make its exclusion seem incomprehensible to-day,
became the third of the *Fünf Albumblätter* published in 1852 in the
Bunte Blätter, Op. 99. The other four appeared two years later as
Nos. 4, 11, 15 and 17 of the *Albumblätter*, Op. 124. No. 4, which is
another *Walzer*, in A minor, is the only one of all the ASCH pieces
which is not written in a flat key and which has to make use of an
enharmonic D sharp for the essential E flat. Its rejection on grounds
of tonality alone is therefore the more easily intelligible. The
Romanza in B flat, No. 11, which emphasizes the ASCH motto
by stating it in octaves, may have been turned down because the
middle section tended to duplicate *Reconnaissance*. The remaining
Walzer, No. 15 in A flat, has no definite ASCH connections, but
is a distant relative of the *Sehnsuchtswalzer*. So strong, however, was
Schumann's obsession by the ASCH motto that he had no com-
punction in superimposing it upon pieces not originally conceived
on that basis. Even *Eusebius*, one of the main props of *Carnaval*, was
not primarily an ASCH piece, as may be noted from the sketches
dated October 1832 in Sk. II. No. 17 of the *Albumblätter*, Op. 124,
Elfe, too, was an ASCH piece only by adoption, for, as we have
already seen, it started its career as a sketch for *Papillons* (Ex. 15),
only to be remodelled subsequently in accordance with Schumann's

Ex.15

(or Ab)   next four bars
                                             as in published
                                             version.

ruling passion. Was ever a composer, so prodigal of ideas as was
Schumann, so persistently economical in his use of them? How
different from Schubert, who, if he were not satisfied with a composition, simply left it unfinished and went on to write something
entirely fresh!

It will hardly have escaped attention that almost every one of
Schumann's works so far mentioned in these pages was subjected to
a process of revision, drastic or otherwise, before it appeared in the

D

version familiar to us today. Now that the works in sonata-form come up for consideration, Schumann's tentative, haphazard method of composition will be seen in a still clearer light, for no work in this section of his production escaped some kind of alteration between the time of its conception and completion, whether in material, arrangement, title, dedication, or merely in opus-number. Even his very first single movement in sonata-form was planned in 1829 as an *Étude fantastique* in D major (for Clara), but by the time it was simplified, completed and published in 1834, it had become the *Toccata* in C, Op. 7, dedicated to 'son ami, Louis Schunke'. It still retained much of its étude character and stands to this day as a monument to the composer's own efficient performing technique and to his familiarity with the *Études* of Moscheles, particularly Op. 70, No. 9.

Schumann wrote his three principal Sonatas by instalments between 1833 and 1838. The composition of each of these works, the F sharp minor, Op. 11, the F minor, Op. 14, and the G minor, Op. 22, occupied him for a year or so and occasioned him more changes of mind than did any of his shorter works. Before he had embarked upon any of the large-scale works he had already tried to write a Sonata in A flat as early as 1830, and one in B minor in 1831 which he intended to dedicate to Moscheles, who was ultimately the recipient of the F minor. Of the A flat only two movements were written; both remain unpublished; their chief themes are shown in Ex. 16.

Of the B minor only the first movement survived to emerge as

Ex.16

a) Allegro

b) Adagio

the *Allegro*, Op. 8, dedicated to Ernestine von Fricken. We have already seen that this movement derived assistance for its introduction and coda from a sketch that was either a discarded *Papillon* (according to Gertler) or a variation on the Paganini theme (according to Schwarz); and other sketches relating to it (in Sk. V) are described by Gertler as being very heavily corrected and very difficult to read. Schumann's career as a composer of sonatas evidently began as uneasily as it continued.

With the compositions already mentioned in this group, two others, not now entitled sonatas but originally intended as such by Schumann, may be included here: the *Fantasie*, Op. 17, and *Faschingsschwank*, Op. 26. Before a survey is made of the purely musical qualities distinguishing all the complete works in sonata-form, a few facts relating to the order and manner of their appearance may be recorded.

The F sharp minor, begun in 1833, was first published, by Kistner, in 1836 under the authorship of 'Florestan und Eusebius', and a second edition, entitled *Première grande Sonate*, was issued in 1840, this time under Schumann's own name. For the first movement Schumann requisitioned a *Fandango, Rhapsodie pour le piano, oeuvre* 4 which he had composed in 1832 and had destined for publication by Hofmeister. Having mislaid it at the time, he had offered Hofmeister the *Allegro*, Op. 8 as a substitute. When the MS. of the *Fandango* opportunely turned up a year or so later,[1] Schumann remodelled it for use in his forthcoming Sonata, as is shown by a sketch (III) which, according to Gertler, manifests a suitable change in mood. He prefaced this revised version with an adagio introduction, to the melody of which he alluded later in the movement and in the second movement, too. This latter, entitled 'Aria', he transcribed from one of his early songs, *An Anna*, composed in 1828, transposing it from F to the more appropriate key of A major and making a few adjustments which are specified by Professor Abraham in the article already referred to. That the composition of the remaining two movements also caused Schumann trouble is revealed by sketches indicating a number of alterations in the planning, especially in the key-system of a section towards the end of the finale. (A complete sketch of this movement is in the Prussian State Library.) Among these sketches, one, which is pianistically the most interesting, refers to the opening of the first trio (third movement), where the theme in the middle

[1] The first page is reproduced in facsimile on p. 57 of Abert's book (see Bibliography).

voice is reinforced at the octave below over a pedal bass so that the melody stands out the more clearly, though the resulting texture lacks the resilience of the final version.

The F minor and G minor Sonatas overlapped each other to some extent as regards dates of composition, and the F minor bears an earlier opus-number than the G minor because the first edition was in print in 1836, some time before the G minor was completed. Schumann had designed the F minor as a Sonata in five movements, but he acceded to the request of his publisher, Haslinger, in cutting out the two scherzi and allowing the work to appear in 1836 as *Concert sans orchestre*. In 1853 Schumann reissued it in accordance with his own intentions and, as the G minor Sonata had meanwhile appeared in 1838 as *Deuxième grande Sonate*, the F minor was numbered *Troisième grande Sonate*. Its construction now comprised several alterations. Some ornamental passages in the first movement were revised; the second scherzo was restored as the second movement; and the finale, originally presto in 6/16 had become presto possibile in 2/4 with some changes in notation. The final edition came out in 1862, when it had been revised by 'DAS' (Dr. A. Schubring).[1] The neglect of this Sonata, in many ways more interesting than its two fellows, may perhaps be ascribed to the changes in construction and title which chequered its early career. At the time of its first publication Moscheles expressed his opinion to Schumann that 'the work did not fulfil the requirements of a Concerto though it possessed the characteristic attributes of a Grand Sonata in the manner of Beethoven and Weber, and that its prevailing seriousness and passion were the very reverse of the attributes expected by a concert audience of those days.'

The material of the G minor occupied Schumann's thoughts intermittently during a whole decade (1828–38). The first and third movements were composed in June 1833 and the second, andantino, which had been written as an independent piece in June 1830 (Sk. II), was an enhanced transcription of his song *Im Herbste* composed as early as 1828. The definitive finale was appended only in 1838, when it replaced one written in 1835 with which Schumann was dissatisfied. To complete the documentation of this long-drawn-out process of creation, it should be added that the tempestuous principal subject of the opening presto had originally been planned as an andante (Sk. II, p. 5).

[1] The first scherzo was published separately in 1866 and was included in the Supplementary Volume of the *Gesamtausgabe*.

The *Fantasie*, Op. 17, was composed in its first form in 1836, in which year Schumann wrote to Kistner outlining a grandiose scheme for its publication[1]—under the title *Ruinen, Trophäen, Palmen: Grosse Sonate für das Pianoforte, Op.* 12—as a contribution to the proposed Beethoven Monument, from 'Florestan und Eusebius'. He wrote a high-sounding dedication, offered suggestions for a spectacular cover with 'Obolus auf Beethovens Denkmal' in gold lettering on a black background, and told Kistner that the Sonata was remarkable in itself, containing, as it did, a reference to the 'adagio' (*sic*) of the Seventh Symphony.[2] Either Kistner was not enthusiastic or Schumann changed his mind, for the work remained unpublished until 1839 when it appeared as *Fantasie*, Op. 17, bearing a quotation from Schlegel, a dedication to Liszt and the imprint of Breitkopf and Härtel. The proposed titles and the reference to the Seventh Symphony had disappeared, and by a strange irony of fate, it was the boyish *Polonaises*, Op. III, first published nearly a hundred years later, which were ultimately vouchsafed the ceremonial black cover with gold lettering which ill accords with their irresponsible mood.

Faschingsschwank aus Wien, Op. 26, which Schumann described in a letter to Simonin de Sire, the dedicatee, as a 'great romantic sonata', was composed in 1839. Four movements were written in Vienna; the fifth—the only one in conventional sonata-form—was added after his return to Leipzig. The work was published complete in 1841, the fourth movement (*Intermezzo*) having, however, been printed in December 1839 as a *Fragment* 'from the *Nachtstücke* to be published shortly' in the Supplement to the *Neue Zeitschrift für Musik*. The title of this opus harks back to one Schumann had previously contemplated bestowing upon *Carnaval—Fasching: Schwänke auf vier Noten*—and indicates that his former delight in giving musical expression to the spirit of the masquerade had been reawakened by his sojourn in cosmopolitan Vienna.

[1] Printing this letter, Erler (*Robert Schumanns Leben*, Vol. I, p. 102) draws attention to the curious parallel lines at bars 79–80 and the corresponding passage later. Schumann's instruction to the engraver to 'engrave this passage exactly like this' is frequently ignored in modern editions—but not by Breitkopf.—*Ed.*

[2] Another quotation from Beethoven remains: from the sixth song of the cycle *An die ferne Geliebte*. The whole first movement hints at it, and it emerges clearly at the end. The words are a dedication—'*Take them, then, these songs* which I sang to thee, Beloved' (Ex. 111 *b*)—and the quotation hints both at Beethoven and at Schumann's own 'distant beloved'. Is it fanciful to detect other references to the Beethoven cycle in the *Fantasie*, e.g. to the last page of the songs in the triumphant second movement?—*Ed.*

From Schumann's desultory and laborious manner of writing sonatas it would appear that while he was not naturally drawn to this branch of composition, he was resolved to find his own way to the solution of the problems of creating large-scale works in established forms. His gifts were not those of a clear-sighted architect, and his sonatas consequently convey little sensation of being compact structures whose ground-plan was determined from the very beginning. Yet though his long-range architectonic planning was deficient, his artistic power of filling large spaces with enchanting musical images was highly developed. If the longer movements of the sonatas are viewed as great mural decorations, resplendent with bold outlines and intensive colouring, they exercise an immediate attraction and reveal the weaknesses in their construction only upon closer analysis. Schumann often became so deeply absorbed in the musical ideas themselves that he lost sight of the aspects of formal symmetry and key-relationship. He would repeat a phrase sequentially until it became tiresome, maintain a rhythmic or metrical figure for so long as to produce monotony, or would cut up a movement into self-contained sections in a manner which deprived it of any sense of wholeness or inevitability. Even so, the best of the Schumann sonata-movements, though they may be lacking in the dramatic tension which is one of the prerequisites of classical sonata-form, are endowed with lyrical and pianistic interest strong enough to outweigh their disadvantages in other respects. They would not otherwise have held the affections of pianists continuously for over a hundred years.

It is idle to attempt to criticize the works of this group according to recognized classical standards, for when Schumann followed the traditions of sonata-form most closely, the movements he produced were far less convincing than when he threw convention to the winds and tumbled out the wealth of his ideas in picturesque disarray. The *Toccata*, whose formal planning is merely stereotyped, holds its own as a concert piece by reason of its compelling virtuosic qualities although they are the very negation of established sonata style. On the other hand, the perfunctory *Allegro*, Op. 8, though formally more ingeniously organized, finds little favour with performers on account of its undistinguished material. Schumann himself stigmatized it as an 'Allegro di bravura' in which 'there was not much besides good intentions'. The conventionally designed finale of the *Faschings-schwank*, notwithstanding its impetuous progress, sounds prosaic when placed alongside either the regular but impassioned first-movements of the *Fantasie* and the F minor Sonata, or the finale of the latter, whose myriads of tameless semiquavers lend it the character of a superb concert-étude. It was the development-section which was Schumann's stumbling-block. Sometimes he omitted it altogether and lengthened the movement with a coda, as in the finale of Op. 11, or he replaced it by a self-contained interlude (Op. 11 and Op. 17,[1] first movements) to counteract the overstatement of thematic material in the exposition and recapitulation. Or he even repeated the 'development' in the recapitulation, as in the first-movement of Op. 14, which incidentally tends to rondo-form on account of the three-fold repetition of the introductory material. The first movement of Op. 11 has the character of a free improvisation in the grand manner. That of Op. 22 is far more regular in construction, but even here Schumann was so ill at ease in the so-called development section that he was driven to dulling the effect of the recapitulation by reverting to the tonic key and exploiting the principal subject long before either was due for re-establishment.

Nevertheless, if Schumann found it difficult to come to terms with the sonata as it was cultivated by his predecessors, he showed great enterprise in instilling each of his own works of this kind with new life. He never planned two of them alike, nor did he even write two movements quite similar in construction or in style. His choice of key-relationship between the movements of a complete work, or of the order of their appearance within it, differs in every case. Of the five slow movements, the two based on songs (Opp. 11 and 22) are treated in diverse manner in spite of the similarity in the style of their material; another (Op. 14) is a set of variations; one (the finale of Op. 17) is an extended dual form new to Schumann, and the last, (Op. 26) a miniature in episodical form. Each of the scherzi has an individual design, and whereas that of Op. 22 is brief and to the point, and the scherzino of Op. 26 is a fragment of repetitive mosaic, the scherzo of Op. 14 is long, intricate in texture and subtle in structure, and its rejected companion (Op. posth.) is a thrilling study in cross-rhythms. The corresponding movement of Op. 11, a scherzo with two trios, the second of which is an intermezzo in the style of a burlesque, has affinities with older rondo form, as has also the first movement of Op. 14. With these movements, the finale of the *Études symphoniques* may also he mentioned as a type of rondo in which both episodes comprise the same material presented in

[1] Although the 'Legendenton' melody of this interlude in Op. 17 is a transformation, if not the original form, of one of the themes of the exposition.

different keys. Of the other movements more specifically in rondo-form, the moderato of the *Fantasie* and the finale of Op. 22 both blend the elements of older and modern rondo, as does also the discarded finale of the latter work—Schumann's most lengthy and least coherent sonata-movement. In all these three movements, each of which has an extensive bravura coda, Schumann mustered so large a retinue of ideas that he had difficulty in ordering their procession. On the other hand, in the opening allegro of the *Faschingsschwank*, a long movement of a ritornello type unparalleled in any other of his piano works and only nearly approached by the fifth *Novellette* or faintly echoed in the first *Nachtstück*, he accorded to the copious material a more regular, sectional treatment which greatly enhances its effectiveness.[1] The one subsidiary movement in this group, the *Intermezzo* of Op. 26, consists of nothing but the alternation of two thematic periods at different pitches and in different keys, but it is nevertheless an expressive tone-poem.

This particular movement may serve as a connecting link between the works of large dimensions just discussed and those of smaller stature about to be surveyed, since it happens to illustrate Tovey's statement that Schumann's pianoforte lyrics 'depend on the simple and effective alternation and contrast of vividly characteristic self-contained musical strophes'. Schumann's supreme gift as a composer for the piano—his power of expressing a very great deal in a very small space—is exemplified to perfection in the many sets of short pieces which he wrote during his first-period, beginning with the *Intermezzi*, Op. 4 in 1832, and ending with the four short movements comprising Op. 32 in 1839. Leaving out of account the perennially beloved *Papillons* and *Carnaval*—two collections of short pieces so individual that they had necessarily to be reviewed here in a category of their own—the sets which now come under observation include some of Schumann's most warmly admired and frequently performed small-scale works. That he wrote them from inner conviction and with comparative ease is proved by the fact that this group of compositions, in contradistinction to some of the others, provides few instances of any outstanding 'variations' in conception. The first set certainly underwent trifling modifications. Its opus-number was advanced from 3 to 4; the title, originally *Pièces phantastiques*, reduced to *Intermezzi*, and the dedication transferred from

[1] I fancy I detect between the appearances of the ritornello the masked figures of Chopin (the first G minor episode), Mendelssohn (the second G minor) and Schubert (the F sharp major). Perhaps the E flat mask conceals Schumann himself (cf. *Grillen*, Op. 12, No. 4).—*Ed.*

Clara to J. W. Kalliwoda. The *Davidsbündlertänze* appeared in two
successive editions with several differences in material and format.
A second, slightly revised edition of *Kreisleriana* was issued twelve
years after its original publication, and the dedication, at first
intended for Clara, bestowed upon Chopin. The separate numbers
of Op. 32 were composed at different times and places and were
only subsequently strung together for publication. Otherwise, the
composition of the works in this large group proceeded rapidly.
The *Intermezzi*, Op. 4, 'extended *Papillons*' according to Schumann,
were composed five years earlier (1832) than any of the better-known
collections of single pieces. They hardly bear comparison with any
of their exquisitely finished successors, but they are of particular
interest in being the first set of pieces which Schumann wrote in
more extended form than hitherto. Their only predecessors had
been nearly all very short, and none of them was so highly organized
as are most of the *Intermezzi*. All but one of these is in episodical
form with an independent 'alternativo', the only exception being
No. 4, for whose slighter stature Schumann had his own good reason:
it is mainly a transcription of yet another of his songs belonging to the
year 1828. Unlike its fellows in Opp. 11 and 22, however, it is preluded
with a little phrase which recurs at the end of each verse and accen-
tuates rather than disguises the vocal, strophic origin of the movement. This phrase and the brief, irrelevant coda which are both
taken from a rejected 16-bar *Papillon* in 3/4 time, are to be found in
Sk. III, together with a sketch for each section of the fifth *Intermezzo*.
(The origin of the 'alternativo' of the sixth has already been referred
to on p. 34.) Another phrase of No. 4 comes from a Piano Quartet
(see pp. 138–9).

While the thematic material of the *Intermezzi* is not on the whole
intrinsically attractive, the deft organization of all the movements—
except the pre-fabricated No. 4—compels admiration. Bar-to-bar
analysis reveals many interesting features, especially in the da capo
repetitions, in which phrases and sections are often re-arranged in
varying order (Nos. 1 and 6), at different pitches (No. 2) or with the
L.H. and R.H. parts inverted (No. 2), and in which the texture is
modified in some manner to secure diversity. Gertler considers
Op. 4 to be the least unified of all the Schumann pianoforte cycles
although it is held together by points of similarity between the
separate items. Indeed, Schumann could hardly have intended them
to be played independently for they manifest a certain sense of continuity and lead into each other satisfactorily, even when they are

not explicitly marked 'attacca'. Among the various points of similarity between them, the following are selected as being typical of
Schumann's pianistic style as a whole: the texture of quavers in
triplets in Nos. 2 and 6; the occasional appearance in the 'alternativo'
of the principal figure of the main section (Nos. 1 and 5); a double-
octave call to attention (Nos. 2 and 6); a decorative passage inserted
for purposes of colour (No. 1, bars 21–3 of D major section, and
No. 5, last 4 bars of 'alternativo'); a bar or two marked 'adagio' in
the midst of a presto (No. 1) or of an allegro (No. 5); intricate cross-
hand passages (Nos. 2 and 5), and the dance-like character of most
of the 'alternativos'. Schumann signalized his adherence to romantic
ideals by attaching a poetic quotation ('Meine Ruh' ist hin') to the
middle section of No. 2.[1] He also looked both before and after to
his own compositions, using in the 'alternativo' of this *Intermezzo* a
type of figure—two notes against one in the same hand (bars 9–15)—
which he had employed in Vars. 1 and 4 of Op. 1, weaving the
'Abegg' motto into the texture of No. 6 (bars 42–44), and hinting in
two places in No. 5 at the brilliant coda of the first movement of
Faschingsschwank (bars 45–6 of the main section and 59–63 of
'alternativo').

During the five years between the completion of the *Intermezzi*
and the composition of the next two series, *Fantasiestücke*, Op. 12,
and the *Davidsbündlertänze* in 1837, Schumann was fully occupied in
writing the several works of different types which have already been
surveyed. The only other short pieces belonging to this intervening
period are the miniatures later included in the *Albumblätter*, Op. 124:
Nos. 1, 3, 12, 13 and 15 of which were composed in 1832, No. 2 in
1833, Nos. 4, 11 and 17 in 1835 and 5 and 7 in 1836. Some of these
had originally been intended for other purposes: the ASCH pieces
mentioned earlier, Nos. 4, 5, 11, 15 and 17 of Op. 124 (and No. 6
of the *Bunte Blätter*, Op. 99), No. 2, *Leides Ahnung*, one of the
Beethoven variations, and No. 3, *Scherzino*, a discarded *Papillon*.
Among the others, two of the earliest, No. 1, *Impromptu*, and No. 12,
Burla—both lively compact pieces of short sequences and reiterated
metrical figures—exhibit one of Schumann's less pleasing idiosyncrasies: his tendency to invent monotonous sequential texture.
Another, No. 13, *Larghetto*, not only typifies his not infrequent practice of hovering between major and minor, but is of additional

---

[1] Boetticher (*Robert Schumann in seinen Schriften und Briefen*, p. 75) quotes a
diary entry, 'The opera without text—But my whole heart is in thee, dear fifth
Intermezzo, that was born with such unutterable love!'—*Ed.*

interest in foreshadowing the introduction to the slow movement of his much later String Quartet in F. The two latest, No. 5, *Fantasie-tanz*, and No. 7, *Ländler*, respectively display attractive characteristics of his pianistic style: the former the unhurried passage of an eloquent melody in the left hand beneath an overlay of scurrying semiquavers in the right, and the latter, the introduction of rhythmical contrast into a dance movement by the insertion of a series of syncopations between the phrases which follow the traditional dance-measure. The next of the *Albumblätter*, No. 8, *Leid ohne Ende* was written in 1837, in the same year as the *Davidsbündlertänze*, Op. 6, and the *Fantasiestücke*, Op. 12, with both of which it has several stylistic points in common, as will later appear. The *Davidsbündlertänze* are one of Schumann's most subjective works. He had already published compositions under his duple pseudonym, 'Florestan und Eusebius', and now, in addition to printing the two names on the title-page (for the last time as a composer), he appended to each of the separate pieces the initial of one or other—or both—of these fictitious person-alities, according to whether the musical content was the expression of the passionate or the dreamy side of his nature. The music thus conceived is so intimate in its delineation of personal moods that possibly it can be enjoyed and appreciated to the full only by players or listeners who have been initiated into the ways of thought of the imaginary *Davidsbund* which was so lively a reality to Schumann himself. No one who has ever heard the traditional interpretation of this work by a Clara Schumann pupil can have failed to perceive that the performer regards the *Davidsbündlertänze* as the quintessence of Schumann's pianistic art.

On its first appearance it was entitled *Davidsbündlertänze* and was published by Friese of Leipzig in two books of nine pieces in each. A four-lined verse—an 'old saying'—was printed on the cover and the performing directions for each piece were given in German instead of the customary Italian. A note above the last piece in each book indicates that it portrays respectively Florestan's distressful state of mind and the tranquil ecstasy of Eusebius. A second edition of the work was published by Schuberth in 1850–1, by which time Schumann had decided to omit the word 'dances' from the title, and the motto verse, too; to exchange one of the racy performing direc-tions for another more sober, and to expunge the romantic descrip-tive notes. He added the sub-title 'Characteristic pieces'. The textual revisions of Nos. 1, 3, 6, 8, 9, 11, and 13 are too slight in import-ance to specify here, except that of No. 9, where the matter-of-fact

last bar replaces the subtle ending of the first edition—an example
of the deliberate supersession of a mysterious conclusion by a
prosaic one, such as we noted earlier during the comparison of the
two versions of the final bars of the *Impromptus*, Op. 5 (see p. 22),
and shall encounter again in Nos. 4 and 5 of *Kreisleriana*, Op. 16.
A third edition of *Davidsbündler* comprising the textual readings of
both the preceding was issued in 1861 under the editorship of 'DAS',
who explained in the Foreword that Schumann had used the title
'Dances' only to emphasize the relationship of the work to its
predecessor, *Carnaval*, in which the *Davidsbündler* had marched to
the strains of the 'Grossvatertanz' in their assault against the Philistines. Musical cross-references between the two works confirm this
relationship in the same way that an extract from *Papillons* inserted
in *Carnaval* indicates the similarity in mood between those two
compositions. The *Davidsbündler* and *Carnaval* are connected by a
reminiscence of the 'Grossvatertanz' in one of the former, which
also includes a brief but direct quotation from *Promenade*, the ante-
penultimate movement of *Carnaval*. Moreover, inconclusive endings
of individual pieces—occasionally even in a different key from the
beginnings—are distinctive features of *Papillons*, *Carnaval* and
Davidsbündler alike. The last-named differs in one important respect
from the other two, as also from most of Schumann's earlier compositions, in lacking any recorded preliminary sketches; a proof that
he wrote it without tergiversation. Indeed, in a letter to Clara, from
whom he had borrowed a musical motto for the beginning of the
first piece, he wrote, 'If ever I was happy at the piano, it was when
I was composing these.'

The movements of the *Davidsbündlertänze* are alternately restless
and contemplative. The combination of triple and duple time in
No. 10; the three concurrent opposing metrical units in No. 2; the
bi-planal pungencies in the D major section of No. 6 and numerous
unprepared discords, especially those in Nos. 2 and 9, all represent
persistent mental conflict. On the other hand, the smoothly flowing
melodic line in Nos. 5, 11, and 14, and the stabilising of the harmonic
progressions by pedal-points, particularly in No. 17, betoken peace
of mind. Schumann's pianistic texture had been growing progressively more intricate, but never had he written quite so cryptically
as in Nos. 2, 7, and 9. It was rare, too, for him to invent phrases of
uneven bar-lengths. In No. 8, however, he showed that he could
construct a complete piece from such material, for it consists of three
successive seven-bar phrases followed by one of five-bars. Only in

two of the *Davidsbündlertänze* did he revert to his early practice of writing in variation-form—although here only on a miniature scale— in Nos. 11 and 5. The melodic line of the latter has affinities with that of *Leid ohne Ende*, Op. 124, No. 8. In view of the fact that both pieces were composed in the same year, it may even be surmised that this isolated *Albumblatt* was at one time intended for inclusion in the *Davidsbündlertänze*, more especially as the unhurried broken-chord ornaments in the left-hand also have their counterpart in Op. 6 in the leisurely left-hand arpeggi of Nos. 1 and 7.

In the *Fantasiestücke*, Op. 12, originally published in two books of four pieces in each, Schumann broke new ground. He produced his first set of pieces of varying length which, although they are all composed in flat keys and form a homogeneous whole, can be played independently of each other without serious loss of effect. The *Fantasiestücke* written in 1837 and *Carnaval* published in the same year, were the first piano works in which he used titles for each individual movement. Writing to Moscheles that year about *Carnaval*, Schumann said, 'I added the titles afterwards, for is not music always sufficiently expressive in itself?'; and a year or two later he told Simonin de Sire that 'the titles of my compositions never occur to me until I have finished writing.'[1] His consistently apt choice of titles for his piano compositions has undoubtedly contributed towards a fuller realization by the performer of the imaginative qualities of the music itself. Besides *Carnaval* and the *Fantasiestücke*, all the other sets of piano works bearing separate titles— *Kinderscenen*, *Jugend-Album*, *Waldscenen*, and *Albumblätter*—have always made a special appeal to the interpretative musician.

In point of formal structure the *Fantasiestücke* are much more complex than any of their predecessors, and their pianistic lay-out is more varied. No two pieces are alike in shape, style or mood. Tovey maintains that 'the true aesthetic analysis of a *Novellette* or *Fantasiestück* of Schumann would mean an analysis of the function and balance of practically every note in each section; and such an analysis would be not only tedious in the extreme, but hideously difficult to understand'. It would, indeed, be tedious to write or to read any such analysis, but it is absorbingly interesting to take the pieces themselves, to sketch even the roughest outline of their main structural features, and in so doing to become aware of the mastery of Schumann's small-scale designing and of his infinite resource in

[1] A ninth *Fantasiestück*, suppressed, and published only in 1935, never reached the stage of having a title.—*Ed.*

devising modifications of established plans. Most of the *Fantasiestücke* sound at a first playing to be cast in episodical form, but closer
inspection reveals that *Grillen* is almost a true example of sonata-rondo
form; that *Fabel* is built up archwise, its several sections recurring
after the central episode in the reverse order from that of their original
appearance; that *Aufschwung* and *In der Nacht* both display the key-
relationships of sonata-form; that in *Traumes Wirren* the return of
the main section is anticipated by a paragraph enlivened by the
sudden emergence of a wisp of the opening subject deceptively
transposed a semitone above its native pitch; and that *Ende vom Lied*
is the only one of these movements which has a literal repeat of its
opening section after the longish interlude, and an entirely fresh coda
in which a figure from the main theme appears by augmentation.
As for *Des Abends* and *Warum*, they are miracles of imaginative construction. In the first-named, the complete tranquil substance
appears twice over, as if it were an image and its reflection in a
mirror. Thereafter, the perpetually liquescent figuration of which
the movement is wrought continues for a while so that it may carry
the music to vanishing-point. *Warum*, actually in lilliputian episodical form, is dominated by a plaintive, questioning theme which
insinuates itself into the texture of gently beating chords, gradually
threads its way through the formal barriers to make a last, threefold
attempt to find a solution of its questionings, and then falls into
inconclusive silence. The movement is a masterpiece of lapidary
art. It is remarkable that among the eight *Fantasiestücke*, two should
be almost unbroken moto perpetuos, and that these two, both tissues
of semiquavers, should stand in sharp mutual contrast in respect of
atmosphere and expressiveness, the almost static *Des Abends* being
the very antithesis of the wildly dynamic *In der Nacht*. The latter was
Schumann's acknowledged favourite of all the pieces in Op. 12,
possibly because of the extra-musical significance it acquired for him
when he found to his delight that 'it contained the story of Hero and
Leander.' To only one of the movements of Op. 12 did Schumann
make a tentative sketch: to *Traumes Wirren* (Sk. II). It shows the
right-hand part of bars 1 and 2 as they stand in print but gives
the left-hand part in widespread broken-chord formation. Gertler
describes these five bars as being less telling than the finished version.

Schumann was nearing the summit of his powers as a composer
of piano music. In 1838, the year he went to reside in Vienna, he
wrote the thirteen pieces of *Kinderscenen*, Op. 15, the eight of
Kreisleriana, Op. 16, the eight *Novelletten*, Op. 21, the first three of

the four items of Op. 32, nine miniatures later relegated to *Album-blätter*, Op. 124, and to *Bunte Blätter*, Op. 99, and incidentally the definitive finale of the G minor Sonata. Yet even this abundant production was surpassed in the following year which saw the composition of the three long soli, *Arabeske*, Op. 18, *Blumenstück*, Op. 19, *Humoreske*, Op. 20 (each of which is a concretion of many well-defined sections), the four *Nachtstücke*, Op. 23, while he was still in Vienna (the *Faschingsschwank*, too, belongs to this period); and of the three *Romanzen*, Op. 28; the last number, *Fughetta*, of Op. 32; and three more trifles for Opp. 124 and 99 after his return to Leipzig. The large number of these works and the similarity in scope of some of them, not to mention limitations of space in this chapter, make it impossible to undertake a detailed analysis of every separate opus. Each of them will, however, be considered briefly as a whole work and its general tendencies noted in passing. A review of their more particular characteristics will be included in a summary subsequently to be made of the chief stylistic features distinguishing the complete series of piano works of Schumann's first period down to the end of 1839.

The first work of 1838 was Op. 15.[1] In March that year, Schumann told Clara that he had suddenly composed 'about thirty quaint little things from which I have selected twelve and called them *Kinder-scenen*.' The titles, he told Dorn later, were 'merely hints as to treatment and interpretation'. The items of this opus, together with the little E flat movement, No. 8 of *Bunte Blätter*, Op. 99, which may have been a rejected *Kinderscene*, are the simplest of all the works of this period in both conception and outline. They comprise almost exclusively tiny pieces in episodical form, with here and there a monothematic prelude or a miniature based on one single phrase or figure repeated endlessly throughout. Of the last-named type, No. 5, *Glückes genug* is a conspicuous example. Schumann marked it to be repeated da capo, as though to indicate that the piece had neither beginning nor end and that it might be played ad infinitum. No. 11, *Fürchtenmachen* consists of alternating sections in contrasted moods and different tempi, in which respects it is an attenuated reflection of *Fabel*, Op. 12, No. 6. Only the epilogue, No. 13, *Der Dichter spricht* is of meditative, improvisatory character.

If *Kinderscenen* represents Schumann at his most naïve and genial as yet, *Kreisleriana : Phantasien für das Pianoforte*, Op. 16, written

[1] Originally 'to have been the beginning of the *Novelletten*' (cf. letter to Raymond Härtel, 21 March 1838).

in the following month and within the space of only a few days, gives expression to his most inward thoughts. His utterance in *Davids-bündlertänze* had now and then been cryptic; in *Kreisleriana* it is often recondite in the extreme, though here, as in Op. 6, brooding mystery is offset by bustling activity. 'Never was Schumann more truly a tone-poet than in this work', writes Wasielewski. The collection of pieces has an enigmatic background. It purports to delineate the rambling confessions of Ludwig Böhner, a gifted but unsuccessful Thuringian composer and conductor whom Schumann regarded as the original of E. T. A. Hoffmann's Kapellmeister Kreisler in his *Fantasiestücke in Callots Manier*—though present-day German literary critics hold other views on the subject. Schumann had heard the eccentric Böhner improvise in Leipzig in 1834 and had at one time thought to portray him in words in the *Neue Zeitschrift für Musik*. Instead, he immortalized him in the music of *Kreisleriana*. The work is a particularly coherent whole. The fundamental tonality is G minor; three of the pieces are in that key, three in the relative major, while the two others are respectively in the nearly related keys of D minor and C minor. Each movement would lose much by being performed away from its context, especially as two (Nos. 4 and 7) end inconclusively—as did also No. 5 in the first edition—so that they must be played in conjunction with their immediate successors. Nos. 4 and 6 are the most abstruse, and for these two intensely personal lento movements, Schumann designed a structure approximating to a recitative and aria, with a summary of the recitative as coda. The closing bar of each is marked adagio, as is the final four-bar phrase of No. 2. The last-named, one of the longest, is in the form of a minuet with two independent trios styled 'Intermezzi I and II'. The principal section, the most placidly expressive of the sustained movements of this opus, has affinities in mood and texture with the short *Impromptu*, Op. 124, No. 9, and with the B flat section of the fifth *Novellette*, Op. 21, which were both written in the same year and the same key. Other single movements of this period which plumb the depths of labyrinthine thinking are the brief E flat minor *Albumblatt* of *Bunte Blätter* (Op. 99, No. 7) and the *Romanze* in F sharp, Op. 28, No. 2. The intermezzo of the third *Novellette*, too, contains some dark sayings. They probably had a literary significance for Schumann, for when he printed this section as a separate piece in the *Neue Zeitschrift für Musik* (22 May 1839) he prefixed to it a quotation from *Macbeth*, 'When shall we three meet again?' Indeed his 'Haushaltbuch' records: 'Saturday,

3 March 1838, made Macbeth-Novellette'. The tumultuous urgency of the quick movements of *Kreisleriana* re-emerges in the 'Sehr rasch' in E minor, No. 2 of *Bunte Blätter*, and the *Gigue* of Op. 32. The latter bears a strong resemblance in spirit and in metrical figuration to No. 8 of Op. 16, and the likeness is accentuated by both pieces being in G minor: another instance of Schumann's frequent habit of using identical keys to denote similarity of mood. In *Kreisleriana* he also demonstrated his increasing preference for composing in older-rondo form. Several of the pieces, notably Nos. 2, 6, 7, 8, are constructed in some small-scale variety of this form. They are therefore comparable in structure with their relatively gigantic contemporaries, some of the *Novelletten*, Op. 21, the sizable pieces of Opp. 18, 19, and 20, as well as with the *Nachtstücke*, Op. 23, the *Romanzen*, Op. 28, and the *Scherzo* of Op. 32.

With the *Novelletten*, originally published in two books with four in each, Schumann launched a series of compositions in a style he had not as yet essayed. Hitherto he had delineated moods (*Fantasiestücke*), emotions (*Davidsbündlertänze* and *Kreisleriana*) or a succession of related images (*Carnaval*). Now he wrote music of a kind he described as depicting 'longish, connected tales of adventure'.[1] The *Novelletten* are 'closely connected, were written with great enjoyment and are on the whole light and superficial, excepting one or two sections where I go deeper'—so he wrote to Hirschbach in 1839. The pieces are resplendent with a multitude of brilliant ideas presented in bold and effective pianistic terms. Their impulsive style offers the strongest imaginable contrast to the introspective *Davidsbündlertänze* and *Kreisleriana* and is the apotheosis of romantic exuberance. Structurally the *Novelletten* are extremely diverse. The shortest (No. 7) is a compact rondo in which the first episode is a development of the refrain; the most extensive (No. 8), which is more than three times the length of its predecessor, is a dual movement wherein a pair of scherzos, each with two trios, is made to cohere by a theme in long notes designated 'Stimme aus der Ferne' common to both sections. Between these dimensional extremes, the other movements, which are more moderate and uniform in length, conform to either rondo or episodical type, though each has some interesting variation in design such as: the recurrence of the refrain,

---

[1] A diary entry for 22 April 1838, reads, 'Sent Liszt the Saracens'. Boetticher says this refers to one of the D major *Novelletten* 'which originally bore the inscription *Sarazene und Suleika*'. In a letter to Clara (6 February 1838), Schumann says he has composed 'during the last three weeks . . . jokes, *Egmont*-stories, family scenes with fathers, a wedding. . . .'.

E

either in an alien key (No. 1), by implication instead of direct statement (No. 4), or ritornello-wise (No. 5).[1] No. 6 is an apparently
haphazard succession of vivid phrases with only an occasional restatement of any one of them, and even then in an unexpected key. It is,
indeed, a breathless narrative. One additional *Novellette*, omitted
from Op. 21 and eventually included as No. 9 in Op. 99, is a simple
duo-thematic miniature, but it breathes the same ardent spirit as its
powerful namesakes. Other contemporary miniatures of similar
character which were, however, published later, are Nos. 1–3, 5,
and 10 of Op. 99,[2] and four pieces in Op. 124: No. 10, *Walzer*,
No. 14, *Vision*, No. 18, *Botschaft* and No. 19, *Fantasiestück*. This last
title, used by Schumann several times during his career (for Opp. 12,
88, 111, &c.) was one of those he borrowed from E. T. A. Hoffmann,
another being *Nachtstücke*, which he gave to the set of four movements, Op. 23, composed in 1839.

An expansive mood pervades these last-named pieces despite the
title, which, tenebrous as it is, replaces another, definitely lugubrious.
'While I was composing', wrote Schumann in April 1839, 'I kept
seeing funerals, coffins, and unhappy despairing faces, and when I
had finished, and was trying to think of a title, the only one that
occurred to me was *Funeral Fantasy*.' The four pieces were originally
headed *Funeral March, Strange Company, Nocturnal Carousal* and
Round with solo voices. Yet they are hardly elegiac in temper though
they fluctuate enchantingly between the major and minor modes.
The first begins deceptively in the supertonic minor, and Nos. 2 and
4 (as well as No. 1), each with an ambiguous diminished-seventh
chord. Only in No. 3 is the opening section convinced of its major
modality from the very beginning. Like *Kreisleriana*, the cycle is
strongly unified in tonality. The initial movement is in C, Nos. 2
and 4 are in F, No. 3 is in D flat, and the subsidiary portions in each
are all in flat keys, except an episode in No. 3, whose sudden flight
to a sharp key, and equally abrupt return to a flat one lend the movement a refreshing touch of chiaroscuro. The piece is in the form of a
scherzo and two trios, with the eight introductory bars subtly meta-
morphosed into a modulatory link before the last appearance of the

---

[1] The 'Haushaltbuch' dates No. 5 precisely 'Up to 11 March 1838. . . . *Glückes
genug* and polonaise for the *Novelletten*. Monday, 12.3. composed at the polonaise
for the *Novelletten*'.

[2] According to Boetticher (*Robert Schumann: Einführung in Persönlichkeit und
Werk*), Op. 99, No. 1 was originally entitled *Wunsch* and dedicated to Clara at
Christmas, 1838, and the *Präludium*, No. 10, is built from the ruins of two unsuc-
cessful fugues.—*Ed.*

refrain. The third *Romanze* of Op. 28 is a longer and more developed species of this structural genus, wherein the contrasting episodes are specifically labelled 'intermezzi' and in whose final reprise variety is secured by the two main sections of the refrain recurring in inverse order. The *Drei Romanzen*, Op. 28, stood high in Schumann's own estimation; he ranked them with Opp. 12, 16, and 21 as being amongst his best compositions for piano, and evidently intended that they should be played as a group. The mutual key-relationship is designed to ensure continuity while at the same time avoiding monotony. There is great contrast of mood, too, between the semplice F sharp, No. 2, whose hypnotic tranquillity emphasizes the animation of the two other movements, No. 1, a restless moto perpetuo in B flat minor, and a segmented finale in B major, alternately jerky and fluent in metrical outline. In this respect the last-named is a near relative of the shorter and more gracious *Scherzo* of Op. 32 (No. 1), while the moto perpetuo (Op. 28, No. 1) just mentioned is twin brother to the *Romanze*, Op. 32 (No. 3), being just such another unflagging sweep of semiquaver triplets in 2/4 time in the minor mode, this time marked 'Sehr rasch und mit Bravour'. A further member of this precipitate family is the *Intermezzo* in E flat minor, No. 4 of the *Faschingsschwank*, which though in common time, carries on the traditional figuration 'mit grösster Energie'. Op. 32 is a strangely heterogeneous collection. With the two intensely romantic creations, *Scherzo* and *Romanze* just mentioned, it combines two brief movements in mildly polyphonic style: a *Gigue*, No. 2, which is Handelian in spirit, and a *Fughetta*, No. 4 which trips along gaily in 6/8 time and whose harmonies are spiced with mordant semitonic clashes. Moreover, as these two latter had been printed as separate pieces in the Supplement to the *Neue Zeitschrift für Musik* in 1839 (Heft 5) and 1840 (Heft 10) respectively, it would seem that the publication in 1841 of all four movements as a complete opus was a matter of expediency rather than of deliberate planning.

Only three compositions belonging to this culminating period of Schumann's creative activity now remain for discussion: *Arabeske*, Op. 18, *Blumenstück*, Op. 19 and *Humoreske*, Op. 20—a triad of works progressively more intricate in their rondo construction and increasingly typical of Schumann's individual style. He described them as 'variations, but not upon a theme', and they illustrate his use of variation as a formative principle inasmuch as the thematic material of each undergoes varied treatment as it proceeds. The *Arabeske* is a straightforward, conventionally planned rondo in C major, but the two minor episodes, each in a different key, are well contrasted to the main substance in both mood and texture, and the detached coda, too, provides fresh material and a new tempo. The *Blumenstück* on the other hand, though an entirely novel type of rondo, is almost completely lacking in contrast. Every one of the five self-contained, numbered sections is in a nearly-related flat key, and throughout the entire piece, which is nearly two hundred bars in length, there are only seven infinitesimal breaks in the constantly changing pattern of eight semiquavers to the bar—and these at cadence-points where such intermissions are almost inevitable. The interest of the *Blumenstück* lies, however, in the unwonted arrangement of the sections. No. I is the introduction which never recurs; No. II, the principal refrain which reappears three times in shortened form and in different keys or mode. The three remaining sections are the episodes, of which Nos. III and V occur only once each, and No. IV twice in identical terms. The element of variation in this work consists in the recurrence of the same theme in fresh keys and different sections, and in the interchange of thematic figures and phrases between the upper, middle, and lower parts of the texture. Schumann considered Opp. 18 and 19 as of less importance than Op. 20 about which he wrote enthusiastically to Clara in March 1839. 'I have been all the week at the piano, composing, writing, laughing and crying, all at once. You will find this state of affairs nicely described in my Op. 20, the *Grosse Humoreske*—twelve sheets composed in a week.' And twelve such sheets, too! In a modern edition they run to twenty-nine pages of kaleidoscopic music which defies exact formal nomenclature. Leaving out of account the several indications of repeats, there are more than thirty double-barlines denoting breaks in the continuity, as well as numerous changes in time—and key-signatures and constant variations in tempi such as characterize many of Schumann's longer movements. Over and above the nine different metronome markings in this work, there are frequent directions for increasing the pace, while an occasional short adagio passage indicates Schumann's realization of the fact that the performer sometimes needed to draw breath. Despite its length and its division into these many sections, some of which are complete in themselves, *Humoreske* is not a sonata, neither is it a set of variations, even in the Schumannesque meaning. It is, however, invested with attributes of rondo-form in that one or two of the sections recur in part or in whole, albeit at irregular intervals. Playing the work gives one the sensation of looking through a whole portfolio of coloured

prints depicting a varied landscape, and of turning back every now
and again to refresh one's memory of some particularly striking
scene.

Humoreske is not only vivid and interesting in its thematic material
and pianistic layout. It possesses an additional fascination in being
an anthology of nearly all the distinctive lineaments of Schumann's
first-period style, from a perusal of which a musician unacquainted
with the composer's other piano works might gain a reasonably clear
idea of his individual manner of writing for the instrument. It may
therefore form a starting-point for the summing up of such outstanding features as occur in it, as well as of others which have not
already been mentioned and exemplified earlier in these pages.

In the first section alone, three typical details may be observed: (*a*)
the opening of the movement with a chord chromatic to the key, such
as was recently noted in the movements of *Nachtstücke*, and as may
be found throughout Schumann's work from the very beginning—
from the *Polonaises*, Op. III, No. 3, *Abegg* Variations (Nos. 1, 2, and
finale), *Papillons* (Nos. 6 and 11), *Carnaval* (*Valse noble, Coquette*,
&c.) down to his last opus for piano solo (133); (*b*) the exact and
immediate repetition of a complete phrase, here, in *Humoreske*, the
four opening bars, and also in *Novellette*, No. 1 (opening of first trio),
Carnaval (*Pierrot*), *Kinderscenen* (Nos. 1, 3, 4, 8), &c.; (*c*) the echoing
of a series of right-hand melody-notes an octave below and a beat,
or fraction of a beat, later in the figure of accompaniment, as instanced
in the introduction to *Humoreske*, the coda of *Arabeske* and in
Davisbündlertänze (No. 4) though there, as also in *Fantasietanz*, Op.
124, No. 5, in inverse position. Another, somewhat enigmatic variety
of this kind of texture occurs at the beginning of the G minor (pre-
cipitoso) section of *Humoreske*, where the uneventful melody written
on a third stave between the treble and bass parts almost entirely
coincides with notes struck by the right or left hand, either at the
same pitch or an octave higher, just as in *Blumenstück* (section III)
the middle part is written in duplicate for both hands during an entire
passage. Such 'paper' effects, which exercise the ingenuity of the
performer as to how best he can interpret them, are rivalled by some
of Schumann's cross-hand passages which, owing to the close inter-
locking of the fingers are extremely difficult to negotiate. A passage
of this kind is to be found in the intermezzo of *Humoreske*, where
rapid octaves in the right hand almost annihilate the efforts of the
left hand to penetrate them; another is in *Davidsbündlertänze*, No.
16, in the course of which the two hands in double octaves become

increasingly interdigitated, and yet another is a series of short runs in contrary motion in the presto of *Romanze*, Op. 28, No. 3, which presuppose two keyboards for their ideal performance, as do several even more ticklish cross-hand passages in the scherzo of the F minor Sonata. When Schumann used the device simply for the purpose of imitating orchestral effects, as in the finale of the *Faschingsschwank* and *Étude II* of Op. 13, the execution of the passages causes no difficulty.

Returning to *Humoreske*, we find that the first section in 2/4 succeeding the introduction provides an example of Schumann's habit of repeating a bar within a phrase, to which the closest parallel is the opening phrase of *Arabeske*. In the instance in *Humoreske*, the bar in question, a little up-rising figure, is not only repeated several times during one paragraph, but nine times in all within the section of forty-three bars—five times in the tonic alone. Later, a much reiterated two-bar figure forms the basis of the complete intermezzo section. Long stretches of one type of metrical figuration occur at several points during the progress of *Humoreske*, and are so common a feature of all Schumann's piano works that they require no further specifying. The repetition of a phrase at the octave above, such as occurs in the 'Wie ausser tempo' section and the final allegro of *Humoreske* is also of frequent occurrence elsewhere, as is the restatement of a whole paragraph in a fresh key, exemplified in the D minor-A minor portion of *Humoreske*, the intermezzo of *Novellette* No. 2 and the *Scherzino* of the *Faschingsschwank*. This is to name only a few instances and to omit any which occur for traditional structural reasons in movements in sonata-form. Another, similar but more unusual device often employed by Schumann, though not in *Humoreske*, is the repetition of a long or short portion of a movement at the interval of a semitone. Examples occur in the middle section of *Aufschwung* (4-bar phrase in G, then in A flat) and *Traumes Wirren* (opening theme in F, later in G flat), in the second movement of the F minor Sonata (central portion), in *Nachtstück* No. 2 (link following first episode) and No. 3 (starting at 46th bar from end), the *Novellette* No. 6 (C major portion afterwards in B major) and in many other, later works.

Some of Schumann's most typical characteristics as a melodist may also be seen in *Humoreske*, the melodic line of which furnishes examples of the falling interval of a fifth (opening, and D minor-A minor sections) and of a third (con intimo sentimento); the rise of a sixth followed by the fall of a tone (G minor and later B flat sections); the repetition of a note in a descending line, and above all, numerous step-wise progressions, both upwards and downwards. This latter is one of the most frequent of all Schumann's melodic devices and may be seen in nearly the whole of his piano production both early and late, especially in the Sonatas and the *Fantasie*, Op. 17, the principal subjects of whose opening movements all comprise fragments of a descending scale. His melodies are devised on this scalewise plan far more often than in broken-chord formation, though this latter type occurs in many of his compositions, from the theme of the *Abegg* Variations, Op. 1, down to the *Gesänge der Frühe*, Op. 133. Throughout Schumann's first period, his melodic invention was almost exclusively instrumental rather than vocal, and his melodies, which were generally an integral part of the texture, could only seldom be effectively detached from it. Not till about 1838 did he realize the possibilities of treating melody independently of the surrounding figuration, nor did he find his way to a more definitely vocal type until he had written many songs. Few of his earlier works contain eminently singable melodies.

In respect of harmonic progressions, *Humoreske* shows passages (at the very end of 'Con intimo sentimento' and at the 'Stretta') which are typical of the same predisposition towards suspensions, anticipations and retardations in either two or more parts, which Schumann had manifested from the beginning of his career, and which may be noted specially in *Papillons* (No. 1), *Davidsbündlertänze* (No. 9), *Carnaval* (*Chiarina, Coquette, Pause*), the G minor Sonata (transition in first movement) and particularly in the allegro of the *Faschingsschwank* (at the end of the E flat interlude). His use of the chord of the supertonic with raised third—the dominant of the dominant—to precede the dominant chord at a perfect cadence, one of his most characteristic progressions, especially at the end of a movement (*Kreisleriana*, No. 2, and *Leid ohne Ende*, Op. 124) is exemplified in *Humoreske* at the close of the adagio bars preceding 'Semplice e con tenerezza' in the centre of the work. Pedal-points, upper, lower or interior, were among his most favoured devices, and their occurrence is so common throughout his production as not to require particular comment. One in *Humoreske*, a combination of all three, is however, of special interest. Between an upper B flat and a lower double-octave D, all in minims, and an interior D reiterated in crotchets, a single line of diminished-seventh arpeggio makes its way down the keyboard twice in succession. Occasionally Schumann broke up a pedal-point into a lively figure (*Novellette*, No. 5, last paragraph), or he converted it into a short stretch of basso ostinato

(*Novellette*, No. 8, before and after the beginning of the 'continua-zione'). In the theme of *Études symphoniques*, he resolved an interior pedal into a trill.

Schumann's proneness, from his youth up, to exploit the chords of the dominant- and diminished-seventh may be seen in the finale of *Humoreske*. His typical use of these chords, either broken or in arpeggio, as figures of accompaniment is to be found in the first and last movements of the *Fantasie*, Op. 17, or as a purely decorative passage in *Études symphoniques*, Var. 9. He sometimes made a very sudden transition from one key to another for the purpose of creating a dramatic contrast. An example may be observed in *Humoreske* (un poco pomposo) where a sforzando chord on A flat drops unexpectedly to a *pp* dominant seventh on D natural—an effect which is paralleled by the *ppp* dominant seventh chord on E flat which suddenly cancels out the low sforzando chords of F minor at the end of *Paganini* in *Carnaval*. Schumann often let the music hover between two keys, keeping the listener in suspense as to which will eventually pre-dominate: in *Études symphoniques* (Var. 6); *Carnaval* (*Florestan*, in which G minor and B flat major struggle in vain for supremacy until the very last note), and the finale of the F sharp minor Sonata in which the tonality shifts so constantly as to necessitate six alterations in the key-signature. Enharmonic modulations he generally reserved for conveying a sudden sense of remoteness, as in *Davidsbündlertänze* (No. 17, 'Wie aus der Ferne', bars 24–25, &c.), *Carnaval* (*Reconnaiss-ance*, A flat minor to B major) and *Scherzino*, Op. 26 (32 bars before the end). When he wished to create an atmosphere of vagueness or mystery, he obscured the tonality with furtive ornamental passages comprising many intervals of semitones, either in the middle of the keyboard (in *Humoreske* at 'stretta'), the *Intermezzo* of the *Fasch-ingsschwank*, and central section of the *Romanze*, Op. 32, No. 3; in more extended compass in *Intermezzo*, Op. 4, No. 5 (just before da capo) and in *In der Nacht*, Op. 12, or in the lower reaches in *Études symphoniques* (Var. 9) and *Allegro*, Op. 8 (ending). Cloud-effects of a more vivid hue he conjured up by the sheer speed of scudding harmonic progressions in detached chords, or of rapidly flowing passages in which chords and passing-notes coalesce into a maze of sound. Both these types are in evidence in the windswept No. 13 of *Davidsbündlertänze*.

One of the most distinctive elements of Schumann's style, his insistence upon rhythmical displacements, syncopations, and com-binations of conflicting or complementary metrical units has inevitably been stressed throughout these pages. A couple of further typical details exemplified in *Humoreske* remain to be noted. The first is the sudden braking of the speed of an impetuous movement by a few lifeless bars of long notes, which takes place at the change of key-signature before 'come sopra', when a series of nine 4-bar blocks of tied minims unaccountably arrests the progress of the animated crotchets and semiquavers in 2/4 time which precede it. It was possibly Schumann's temperamental restlessness and his technical inability to build up a long movement to a satisfactory rhythmical climax by structural means that caused him to resort to this drastic device—and to its converse, the performing direction, 'faster and faster' he so frequently used—as well as to those of interpolating adagio bars or phrases at points of stress and at the ends of pieces, and of using extended plagal cadences to allow movements to come to rest more gradually than was otherwise feasible. A notable example of the last-named occurs at the end of the rejected finale of the G minor Sonata. Allied to this practice of utilizing extraneous resources of expression was Schumann's habit of writing a separate final section to some of his pieces, an outcome, perhaps, of a trait first shown in the valedictory endings of Op. 12 (*Das Ende vom Lied*) and Op. 15 (*Der Dichter spricht*), where the composer seems to turn to address his listeners personally, as he did in the long postludes to some of his songs (*Die alten, bösen Lieder, Am leuchtenden Sommermorgen, Im Rhein, im heiligen Strome*, &c.). In *Humoreske*, the lengthy final section is headed 'zum Beschluss' and consists, like the 'zum Schluss' of *Arabeske* and 'Fortsetzung und Schluss' of the eighth *Novellette*, largely of fresh material, though each of these three sections makes the effect of being a meditation upon all that has gone before. The other typical rhythmical detail is the lavish use of a certain pattern of notes, a characteristic Schumann finger-print, consisting of four semiquavers, the first of which is also a dotted quaver, sustained until released by the fourth semiquaver. As it comprises both a melody and its accompaniment it lends itself to exploitation for longish periods, as in *Humoreske* (molto vivace), *Allegro*, Op. 8, *Kreisleriana* (No. 2, intermezzo II), *Novellette*, No. 2, and elsewhere. This pattern is not, however, entirely of Schumann's own devising, for Schubert had made it the basis of the first variation in his *Impromptu* in B flat, Op. 142, and Weber had used it in the Rondo of his Sonata in A flat. Schumann was additionally indebted to Schubert for the polonaise-rhythm which he incorporated into many of his works from the early duets onwards, and it may even have been Schubert's practice of using dance-measures in many of his piano sonatas which led Schumann to introduce the rhythm of the polonaise, the waltz and the mazurka into his own Sonata in F sharp minor, and to adapt another type of dance, his so-called *Fandango*, as the first movement of the same work.

The intensely polyphonic character of Schumann's pianoforte texture was due not only to his close study of the works of Bach, but in part to his familiarity with many of Beethoven's compositions, especially the variations. From Bach he acquired an understanding of the principles of strict counterpoint and of the art of fugue, and possibly his own predilection for busy sequential figuration in two or more parts; from Beethoven, the concise canonic imitations and the expressive harmonic polyphony which are so constant a feature of all his works and which may be seen in all their typically Schumann-esque intensity in *Humoreske*, especially in the 'semplice e con tenerezza' and the final sections.

A few of Schumann's most characteristic methods of treating the thematic material may be seen in the following works: *Fantasie*, Op. 17, second movement (A flat section), where a melody in the middle voice is played by the right hand on the weak beats while upper and lower parts in decorative figuration maintain a comple-mentary rhythmic framework; *Étude symphonique*, No. XI (Var. 9) throughout which the left hand supplies a murmuring accompani-ment of demisemiquavers to the leisurely two-part playing of the right hand; *Fantasie*, third movement (F major section) and trio of *Scherzo* in F minor (op. posth.), where the melody runs in octaves divided between the two hands in treble and tenor while alto and bass are each entrusted with a different line of accompaniment, and *Nachtstücke*, No. 1, in which a predominantly chordal texture com-prises much individual part-writing including the appearance of the opening right-hand treble theme by inversion in the tenor and bass, and in canon at the octave throughout the whole middle section.

Schumann seldom left wide gaps between the right and left-hand parts, and a passage such as the penultimate phrase of the 'Aria' in the F sharp minor Sonata is rare. The centre of the keyboard was his main sphere of action, and when he deserted it for the heights or depths, he generally kept both hands reasonably near together, as in the endings of Op. 6, No. 4, Op. 12, No. 8, Op. 15, Nos. 6 and 8, Op. 16, No. 8, and Op. 23, No. 1—though not always with such tellingly resonant effect. For instance, some of the close polyphonic writing in the finale of *Humoreske* sounds obscure owing to its low register. In point of performing technique, many of Schumann's first-period works make heavy demands upon the player, not only by reason of the complexity of their texture, but on account of the many wide stretches (*Toccata*, Op. 7) including innumerable tenths (Sonata, Op. 11, finale) and the frequent, even wider leaps for both hands (*Paganini Étude*, Op. 10, No. 1), often in contrary motion (Op. 17, second movement, coda), as well as page after page of brilliant and exhausting passage-work. The Sonatas and some of the longer works can be adequately performed only by very highly qualified players, and many of the shorter pieces which are technically less exacting require extremely skilful interpretation.

After 1839, Schumann's output for piano solo was never again to be so rapid, concentrated or extensive, and only rarely so spontaneous. Moreover, after the composition of the first movement of his Piano Concerto in 1841, and of the Piano Quartet and Quintet in 1842, his production of keyboard music was to be directed into fresh channels. Before, however, pursuing his several new ventures, each in its own separate category, we may stop to examine the few little pieces he composed during this three years' interval. In 1840, he was so intent upon writing songs that he entirely neglected the piano as a solo instrument. In 1841, while his pianistic activities were centred in the Concerto, he found time to write four short soli: the well-known *Schlummerlied* later included in *Albumblätter*, Op. 124 (No. 16), and three pieces for *Bunte Blätter*, Op. 99 (Nos. 4, 12 and 13). The first of these (No. 1 of *Fünf Albumblätter*), the wistful miniature in F sharp minor whose artless exterior conceals a particularly subtle arch-wise construction, was to become the theme of Brahms's *Variations* for piano, Op. 9. The others are the longer and more genial *Abendmusik* in B flat and *Scherzo* in G minor.[1] These two pieces, and the *Schlummerlied* display interesting structural details and show that Schumann's long-standing affection for rondo- and variation-form was undiminished. Though each of the three is designed in a different variety of episodical-form, all make the impression of being rondos: the *Schlummerlied* by the fourfold appearance of the opening section, and the *Scherzo* by the ritornello-like recurrence of the principal phrase which also undergoes development throughout the main section. This piece partakes of the formal design as well as the unquenchable gaiety of the first movement of

---

[1] According to Boetticher (*Die Musik*, October 1941) the *Scherzo* originated as the trio of a projected symphony, earlier than 1833. At any rate it is identical with the scherzo of the C minor Symphony projected in 1841 (cf. p. 219).—*Ed.*

the *Faschingsschwank*. *Abendmusik*, sub-titled 'Menuet', combines the attributes of variation with those of rondo, both the principal themes recurring several times, either with discreet melismatic decoration or in different keys, while the trio, in G flat, which opens with a brief quotation from the G flat section of *Grillen* (Op. 12), is even more persistently syncopated than its prototype. The third beat of every bar throughout this section is tied over to the succeeding first beat, the normal accentuation being thus continuously displaced until the more straightforward 'Menuet' returns to stabilize the rhythmic scheme.

The year 1843 saw the composition of two more pieces of similar type: *Wiegenliedchen*, Op. 124, No. 6, a diminutive, unsophisticated cousin of *Schlummerlied*, and *Marsch*, Op. 99, No. 11, whose typical 'marcia funebre' rhythm lends it a character far more genuinely elegiac than the first movement of *Nachtstücke* (Op. 23) originally entitled *Funeral March*. The main section, which is more deftly organized than many of Schumann's pieces of this kind, resembles an eighteenth-century type of binary movement, in that the figures and phrases of the first half are re-arranged in the second in different order and fresh keys, the two sections balancing rather than exactly corresponding to each other. The fragmental construction of the *March* is effectively offset by the unbroken succession of quaver triplet chords forming the trio, whose three long phrases overlap one another in a manner rare in the composer's usually square-cut measures.

The same year, Schumann inaugurated a new period of composition in characteristic fashion with a set of variations which was, however, of a straightforward, melodic type such as he had never attempted before. Equally characteristically, he straightway 'varied' it. The *Andante* for two pianos, Op. 46, was not originally written exclusively for the pair of keyboards, nor was it the conventional set of eight variations and coda well-known to duettists today. It was conceived as a chamber work in which the two pianos were companioned by two 'celli and a horn.[1] After the first rehearsal, Schumann withdrew the work as unsatisfactory. Possibly the circumstance that his lodgings provided insufficient space for so unwieldy a combination of instruments and that he had to petition Breitkopf and Härtel for a room for the rehearsal made him realize that opportunities for performance would be restricted. He accordingly re-wrote the composition for the two pianos alone, in which

[1] See p. 174.

much revised form it was first performed by Clara Schumann and Mendelssohn and published in 1844. The original version did not appear in print until 1893, when it was included in the Supplement of the *Gesamtausgabe* of his works. It had, meanwhile, been performed by Clara and Brahms in Vienna in November 1868. The *Andante* as it now stands is an undeniably effective piece of decorative piano-writing, but it is by no means representative of Schumann's finest art and skill as a composer of variations. The repeat of each section of the theme and the threefold reiteration of its most characteristic two-bar phrase, as well as the almost unbroken antiphonal treatment and melismatic figuration throughout the work lend it a monotonous character which is, however, less pronounced in the original version owing to the greater variety of tone-colour. For instance in Var. 7 (E flat, marcato) the horn stood on a level of importance with the pianos, announcing a distinctive figure which was echoed by chords on both keyboards; in the following triplet variation, all three instruments took it in turn to play an expressive chromatic melody with the pianists, and the variation ended with an eloquent grupetto for the horn, which now sounds merely tame under the fingers of the pianist. The supersession of this colourful version of the *Andante* by the comparatively uneventful one for the two pianos unaccompanied constitutes a distinct loss to the province of chamber-music.

Schumann's only remaining three sets of variations for piano, which are of small interest compared with those of his first period, were not written until ten years later than the *Andante*, but they will be mentioned at this point to complete the survey of this category of works. The immediate, though remote, successor of Op. 46 is the set forming the second movement of the Sonatina, Op. 118, No. 1, composed in 1853. Its principal distinction is the brevity of the theme, which is only six bars in length, but here, as in the theme of Op. 46, repetition in the melody—though only of one bar—tends to become wearisome during the five variations, especially as they follow both the rhythmic and melodic outline unswervingly throughout. The only relief from this routine treatment is provided in Var. 2 by the transference to the tenor voice of the melodic line, which is otherwise always prominent in the uppermost part of the texture; to the replacing of the minor mode by the major in Var. 4, and to the coda of four bars which eventually breaks the spell of the recurrent six-bar periods. Even bearing in mind that this movement was written for a child to play, it may be admitted that in spite of the unfailingly charming figuration, it lacks Schumann's usual inspiration and resource.

On the other hand, the five pieces of *Gesänge der Frühe*, Op. 133, inspired in October of the same year by Hölderlin's 'Diotima' poems, while not comprising a set of variations in the accepted sense, are nevertheless 'variations' according to the Schumannesque conception of the term, though unfortunately at its most obscure. In each of the pieces, the individual theme is worked several times, either in whole or in fragments, and in each, too, a climax occurs twice, each time upon the second-inversion of the tonic chord, generally in connection with an entry of the theme. Moreover, slight mutual thematic reminiscences may be traced between some of the pieces. Schwarz gives it as his opinion that, in view of the coincidence of the essential formal and harmonic structure on the one hand, and of the working of the same thematic substance on the other, the five pieces of Op. 133 may justifiably be considered as 'variations' in an even stronger sense than the individual numbers of *Carnaval*. Notwithstanding this reasoned apologia by a scholarly critic, it is difficult, in considering the pieces from the purely musical and expressive points of view, not to be disappointed in their only very occasional clarity and beauty. The part-writing in the more polyphonic items (Nos. 1 and 5) is inert and the decorative texture elsewhere frequently awkward and ineffective. Schumann, who had always composed at the piano until 1845,[1] had by now long ago relinquished this practice, and in relying upon his eye rather than on his fingers, he sometimes produced results which are profoundly unsatisfactory to the performer. In No. 1, for instance, the ingenuity on paper of a four-fold stretto of the main theme during the last few bars cannot atone for the unpianistic texture it occasions, nor does the tossing of an already jagged theme from one much-engaged hand to the other conduce to a convincing interpretation of No. 2. The harmonic scheme of No. 3 is greatly disorganized by the efforts of the bass part to maintain an independent broken-chord figuration in octaves which constantly obstructs the logical progressions by intractable 6/4 chords. The gracefully flowing figuration in No. 4 is stultified by the indecisive theme, and the semiquaver clouds which encompass the melody-notes of the last piece cannot conceal the weakness of its harmonic basis. Who, among practising pianists, would join with Schwarz in

---

[1] 'From 1845 onward, when I started to invent and work out in my head, a quite different way of composing began to develop' (diary entry quoted by Kreisig, *Zeitschrift für Musik*, 1925, p. 166).

speaking of this laboured production of Schumann's clouded middle life in the same breath with *Carnaval*, one of the most spontaneous creations of his exuberant youth?

The last set of piano variations, which was also Schumann's last composition of any kind, combines something of the transparency of the Op. 118 movement with the ingenuity of Op. 133, and even with a dash of the virtuosity of the *Études symphoniques*. It was composed in 1854, under circumstances so tragic that its predominant lucidity is a matter for wonder and admiration. When he wrote down the theme in the night of 17 February that year, Schumann, whose mind was by now seriously deranged, believed that it had been dictated to him by spirits, whereas it was in reality simply a variant of the principal subject of the second movement of his own Violin Concerto composed a few months earlier.[1] During the following ten days, until his mental agony became unendurable, Schumann proceeded to compose some of the variations, and after his partial recovery from the disaster of 27 February he resumed work upon them, eventually leaving five variations finished, but the set as a whole uncompleted. The theme of twenty-eight bars in E flat, which is the longest of all the Schumann variation-themes and which, like those of Opp. 46 and 118, is extended by the repetition of one of its characteristic segments, was first printed by Brahms in 1893 in the Supplement of the *Gesamtausgabe*. The variations themselves remained unpublished until Karl Geiringer edited them from the original manuscript for Hinrichsen's Edition in 1939. The rhythmic structure of the theme is preserved intact throughout the five variations, as is also the melodic line which remains perpetually in the right hand except in Var. 3 where it is allotted almost exclusively to the left hand which only occasionally allows it to rise to the surface in the treble. In the first variation, it dominates the scene; in the second, it yields pride of place to the tenor with whom it runs in almost exact canon at the octave, a beat apart in the first section and at two bars' distance in the second. It pursues an uninterrupted course in Var. 4, undeterred by its transposition a major third higher into the key of G minor, while in the last variation, where it is restored to E flat though metrically displaced and attenuated in note-value, it secures recognition only by maintaining a running fight against a throng of demisemiquavers which collide with it at discordant intervals to the very end. One single final bar of undisturbed

---

[1] See Ex. 134; a still earlier version of the same thought occurs in the middle section of *Vogel als Prophet*, Op. 82, No. 7.—*Ed.*

tonic harmony resolves the persistent conflict. This is the variation which displays the same high quality of invention as was manifested twenty years earlier in the *Études symphoniques*.

Schumann completed the Piano Concerto in 1845 and in the same year embarked upon a kind of composition which was not only entirely new to him and in the strongest possible contrast both to the contemporary Concerto and to all his preceding piano works, but which was designed for a type of keyboard instrument hitherto unexploited as regards original composition. Schumann had first made acquaintance with the pedal-piano at the Leipzig Conservatorium where one had been installed for the use of the organ students. When he had moved to Dresden and had begun, early in 1845, to initiate Clara into the serious study of contrapuntal works, he hired a pedal-attachment for his own piano to facilitate these joint studies, and forthwith started to compose works suitable for performance on the enhanced instrument. The experience he had gradually acquired in writing orchestral and chamber works during the previous three or four years had made Schumann dissatisfied with the limitations of the keyboard. The pedal-piano offered wider scope for his increased powers as a contrapuntist and an orchestrator, and he took eager advantage of it, hardly stopping to reflect how slight were the chances of performance of works for this rare and cumbersome instrument. So completely was he carried away by the exciting possibilities of the new medium that when he had persuaded his reluctant publisher into undertaking to print two sets of pieces for it, he even considered it advisable to swear him to secrecy lest news of the forthcoming publication should leak out and other composers should anticipate his own novel idea. Today the pedal-piano is virtually extinct, at least so far as concert performances are concerned, and in their original form, the *Six Studies*, Op. 56, and the *Four Sketches*, Op. 58 (sub-titled 'also for pianoforte for three or four hands') have become almost exclusively the property of organists in public or of piano-duettists in private. The *Six Fugues*, Op. 60, which were written specifically 'for organ or pedal-piano', are, however, not infrequently heard upon the former. Schumann did not altogether deny the piano a share in these contrapuntal activities of 1845. He endowed it with a group of *Four Fugues*, Op. 72, and the tiny canon in D which he added as the last number of the *Albumblätter*, Op. 124. Three years later he wrote *Kanonisches Liedchen* and *Kleine Fuge* for inclusion in his Op. 68. Lastly, in 1853, he composed the set of *Seven Pieces in Fughetta Form*, Op. 126, as well

as the jaunty canon in B minor which forms the second movement
of the Sonatina, Op. 118, No. 2. The only remaining piece belonging
to this category, the brief canon on F. H. Himmel's song *An Alexis*
which was included in Julius Knorr's Op. 30, bears neither opus-
number nor date of composition. It was printed in the Supplement
of the *Gesamtausgabe* in 1893.

From a study of the polyphonic elements in Schumann's pianoforte works up to 1845[1] it is not difficult to foresee, either that his
constant aptitude for devising short canonic imitations and his predilection for employing contrapuntal devices would one day develop
into a capacity for composing full-length accompanied canons such
as the *Six Studies*, Op. 56, or that the writing of the desultorily
fugal finale of the *Impromptus*, Op. 5, would eventually lead to the
production of the set of short *Fugues*, Op. 72, which Schumann
himself considered only as 'characteristic pieces in the severe style'.
Nevertheless, it requires a very considerable effort of the imagination
to detect in the composer of *Carnaval* the future author of another
series of movements 'sur quatre notes': the *Six Fugues on the name
of BACH*, Op. 60. For whereas the letters ASCH had stimulated
Schumann to the creation of one of the most romantic compositions
of his first-period, the name BACH was to incite him to summon
up the whole impressive array of contrapuntal profundities which
went to the making of the most severely classical work of his entire
career. 'This is a composition at which I worked for a whole year
in order that I might make it worthy of the great name it bears, and
which I believe will outlive all my others'—so he wrote to his publisher in 1846. There was no question here, as with Opp. 56 and 58,
of producing a work whose novelty should intrigue the public, but
of paying homage to the master whose compositions had ever been
his inspiration and whose fugues he described as 'characteristic
pieces of the finest kind' and as 'truly poetic creations'.

The comparatively slight pieces for the pedal-piano, charming and
deft as they are, show few signs of such concentrated devotion to the
ideals of polyphony as do the strict *Fugues* of Op. 60. Op. 56 manifests both the strength and weakness of Schumann's equipment. The
former consists chiefly in his unfailing inventiveness as regards
animated figuration, and is shown to its greatest advantage in the
crisp and lively No. 5; the latter, in his fatal tendency to repetitious
treatment of material, such as mars the otherwise graceful No. 2
wherein the canon at the unison in the two upper voices at the

[1] On Schumann's fugal studies, see p. 261.—*Ed.*

F

distance of one bar inevitably gives rise to an almost ceaseless procession of bars grouped in pairs. This opus, whose key-relationship is unified, is notable for the diversity of style among the six pieces and for the well-balanced combination of the strict elements with the free. Only the first piece, which is the most Bachian in its clear lines and transparent texture and in which the canon runs uninterrupted at the octave throughout, is not typical of the composer. The others bear his characteristic imprint as regards form, content, and texture and are pre-eminently romantic in style. All are episodical in structure, but each, except No. 6, makes the impression of being *durchkomponirt* owing to the uniformity of its individual figures of accompaniment. The canon is not always maintained at the same interval or distance throughout a whole piece. In No. 4, in which it starts at the fifth and is later shifted to the octave, the canon occurs alternately at the distance of three, two, or one bars; in No. 6 it proceeds, at the octave, only during the first and last sections, which are mainly in four-part chordal harmony. The contrasting central episode comprises a brief five-part fugato on a flowing four-bar subject. In all the six pieces, the pedal-part, which is absolutely integral to the harmonic scheme, is of varying intrinsic interest, and only in No. 5 does it participate very reticently in the purely decorative texture, and in No. 6 play a small but essential role in the main canonic proceedings.

In the *Four Sketches*, Op. 58, Schumann cast off the shackles of polyphony, and except in the middle section of No. 2 where he introduced a few prominent canonic imitations, he luxuriated in a kind of texture which was not only predominantly homophonic, but frequently homorhythmic (in Nos. 1 and 2) and even occasionally unisonic (in No. 3). The key-system of this complete work bears a likeness to that of the *Nachtstücke*, and there are other similarities between the two sets: the major-minor fluctuations in the opening pieces of each, and the metrical outline of both the third movements. The performing directions, 'lebhaft' and 'markirt' common to both, betoken a likeness in mood, though Op. 58 is far more spirited than its forerunner and frequently attains the untrammelled exultancy of the *Faschingsschwank*—which, indeed, it recalls with harmonic progressions in No. 1 and with the waltz-rhythms which characterize all four pieces. The pedal-part throughout Op. 58 has no purely independent existence except in the tiny solo metrical figure of No. 4, and the whole could be incorporated into the keyboard part in such a manner as would not entail any more wide left-hand stretches or arpeggio chords than are customary in many of Schumann's piano works. By the time he wrote this second group for the pedal-piano, his enthusiasm for the contrapuntal possibilities of the instrument had evidently waned. Whether the thumb-nail canons, Op. 124, No. 20, and *An Alexis* were devised for it or for the ordinary piano can hardly be determined from the internal evidence which is ambiguous. The matter is of little consequence, for the first, which could well do with pedal facilities for its distant bass, is so crude in part-writing as to discourage performers, and the second, more compact and gracious, too slight to attract them.

There is no ambiguity as to the composer's intentions regarding Op. 60, for even if he had not explicity marked the BACH fugues 'for organ', it would be obvious from a glance at the score that these complex, extended pieces could not be effectively interpreted upon any other instrument. The intricate texture demands not only the manuals and pedalboard for its adequate performance, but all the resources of registration for imparting the variety of tone-colour necessary to relieve the monotony of the figuration. Tovey's statement, that Schumann, 'besides being the great Romantic seer, was one of the most learned contrapuntists who ever lived', is substantiated in these fugues, which bristle with the many abstruse devices which are taken as a matter of course in the works of Bach, but which, coming from Schumann's pen arouse sheer wonderment. Yet, when the player has scanned the pages and noted with increasing admiration the numerous learned contrapuntal expedients employed: the presentation of the theme by augmentation, diminution, and inversion, both successively and concurrently, its appearance in double counterpoint and in stretti maestrali, to say nothing of its entries per arsin et thesin, and per modo retrogrado (sometimes in combination with modo ordinario), what distinctive musical features can he trace to reassure him that this erudite Schumann is still the same composer who not long since had displayed so many other, less forbidding facets of his style in the resplendent *Humoreske*, and throughout whose entire production the purely expressive element had played so indispensable a part? At the very outset he may observe that the four-note theme, which happens to comprise two pairs of semitones, bears an affinity to the preponderantly semitonal theme of the finale of the *Humoreske*, the close texture of whose working-out section resembles that of Fugue No. 1. He may also opine that the several guises, tonal, metrical, and expressive, in which the BACH theme appears as the subject of each fugue, owe something of their diversity to Schumann's considerable experience in re-shuffling the four notes of his *Carnaval* motto, and that its many permutations and combinations throughout the episodes are a consequence of his extensive practice in writing variations; that the cloud of murmuring semiquavers at the end of the vivacious second Fugue is the counterpart of many such passages in the sonatas, *Fantasiestücke* and shorter pieces, and that the few laconic statements of the subject in the depths of the pedal-part in No. 3 indicate the same mood as do the low-pitched cryptic comments in *Kreisleriana*; that the performing direction, 'faster and faster' in Nos. 3 and 6 and the holding up of the rhythmical flow by passages of longer notes in No. 2 indicate the same innate impetuosity and the same technical inability to arrive at a convincing climax by recognized structural methods which the composer had shown so markedly in *Humoreske*. Finally, the player may come to the conclusion that these learned fugues, viewed as whole movements, may be considered typical of the composer in that their texture never lacks interest, but that their formal construction is unconvincing. It was not in Schumann's nature to write long pieces in which there were few possibilities of vivid contrast. His whole art of composition rested, as we have already seen, upon the alternation of contrasting sections, and when he was precluded by the dictates of fugue from resorting to his customary, effective methods of balancing one type of picturesque section against another, he could do little but spin a web of monochrome figuration. Even though the constitution of the double-fugue presented opportunities of securing contrast, he was unable to take full advantage of them, and when he had introduced the new second subject in part two of Fugue No. 6, he still gave no respite to the persistent figures of triplet crotchets which had accompanied the BACH subject almost all the way through the first part of the fugue. The only appreciable contrast in Op. 60 is that provided by the differences in mood and tempi between the individual fugues: the sprightliness of Nos. 2 and 5 as compared with the solemnity of Nos. 1 and 3 and the inscrutable deliberation of No. 4 with the extreme urgency of No. 6.

Fortunately for the solo pianist, Schumann's sojourn in the rarefied atmosphere of the fuga ricercata was of brief duration. The *Four Fugues*, Op. 72, are of an altogether less scholarly variety although they are by no means devoid of some of the more recondite concomitants of their species. Owing to their greater conciseness, however, the uniform texture of each separate fugue tends to endow it with a sense of homogeneity such as we noted in some of the short monothematic pieces of Schumann's first-period: for example, the *Burla* of Op. 124, the *Albumblatt*, Op. 99, No. 5, some of the *Kinderscenen*, Op. 15, and the second *Nachtstück*. Moreover, the qualities of these little fugal works as 'characteristic pieces'—Schumann himself originally called them *Vier Charakterfugen*—far outweigh their purely technical interest, considerable though it is. The decorative harmonies and eloquent tenor part of the final phrase of Fugue No. 1 exert a stronger fascination than does the skilful combination of the subject with its own augmentation a few bars earlier, and the vitality of the material in No. 2 is more immediately arresting than the great ingenuity with which it is treated throughout its course.[1] The third fugue, whose furtive, serpentine subject—so strangely like that of Chopin's study in the same key (No. 1 of *Trois Nouvelles Études*, published in 1840)—winding its way through a tissue of chromaticisms, is arrested for one fateful moment while the tonic, suspended between four ominously repeated chords of the dominant relapses into an even more fateful and expectant silence after its resolution on the leading-note, achieves a stronger and more artistic climax than any of its fellows in Op. 60. The deep-set melancholy of this romantic F minor movement is perfectly counterpoised by the infallible good humour of its successor in the major mode. This last fugue, light-hearted as any *Papillon*, maintains an unbroken flow of repartee between the four well-matched voices until it ends, less wittily but more feelingly, with three direct statements of the subject, differently harmonized and finally clinched by the composer's most characteristic cadence. Another characteristic Schumannesque touch in Op. 72 is the opening of one of the pieces, out of its basic tonality: in this instance, the third fugue, with notes implying the subdominant. Schumann evidently prized this fugue for he sent it to his friend J. J. Verhulst in Amsterdam for inclusion in an Album published by the Dutch 'Maatschapij tot Bevorderung der Toonkunst'.

Eight years were to elapse before Schumann wrote his last set of movements in polyphonic style. The *Seven Pieces in Fughetta Form*, Op. 126, written between 28 May and 9 June 1853, show no diminution in his powers either as a contrapuntist or as a composer of 'characteristic pieces'.[2] Moreover, the Fughettas are distinguished

---

[1] Boetticher (*op. cit.*) tells us that on the original sketch of this fugue, Schumann wrote 'dabei furchtbar [word scratched out] 1845'. Bars 78–80 were an afterthought not in the sketch.—*Ed.*

[2] A great number of sketches for Op. 126 are printed by Boetticher (*op. cit.*).—*Ed.*

by much greater clarity and charm than the contemporary *Gesänge der Frühe*[1] in which, as we noted earlier, the polyphonic and harmonic elements are never convincingly integrated. The prevailing spirit of Op. 126 is, however, possibly too subdued for the work to be satisfactorily performed as a whole. It is predominantly in the minor mode: Nos. 1, 5, and 7 are all in A minor, Nos. 2 and 4 in D minor, and only Nos. 3 and 6 in F major. It consequently lacks tonal variety, and the tempi, too, are more often deliberate than lively. All the pieces are short—the longest is only 53 bars—and in each the constant entries of the subject are seldom interrupted by even the shortest episodes. When, as in Nos. 1 and 5, the subject is of purely melodic interest and lends itself more readily to harmonic than to polyphonic treatment, the piece assumes the aspect of a miniature set of continuous variations. This is particularly noticeable in No. 5 wherein the figures of accompaniment increase in floridity from duplets to triplets and quadruplets in the manner of the early classical variation. The charm of Op. 126 lies in the intrinsically attractive thematic material and in the distinctive character of each fugal subject whether it is meditative or energetic. While the part-writing is full of vitality, the texture is harmonically more gracious than in some of Schumann's other contrapuntal compositions, and in the two 3-part Fughettas (Nos. 1 and 6) it is outstandingly transparent. The latter, a moto perpetuo of semiquavers in 12/16 time, has a striking subject implying tonic and dominant harmonies which are, however, momentarily obscured by heavily accented unessential-notes on the main beats. The counterpointing of these indomitable auxiliary-notes occasions a number of fierce clashes between the three highly independent voices, a twice repeated sequence of ninths between the extreme parts being especially piquant. A modal flavour haunts some of the pieces, notably Nos. 5 and 7, throughout whose course the indecision of the respective subjects as to whether they belong to A minor or C major leads to many tonal ambiguities and to some surprising false relations. The poetic feeling in Op. 126 is so strong at times as to suggest that, had he not felt himself bound

[1] Though admittedly Schumann's own opinion was exactly the opposite. He writes to the publisher, F. W. Arnold (24 February 1853): 'I should prefer the Fughettas not to appear, on account of their mostly melancholy character, and offer you another, recently finished work *Gesänge der Frühe*, five characteristic pieces for pianoforte dedicated to the poetess Bettina. They are pieces depicting the approach and waxing of the morning but more as expression of feeling than painting (*mehr aus Gefühlsausdruck, als Malerei*). As these compositions will undoubtedly find more sympathy than the Fughettas . . . I beg you to let me have a prompt reply about them.'

by the conventions of the 'severe style', Schumann might have given the little pieces imaginative titles such as he had bestowed fifteen years earlier upon his *Kinderscenen* and more recently upon the majority of the items in the *Album für die Jugend*, Op. 68. In the last-named work, the concise *Kleine Fuge* in A major (No. 40) is similar in manner and content to the more cheerful pieces of Op. 126. Its brisk subject is adumbrated in the preceding *Vorspiel*, a flowing movement in the style of a Bach Invention. The *Kanonisches Liedchen* in A minor (No. 27) portrays the same wistful mood as do the Fughettas in that key, though a brief interlude in the tonic major temporarily dispels the clouds. This concentrated little piece, the last in the group of contrapuntal works, is a perfect example of the composer's power to sublimate canonic means to an artistic end. Within a four-part texture, the canon between treble and tenor proceeds with such assured smoothness and effortless grace that its strict contrapuntal mechanism might well escape detection by any but the most expert ear.

The forty-three small pieces of the *Jugend-Album*, Op. 68, which Schumann wrote in 1848, were the first of a series of little works for piano solo and duet, to the composition of which he was stimulated primarily by the necessity of providing elementary teaching pieces for his own children. The other works belonging to this group are *Drei Sonatinen für die Jugend*, Op. 118 (1853), and the two sets of duets, *Zwölf Klavierstücke*, Op. 85 (1849), and *Kinderball*, Op. 130 (1853). Schumann, who was exhausted after the completion of his biggest single work, the opera *Genoveva*, found the production of the miniatures of Op. 68 a highly congenial and recreative task, more especially as they were the first piano soli he had written since indulging in the orgy of contrapuntal studies throughout 1845. He told Carl Reinecke that he felt as if he was starting to compose again from the very beginning, and so greatly was he fascinated by this fresh occupation that he wrote the whole of the pieces within sixteen days, the first seven in time for the seventh birthday of his eldest child on 1 September, and the remainder in the ensuing fortnight. The completed *Album für die Jugend* was published in December the same year by Schuberth of Hamburg, who suggested this title in preference to the composer's own choice of *Weihnachtsalbum*. A facsimile reproduction of a manuscript sketch-book of Schumann's relating to the work was issued by Schott in 1924 with an editorial preface, by Lothar Windsperger, which includes a comprehensive analysis of the points of correspondence and divergence between the sketches and the printed pieces. From this 34-page facsimile it is possible to observe at first hand a few of Schumann's idiosyncrasies when he was carried away by enthusiasm for a new idea. For example, he scribbled down some of his thoughts in such feverish haste that he did not even stop to see if he had opened the book the right way over, and several of the pages have consequently to be held upside down to permit of the sketches being deciphered. Moreover, their haphazard arrangement throughout the book, their frequent illegibility and few corrections bear additional witness to the composer's state of excitement at the time of their conception.

The contents of the sketch-book may be summarized as follows:

(1) It contains 37 of the 43 published pieces, the omissions being Nos. 7, 12, 18, 30, 33, and 42. Of these 37 sketches, about 20 correspond almost exactly with the definitive versions, the two principal exceptions being (a) that *Sizilianisch* (No. 11) originally comprised two pieces of this name, the second of which was ultimately incorporated in the first as a trio and its former notation in quavers altered to semiquavers; and (b) that in *Nordisches Lied* (No. 41) the GADE motto was formerly placed in the alto instead of in the treble line.

(2) Among about a dozen sketches which Schumann eventually decided not to publish are four pieces, almost completed but rather tentative in character: *Guguk im Versteck*, *Lagune in Venedig*, *Haschemann*, and a tiny waltz, which are printed in full in the supplement to the facsimile. The other rejected sketches include the opening of a study for the left hand and an extremely elementary little piece designated *Für ganz Kleine*, as well as several studies in canon, and a round for three voices.

(3) A few of the sketches appear in two different workings, notably *Volkslied* (No. 9) the second version of which Schumann marked as 'better than the first'.

(4) In every sketch, except *Stückchen* (No. 5), the figure of accompaniment is noted down in addition to the melodic line.

(5) Some sketches have no titles at all; others have different titles from those they bear in the printed version. For instance, *Mignon* (No. 32) was formerly *Seiltänzerin*, *Sylvesterlied* (No. 43) was *Zum Schluss*, &c.

Apart from the actual sketches, the manuscript book contains several entries regarding Schumann's projects for his little educational work. He originally intended to include extracts from the works[1] of nine well-known composers, from Bach to Spohr, as well as other pieces of his own composition, the proposed titles of which he noted on the first page, though he did not avail himself of them in this opus. One, *Bärentanz*, was transferred to the inimitable second duet of Op. 85; another, *Puppenliedchen*, cropped up later in a slightly different form as *Puppenwiegenlied* in Op. 118, No. 1. Three of the pages are inscribed with some of the *Musikalische Haus-und Lebensregeln*—31 out of the total 68 which Schumann first printed in the *Neue Zeitschrift für Musik* in 1850, then added as a supplement to the second edition of the *Jugend-Album* in 1851 and finally printed in his collected writings in 1853.

The educational value of the *Jugend-Album*, Schumann's *Mikrokosmos*, has long been proved, and needs no further appraisal. Its importance as pure music is more debatable, but for the student of his works, this midgetry is of undeniable interest. Schumann had written miniatures for the piano at every stage of his career, but never before in such large numbers, in so short a period, or so limited in scope. A certain measure of monotony in the collection of 43 simple pieces is inevitable. It is, however, mitigated by the fact that only the first 18 are intended for the beginner and the remaining 25 for the more advanced student. On the other hand, it is accentuated by the large and unnecessary amount of repetition of whole sections, phrases and figures in the individual pieces, by the restricted key-system and by the unaccountable avoidance of the use of triple time. Only the 'easy' keys are employed, nearly a third of the pieces are in A, and every movement throughout the series is in either simple quadruple, or simple or compound duple time—a strange neglect of one rhythmical aspect of a young player's equipment. These sundry disadvantages are, however, to a great extent balanced by the engaging quality of much of the thematic substance and by the diversity of treatment which Schumann accorded to it. The various kinds of form available for the purposes of this small-scale work are naturally limited. (*a*) The largest number of pieces of any one type are binary in mould, and in these Schumann used many different methods of arranging the material. (*b*) Several of the other pieces are in episodical form, Nos. 17, 23, and 39 of which have independent and poetic codas, and No. 36, an introduction and coda of similar material. The last-named belongs to the very few movements (Nos. 21, 34, and 41) which begin out of the key. (*c*) Of the

---

[1] Or pieces 'in the manner of'; the list of names occurs on the same page as the sketch for *Erinnerung an Felix Mendelssohn-Bartholdy.—Ed.*

three rondos, No. 18 is much enlivened by the recurrences of refrain and episodes in unorthodox keys, but No. 19 is a rondo only in intention, for the refrain is truncated and suppressed on both its attempted reappearances. No. 39, *Winterzeit II* is refreshingly irregular in construction as befits so poetic a conception. (*d*) Four items may be assigned to the category of variations: in each of three of them (Nos. 8, 9, and 23) a phrase reappears intact in a new guise; the fourth (No. 41) is a minute set of variations upon the name GADE, Schumann's Danish contemporary and friend. Moreover, No. 42, *Figurierter Choral* may be considered as a 'variation' upon No. 4, *Choral*, which is transposed into a fresh key, its melodic outline altered in two bars, the sparse texture enhanced by a flowing middle-voice and the whole rounded off with an ornamental coda. The tune of the *Choral* in question, 'Freu dich sehr, o meine Seele', often used by Bach, proceeds almost entirely in conjunct motion. Hence, perhaps, its particular attraction for Schumann whose predilection for writing his own melodies on this plan we have already noted earlier.

Among the rarer species, one (No. 23) is a diptych; another (No. 35) is a prelude—(its resemblance to the first Prelude of the *Forty-Eight* can hardly be overlooked)—and one (No. 31) differs from every other piece in the whole album by being a continuous sweep of fifty-five bars without any separate sections, repeats or decisive cadences, and with only a couple of quaver rests throughout its course. Many of the pieces are notable for continuity in the arrangement of their material, but not one of them defies dissection so effectively as does this triumphant *Warrior's Song*. Several pieces are monothematic, the most outstanding example being No. 34, *Thema*, in which a dotted metrical figure distributed between all four voices in turn seems to engrave one pregnant thought ever more deeply upon the listener's mind. It bears a strong resemblance to *Leides Ahnung*, Op. 124, No. 2. This *Thema* is one of the extremely few pieces in the *Jugend-Album* which possesses an 'inscriptional' quality such as distinguishes some of the shorter of the Beethoven *Bagatellen*. It is in itself Beethovenian in both content and style, some of the harmonic progressions recalling the thirtieth of the *Diabelli* Variations. An additional link with Beethoven is forged by No. 21, a free improvisation on the phrase 'O Dank! ihr habt mich süss erquickt' from the terzetto, *Euch werde Lohn in bess'ren Welten* from *Fidelio*, and a Schubertian touch may be discerned in the quiet plain-octaves passage which opens *Winterzeit* (No. 39), the 'impressionist' sketch already mentioned as a rondo. The A major movement, No. 28, written to commemorate the anniversary of Mendelssohn's death, is not the only piece bearing traces of this composer's manner. It is also apparent in Nos. 13 and 26. More characteristic of Schumann's own distinctive style is the harmonic polyphony of *Scheherazade*, No. 32, and the texture of *Kleine Romanze*, No. 19, in which the melody played by the right hand is doubled by the left hand in the tenor part, just as it is in another of the composer's *Romanzen*, No. 11 of Op. 124.

When Schumann composed the *Zwölf Klavierstücke*, Op. 85, for piano duet in the following year, he recaptured the untrammelled mood of the *Jugend-Album*; but by the time he came to write the *Drei Sonatinen für die Jugend*, Op. 118, for piano solo immediately after the Fughettas, Op. 126, in 1853, it had fled almost beyond recall, and only a few of the shorter movements approach the pieces of Op. 68 in imaginativeness and perspicuity. Each of the Sonatinas, which are dedicated to his three eldest daughters respectively, consists of four movements, the third and fourth of which bear 'characteristic' titles, and a feeling of unity is imparted to the cycle by a quotation in the finale of No. 3 from the first movement of No. 1. Schumann originally wrote the first Sonatina as *Kinderscenen*. It is the shortest and simplest both in structure and style, and the one most likely to appeal to a young player. The first and third movements are in episodical form, the latter, a charming, dreamy *Lullaby* (*Puppenwiegenlied*). The second is the concise set of variations referred to earlier in these pages in its own category,[1] and the last movement a *Rondoletto*. In each of the two other Sonatinas, both the first and the last movements are in longish sonata-form and are so prolix in construction and commonplace in material as to be uninteresting to either young or older performers. The slow movement of No. 2 is indeterminate in form and sluggish in style; that of No. 3, rhythmically laborious, and only the scherzos: *Canon* (No. 2) and *Zigeunertanz* (No. 3) are vivacious and convincing in spite of their repetitive character. Schumann seems to have lost touch with the realities of educational music, for how else could he have failed to perceive that the long, rambling movements were beyond the interpretative powers of youthful performers, that some of the more involved figuration was too exacting for their inexpert hands, or that decorative chromatic passages such as those in the andante of No. 3 required extremely skilful pedalling? And why did he make so

[1] See p. 69.

little use of the available opportunities for rhythmic variety? Only
two of the twelve movements of Op. 118 are in triple time. The last
of Schumann's works for children, the duets, *Kinderball: Sechs
leichte Tanzstücke*, Op. 130, also written in 1853, suffer from the same
disabilities as the Sonatinas. They are, in the main, too advanced
in technique for the young, too limited in scope for the adult and
musically too slight to hold the affections of either type of performer.

Schumann's output of piano duets, five sets in all, is neither large
nor intrinsically important, but it is interesting when studied in
relation to his compositions for the solo instrument. We have already
seen that his first extant work of this kind, the *Eight Polonaises*,
Op. III, composed for performance by his brothers, was produced
in 1828, a short time before any of his published soli. Now we are
confronted with the curious fact that he did not write a second set
of duets (Op. 66) until twenty years later, and even then, some considerable time after he had produced all his finest solo compositions
and when his creative powers were no longer at their zenith. Any
compelling external cause for his return to duet-writing at this
particular juncture eludes discovery. Ever since his marriage in
1840, an ideal duet-partner had been constantly at his side, yet he
had written nothing for four hands on one keyboard. In 1848, when
he wrote the six elaborate 'Impromptus' for duet, *Bilder aus Osten*,
Op. 66, his children, for whose musical education he was later to
compose easy soli and duets, were too young to be considered as
performers of any music except the very simplest. In his preface to
Op. 66, Schumann stated that the immediate and overwhelming
inspiration of the 'impromptus' had been his reading of Rückert's
*Die Verwandlungen des Abu Seid von Serug, oder die Makamen des
Hariri* (free translations, in rhymed prose and verse, from the Arabic),
but there still seems no intelligible reason for his having re-interpreted
these oriental stories in terms of the piano duet rather than in those
of the orchestra or of chamber music. The production of the three
remaining sets of duets is more easily explicable. Owing to the
popular success of the *Jugend-Album* in 1849, Schumann's publisher
Schuberth asked him to compose a set of duets of similar character
so that their publication might coincide with that of the second
edition of the *Jugend-Album* in 1851. The composer readily com-
plied with the request and wrote the *Zwölf Klavierstücke*, Op. 85,
'for children young and old' in September 1849. Once he had become
accustomed to the idea of writing duets for the combined purposes
of instruction and entertainment, he found little difficulty in producing

other works of the same kind: *Ballscenen*, Op. 109, in 1851 and finally *Kinderball*, Op. 130, in 1853, two sets of dance-movements which make the impression of having been written without the conviction and zest which distinguish their highly imaginative forerunners in Op. 85.

The *Polonaises*, Op. III, already mentioned earlier as being the thematic source of some of the *Papillons*, possess additional points of interest for the student of Schumann's keyboard works, who may trace in these incunabula some of the characteristics of his style as a composer of both soli and duets. It may not, perhaps, be altogether fanciful to surmise that the composer's music for the solo instrument owes something of its complex nature to the fact that he wrote duets before he wrote soli, and that having thus early become accustomed to weaving a comparatively intricate texture for four hands, he inevitably worked on similar lines, making only unavoidable modifications, when writing for two hands. Moreover, in translating some of the passages from the duet *Polonaises* to the solo *Papillons*, he even discovered fresh possibilities of elaborating the texture. The fifth *Papillon*, one of the very earliest examples of typically Schumannesque harmonic polyphony, is even richer in essential part-writing than is the trio of the seventh Polonaise from which it is derived.

Schumann was without doubt indebted to Schubert for the idea of writing Polonaises for four hands, and a comparison of his own Op. III with his predecessor's Opp. 61 and 75 reveals similarities in style between the works, such as the predominantly chordal and metrically vigorous character of the polonaises, the melodic charm of the trios, and the canonic imitations which occur in the trios of Op. 61, No. 4, and Op. 75, No. 4, and abound throughout Op. III. Schumann also followed the example set by Schubert in Op. 61 in omitting to plan an orthodox scheme of key-relationship between the separate pieces. There is no coherence in the sequence of tonalities used for the *Polonaises*, Op. III, four of which are in sharp and four in flat keys. The confusion is intensified by the unusually abrupt cleavage between the respective tonalities of the fifth polonaise and its trio, the former being in B minor and the latter, which wanders in and out of several keys, fundamentally in C major. Schumann generally wrote his contrasting section in a nearly related key, and only in a few pieces, such as Op. 85, No. 9 (*Am Springbrunnen*) did he go even so far afield as B flat for the central episode of a movement in D major. On the other hand, he aimed at securing unity among a group of movements by the quotation in one of a motive or phrase from another, as he was later to do in the *Davidsbündlertänze* and the *Jugend-Sonatinen*. In Op. III, No. 2, a figure in bar 5 is used as principal motive in the trio; in Polonaise 3, descending scale-figure referred to in trio 8; Op. 66, quotation of opening subject of No. 4 in coda of No. 6. Several of the stylistic details in the *Polonaises* prefigure those in his later works for piano solo and require no specifying here. A few others which recur in his subsequent duets are as follows:

(*a*) The treating of a short phrase by canon at the octave two or four bars apart, between the two hands of one player: Op. III, trio No. 6; Op. 85, No. 8, and Op. 130, No. 5 (coda), between primo and secondo, one bar apart.

(*b*) The shaping of phrases into unusual bar-lengths—a comparative rarity in Schumann's production as a whole: Op. III, trio 2, (7 bars), No. 3, (9 bars), Op. 66, No. 1, B flat section (*every* phrase), Op. 85, No. 1 (9 bars), No. 2 (6 bars), No. 3 (10 bars), Op. 109, No. 2 (9 bars), Nos. 5 and 9, &c.

(*c*) The use of a single-line melismatic passage for expressive purposes: Op. III, trio No. 7, Op. 109, Nos. 4 and 6.

(*d*) The maintaining of a continuous, murmuring figure of semi-quavers alternately in the right and left hands of either one or both players: Op. III, trio No. 3 (secondo), Op. 85, No. 9 (both); or of broken octaves divided between the two hands of one player, Op. III, trio No. 3 (primo) and Op. 66, No. 6 (secondo).

(*e*) The construction of a whole movement from one, or at most, two melodic figures treated plastically: Op. III, trio 8, Op. 66, No. 4, Op. 85, No. 6, Op. 130, No. 4.

(*f*) The use of very low pitch, either for single passages in secondo's part which overweight primo's: Op. III, trio No. 8, Op. 66, Nos. 1 and 6; or for a whole movement, Op. 130, No. 6 (*Ringelreihe*) which is consequently so heavy and clumsy throughout as to suggest that this 'round dance' is being performed by giants rather than children.

The division of the musical and technical interest between the two players of Schumann's duets is unequal. In few of the works does the substance afford opportunities for genuine ensemble playing as, for example, in Op. 66, Nos. 2 and 4, and Op. 109, No. 5, where motives are passed to and fro between primo and secondo, and only occasionally are the players made acutely aware of their interdependence when, for instance, their parts overlap and necessitate mutual hand-crossings (Op. III, No. 6, Op. 109, No. 8). In general, the partners are either given the same type of figuration and are obliged to follow each other closely, or secondo is treated merely as an accompanist to primo. In this case, however, the accompaniment allotted to him is frequently intrinsically interesting and finely contrasted with primo's part. In the first trio of Op. III, secondo supplies a uniform, dotted figure—a kind of basso ostinato—below primo's flowing triplets, and in the eighth trio, he maintains an expressive, almost cantabile commentary upon the ingenuous melody which primo plays in single notes or unison octaves. Indeed, in almost all the trios of this opus, except No. 3 where the partners are reasonably unanimous, each player is enabled to pursue an independent course, and in Op. 85, similar methods of distributing the interest are employed even more effectively. In this later set of 'characteristic' pieces, which all bear imaginative titles, much of the picturesque atmosphere is evoked by the skilful opposition of the forces of each player. For instance, in No. 2, *Bärentanz*, secondo, impersonating the elderly bear, growls throughout the entire movement on one repeated low doubled fifth darkened by chromatic acciaccature, while primo plays the part of the cub in gambolling semiquavers high in the treble; in No. 5, *Kroatenmarsch*, secondo has to be content with acting as drummer to primo's band of wind-instruments; in No. 11, *Gespenstermärchen*, he maintains a ceaseless undercurrent of breathless semiquaver whispers to primo's horrific narrative in slower notes, and in the last movement, *Abendlied*, undertakes the sole responsibility of providing the harmonic foundation in pianissimo chords to an upper part so exiguous that it is played by primo's right hand alone. In other movements of Op. 85, however, especially Nos. 9 and 10, *Am Springbrunnen* and *Versteckens*, the status of the players is equal. Of all the five sets of Schumann's duets, this opus, which might well form the background to a miniature ballet, consistently affords the greatest enjoyment to the players themselves. It also recalls more strongly than do any of the others the happiest features of the composer's first-period style. Like the *Jugend-Album*, to which it is a companion, it is somewhat restricted in tonal range, only the 'easy' keys being used, except for *Abendlied*, which movement in D flat illogically concludes the series which began in C.

Bilder aus Osten, Op. 66, is unique among the works for four hands in having a really homogeneous key-system. Three of the six pieces are in the basic tonality of B flat minor, two are in D flat major and one in F minor. The rhythmic scheme is unfortunately only too homogeneous; none of the pieces is in triple time. The work stands alone, too, among all Schumann's complete sets of individual pieces for the keyboard, either solo or duet, in having been *avowedly* composed in response to a single definite literary stimulus. Schumann did not pretend to have portrayed any particular event from the *Makamen*, except in the last movement, 'Reuig, andächtig', where the hero, Abu Seid, is delineated as repenting of his former riotous living.[1] But he did claim to have expressed in music the fundamentals of oriental poetry and thought as presented by Rückert in his German version of Hariri. The musical substance of Op. 66 is, however, no less occidental than that of Schumann's other compositions, and even if the player is aware of the composer's intentions, he must search deeply for any specifically oriental attributes—except perhaps for the profusion of repetitive figuration and the rarity of breathing-spaces which are commonly considered to be characteristics of exotic music, but which are already prominent features of Schumann's style. In its generally straightforward, vivid narrative style, the work is a small-scale counterpart of the *Novelletten*, Op. 21. Yet the composer seems to have felt that he had written in a new style, for he asked his friend Karl Brendel to feel his way gradually into the pieces and not to judge them from a single hearing.

The player who looks at a copy of Schumann's *Ballscenen*, 'nine characteristic pieces', and finds that it opens with a movement entitled *Préambule* and closes with a *Promenade*, may reasonably hope to discover in this Op. 109 a reflection, however pale, of the composer's Op. 9. But *Ballscenen* is no *Carnaval*, evoking the spirit of the masquerade in sensitive musical imagery. It is simply a collection of conventional dance-movements representative of sundry nationalities, Polish, Hungarian, French and Scottish. The *Polonaise* (No. 2), for all the Chopinesque tinge in the third phrase, sounds much less spontaneous than its far-off prototypes in Op. III; the *Ungarisch* (No. 4) is emphatic and repetitive without conveying any real sense of abandon, and the two *Walzer* (Nos. 3 and 8) are denied the easy lilt of *Valse noble* by jerky metrical figuration in both parts in the first, and a heavy bass and obstructive accentuation in the second. The *Mazurka* (No. 6) 'sehr markirt' is, however, invigorating from the outset; the *Française* (No. 5) executes its steps with determination and the *Écossaise* (No. 7) is appropriately sturdy. In the last-named, secondo, whose role in this opus is otherwise undistinguished, rivals primo in independence and importance. In *Promenade* he has a chance of producing some good percussion

---

[1] His own copy of the book (in the third edition, Stuttgart, 1844) shows crosses against *Makamen* 2, 6, 7, 13, and 16 in Vol. I and 24 in Vol. II.—*Ed.*

effects, while in *Préambule* he is much more actively employed than his partner. This introductory movement affords the only reminiscence of *Carnaval*. It closes firmly with four repeated forte chords of G major, and then, without a moment's pause, springs to life with a chord of the dominant seventh on A in preparation for the brief modulatory passage leading into the ensuing *Polonaise* in D. It is just such a sudden transition as that from the end of *Paganini* to the repeat of *Valse allemande*, though it is certainly less thrilling. The square-cut, aggressive *Promenade* of Op. 109 bears no resemblance whatever to its eloquent namesake in Op. 9.

Kinderball, Op. 130, 'six easy dance-movements', already mentioned here in the category of pieces for children, differs from its predecessor, Op. 109 in dimensions rather than character. The whole work is on a small scale, and each movement, except the leaden-footed finale, *Ringelreihe*, is more concise than any in Op. 109. Four of the dances exemplify types already included in the previous opus, and each makes a happier impression. The slow *Polonaise* (No. 1) is more dignified and melodious; the *Walzer* (No. 2) flows unimpeded by rhythmical obstructions; the *Française* (No. 5) trips more featly than its forbear and primo's part in the *Écossaise* (No. 4) contains the most fluent and bewitching piano writing in either of the two collections. The *Menuett* (No. 3), marked 'Gravitätisch', composed three years before the other movements, consists entirely of four-bar periods, but the structural monotony is neutralized by the varied metrical scheme, and the accentuation, which generally falls on the second beat, lends the movement the stately character of a sarabande. This unimportant, but not altogether unattractive opuscule was written in three days in September, 1853, soon after Schumann had completed his longish *Konzert-Allegro*, Op. 134, for piano and orchestra. Its triviality is scarcely a matter for surprise.

Three sets of piano soli, which do not belong to any of the categories of Schumann's last-period works described in the foregoing pages, now remain for discussion: *Waldscenen*, Op. 82, *Vier Märsche*, Op. 76 and *Drei Fantasiestücke*, Op. 111. The first, composed between 29 December 1848 and 6 January 1849, differs from the composer's other sets bearing descriptive titles in that each piece was originally headed with a poetic motto,[1] of which that to No. 4—*Verrufener Ort*, as it was originally called—was the only one preserved. Thus *Eintritt* was headed:

---

[1] See Boetticher's *Robert Schumann: Einführung in Persönlichkeit und Werk*, p. 634.

G

Wir gehn auf tannumzäuntem Pfad
Durch schlankes Gras, durch duft'ges Moos
Dem grünen Dickicht in den Schoss.

The second piece, first entitled *Jägersmann auf der Lauer*, was prefaced by the poem 'Früh steht der Jäger auf' from Heinrich Laube's *Jagdbrevier*, while the *Jagdlied* (originally *Zur hohen Jagd*) was inscribed 'Frisch auf zum fröhlichen Jagen', the first line of another of Laube's hunting poems.[1] The motto of *Vogel als Prophet* was 'Hüte dich! sei wach und munter', and the final *Abschied* was headed by the verse

> Leise dringt der Schatten weiter,
> Abendhauch schon weht durchs Tal,
> Ferne Höhn nur grüssen heiter
> Noch den letzten Sonnenstrahl.

In his monograph on Schumann, Cesare Valabrega devotes a whole section entitled 'La natura nella sintesi artistica Schumanniana' (pp. 17–44) to a detailed description of *Waldscenen*, which he considers as one of the composer's most typical works, and which he selects as the basis of a long dissertation upon his power of translating into music 'both the profundity of cosmic life and the most complex sensations which the human spirit derives from it'. If, however, *Waldscenen* is considered simply as music for performance rather than for philosophical discussion, the nine pieces are found to be so unequal in stature that the cycle is rarely played in its entirety. Despite variations in tempi and contrast in mood between the separate movements, the whole tends to become monotonous owing to the restricted tonal scheme and to the absence of any movement in triple time. Only two of the pieces, the etherealized *Vogel als Prophet* and the romantic *Verrufene Stelle*, which are representative of Schumann's highest powers as a tone-poet, are frequently performed. They almost completely overshadow the remaining movements, which are of comparatively slight importance though they are not altogether without interest and charm. The faery *Eintritt* (No. 1), in which the curtain rises upon the forest scene, opens with a subdued motive which suggests a horn-call with its own immediate echo; the evanescent texture of the four bars after the first repeat

---

[1] Five of which were also set by Schumann a few months later (May 1849) for male chorus and four horns, as *Jagdlieder* (originally *Lieder zur Jagd*), Op. 137. Two of the settings show some thematic affinity with the piano pieces inspired by the same poems: compare Op. 137, No. 1, with Op. 82, No. 8, and Op. 137, No. 4, with Op. 82, No. 2.—*Ed.*

conjures up the dappled shade of the woodland brake, and later, the distant spacing of treble and bass-parts, with the sustaining-pedal bridging the gap, produces an effect of remoteness and mystery. The endings of both the D minor movements, *Jäger auf der Lauer* (No. 2) and *Verrufene Stelle* (No. 4) are given an eerie twist by the alternation of contradictory major and minor triads; the guileless treble-line of *Einsame Blumen* (No. 3) is enhanced by the echoing middle voice which every now and again makes a semitonal impact upon it, and the elusive formal design of *Freundliche Landschaft* (originally *Freier Ausblick*) (No. 5) beguiles the tedium of its figuration. Only *Jagdlied* (No. 8) introduces a strenuous element hitherto little apparent except in *Jäger auf der Lauer*. All these pieces are of predominantly instrumental type and their texture is imaginatively woven. In *Herberge* (which was first conceived as *Jägerhaus*) (No. 6) and *Abschied* (No. 9), which are more purely melodic, the material is subjected to a kind of treatment which exaggerates its inherent sentimentality, especially in the protracted codas. Although Schumann allowed *Verrufene Stelle* to keep its poetic motto, the musical content corresponds so perfectly with the ghostly title that the player hardly needs further suggestions as to performance. The sparse texture, expressive part-writing, eloquent passages in the lower register of the keyboard, and the generally mysterious atmosphere lend this piece a character similar to that of the more reflective movements of *Kreisleriana*. The exquisite line-drawing in the first and last sections of *Vogel als Prophet* (No. 7) is of like nature to that in Var. 7 (Etude VIII) of the *Études symphoniques*, but is infinitely more tenuous. There, the figuration ranges high and low over the keyboard, each entry of the melodic fragment being quickly followed by another in a different voice or register while the texture is amplified by chords and intensified by strong accents and sforzandi. Here, the thin melodic line remains almost exclusively in the upper or middle register above light harmonies, and even when it is intermittently counterpointed, the answering voice seldom descends below the tenor compass. The slenderness of the figuration is accentuated by the chromatic auxiliary-notes which usurp the place of the essential notes on almost every beat and produce a succession of piquant sounds. The tranquil chordal middle section in G major throws this fine-spun filigree into even stronger relief.

The *Vier Märsche*, Op. 76, reveal Schumann in an entirely different light. He is no longer the sensitive nature-poet, but an ardent republican giving rein to his feelings concerning the political

disturbances of 1849 by writing piano music far more stirring than
had been his wont since the culminating period of his production in
1839. He composed the first march while returning to Dresden after
taking refuge at Kreischa in June 1849, and the others during the
ensuing few days. The completed set was forthwith dispatched to
Leipzig for immediate publication, with a special request for the
printing of the significant date in the largest possible figures.[1] The
rousing Marches, all in common time, are very different in character
from either of the two which had long ago preceded them: the
spirited *Davidsbündlermarsch* in triple time at the end of *Carnaval*,
and the slow, sustained *Marsch und Trio*, Op. 99, No. 11, alla breve.
Schumann had previously shown a preference for this latter, 'marcia
funebre' type, choosing it, as we have already seen, as the basis of
his *Études symphoniques*, and also for the slow movement, 'in modo
d'un marcia' of his Piano Quintet. Now he was all fire and energy—
so fiery, indeed, that he relinquished his customary segmental
manner of composition (though not his ineradicable habit of repeating brief phrases) and was able to carry through the writing of these
longish movements without needing to arrest their triumphal progress by the insertion of conventional, self-contained trios of
markedly different style. Certainly, each march has a well-defined
central section which provides contrast either in key or tempo, but
it does not occasion any serious break in the continuity, except in
No. 4, where the transition from E flat to B major calls for a momentary respite in the metrical routine. To this movement, however,
Schumann could not desist from appending a detached coda in
which to refer to material in the other marches and to sum up the
entire series, as was so frequently his custom. The pianistic texture
in all four movements is rich and full of variety. Rhythmical and
lyrical interest are evenly balanced. Strongly accentuated figures
alternate with flowing passages in which a gracious melody is
accompanied by pulsating chords, more often than not in triplets.
Much of the writing recalls the superb style of the *Études symphoniques*, the *Fantasie*, Op. 17, and the more brilliant sections of the
Faschingsschwank and seems to suggest that the political enthusiasms
now agitating Schumann had resuscitated some of the passionate
emotions of other kinds to which he had given such vigorous
musical expression during his younger and more care-free days.
The third March is entitled *Lager-Scene* and is in slightly slower

[1] For further details, see G. Abraham, 'On a Dull Overture by Schumann',
in *Monthly Musical Record*, December 1946.

tempo than the others though the middle section is marked to be played quicker. This whole movement is in the nature of a 'characteristic piece' and is rounded off with a picturesque coda in which the bustle and stir of camp life die away into the silence of the night. In the B major section of No. 4, at bars 5 and 6 after the repeat, there is an unmistakable reference to the opening notes of the 'Marseillaise'. Its particular subtlety consists in its being nothing more than a slight readjustment of the phrase with which the section begins. When the quotation is followed shortly after by the original phrase, the ingenuity of its incorporation in the texture is seen even more clearly in retrospect.

To this same series of marches—known in the Schumann circle as the *Barricade Marches*—belongs another, *Geschwindmarsch*, which Schumann had originally intended to place between Nos. 3 and 4, but which he cut out and included, with a modified key-scheme and a new ending, as No. 14 of the *Bunte Blätter*, Op. 99; the original version of the March was published as a supplement to *Die Musik*, May–June 1941. It is quite different from the others, firstly on account of its duple time-signature and much quicker pace, and secondly, because Schumann not only reverted to his custom of balancing one brief section against the other by translating phrases bodily into fresh keys, but constructed the whole march almost exclusively out of two-bar fragments. The thematic material itself is bright and attractive, yet its generally finicking and often witty treatment lend the piece the character of a march for tin soldiers rather than for perfervid republicans. Perhaps that was the reason for Schumann's discarding it from Op. 76. Its persistent meticulousness is redeemed in the definitive version at the very end by a fascinatingly sleek passage of descending chromatic harmonies in crotchets leading to an unexpectedly restful plagal cadence, whereas the original had ended with a powerful crescendo and crashing *fff* chords. With this sprightly little movement, which in point of both style and content might have been written by Grieg, Schumann concluded the series of occasional pieces he had composed spasmodically throughout his career. He finally gathered them into the two collections, *Bunte Blätter*, Op. 99, and *Albumblätter*, Op. 124, and had them published in 1851 and 1854 respectively. He held no very high opinion of the pieces, but thought they would be of interest to his friends as examples of 'musical moods'. His own title for the series was 'Spreu' ('Chaff'). Incidentally he wished the *Bunte Blätter* to be literally 'leaves of many colours' and discussed with his publisher, F. W. Arnold, the possibility of issuing each piece with a wrapper of colour 'corresponding to its character'. For the *Drei Stücklein*, Nos. 1–3, he chose green.[1]

If Op. 76 is to some extent reminiscent of various works written during Schumann's first period, Op. 111 is evocative of one in particular, its namesake, Op. 12. The *Fantasiestücke*, Op. 111, consists of three pieces, all in flat keys, as are those of Op. 12, and marked to be played without a break for they are rather more interdependent than their forbears. Although they bear no individual titles, it is difficult not to associate the turbulent No. 1 with *In der Nacht*, from which it borrows a melodic phrase; to regard No. 2 as a wistful though less perplexed analogue of *Warum*, or to relate the robust tunefulness of No. 3 to certain passages in *Fabel* and *Das Ende vom Lied*. The first movement of Op. 111, Molto vivace ed appassionato, in C minor, another of Schumann's moto perpetuos in triplets, contains only one fragment of pure melody, the quotation from *In der Nacht* already referred to. It is of definitely instrumental type after the manner of Brahms's Intermezzo in A minor, Op. 118, No. 1, and is bi-partite in structure, the second half being in the nature of a freely varied replica of the first. A ritornello tinge is imparted to the movement by the recurrence every now and again of the opening bar. There are several climaxes, but no one decisive culminating point, in which respect it differs fundamentally from the Brahms Intermezzo. The movement is a decoration rather than an experience, yet it is a complete and convincing whole and is pianistic in Schumann's best first-period style. The tranquillizing second movement, an Andantino in A flat in triple time, is composed largely of light, sustained homorhythmic chords and is a perfect foil to the C minor. It opens with an ear-haunting phrase which recurs in whole or in part so often that it seems to constitute the entire piece. It does not ask a question, but gently states a simple fact which no one could find it in his heart to gainsay. The central episode, which flies back to the key of C minor, the quaver triplets and the more complex texture of the first movement though not its rapid tempo, conveys the feeling that a recollection of his recent agitation had momentarily disturbed the composer's new-found tranquillity. It is, however, restored by the repetition of the A flat section, in whose little coda the oft-repeated statement is finally affirmed more gently and persuasively than ever. This blessed quietude is immediately dispelled by the forcible third movement in C minor wherein a square-cut

[1] Cf. Boetticher in *Die Musik*, October 1941.

melody, made more conspicuous by an accompaniment of chords in both hands on the weak beats, unfolds itself in a series of two-bar phrases. The melody, which is just tolerable in the minor mode, becomes almost unbearably complacent when played in the major mode in the most resonant part of the keyboard, with accompanying chords pulsating above and below and a heavy bass-part. The lighter, more gracious texture of the pianissimo middle section and coda comprises the same kind of wide spacing with mild discords between the extreme parts, and the type of eloquent single-line passages, in upper, lower, and middle voices which distinguish some of the movements of *Waldscenen*. The obstinate two-bar rhythm, however, precludes any organic growth or expansion of the thematic substance, and the movement as a whole forms an unsympathetic ending to a cycle which begins so ardently, continues with such infinite placidity, and contains so much truly grateful pianoforte writing.

Looking back over Schumann's later period of composition we cannot fail to note that, for all their quantity and variety, the piano works, solo or duet, comprise few of great intrinsic value and many which would hardly have survived until today had they not been written by one whose earlier compositions had secured him imperishable fame as a pianists' composer. Many of the later-period works are little known, even among musicians. Very few of the solo pieces find their way regularly into recitalists' programmes and none of the duets ever appears in public. The *Variations for Two Pianos* are given only an occasional hearing, for despite the present rage for two-piano playing, performers apparently prefer to bring forward exciting new transcriptions of well-known solo works rather than resuscitate one designed originally for the two keyboards, even by a composer of established reputation. Yet, when it is remembered that after the peak year, 1839, not only were Schumann's creative activities no longer centred in solo piano music, but that his physical health was beginning to deteriorate so that he could no longer compose with the same zest and vigour as in earlier years, the decline in quality of his later-period works is the more easily understood.

Schumann's piano compositions are intensely intimate; they stand or fall by the vividness of the experiences which inspired them. His youth had been passed in a ferment and the music he wrote in early years had been the principal outlet for all his glowing literary enthusiasms, poetic idealism, and artistic aims. By 1840 he had already won recognition as a composer; the conditions of his life were more stable; his youthful ardours had to some extent died down and his experiences were no longer of the same passionately romantic kind which called for instant translation into subjective piano music. For a whole year he poured his feelings into songs. Then he turned to chamber, orchestral, and choral music, and only later came back to the piano which he was henceforth to utilize either for abstruse purposes such as the contrapuntal works of 1845; for educational projects, as in the pieces for children; for political propaganda in the *Vier Märsche*, Op. 76; and only infrequently and rather half-heartedly for the purely imaginative type of music in which he had formerly excelled. Moreover, after 1844, in which year Schumann relinquished his editorship of the *Neue Zeitschrift für Musik*, he had much more leisure than hitherto, and tended to compose more for the sake of composing than because of any inner necessity; and after 1845, as we have seen,[1] he began to 'invent and work out' in his head.

There are few fundamental differences in actual pianistic style between Schumann's first- and later-period compositions. He continued to use most of the devices familiar to students of the main body of his work, but his later music calls for less virtuosity on the part of the performer. It contains fewer wide leaps and stretches or difficult cross-hand passages, and though the texture is often as intricate as that of former years, the melodic content is more pronounced and rhythmic displacements are fewer. Some of the part-writing is lacking in clarity, the basses have become heavier, feminine endings are more common, and the element of repetition is greatly increased. The basic difference, however, consists in the decreased intensity of the inspiration. The later 'characteristic' pieces viewed as a whole indicate a change of mood from the poetic to the prosaic. Here and there an example of the composer's former stylistic witchery enchants the listener and reminds him of the first-period works. Such pieces as *Vogel als Prophet* and *Verrufene Stelle* (Op. 82), *Theme, Winterzeit, Knecht Rupprecht* and No. 30 of Op. 68, the second *Fantasiestück* of Op. 111 and *Versteckens* and *Gespenster-märchen* (Op. 85)—to name some of the more fantastic works of 1848-9—could have been written by no one but Schumann at his best. They bear his magic imprint while many of their fellows might easily have come from the pens of his contemporaries and disciples, Kirchner, Gade, Jensen, and Sterndale Bennett. The many conventional piano pieces of Schumann's last period may add nothing to his reputation. When, however, they are considered in relationship

[1] Cf. p. 70.

to the production of his best and most fruitful years, they may serve to emphasize the unique and inimitable quality of his splendid earlier works. Even if Schumann had written nothing after his thirtieth year, he would still be entitled to his unassailable position as one of the most individual and imaginative of all composers of piano music.

CHAPTER III

THE SONGS

By Martin Cooper

'Do you, I wonder, feel as I do?' wrote Schumann to Hermann Hirschbach in June 1839. 'All my life I have thought vocal music inferior to instrumental and have never considered it to be great art.' Only eight months later, in February 1840, he wrote of 'composing nothing but songs' and in a letter to Clara, 'Since yesterday morning I have written nearly 27 pages of music—something new, of which I will only say that I laughed and wept for joy as I wrote. . . . Oh! Clara, what a joy it is to write for the voice, a joy I have lacked too long.' That is the typical Schumann, a theorist whose theories are always apt to be contradicted by the mood of the moment, emotional and unpredictable and glorying in the quick succession of extremes of feeling, the sun chasing the clouds, laughter and tears at one and the same moment, creating in his music the rainbow effects which he so much admired in the prose of his beloved Jean Paul. Up to the age of thirty the piano had been virtually his only confidant—for that is exactly what Schumann's piano music represents, confidences —but with the final blooming of his love for Clara Wieck he felt the need of a still more personal and intimate form of expression. Of Schumann's 250 odd songs very nearly half were written in the year of his marriage (1840) and that half contains almost all the best songs he was ever to write.

In spite of his letter to Hirschbach, Schumann had already tried his hand at song-writing before 1840. His Op. II originally consisted of eleven songs dedicated to his three sisters-in-law. Three of these were published by Brahms in the supplementary volume of the Collected Edition; six by Geiringer in 1933, and one—a setting of Goethe's *Der Fischer*—as a supplement to the *Zeitschrift für Musik*, also in 1933.[1] But Schumann was not satisfied with them as songs and used three of them in his piano-works of the '30s. *An Anna II* (composed 31 July 1828) appeared as the Aria in the F sharp minor Piano Sonata; *Im Herbste*, as the andantino of the G minor Piano Sonata; *Der Hirtenknabe* (composed August 1828) in the Intermezzo,

---

[1] The eleventh, Jacobi's 'Klage', was apparently never finished.

Op. 4, No. 4. In fact the new lyrical impulse which Schumann brought to his piano-writing made the distinction between instrumental and vocal music more blurred than it had ever been before; and made him, too, the ideal link between Schubert and the next generation of song-writers for whom voice and instrument were of equal importance. His literary taste and affinities gave him a feeling for prosody and a sensitiveness to the atmosphere of a poem such as no previous song-writer had ever had. A glance at the list of poets set by the mature Schumann gives an idea of his literary taste. Heine easily heads the list, with 42 poems. Then come Rückert (27), Goethe (19), Eichendorff (16), Justinus Kerner (14), Chamisso (11), Lenau (10), Burns (9), Geibel, Mary Queen of Scots, and Hans Andersen (5 each), Mörike and Hoffmann von Fallersleben (4 each), Schiller (3), and Tom Moore (2). Of nonentities he hardly ever set more than a single poem, except in the case of the young poetess Elisabeth Kulmann, whose romantic life and early death at the age of seventeen led Schumann into mistaking her for a genius. 'Wilfred von der Neun' (whose real name was Toepff) was no more than a talented amateur, but his poems at least provided Schumann with the larger and vaguer background that he needed in 1850 and they are certainly superior to the pretty platitudes of Elisabeth Kulmann.

Heine was the ideal poet for Schumann not only because a certain spiritual affinity existed between them, showing itself in the deliberate cultivation of sharply contrasted emotional moods within a single lyric; but also because of the conciseness and point of his style. Schumann, with his admiration for Jean Paul, was quite happy dreaming his way through the most circumstantial and flowery writing, pursuing the most far-fetched metaphors to their logical and ludicrous conclusions, savouring the extremes of comedy and sensibility on the same page and quite oblivious of the absence of plot or formal arrangement.[1] Heine's poetry served him as an unconscious discipline, curbing his natural tendency to divagation and forcing him to come to the point, to condense his emotions to their sweetest

[1] In case the reader may tire of reading the name of Jean Paul repeatedly or may suspect that modern denigration of his style is unjust I choose at random one of his high-flown metaphorical passages. This is taken from the *Flegeljahre* and Vult is speaking. 'O reiner, starker Freund, die Poesie ist ja doch ein Paar Schlittschuh, womit man auf dem glatten, reinen, krystallnen Boden des Ideals leicht fliegt, aber miserabel forthumpelt auf gemeiner Gasse'. ('My pure, strong friend, poetry when all is said and done is a pair of skates, on which one can skim lightly over the smooth, clean crystal surface of the Ideal, while in the ordinary street they make one's progress a wretched hobbling.') Compare also the quotations in the previous chapter (pp. 37–8).

and their bitterest. When, in July 1828, Schumann sent his first songs to Gottlob Wiedebein, the Brunswick *Kapellmeister*, the advice he received was to 'look to truth above all. Truth of melody, of harmony, of expression—in a word, poetic truth.' It was really Heine who enabled Schumann to follow that advice.

Thirty-seven of the forty-two Heine settings were composed in the year 1840. Heine's ballad *Belshazzar* was one of the first poems he set, on February 7 of that year (although it only appeared six years later, as his Op. 57) while the first of the opus numbers consisting of songs was the Op. 24, the *Liederkreis* of Heine poems, dedicated to Pauline Garcia. His Opp. 25, 27, 30, 31, 35, 36, 37, 39, 40, 42, 45, 48, 49, 53, 57 were all written the same year and a study of these songs alone would give a complete idea of Schumann as a song-writer. In the next twelve years he never wrote anything better and only occasionally anything nearly as good as appeared in this sudden enormous spate; and as he grew older his literary instinct seems to have faltered. How important this was to the quality of his music he was himself perfectly aware. 'Parallel to the development of poetry, the Franz Schubert epoch has been followed by a new one which has utilized the improvements of the accompanying instrument, the piano', he wrote in his *Observations on Composers and Composition*. 'The voice alone cannot reproduce everything or produce every effect: together with the expression of the whole, the finer details of the poem should also be emphasized. All is well as long as the vocal line is not sacrificed.' It is not surprising to find the piano playing a more prominent part in the songs of 1840 than in the later ones, for Schumann was still first and foremost a pianist at that point. What is more surprising is that no single one of these early songs is a piano solo with obbligato voice. (In fact it is possible to detect, on internal evidence alone, the authorship of No. 2 of Op. 37, one of the three songs contributed by Clara to the twelve settings of poems from Rückert's *Liebesfrühling*. 'I have no talent at all for composition', sighed poor Clara and certainly *Er ist gekommen* is simply a piano solo with a voice part added, just such as one would expect a piano virtuoso to write). The preludes and postludes, generally considered to be typical of Schumann's song writing as a whole, most frequently occur in the 1840 songs and are nowhere so prominent as in the *Dichterliebe* and *Frauenliebe und -leben* series. Another feature which is strongly characteristic of the 1840 songs and hardly appears afterwards is the turn. This appears in *Widmung*, *Lied der Suleika* (Ex. 17), *Aus den östlichen Rosen*, *Er, der Herrlichste von allen*

and *Helft mir, ihr Schwestern* but on the rare occasions when
Schumann uses it in his later songs (*Himmel und Erde*, Op. 96, No. 5,
for example) it strikes a false note and seems out of style. Whether
the turn is to be considered as fundamentally a pianistic trait—a
habit of the fingers in a composer much given to improvising—or to

Ex. 17

be related to Schumann's unconscious imitation of the operatic style,
it remains a distinct mark of the year 1840. *the turn in the songs*

The piano obviously suggested another trait which is common
throughout the whole range of Schumann's songs but particularly
so in those of 1840. This is the anticipation of the voice by the
piano or vice versa, such as we find in *Es treibt mich hin,*
Intermezzo and *Aus den hebräischen Gesängen* (Ex. 18) in one form
and in *Stille Liebe* in the other. Occasionally this device of syncopation, which became almost a mannerism in Schumann's piano works,

Ex. 18

is used with programmatic effect, as in *Lieb' Liebchen* where it represents the beating of the lover's heart and gives rise to the subtly
dramatic ending of each quatrain, where the words 'Totensarg'
(coffin) and 'schlafen kann' (can sleep) are left hanging in the air by
an accompaniment which has come to an end a bar earlier. These
illustrations or programmatic devices are rare in Schumann's songs,
but when he attempts them they are almost always carried out with
the finest musical sensitiveness and never exaggerated. The fall of
the rose petals in *Der Hidalgo* and the rippling of the waves in
Aufträge are effective because of their simplicity and their musical
unpretentiousness; but Schumann is at his happiest when he is suggesting another musical instrument. The Romantic predilection for
the horn and its associations with hunting, with the life of the forest
and knightly adventure, finds expression in innumerable songs of
which *Waldesgespräch, Der Knabe mit dem Wunderhorn* and the late
Der Gärtner are only typical examples among many others. The
organ-like piano part of *Stirb' Lieb' und Freud'* suggests the cathedral setting of the poem and the harp-player's broken chords are
discreetly suggested in *Wer nie sein Brot mit Tränen ass* and *Wer sich
der Einsamkeit ergibt*. In a more humorous vein is the suggestion of
the military band in *Husarenabzug*, the brilliant imitation of a
wheezy concertina in the first of the *Der arme Peter* songs and the
guitar in *Der Contrabandiste*. Occasionally Schumann writes a whole
dance movement where the poem demands it, as in *Es ist ein Flöten
und Geigen* (No. 9 of the *Dichterliebe*) and *Der Spielmann*, but even
here the voice is never overridden.

If we had not his own word for his dislike of Spohr's chromaticism,
we might be surprised by the very sparing use of chromatic melody
or even strongly chromatic harmony which we find in Schumann's
songs. A considerable number suffer from a tendency to the opposite
extreme, unrelieved diatonic harmony only too often combined with
a square march rhythm, also unrelieved. This can generally be
traced to Schumann's desire to write something in either ballad or
folk-song style (e.g. *Sonntags am Rhein*) or else to an attempt to
recapture the carefree, youthful atmosphere of the *Knaben Wunderhorn* (*Freisinn, Frühlingsfahrt* or the 6/8 swinging march of *Wanderung*
and *Der Knabe mit dem Wunderhorn*). This rhythmic monotony was
already a noticeable trait of some of the longer movements of the
piano works (the last of the *Études symphoniques* for example) and a
tendency to square-cut rhythm remained with Schumann throughout
his life. His rare use of chromatic sequences and harmony in the

songs is often dictated by the text and he obviously felt very strongly the atmosphere of extreme melancholy, even verging on despair, which such passages produced. In this he was still a child of the eighteenth century. On the other hand his love of quick transitions of mood made him on the whole avoid complete songs in what he felt to be this exaggeratedly melancholy manner. *Aus den hebräischen Gesängen* and *Einsamkeit*, with their strongly chromatic, melancholy opening sections, both have comparatively diatonic middle sections in the major key and only *Zwielicht*, which is considerably shorter, is allowed to remain in the mood of unrelieved, chromatically coloured gloom throughout. This sparing use of what he plainly felt to be an extreme atmospheric effect makes it all the more effective, and on the very few occasions on which Schumann falls into a strongly chromatic manner in order to express anything but melancholy the result is unpleasantly saccharine and reminiscent of the worse hymn-tunes of John Bacchus Dykes. This resemblance is strongest, perhaps, in *Wehmut* where both tempo and rhythm suggest the hymn-tune; but *Nur ein lächelnder Blick*, where the chromatic alterations in the melody are combined with a slow 6/8 rhythm and an abysmally vapid poem, may be considered the parent of countless Victorian drawing-room songs which delighted our grandparents but arouse nothing but distaste in us.

The quality which is most typical of Schumann's songs, his most individual contribution to the development of the German *Lied*, is really a noble variety of this sentimentality, the lily which festering in *Nur ein lächelnder Blick* smells more rank than any weed. The German word for it is 'Innigkeit' and it is virtually untranslatable by any single English word. 'Innigkeit' is a variety of warm, intimate and meditative emotion, essentially self-conscious and therefore dangerously closely allied to sentimentally but saved, at least in its nobler manifestations, by a genuinely childlike simplicity. When this simplicity is also self-conscious, its childlike language becomes something like baby-talk and 'Innigkeit' is then indistinguishable from archness and sentimentality. It is remarkable how many of Schumann songs bear the superscription 'Innig' (*Nur ein lächelnder Blick* among them) and how typical, for good and for evil, these songs are in almost every case—*Widmung, Schöne Fremde, Was will die einsame Träne* for example on the credit side and *Frage, O ihr Herren, Liebesbotschaft* and *Er, der Herrlichste von allen* on the debit, among many others of both complexions. On the whole it is the 'innig' side of Schumann that dates his music most noticeably, just as it was this which endeared him to our grandparents. The circumstances in which the 1840 songs were written—on the eve, or immediately in the wake, of an extremely happy marriage—sometimes give their lyricism a domestic, conjugal quality which may strike the modern listener as a little complacent. Certainly the humble adoration of the chosen male that breathes from the poems of Chamisso chosen by Schumann for his *Frauenliebe und -leben* wakes very little echo in a modern listener. It reflects rather the feelings that the nearly 40-year-old Chamisso was delighted to find in his 18-year-old bride, but to a modern taste there is something supremely unattractive in the poet making his bride speak of herself as a 'nied're Magd' (lowly maiden) who only asks to gaze on her husband in all humility ('nur in Demut ihn betrachten') and is blinded by the beauty and amazed at the condescension of so superior a being. We feel that to be false, possibly quite unjustly: but if not false, then at any rate the prelude to a *Frauenleben* bounded by the 3 ks—'Kirche, Kinder und Küche'. It is perhaps significant that the second song of the cycle (*Er, der Herrlichste von allen*) is not only the most abject in sentiment but also the least successful musically, with its square dotted rhythms and hammered accompanying chords extending uninterruptedly over four pages. Rückert's two poems in a similar vein (*Lied der Braut*, Nos. 1 and 2) show the girl torn between her love for her mother and her husband. Here again a modern reader of the poems might divine a certain gloating over the situation, comparable with the excessive interest shown by elderly spinsters in the details of a wedding-day programme or the exact disposition of bedroom furniture in the household of a newly-married couple. But Schumann extracts the last ounce of sentiment from the poems, down to the sighing 'lass' mich' with which No. 2 closes, without self-consciousness and therefore without offence.

Nevertheless, it is a very welcome change to move on to the quite unmatrimonial sentiments of Heine, to find for a change the male sunk in hopeless adoration and to savour the caddish and venomous revenge reserved for the last line or couplet of a poem that seems to start in tremulous humility. Not that Schumann ever achieves real venomousness; to see how far he falls short of the possibilities we have only to compare his setting of *Anfangs wollt' ich fast verzagen*, a solemn and resigned chorale, with Liszt's wonderful dramatic miniature. Nor did Schumann attempt to set *Vergiftet sind meine Lieder*, which is perhaps Liszt's masterpiece; the venomous quatrain in the style of Martial could hardly have appealed to the composer of

Frauenliebe und -leben. Even so, the lyricism of the *Dichterliebe* is a far lighter, more mercurial, more *musical* lyricism than anything that Chamisso ever achieved, for all his French blood. Of the nine songs of the Heine *Liederkreis* (Op. 24) only two come up to the level reached by all sixteen of the *Dichterliebe*. The two sets are virtually contemporary, the *Liederkreis* songs composed between 1–9 May and the *Dichterliebe* begun on 24 May and finished on 1 June; so that the difference in quality can only be connected with the choice of poems. *Ich wandelte unter den Bäumen* and *Lieb' Liebchen* (Nos. 3 and 4 of the *Liederkreis*) would not be out of place in the *Dichterliebe* any more than the four songs which originally belonged to the set but were only published at the very end of Schumann's life or posthumously. These are *Dein Angesicht* (Op. 127, No. 2), *Es leuchtet meine Liebe* (Op. 127, No. 3), *Lehn' deine Wang'* (Op. 142, No. 2) and *Mein Wagen rollet langsam* (Op. 142, No. 4, wrongly said by Dr. Ernest Walker to be Schumann's last song: it was actually composed on 29–30 May 1840).

What distinguishes all these Heine settings from the remainder of the *Liederkreis*, and from all but a few isolated songs spread over the rest of 1840 and the rest of Schumann's life, is not only their intensity of feeling but their economy of expression. Already in *Ich wandelte unter den Bäumen* we meet for the first time that astonishing blend between the simplest folk-song manner and the most subtle and highly organized psychological suggestion, which is the distinguishing

Ex. 19

note of the *Dichterliebe*. Schumann begins the voice part with a perfectly simple diatonic melody, rhythmically devoid of any subtlety whatever; the accompaniment follows the voice exactly. But after two lines, 'da kam das alte Träumen, Und schlich mir ins Herz hinein', the 4/4 rhythm is interrupted by an inimitable triplet phrase which is twice echoed in the piano part (Ex. 19). The second quatrain repeats this pattern and then, with a sudden change—not really a

H

modulation in spite of the dominant minor ninth—the key shifts from G major to E flat major and the triplet rhythm returns, though at a slower tempo, as the birds offer to tell the poet the magic word they have overheard, the secret of his love. But he will not be robbed of his grief and the folk-song melody returns, only to dissolve into a kind of arioso recitative at the twice repeated 'ich aber Niemanden trau' which dies away in a whisper. The eeriness of the whole poem arises from the suggestion of the 'secret' which the poet refuses to be told, although it would lighten his grief. It is this which gives the neurotic, 'psycho-analytical' atmosphere to so many of Heine's poems, the suggestion of a split personality and a self-torturing, masochistic rapture beneath the conventional roses and nightingales. Here, in *Ich wandelte unter den Bäumen*, Schumann juxtaposes but does not mingle the two personalities. In the *Dichterliebe* his method is far more subtle, for he makes the two 'persons' speak at the same time. Heine plainly enjoyed the torments of unrequited love— 'Liebesleid und Weh'—quite as much as the pleasures of mutual passion, which were the only thing that interested Chamisso. (How profoundly disturbed Chamisso was by any less conventionally happy amorous situation is shown by his pathetic poem *Was soll ich sagen?*, which Schumann seems to have set without really understanding its significance. Chamisso remained Frenchman enough to be mortally embarrassed by an amorous, as opposed to a specifically erotic, relationship between an old man and young girl.)

Schumann, with instinctively right judgement, chose miniature poems of Heine, almost all of them in the extremely simple style of the folk-song. Only one—*Die Rose, die Lilie*—is as simple in matter as it is in manner and Schumann's setting is as natural and unclouded as the poem. In all the other poems Heine's simplicity of manner is deceptive and what begins apparently as a straightforward lyric assumes before the end the complexion of an enigma or a satirical epigram. *Wenn ich in deinen Augen seh'*, for example, starts like a folk-song and continues conventionally enough until the last couplet. Then, instead of the lover's happiness being full when the girl confesses her love for him, we find the exact opposite, tears: 'Doch wenn du sprichst: ich liebe dich! so muss ich weinen bitterlich'. Schumann starts in a straightforward G major, modulating to the subdominant by means of supertonic minor harmony (which we shall see later to be typical). The first hint of some strange fly in the ointment is the chord of the diminished seventh on the word 'sprichst' but, by a stroke of genius, the actual words 'weinen bitterlich' are in no way underlined harmonically and only the piano postlude gives the hint of something mysterious and uncompleted, by converting the tonic of G major immediately into the dominant seventh of C major so that the tonality of the whole postlude hangs ambiguously between the two keys of C and G. Sometimes the piano part alone suggests the mystery beneath the poem's surface from the very beginning. The chord of the German sixth with which *Am leuchtenden Sommermorgen* opens and the syncopated accents throughout the piano part mentally prepare the listener for the wonderful modulation to the key of G major and the close, once again on the German sixth, which Schumann discovered for the gentle, enigmatic entreaty of the flowers: 'Sei unsrer Schwester nicht böse, du trauriger, blasser Mann'. Finally, in the postlude, the picture of the garden is completed and over the slowly rippling arpeggios another voice rises, this time the piano's, answering with wordless consolation the unspoken complaint of the poet. I personally should place this one song among the very greatest miniatures in the whole of music, a faultless dramatic lyric (with the lyricism unbroken on the surface and the drama implicit), the *locus classicus* of 'Innigkeit' at its very best.

The two dream poems of the *Dichterliebe*—in which we should naturally expect the strange and pathological element to predominate —are in marked contrast to each other. *Ich hab' im Traum geweinet* owes a large part of its effectiveness to the long pauses, the unaccompanied phrases of the voice and the sinister dotted quaver figure in the piano part which punctuates the lines of the poem (*cf.* Duparc's *Le Manoir de Rosamonde*). Once again we find extreme agony of mind expressed in the chromatic harmony of the accompaniment to the last couplet, where the voice part ends on a chord of the dominant and out of the key (dominant of A flat in the key of E flat minor). The dream is precise, bitterly clear in every detail. *Allnächtlich im Traume* with its short, gasping phrases and sudden changes of rhythm is the dream which remains clear only as a general impression, all the details being blurred. Schumann's setting has the breathlessness of Heine's poem, the sudden, childish spurts of confidence, ending with the pathetic, frustrated confession, 'und das Wort hab' ich vergessen': the whole point of the dream has eluded him. Singers are apt to take the song too slowly and to make it an expression of bliss, when the sense of both words and music demand an atmosphere of restlessness and anxiety. Schumann never modulates properly to the key of the dominant, either in this song or in *Ich grolle nicht*.

If he reaches the dominant he moves away from it at once, after a single beat, preferring subdominant harmony or, in *Ich grolle nicht*, a maximum of variety without actually leaving the tonic key at all. This is the only one of the *Dichterliebe* cycle with a repeated-chord accompaniment, which is justified by the shortness of the song and the urgent, persistence of the words, the quick mounting to a thunderous climax (where, by the way, the alternative, higher voice part was added by the composer only as an afterthought when the song was in proof). Hardly less of a dream is the last song but one of the set, *Aus alten Märchen*, one of the most successful of Schumann's 6/8 march songs, with the persistent rhythm mitigated by considerably greater harmonic variety and changes in the weight of the accompaniment than in other songs of the same kind. The augmented version of the melody in the last verse, marked 'mit innigster Empfindung,' concentrates the whole weight of the song in the close and makes the sudden evaporation of the whole vision in a series of diminished sevenths both more unexpected and more effective. *Die alten, bösen Lieder*, which ends the set, opens with a dramatic flourish that is very rare in Schumann's songs and the piano part—with its marked resemblance to No. 4 of Chopin's *Études*, Op. 10, which had appeared in 1831—bears the main burden of the musical interest until the, by now familiar, concentration of energy and intensification of emotion which herald the final quatrain. The weighty, mounting octaves in the bass of the piano part recall a similar passage in the first movement of the *Eroica* (probably intentionally), but when the voice has finished the octave portamento rise on the C sharp, the whole mood of the music changes in a moment from brutal violence to tremulous self-pity. This is the reverse of the usual Heine process; the sting is not in the tail of the poem, for once. Instead of a savage or enigmatic close Schumann has dramatic justification for one of his most cherished effects—the sun suddenly bursting through the clouds, a wave of tenderness bursting in upon harsh sarcasm. He achieves this by an enharmonic modulation pivoting on the C sharp which is suddenly treated as the leading note in the key of D major instead of the dominant of F sharp. This lasts only two bars and the voice part dies away over a dominant harmony in the original key of C sharp minor. Then the consoling voice of the piano rises—exactly as in the postlude to *Am leuchtenden Sommer-morgen*—only here the postlude is followed by a further instrumental passage in the nature of an improvisation which rounds off the whole cycle. A descending quaver passage in the right hand is developed sequentially and harmonized with rich chromatic harmony until it finally dies away in a thrice-repeated sigh.

No other poet provided Schumann with the concentrated intensity of feeling and the verbal terseness and economy that were the two things he most needed from a poem. Or if an occasional lyric (Mörike's *Das verlassene Mägdelein* or Ullrich's *Die Fensterscheibe*, for example) has these qualities we still miss the mysterious, charged atmosphere of the Heine settings. Nos. 11 and 12 of Op. 35, *Wer machte dich so krank?* and *Alte Laute*, have something of the same quality; but Justinus Kerner, the poet, was a doctor and an occultist and the mystery behind the poems is objectively imagined rather than subjectively experienced. This accounts for the tame ending of *Alte Laute*, the introduction of the conventional figure of the angel and the correspondingly conventional cadence in the music, which had started so promisingly with the single, tense chord of G major modulating by a chromatic slip of the bass into the tonic, A flat major (Ex. 20). Far more typical of Schumann's general lyrical manner is No. 10 of the same Op. 35, *Stille Tränen*. Kerner's poem is one of the innumerable lyrics inspired by the secret grief

Ex. 20

Das du so krank ge - wor - den

of the poet and the uncomprehending attitude of the world, a Romantic commonplace which he treats no better and no worse than a hundred other minor poets have done. It lacks entirely the drive and bite that Heine's sense of humour and power of self-criticism give to even his most effusive poems; and Schumann's music, for all the beauty of the melody and the richness and subtlety of the modulations, is too discursive and rambling. His repetition of the last couplet, preceded and followed by an interlude and postlude of comparative lengthiness, represents a third of the whole song, which is thus artificially enlarged. There is no case of Schumann's treating a Heine poem in this way, though it becomes almost a mannerism in his settings of other poets. Even the beautiful No. 1 of Op. 39 (the Eichendorff *Liederkreis*) *In der Fremde* repeats the last line simply for the sake of repeating the effective cadence (a G natural in the key of F sharp minor). The other song of the same name in the same set (*Ich hör' die Bächlein rauschen*) repeats the last line of the poem three times without even the excuse of a harmonic or melodic *trouvaille*, and in a really poor song such as *Liebesbotschaft* (Op. 36, No. 6) the general rambling and sectional character of the whole setting is enhanced by a spate of arch repetitions at the end.

Apart from five poems in the *Myrthen* of 1840, Schumann did not attempt to set any but incidental poems of Goethe until the nine songs from *Wilhelm Meister*, Op. 98a. Goethe's balance and serenity, philosophic depth, and dislike of romantic exaggeration all made him a quite unsympathetic figure to the young Schumann; and later in life his attempt to widen his horizon and to achieve a musical language capable of expressing Goethe's thought led him, at least as a song-writer, to go against all his natural instincts—or rather, since instinct generally gets the better of the artist, to give free rein to the most unfortunate of his natural tendencies, rambling and divagation. The lyrics from the *West-östliche Divan* in *Myrthen* are charming and effective even if only one of them, *Lied der Suleika*, really catches the spirit of Goethe; and even there the otiose repetitions are a serious blemish in the setting of such a formal master as Goethe. The ballad of *Die wandelnde Glocke* is one of the better of Schumann's songs in this style. It attracted him from a literary and theoretical point of view but was in no way suited to his essentially lyrical and subjective temperament. The *Wilhelm Meister* songs, on the other hand, are among Schumann's most conspicuous failures as a songwriter. Painfully oppressed by the philosophic significance of Mignon and the old harp-player, he rambles on in a portentous, pseudo-symphonic style, with frequent modulations and unnatural vocal phrases, losing the thread of the poem and of his own musical design, and sometimes, as in No. 6, visibly at a loss how to continue (Ex. 21). Only Philine's *Singet nicht in Trauertönen* is at least half successful, though here again the repetitions of the last line, and then again of the last phrase, are unforgivable.

In addition to settings in ballad style scattered all over his sets of songs, Schumann wrote four sets with the definite title of *Romances and Ballades*, Opp. 45, 49, and 53 in 1840, and Op. 64 in 1847. These contain sixteen songs in all, with texts by Heine, Eichendorff, Mörike, Seidl, Lorenz and von Frölich. In the same category are Heine's *Belsatzar*, Op. 57 (though actually one of the first of the February 1840 songs), Schiller's *Der Handschuh*, Op. 87, and the melodramas or ballads for declamation—Hebbel's *Schön' Hedwig*, Op. 106, and *Ballade vom Haideknaben*, Op. 122, No. 1, and Shelley's *Die Flüchtlinge* ('The Fugitives'), Op. 122, No. 2.

Of the three poems by Chamisso, Op. 31, two are definite ballads,

Die Löwenbraut and *Die rote Hanne*, and the third, *Die Kartenlegerin*, is a romantic genre picture in much the same style. Two of the Heine settings are miniature dramas consisting of three poems each, *Der arme Peter*, Op. 53, No. 3 and *Tragödie*, Op. 64, No. 3. They are very unequal in quality and only one song from each triptych is

Ex. 21

comparable with Schumann's best settings of Heine. The concertina which accompanies Grete's dance with Hans, poor Peter's rival (*Der arme Peter*—1) turns the whole song into a slow country waltz or *Ländler*. Peter's misery finds no expression in the music; he is merely part of the picture, in the true ballad style. The second song in *Tragödie*, on the other hand, is lyrical in character and only successful in comparison with the fatuity of the first, and the sentimental banality of the third, parts. *Belsatzar* starts rather unpromisingly like a piano solo—in fact the semiquaver figure in the piano part which dominates half the song is closely related to a passage in No. 5 of the *Fantasiestücke*, Op. 12 (*In der Nacht*). The great length of the poem, eleven verses of four lines each, made it extremely difficult to avoid monotony; but Schumann succeeded here as he seldom did in later ballad settings. This is chiefly owing to the way in which the piano part becomes increasingly simple and tends more and more to make way for the voice as the dramatic interest of the poem increases. The semiquavers, which are almost continuous in the first half of the poem, give way first to repeated quaver chords, with the accent off the beat, and then to isolated chords merely supporting the voice in the last two verses, where the tempo decreases and the chief point lies in the dramatic recitation of the text ('In langsamern Tempo, leise und deutlich zu recitiren'). The glaring fault of both *Die Löwenbraut* and *Blondels Lied*, rhythmic monotony, was thus avoided in *Belsatzar* as in the lyrical ballad of *Die beiden Grenadiere*. In *Die Löwenbraut* there are forty continuous bars of slow 3/2 time, unrelieved by any variation in the piano pattern which follows the voice exactly. Similarly in the 124 bars of *Blondels Lied* —a 'nicht schnell' 4/4—there are only twenty bars in which the piano part does not follow the voice exactly; often it is in octave unison or in the simplest diatonic harmony devoid of harmonic, melodic, or rhythmic interest. Schiller's *Der Handschuh* is an exciting story told with the obvious and rather self-conscious dramatic effect we should expect. Schumann amuses himself by some equally naïve dramatic effects (major and minor ninth intervals in the voice when the lion roars and lashes his tail) and there is plenty of variation of key and rhythm, so much so in fact that musically the song does not really cohere at all. It is in fact a hybrid between a real ballad such as *Belsatzar* and the declaimed melodramas, in which the actor plays the main role and the music is merely 'background'. Unfortunately this is a role that music obstinately refuses to play and the melodramas are complete failures, though the *Ballade vom Haideknaben*[1] is an exciting story and Schumann's illustrations are often apt enough.

At the opposite extreme to the ballads stand Schumann's salon pieces. They are not many, for the simple reason that Schumann was never by nature a frequenter of salons. Domestic, conjugal felicity, which speaks rather too loudly for modern taste from some of the songs, satisfied both his emotional nature and his demands for the society of his fellow creatures. Nevertheless, every middle-class drawing-room in the Germany of the 1840s and '50s had its cultural pretensions and was, indeed, a miniature salon, if only for the family circle. Albums, pressed flowers, needlework, water-colours, piano duets and, of course, singing all contributed to this specifically domestic form of culture; and though it was only in exceptional salons that these rose much above the status of genteel crafts or

[1] See p. 264.

achieved that of arts, the demand on all artists to produce at least occasional pieces for home use was continuous and, as their works show, fairly continously met. The works of even such a comparative misanthrope as Grillparzer contain innumerable *pièces d'occasion* 'for Miss X's album', 'on a water-colour by Miss Z', and the like, while a socially-inclined artist like Liszt must have had the greatest difficulty in refusing demands which, if satisfied, would have taken up all the time he had for composition. As it is, a large proportion (25 out of 57 in Kahnt's three volumes) of Liszt's songs are settings of elegant trifles written by friends, of both sexes, belonging to the *beau monde*. Schumann was probably less plagued than many artists because of his inclination to solitary brooding, his frequent 'absence' in social gatherings; but it would have been unnatural if there were not some salon pieces among his songs. Indeed, his gifts as a minaturist and his lyricism, though rather intense and highly charged for the drawing-room, fitted him for this minor genre, and there are at least two models of the kind among the 1840 songs, Rückert's *Jasminenstrauch* and Catherine Fanshawe's *Rätsel* (the poem itself consisting of a parlour game and wrongly attributed to Byron). Far more typical of the general level of such works is the song *Liebste, was kann denn uns scheiden*, No. 6 of the poems from Rückert's *Liebesfrühling* which Schumann and his wife collaborated in setting. The four verses of the poem, each starting with the question, 'Beloved, what can part us?', continued with verbal assonances on 'meiden' and 'scheiden', 'mein' and 'dein', and the obvious variations of an arch party-game. (It is worth while comparing the song with Liszt's setting of Charlotte von Hagen's *Dichter, was Liebe sei,*

Ex. 22

mir nicht verhehle, a more personal and dangerous variant of the same game.) The musical interest is virtually non-existent. Both *Röselein, Röselein* and *Schneeglöckchen* (Op. 96) are all more highly developed, more sophisticated salon pieces; and even *Stille Liebe* and *Aufträge* are not really much more. The arch 'question' in the piano part with which *Stille Liebe* opens (Ex. 22), with its superscription 'innig', is comparable with the teasing triplets at the opening of Liszt's *Dichter, was Liebe sei*, though the emphasis is all on emotion in Schumann and on grace in Liszt. In the same way the rippling demisemiquavers that represent the wave in *Aufträge* are a great artist's version of what is in origin no more than a parlour trick.

Among these amusements and accomplishments of the nineteenth century, drawing-room duet-singing had a place which was half artistic and half (shall we say?) social. Music, as Plato knew, is an excellent dissolver of inhibitions and barriers of all kinds and if Edward could persuade Bertha to learn a duet with him he could reckon on the power of both music and text (generally discreetly amorous), the appeal of his own charming tenor, and his exquisite tact and consideration in turning pages, modifying his tone so as not to drown her pretty soprano, the necessity of looking one's partner straight in the eyes so as to ensure a perfect entry of both voices together and a hundred and one delightful details which gave courtship all the excitement of an honourable adventure and a good many of the thrills of the chase. Nineteenth century duets, then, are not to be judged on purely musical grounds. Like modern Russian symphonies, they were strictly *Gebrauchsmusik* and, as such, the capabilities of the performers must not be rated too high by the composer. Of Schumann's thirty-four duets only a handful are of any interest musically. The majority are comparable in interest of design, as in original intention, with the small form of sofa called a *causeuse*, large enough for two people sitting very close together and making no violent movements. Typical of this sort of duet are *Liebesgarten* (which looks like a banal sketch for *Im Walde*, though it was actually written later) and the duet numbers from Rückert's *Liebesfrühling*, including the duet version of *Liebste, was kann denn uns scheiden? Familiengemälde* with its sentimental comparison of the young couple and the old Darby and Joan, is a typical conversation piece in Schumann's most bourgeois manner. The four duets, Op. 78 contain some much better music. The *Tanzlied* is a charming drawing-room game, needing considerably more musical ability than anything of the kind that Schumann had written previously; but I suspect that the boldness of the text ('morgen, o Trauter, dein ganz') confined performances to professional singers in any case. This applies also to the two 'vergebliche Ständchen', *Liebhabers Ständchen* and *Unterm Fenster*. The setting of Goethe's *Ich denke dein* keeps the voices singing mostly in thirds and sixths like all the salon pieces, but it has a pretty romantic sentimentality and must have been a powerful weapon in Edward's amorous arsenal. *Wiegenlied* (Cradle-song for a sick child) has not the mawkish flavour we might expect and though the relation between the two voices is still very primitive and uninteresting, the contrast between triplets and plain four-in-a-bar quavers, the sudden modulations from E minor to C major and from C to E flat, and the exploitation of the passing note (A sharp in the E minor triad) makes the song unique among the simpler salon duets of Schumann. The duets in the *Liederalbum für die Jugend* and the settings of Elisabeth Kulmann (*Mädchenlieder*) are of no interest musically.

There remain the two sets of Spanish pieces, *Spanisches Liederspiel*, Op. 74 (five duet numbers), and the two duets in the *Spanische Liebeslieder*, Op. 138. Spanish pastiche attracted Schumann rather in the same way that Hungarian gipsy pastiche attracted Brahms. In neither case was there any attempt at understanding the different musical tradition, and the resemblance of the result to the original is only occasional and superficial. Nothing further was aimed at, of course, but even so Schumann's Op. 74 does contain some very extraordinary things. Of the duets *Erste Begegnung* and *Liebesgram* have vaguely exotic rhythms, strongly dotted, that is to say, with occasional accents off the beat and some 'passionate' triplets, exactly like Brahms's so-called Hungarian pieces. *Intermezzo* is a very German serenade, more like a cradle-song imitated from German folk-song, such as Brahms affected later. *In der Nacht* again suggests Brahms's future style, in its most un-Spanish combination of Bach-like chromaticism (Ex. 23) and sweet, warm German sentiment. Finally *Botschaft* opens with a direct quotation from the middle section of Chopin's C sharp minor Polonaise, Op. 26, and makes

Ex. 23

considerable demands on the singers in the two really independent vocal lines which only come together for florid ornamentation with wide intervals (Ex. 24). This same tendency to wide intervals is found in one of the solo numbers of the *Liederspiel, Melancholie*, a

Ex. 24

strange and violent little song, again with Bach-like characteristics (Ex. 25)[1] and containing dramatic leaps of ninths, tenths and even in one place a fourteenth, which are most unusual in Schumann's vocal writing. *Der Contrabandiste*, with its guitar accompaniment, coloratura and triplets imitating a horse's gallop, is really a parody and

Ex. 25

quite an amusing one. The guitar is suggested again in the *Romanze* from the *Spanische Liebeslieder*, Op. 138, whose title and pianoforte duet accompaniment obviously gave Brahms the idea for his own

[1] Cf. pp. 261 and 267.

Liebeslieder. None of these solos or duets bears the remotest resemblance to anything genuinely Spanish and the general musical level of interest is below that of the earlier *Liederspiel.* Thus *Bedeckt mit Blumen* is rather like the earlier *Liebesgram,* only less successful, and *Blaue Augen hat das Mädchen* is a much less interesting essay in the German folk-song style than *Intermezzo.* Of the solo songs *O wie lieblich ist das Mädchen* and *Hoch, hoch sind die Berge* are essays in much the same style and their chief distinction lies in the fact that, once again, Brahms (I suspect) had a passage from *Hoch, hoch sind die Berge* (Ex. 26) in mind when he wrote *Vergebliches Ständchen.*

Ex. 26

In between the ballads and the salon pieces, and partaking of the nature of both, come first the *Liederalbum für die Jugend,* Op. 79, and the *Seven Songs,* Op. 104, settings by the child 'poet' Elisabeth Kulmann. Like the *Kinderscenen* for piano, these songs are written for children as they exist in the sentimental imagination of an adult rather than for children as they are. It is possible that in the nineteenth century children could be persuaded to adopt, at least in public and before their parents, some of the qualities attributed to them in the songs—extreme naïveté, love of nature, a sense of pity and at least nascent Sabbatarianism. But that any children, in any country, at any date, should really have been anything but complicated, indifferent to nature, pitiless and impious by nature, I cannot believe. Schumann, then, either writes for the 'Kunstkind', the product of intensive nursery training, or not for children at all. *Schmetterling, Frühlingsgruss, Sonntag, Hinaus ins Freie, Weihnachtslied* and *Kinderwacht* are all carefully simple musically, unctuous in tone and quite devoid of any interest. But spread among these thirty odd songs there are some exquisite miniatures. The first of the two *Zigeunerliedchen* (Ex. 27), for example, and *Der Sandmann* have a lightness and aptness of touch, a sureness of psychological instinct shown in minute detail, such as only Hugo Wolf has equalled. They

are neither folk-songs nor children's songs but spring from a spontaneity of feeling and directness of expression which Schumann at
times possessed in common with 'primitive' people and children.
No child ever thought or felt in terms of Hoffmann von Fallersleben's

Ex. 27

Un - ter die Sol - da - ten ist ein Zi - geu- ner bub' ge - gan- gen

So sei gegrüsst viel tausendmal, holder, holder Frühling but any child
might prick up its ear at a story which began *Unter die Soldaten ist
ein Zigeunerbub' gegangen.* *Des Sennen Abschied* from Schiller's
William Tell might be taken as a companion piece to Lenau's *Die
Sennin* (Op. 90, No. 4) as both depict the descent in the autumn
from the high mountain pastures of the Alps. Schiller's poem is the
shepherd's own song and Schumann's accompaniment suggests a
primitive pipe-tune which gradually dies away in the distance.
Lenau's is a German equivalent of Wordsworth's *Highland Reaper*,
a deeply subjective lyric full of Ruskin's pathetic fallacy (the moun-
tains miss the girl and remember her songs). The harmonic scheme
is correspondingly more rich and complicated and whereas *Des
Sennen Abschied* only modulates occasionally to the dominant or the
relative minor of its tonic C major, the voice part of *Die Sennin* ends
on a chord of the dominant, while the piano part dies slowly away
on a mediant major chord (D sharp major in B major).

The two Goethe settings which have somehow found their way
into the *Liederalbum für die Jugend* are quite out of keeping with the
rest of the contents. Lynceus' song from *Faust*, Part 2, is a monotonous piece in the four-square dotted rhythm beloved by Schumann,
the setting of *Kennst du das Land* obviously belongs to the other
Wilhelm Meister songs in Op. 98a, where it also appears. It cannot
compare with the setting, however faulty, by Liszt or the magnificent
one by Hugo Wolf, but it is very much better than the rest of the
Wilhelm Meister songs and interesting for Schumann's very rare
insistence on the chord of the dominant minor ninth ('Was hat man
dir, du armes Kind, getan?').

Schumann's admiration for the poems of Elisabeth Kulmann,
which issued in his Op. 104 (1851) is explicable partly as the result
of failing powers of judgement, perhaps, but partly also as one of
those quite frequent lapses in taste which may occur to any artist of
a deeply emotional character liable to be influenced by personal

circumstances. Elisabeth Kulmann was born at St. Petersburg in 1808 and lost her father and six of her seven brothers while she was a young child. She herself died of consumption in 1825, after living in poverty with her mother. Her poems show her to have been a sensitive and idealistic young woman, whose imagination was probably stimulated by the disease from which she suffered. She had a poetic facility which enabled her to imitate the lighter, occasional lyrics of the Romantic school with a certain elegance, and a spiritual quality which showed itself in the simplicity and resignation with which she faced death. Schumann was greatly struck by the unusual pathos of her story and, in an introduction which he printed to his settings of seven of her poems, he went so far as to prophesy her universal recognition as a great German poet and to speak of her poems as 'wisdom's highest teachings expressed with a poetic perfection worthy of a master'. It must be remembered that his literary taste was always very personal rather than aesthetically correct, and that to the end of his life he rated Jean Paul as the equal of Goethe and Shakespeare. The settings of Elisabeth Kulmann's songs witness to the soundness of his musical instinct, in any case, for the unpretentiousness of the music exactly matches the poems, with their maidenly lisping of swallows, greenfinches, dead flowers, clouds and the moon. They are of no intrinsic musical interest whatever.

It is an interesting fact, which says much for Schumann's understanding of the nature of vocal music, that the rhythmic complications, anomalies and puns which are such a marked feature of his pianoforte style seldom, if ever, appear in the voice parts of his songs; and hardly ever oppressively even in the piano parts. In fact, as we have already seen, a considerable proportion of the songs suffer from the opposite fault, monotony and jejuneness of rhythm. Schumann always tended to confine his rhythmic experiments to detail, often to inner parts, while the movement as a whole—whether it be orchestral, vocal or chamber music—progresses in uniform, scarcely disguised march time. His most completely successful pieces are generally miniatures and, in the songs at least, the subtlety and effectiveness of his rhythm is generally in inverse proportion to its complexity. Compare, for instance, *Die Fensterscheibe* with *Abendlied*, both from Op. 107. Schumann very seldom changes the time signature in the course of a song. When he does—as in *Allnächtlich im Traume* or *Jemand*—it is for a quite definite dramatic purpose. In some of the most successful songs the piano continues the same rhythmic pattern from beginning to end (*Der Nussbaum*, *Mondnacht*,

Frühlingsnacht and most of the *Dichterliebe* songs) and the voice has its own, perfectly distinct melody which is either completed or commented on by the piano (*Nussbaum*) or leads an entirely separate existence (*Das ist ein Flöten und Geigen*). A note-by-note accompaniment, with the top note of the piano part permanently in unison with the voice, is sometimes skilfully masked by ornamentation, as in *Und wüssten's die Blumen, die kleinen*, or broken up into brilliant fragments, as in *Frühlingsnacht*. It is generally only left quite undisguised in the march songs in 'folk' or student style (*Frühlingsfahrt, Wanderlied* and the rest) and even then not for the whole song in the better examples. Hymns like *Zum Schluss, Talismane*, or *Über allen Gipfeln* are of course derivatives of these march songs; but even in these Schumann generally breaks the plodding 4/4 by some device, the flowing quavers in the middle section of *Talismane* and the festoons of crotchet triplets at the words 'Warte nur!' in the Goethe poem. Occasionally Schumann overworks an idea which is good in itself but loses its initial point by repetition. The piano part of *Muttertraum*, with its wandering semiquavers and cross-bar suspensions, sounds like a two-part invention to which the voice part has been added afterwards and, though it makes an effective opening, it does not seem to correspond to two whole quatrains of Andersen's poem. In much the same way *O Freund, mein Schirm, mein Schutz* (No. 6 of Rückert's *Minnespiel*, Op. 101) seems rather an essay in the style of Bach—perhaps suggested by Rückert's poem, which addresses the earthly much as Bach's cantata arias address the heavenly lover—than a genuinely original inspiration. The exclusive use of passing-note harmony and the same angular rocking rhythm, as of a broken cradle, for nearly fifty bars without a single break is an extraordinary instance of lack of self-criticism in such a self-conscious artist as Schumann. Compare this with a song of much the same length (though admittedly much quicker tempo) like *Ein Jüngling liebt ein Mädchen* where Schumann starts with the idea of a strong accent off the beat and indeed carries it right the way through the song but is careful not to emphasize the syncopated rhythm except in the piano solo passages, prelude, interlude and postlude.

This scrupulousness in his treatment of the poems which he set places Schumann, as we have seen, half way between the unscrupulously musical Schubert and the almost painfully literary Wolf. His two misquotations ('Blätter' for 'Äste' in Moser's *Der Nussbaum* and 'lieblichen' for 'guten' in Heine's *Das ist ein Flöten und Geigen*) are little more than misprints and the only serious criticism that his poets could make of Schumann's settings of their poems is that he tends, for purely musical effect, to repeat their last lines or last phrases. The examples of this are innumerable and I have referred to some already. Even Heine is occasionally mishandled in this way (*Berg und Burgen, Ich wandelte unter den Bäumen*) though generally the construction of his poems makes it virtually impossible without giving the impression of repeating the point of a witty story to be sure that the audience has not missed the point. What led Schumann to offend against literary canons in this way was his desire to impart a dream-like, echo effect to a song, a heightening of emotion as the music dies away in the distance. Sometimes this effect is achieved by a simple repetition of the last phrase, differently harmonized but with no piano postlude, as in *Im Walde*. Sometimes—and this is the more frequent method —the last line or phrase is repeated and a postlude added as well, as in *Stille Tränen, Nur ein lächelnder Blick, Liebesbotschaft* and many others. But the same effect is achieved by purely musical means and without deforming the poem in all Schumann's best songs simply by the piano postlude taken in conjunction with the last line of the poem, as in *Widmung, Der Nussbaum, Mondnacht, Frühlingsnacht, Am leuchtenden Sommermorgen, Jasminenstrauch, Auf das Trinkglas eines verstorbenen Freundes, Die beiden Grenadiere, Die Fensterscheibe*—to choose examples from every date and category. In these songs the musical and literary emphasis coincide, instead of Schumann coming to the end of his poem before the music has reached its natural climax, as in *Stille Tränen*—the most flagrant example of all—where twenty-one bars out of a total seventy are tacked on after the poem has finished, in the form of interlude, repetition of the last couplet and long postlude.

As we have seen, Schumann was conservative in his use of chromaticism, but this does not mean that the songs are in any way poor harmonically. A few, as we have seen, are too rich and a considerable number suffer from a deliberate simplicity employed, often unsuccessfully but always deliberately, for a definite purpose—the creation of an imaginary 'folk', child or student atmosphere. None of Schumann's masterpieces come into either of these classes, the over-rich or the artificially slimmed. In fact, the beauty of his most successful songs depends very largely on the perfect accord between poetical matter and harmonic manner. In setting a simple poem such as Moser's *Der Nussbaum*, Schumann employs a very simple harmonic scheme which does not go beyond the tonalities of the mediant (minor), the subdominant, dominant and supertonic minor. Within

I

these keys there are no further chromatic alterations and the ambiguous chords of the dominant seventh or chromatic alterations of the sixth are instinctively avoided. In an intensely emotional lyric such as Eichendorff's *Mondnacht*, on the other hand, Schumann deploys much more harmonic subtlety. The actual form of the song is simple almost to monotony: the voice part consists of the same eight-bar phrase repeated four times and followed by two four-bar phrases, which lead to the fifth and last repetition of the original phrase slightly varied to make a full close. In *Der Nussbaum*, as in many other songs, Schumann tended to avoid the dominant, to shy off it by a harmonic side-slip (the only occasion where the dominant seventh is used) and to prefer the minor of the mediant or supertonic. In *Mondnacht* the piano prelude modulates to the dominant (B major) within two bars and seems to insist on it until the voice enters and we find ourselves almost immediately in F sharp major, that is to say the key of the supertonic from the point of view of E major (the tonic key) or the dominant from the point of view of B major. This playing with ambiguities of chords of the dominant reaches its climax at the beginning of the last quatrain where, on the word 'spannte' ('spread') an inversion of the dominant seventh in the tonic (E major) suddenly becomes a dominant major ninth in the key of A, as the spreading of the soul's wings is suggested by the wide interval and spreading semiquaver phrase in the piano part. Schumann even ends the voice part on a chord of the dominant seventh, out of the key (A major instead of E) and there are many instances of this, at that time revolutionary, process throughout the songs. In the *Dichterliebe* alone *Im wunderschönen Monat Mai, Ich hab' im Traum geweinet, Das ist ein Flöten und Geigen*, and *Am leuchtenden Sommermorgen* end on chords of the dominant seventh out of the tonic, and *Aus meinen Tränen spriessen, Ich will meine Seele tauchen, Im Rhein, im heiligen Strome, Allnächtlich im Traume, Aus alten Märchen* and *Die alten bösen Lieder* all close either in the key of the dominant or else on a dominant seventh in the tonic. This applies only to the voice parts, of course, and in most cases Schumann makes the piano postlude come to a more or less conventional cadence in the tonic. Not always, however. In *Die Nonne*, for example, both voice and piano part close on a dramatic dominant seventh and in *Die Sennin* the voice ends on a dominant seventh of the tonic and the piano part unmistakably in the key of the mediant. Occasionally Schumann opens a song with a chord of the dominant or diminished seventh (*An meinem Herzen, an meiner Brust* from

Frauenliebe und -leben; Flügel! Flügel! um zu fliegen, Was will die einsame Träne? Die Tochter Jephtas) and even more frequently are whole passages in the course of a song built up on sequences of dominant sevenths. Among the most obvious examples is the quiet middle section of *Widmung* and the magnificent chain of dominant sevenths which leads up to the climax in *Aus alten Märchen* ('und laute Quellen brechen' to the twice repeated 'Ach!'). We have already seen a more sophisticated version of the same thing in *Mondnacht* and there are two other noticeable examples in the Eichendorff *Liederkreis: Schöne Fremde* and *Frühlingsnacht.* All these nocturnes or night pieces are in extreme sharp keys, as though Schumann felt that this blend of richness and ambiguity were his own way of expressing the Romantic adoration of the night— Novalis's 'herrlicher Fremdling mit den sinnvollen Augen, dem schwebenden Gange und den zartgeschlossenen, tonreichen Lippen'. More rarely a comparatively diatonic song will close with a postlude which consists almost entirely of a chain of dominant sevenths (*Schöne Wiege meiner Leiden*, Ex. 28, and *Rose, Meer und Sonne*).

Ex. 28

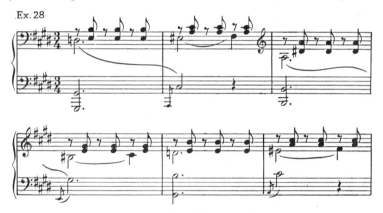

There was nothing unusual in Schumann's use of the dominant seventh; that is to say, there was nothing unusual in the fact that he used it. A far more unmistakable harmonic finger-print of Schumann's is his predilection for—almost his obsession with— supertonic minor harmony (especially, it seems, in the key of A major, where passages in B minor almost always appear sooner or later). The opening phrases of *Was will die einsame Träne* (Ex. 29) and *Lied der Suleika* (Ex. 17) are typical instances, but examples are spread thickly throughout songs of every period. It is dramatically crucial in some of the *Dichterliebe* songs, at 'da ist in meinem Herzen die Liebe aufgegangen' in *Im wunderschönen Monat Mai* and at 'ich liebe dich' in *Wenn ich in deine Augen seh'*. Again in *Was soll ich sagen?* we find the same harmony at the dramatic climax, 'du heissest mich reden'. Sometimes it is reached through the subdominant, as in

Ex. 29

Stille Tränen (C major), where the D minor ('ob allen Landen') is reached through the dominant seventh of F major, the subdominant of the tonic key; or by means of the dominant, as in *Aufträge*. Sometimes it is a mere passing effect, almost always emotional, as in *Heimliches Verschwinden* or *Meine Rose* (Ex. 30); or it is used as an

Ex. 30

ornament to give dramatic emphasis to a phrase, as in the last bars of the voice part of *Ihre Stimme* (Ex. 31).

Another favourite and very effective device of Schumann's, which he uses with great care and never wastes, is enharmonic modulation. The roots of almost all his harmonic experiments can be found in Schubert, including the technique of jumping from dominant to dominant which we have just seen and the turning to the key of the mediant where more conventional composers would have modulated to the dominant ('Zwischendominanten' and 'Mediantenrückung', as the Germans call these devices). The pivoting on a single note we have already met in the last bars of *Die alten bösen Lieder*, where

Schumann used it to express the sudden change in the poet's mood. In *Die Lotosblume, Stille Tränen,* and *Alte Laute* there is no dramatic, literary reason and Schumann is guided by purely musical instinct. The effect is certainly breathtaking when the A flat major breaks in on the C major at 'Der Mond, der ist ihr Buhle' in *Die Lotosblume* and at 'So lang du ohne Sorgen' in *Stille Tränen*: and hardly less

Ex. 31

when the simple, sequential phrases of *Alte Laute* are suddenly transferred from the dominant (E flat) to G flat major, i.e. the key whose tonic is the third note in the minor of the dominant (Ex. 32). This is a sophisticated form of the tendency to mediant harmony which we have already noticed (in *Der Nussbaum*, for example). Although there is no immediate dramatic reason for these enharmonic changes

Ex. 32

Schumann nearly always uses them in songs whose general sense and atmosphere have something eerie or uncanny; and this is obviously in accordance with his general feelings, already noticed, of the extreme power and effectiveness of chromaticism in any shape or form. We have already noticed the enharmonic modulations in two songs from Op. 35, both poems by Justinus Kerner, the doctor and occultist. A third of his poems, No. 6 of Op. 35, *Auf das Trinkglas eines verstorbenen Freundes*, is an unusual combination of Schumann's

extremely rigid, four-square, dotted rhythm—a cross between the
march and a prayer like *Zum Schluss*—with harmonic experimentation which alone suggests to the listener the mystery of the
poem. The piano follows the voice part note by note for three
quatrains, without ornament of any kind apart from the harmonic
colour. At the end of the first quatrain the music has reached what
is presumably the dominant of B flat major (the song being in the
key of E flat). This unison F Schumann now chooses to regard as
the mediant of D flat major and a four-bar phrase, repeating exactly
the rhythm of the first two couplets, now follows in that key. This
in its turn ends on a chord of D flat major with the mediant uppermost and is followed by a four-bar phrase identical with what has
gone before but in the key of F minor (the supertonic minor of the
original E flat, for which Schumann always hankers). The next
quatrain is based entirely on a punning use of the chord on the
flattened sixth of the scale, alternating with the dominant seventh
first in the key of B flat, then of E flat (Ex. 33), and this,

Ex. 33

significantly, is the heart of the poem's mystery, which lies in the
words 'was ich erschau' in deinem Grund ist nicht Gewöhnlichen zu
nennen' ('what I descry in your bowl is not to be spoken of before the
common herd'). After this the last quatrain is devoted to depicting

the slow movement of the moonlight down the valley and the solemn tolling of midnight. This passage is another example of Schumann's chains of dominant sevenths and very effective it is here, with the voice released at last from its note-by-note bondage to the piano and even varying slightly the ♩ | ♩. ♪♩ ♩ | ♩. ♪♩ rhythm which Schumann pursues inexorably throughout the whole song.

Schumann himself was quite aware of the novelty and originality of many things in his songs. On 31 May 1840 he wrote to Clara that 'it often seems to me as though I was treading quite new paths in music' ('als käme ich auf ganz neue Wege in der Musik') and a year later we find him writing to Kossmaly, author of an essay on 'The Song', with proper consciousness of his own originality:

> It vexed me rather that you put me in the second class. I did not expect to be included in the first class but I believe I can claim a place of my own and least of all am I pleased to be ranked with Reissiger, Curschmann, &c. I know that my endeavours and my means far exceed theirs and I hope you will remember that and not call me vain, which I am far from being.

He was generous in proclaiming the influence of Clara on the compositions of 1840. 'When I was composing them', he writes to her, 'I was entirely taken up with you. It is not possible to write such music without a bride such as you—and I mean that as high praise of you.' But the desirability of Clara's influence on the final versions of some of the songs has been questioned. Not her personal influence on Schumann, who told the same Kossmaly that his music had always been 'the expression of himself both as human being and as musician', with no cleavage or hostility between the two. But Clara Wieck was first and foremost a pianist formed in the classical and neo-classical school, with none of the instinctive leanings to Romanticism which her husband had always felt. Her musical taste leaned towards Mendelssohn quite as much as towards Schumann and there is, to say the least of it, a strong tradition (traceable directly to Theodor Kirchner, a disciple and friend of Schumann) that she persuaded Schumann to make various alterations in the text of his songs, always in the interest of academic 'correctness'. Schumann, in his aphorisms, expressed himself quite unambiguously on the subject of revisions:

> Two different readings of the same work are often equally good. (*Eusebius.*)
> The original one is generally the better. (*Raro.*)

And in point of fact the alterations that we can trace from his note-books are seldom of great importance and more often than not aim at perfecting the prosody of a song rather than any specifically musical improvement.

It was Schumann's practice to go on making alterations, which were often continued to the last moment, when the music was in proof. It will only be possible here to give a few typical examples of Schumann's revisions, as any more thorough study would necessitate a prohibitive amount of quotation. Most interesting of all is to see[1] how in many cases the songs which seem the most spontaneous and 'inevitable' were actually those on which Schumann took the longest time to make up his mind. Thus there exist three versions of *Mondnacht* (Schumann gave his mother-in-law a manuscript copy which differs from both the original and the corrected, published version), in which the

Ex. 34

composer seems chiefly concerned with giving the text and his illustrations more perfect expressiveness, though the musical char-acter of the song receives hardly any alteration at all. On the other hand *Frühlingsnacht* has a major alteration of the text of bars 15–17

---

[1] Viktor Ernst Wolff: *R. Schumanns Lieder in ersten und späteren Fassungen* (Leipzig, 1914). Wolff's 'first' versions, however, are themselves fair copies, not initial sketches.

as important as some of the major operations to which Beethoven's sketch-books bear witness. Compare the simplicity and expressiveness, the apparent 'inevitability' of the published version with the fussiness and ineffectiveness of the original (Ex. 34), in which the word 'herein' is repeated for no reason.

On the other hand, was Clara responsible for the 'toning down' of bars 69–76 of *Das ist ein Flöten und Geigen*, in which the chords of the original three-bar version (Ex. 35) seem to suggest either the climax of the festivity or the dagger-thrusts in the unfortunate lover's

Ex. 35

heart—or, knowing Schumann, both? Certainly the contradictory spirit of Jean Paul hangs over the whole song (Schumann probably had the last scene of the *Flegeljahre* in mind, the ball and its extraordinary results for Walt, Vult, and Wina), for over bars 75–8, which show the lover moving slowly away from the scene of his misery, Schumann wrote 'Vivat hoch' which, presumably on reflection, he enclosed in brackets. Dr. Wolff sagely remarks that this outburst is a 'memorial of Schumann's Janus-like temperament. In the heat of creation Florestan was led by his dramatic visions to make such annotations, which Eusebius later bracketed in a moment of cooler reflection'.

The manuscripts of the *Dichterliebe* are particularly heavily scored with revisions. Here again the most apparently spontaneous songs— *Die Rose, die Lilie* and *Hör' ich ein Liedchen klingen*—are shown to be the fruit of considerable reflection, if only on points of prosody, while *Am leuchtenden Sommermorgen* appears as a minutely calculated work of art, each of whose effects is carefully planned and either subtly prepared or deliberately surprising (e.g. the inclusion of two bars in the piano part between the first two lines of the poem, bars 6 and 7, in which the harmonic effect of bars 8–9 is cunningly prepared). Schumann did not immediately make up his mind on the dramatic enharmonic modulation at the end of *Die alten, bösen Lieder*, where (bar 49) the effect of the dissonance was originally intensified by two quavers (E natural followed by C sharp) on the 'und', later replaced

by the less violent single crotchet C sharp. Was this Clara's handi-
work? Certainly I should suspect her influence in the change (bars
59–60) from the unconventional quintuplets in the manner of
Chopin to the conventional gruppetti before the sixth beat in each bar.
Sometimes Schumann's second thoughts seem to have been
definitely disimprovements. Why, for example, did he alter the
opening bars of *Liebesbotschaft*, in which the original version opens
canonically, with one bar of piano solo (bar 1 of the final version)
and the voice following with the same melody one bar later? Clara
cannot have objected to anything so academically respectable as a
canonic imitation. Internal evidence provided by Schumann's very
rare use of canon in a few other songs would suggest that he regarded
this device—as we have seen that he regarded chromaticism—as
producing a definite effect (presumably of ancient, semi-ecclesiastical
venerableness, as in *Auf einer Burg*) and this was certainly out of
place in setting the amorous platitudes of Reinick's *Liebesbotschaft*,
though from the purely musical point of view the song loses interest
in the final version. Schumann would perhaps reply that what
concerned him first and foremost was old Wiedebein's advice, to
'look to truth above all'.

Liszt praised Schumann for choosing as texts for his songs poems
'whose beauty of form proceeded from a feeling capable of a still
higher expression than words could give'. Actually the form of the
poem was the only thing about it which Schumann tended to treat
with little respect, repeating to his heart's content if he felt musically
inclined, as we have seen. But Liszt was right in praising
Schumann's sense of musical possibilities in a poem. There are very
few instances of his setting to music poems complete in themselves
and lacking in the atmospheric suggestion which was the first necessity in Schumann's case. The five poems by Mary, Queen of Scots
(Op. 135) are certainly one example. In translation they lose the
pathos of their sincerity and verbal simplicity (especially No. 5,
Gebet, whose whole charm lies in its tripping Latin assonances); and
it was probably the glamour of the author, unwittingly transferred
to her poems by Schumann (as in the case of Elisabeth Kulmann),
which made him choose such completely un-romantic words. But
in general we have to go forward to Hugo Wolf before we find
another German song-writer with such a fine instinct in choosing
and setting his poems. Brahms was a more perfect craftsman than
Schumann, with a more genuine understanding and less sentimentality in his approach to German folk-song. He was rhythmically far

more adventurous, but at the same time he knew when the listener would have had enough of a good thing and he could never have written a whole song, like Schumann's *Abendlied*, with crossrhythms persisting throughout. On the other hand his North German tendency to sentimental brooding led him to choose poems such as Klaus Groth's *O wüsst' ich doch den Weg zurück*, Daumer's *Wir wandelten* and Almers' *Feldeinsamkeit* for some of what proved to be his most successful songs; and the quality of the poetry had a definite influence on the quality of the music. Schubert might have set such poems with impunity; and Schumann might have conceivably chosen them, though they would have become poor songs, in the second or third rank of his output. Brahms's masterpieces—for masterpieces they are, in their way—are founded on shoddy literary material and emotion, which they faithfully reproduce with great charm. Whereas the great songs of Schumann are a joint triumph for Schumann and Heine or Eichendorff, many of the great songs of Brahms are a triumph (sometimes Pyrrhic) for Brahms alone. It is only in the folk-song pastiche, where Schumann generally failed so signally, that Brahms is consistently his superior. We have only to compare the older man's *Liebhabers Ständchen* or *Unterm Fenster* with his successor's *Vergebliches Ständchen*, *Lied eines Schmiedes* with *Der Schmied*, *Sonntags am Rhein* with *Sonntag* (and the list could be prolonged) to see Brahms's unquestioned superiority in this vein.

Schumann's influence on Liszt as a song-writer was, I rather think, unfortunate. In his settings of Heine, Liszt owes nothing to Schumann; he was a dramatic miniaturist, as we have seen, and a lyrical poem like *Du bist wie eine Blume* appears as an exception. How differently the two men treated even the same poems of Heine can be seen by comparing their settings of *Anfangs wollt' ich fast verzagen* and *Im Rhein, im heiligen Strome*, where Liszt paints and dramatizes phrase by phrase, bar by bar, and Schumann lays down a solid rhythmic pattern which is pursued almost owlishly from beginning to end. It was in his settings of Goethe that I suspect Liszt of following the bad example of Schumann, in wandering from section to section and hammering together what often amounts to four sides, a lid and a bottom all belonging to different boxes. The chronology of Liszt's songs is uncertain, even such a trifle as *Dichter, was Liebe sei* appearing in three different versions dating from 1844, 1855, and 1878. But the majority were written in the '40's, after Liszt settled at Weimar (1842). And certainly a big blowsy song like *Ich möchte hingehn* or the sprawling settings of *Wer nie sein Brot mit Tränen ass*

(1845 and 1860) were written with a full knowledge of Schumann's songs, good and bad. That Liszt did not always distinguish the one from the other is shown in his choice for piano transcription. Thus by the side of *Widmung* and *Frühlingsnacht* stand thoroughly second-rate songs such as *An den Sonnenschein* and (significantly) *An die Türen will ich schleichen* and the rather colourless numbers from the *Liederalbum für die Jugend*. Perhaps the truth is that both Liszt and Schumann suffered, especially as they grew older, from the same, typically Romantic failing—a passion for the vague, large and high-sounding which led both men in their different ways to a form of musical meandering among windy generalities.

Hugo Wolf, who owed much to Schumann, instinctively turned to songs of an entirely different kind. A dramatic miniaturist like Liszt, he developed and made explicit the drama which is often only hinted at by Schumann. The two men's settings of Mörike's *Er ist's* and *Das verlassene Mägdelein* provide typical examples of their different methods. Schumann's setting of *Er ist's* is included in the *Lieder-album für die Jugend* and it has the self-conscious simplicity which, as we have seen, Schumann associated with children. It is marked 'innig', whereas Wolf's mood is clearly shown by 'sehr lebhaft, jubelnd' ('very lively, with jubilation'). Both songs open with two bars for the piano, Schumann's based on a descending scale passage with dotted rhythm, bringing in the voice on his favourite dominant seventh in the key of the dominant (dominant seventh of E in the key of A major) (cf. *Loreley* and *Schöne Fremde*). Wolf merely sets in motion a vigorous rhythmic figure which is to domin-ate the whole song, a broken tonic triad (G major) over which the voice enters with an opening phrase spread over the notes of the triad. At the end of the first quatrain, where Schumann has modulated through the minor of the mediant (C sharp) to a conventional close in the key of the dominant in the interlude for the piano, Wolf has quickly reached the remote key of C sharp major. A comparison of the two settings of the next two lines, with exactly the same rhythm in the vocal parts (Ex. 36, *a* and *b*) will show how completely differently two composers can envisage the same poem. The piano part is of primary importance in each case, of course. Schumann's is actually the more independent, Wolf's more in the nature of an accompani-ment. Both composers instinctively aim at expressing the atmos-phere of expectancy, which is the note of the poem, by a series of generally unresolved dominant sevenths, Schumann's naturally far less sophisticated than Wolf's. Both emphasize the 'Horch!' by a

harped dominant seventh right out of the key of the preceding bars:
but Schumann continues the shy, hesitant ('etwas zurückhaltend')
manner and the rather self-conscious, Dresden-china prettiness
already suggested by the mordents in the piano part, whereas Wolf
quickly works up to his climax and gives final vent to his excitement
in a long piano postlude (twenty-one bars in a song of under sixty).
The last lines of the poem read in Wolf's version:

> Frühling, da, du bist's! (twice)
> Dich hab' ich vernommen!
> Ja, du bist's!

This already has two unwarranted repetitions. Schumann, in a
happy haze, 'innig' rather than 'jubelnd', murmurs the words again
and again:

> Frühling, ja, du bist's! ja, du bist's, du bist's!
> Dich hab' ich vernommen, ja, du bist's!
> Dich hab' ich vernommen,
> Frühling, ja, du bist's! ja, du bist's!
> Ja, du bist's, du bist's, du bist's,
> Dich hab' ich vernommen,
> Ja, du bist's!

Ex. 36

a) Schumann

b) Wolf

There is only the shortest postlude (in which the 'pretty' mordents recur). These are the dangers of 'Innigkeit' and too much Jean Paul, the dreaming aloud and the soulfulness which is not so simple and unselfconscious as it would like to seem, but pins on some arch little ornaments and is not above an occasional simper.

Between the two settings of *Das verlassene Mägdelein* the resemblance is so marked that it is impossible that Wolf had not got Schumann's in mind when he wrote his own.[1] But Schumann's is

---

[1] Since writing this passage and what follows I have found confirmation of this in Mr. Ernest Newman's *Hugo Wolf*, p. 182, note 3, where he says that in a letter to Eckstein dated 27 March 1888, Wolf wrote that he greatly admired Schumann's setting of *Das verlassene Mägdelein* and had no intention of setting the poem himself: but that being deeply affected by the poem the music came to him almost against his will. The comparison of the two settings which follows was written without knowledge of Mr. Newman's (p. 190), with which I am in general, but not complete, agreement, as comparison will show.

a *cri du cœur* whereas Wolf's is a picture. Schumann cares nothing for the suggestion of early morning cold and desolation which Wolf gives in his piano prelude, still less for the sparks which Wolf strikes as the girl lights the fire, interrupting the heavy tread of the rhythm ♩ ♫ ♩ ♫, an exaggeration of Schumann's, which is alleviated by the movement of the inner parts. Schumann places his two-bar piano interlude between the two lines of the poem where the girl lights the fire and then sits gazing miserably into it. Wolf, with a better literary and dramatic instinct, puts his four bars of interlude after the lines and makes them depict the girl's misery, so that his 'plötzlich, da kommt es mir' sounds like a real, sudden memory. He paints the ecstasy of the girl's dream of her lover in three repeated phrases, ritardando, and ending on a pause before the tears start falling hopelessly. Schumann, aware only of the girl's misery, carries straight on from the dream to the tears with an accentuation of the harmonic clash (dominant minor ninth, Ex. 37; cf. *Mignons Lied*)

Ex. 37

Trä - ne auf Trä - ne dann   stür - zet her   nie - der

which is a characteristic feature of the whole song. Wolf, in an era of greater harmonic sophistication, when minor ninths had become small beer, chooses a subtler chord as the symbol of the girl's grief, the augmented triad or 'whole-tone' chord in its various positions. Again, Wolf's postlude, with its bare open fifths, suggests the misery and desolation of the opening, whereas Schumann has no postlude at all but comes to rest on a rather inept 'tierce de Picardie', the tonic triad with the major third instead of the minor. The unusually chromatic harmony in Schumann's setting (in accordance with his regular association of chromaticism with extreme grief) becomes with Wolf something very close to harmonic experimentation, which accords badly with the simple emotion of Mörike's poem and is not justified by any pictorial effect. Not that a comparison of the two songs need result in a judgement of value between them; it is merely instructive to see how differently the two composers work on a given poem which admits (unlike *Er ist's*) of only one emotional approach, from what different angles they approach it and what are the alterations Wolf makes in what is almost certainly an (unconscious) 'rethinking' of Schumann's music as well as Mörike's verses. There are other songs by Wolf which often seem to be sophisticated re-thinkings of Schumann's material. The two *Zigeunerliedchen* from the *Liederalbum für die Jugend* have already been mentioned on pp. 117–8 and a comparison between the first of them (*Unter die Soldaten*, Ex. 27) with say the opening of Wolf's *Schweig einmal still* (*Italienisches Liederbuch*, Vol. 3, No. 43) will give an idea of what I mean. Wolf's soldier songs, also, seem to hark back to Schumann's (compare, for example, Schumann's *Die Soldatenbraut* with Wolf's *Der Tambour*) though again the later songs have a variety, both rhythmic and harmonic, and a dramatic sophistication which often make the earlier seem homely and naïve in comparison.

In Schumann's special domains he is supreme and need fear no comparison: the romantic night-pieces like *Der Nussbaum*, *Frühlingsnacht*, *Mondnacht*, *Schöne Fremde* or what may for want of a better title be called psychological, rather than dramatic, lyrics as those of the *Dichterliebe*, *Wer machte dich so krank?*, *Die Fensterscheibe*. In the night-pieces he found musical expression for a specifically new, romantic emotion. (New to music, that is to say; Novalis's *Hymnen an die Nacht* were nearly fifty years old in 1840, while Edward Young, whose *Night Thoughts* originated the cult, had died as long ago as 1765.) In Schubert's *Nacht und Traüme* there still remains something of the eighteenth century, a marmoreal serenity and an absence of the 'Orphic' or 'Dionysian' quality which begins to appear in Schumann's night-pieces (*In der Nacht*, from the *Fantasiestücke* for piano, for example, as well as the songs) and found its fullest expression in that 'vast nocturne', Act II of *Tristan*. It is a specifically German quality, quite unlike the elegant melancholy of Chopin's Nocturnes or Tom Moore's *At the mid hour of night*, no less beautiful for being tributes to a literary fashion but only incidentally night-pieces, whereas Schumann's music really suggests another world of feeling, solemn and mysterious, peopled with poetic imaginations which would fade in the light of common day, and foreshadow Tristan's 'göttlich ew'ges Urvergessen'.

To speak of Schumann as merely a miniaturist is a by now

dangerous platitude; but it is certainly true of Schumann as a song-writer. He managed his larger songs worse than any of the great German song-writers, Schubert, Brahms or Wolf; but in return he showed himself a master of pregnancy and compression in the psychological lyric, a genre which is virtually his invention. He was not a dramatist like Wolf; we have seen how differently the two men reacted to the same poem. But Schumann's literary background and his reading had given him an instinctive understanding, a psychological acumen, which combined with his lyrical gift and his own intensely emotional character to create something like a new form. While much of Schumann's music, including a considerable proportion of his songs, bears the traces of the naïvely emotional and complacent background which determined the composer's mentality, there remains an irreducible minimum of works which have that ageless quality which is the only certain hallmark of genius. At the very centre of that core are the great songs, so that if future generations remember Schumann for nothing else he can hardly fail to be counted among the very greatest of the German song-writers.

CHAPTER IV

THE CHAMBER MUSIC

By A. E. F. DICKINSON

WE may take it that the bulk, perhaps the entire content, of Schumann's chamber music was 'romantic' and 'unnecessary'. It was not in the first place something for the composer to play with odd string-players, like Beethoven's Op. 1 Trios or Brahms's Op. 8, or something for a habitual and handy ensemble, such as prompted Beethoven to his Op. 18 and Op. 59 sets, or started Schubert writing quartet after quartet until eventually he achieved the D minor, far beyond the utility level. Nor did the Schumann quartets overflow, as Schubert's appear sometimes to have done, from a song-composition evoked but not satisfied by the setting of verse and poetry to music; nor did they arise as practical substitutes for orchestral writing, as the dynamic of Schubert's again suggests from time to time. The quartet medium had naturally attracted the notice of a composer who brought to his creative activity a wide and sympathetic survey of the known musical heritage, in which the German tradition (in the widest cultural sense) predominated, and once during his earliest pianistic period in 1829 he toyed with the piano quartet. Only short excerpts from this C minor Quartet have been published.[1] One phrase from the trio of the scherzo (Ex. 38) is interesting in that

Ex. 38

---

[1] In H.F. Redlich's articles in the *The Monthly Musical Record*, July–August and December 1950, and January 1951.

Schumann spoke of it as 'a passage in one of my compositions of which I said to myself it was *romantic*, where a spirit different from that of the old music revealed itself to me'; as Dr. Redlich has shown, he used it again in the Intermezzo, Op. 4, No. 4.

In the April of 1838 he wrote a string quartet (lost) which he described as 'only an essay' and then in 1839 the beginnings of three quartets (also lost) which he told Clara were 'as good as Haydn'. In 1840 the piano works, having shown a marked development of mind without reaching any particular point of convergence comparable to Beethoven's Op. 31 sonatas, ceased abruptly; the piano-writing continued characteristically but sporadically in the song-output with which in this year Schumann celebrated the end of his long struggle with the father of Clara Wieck, now Clara Schumann. In the following year came two symphonies (Nos. 1 and 4) and the Fantasia which later expanded into the Piano Concerto. In 1842 Schumann was studying the quartets of Haydn, Mozart, and Beethoven; and in his retrospect of musical life in Leipzig in 1837–8, in the *Neue Zeitschrift für Musik*, Schumann wrote with reverence of Beethoven's Quartets in E flat (Op. 127) and C sharp minor, and also of Schubert's D minor. The scope of quartet-writing, from the songfulness of *Death and the Maiden* and many Haydn moods to the finer thought of Mozart and the sublime absorptions of Beethoven's, was apparent. The fruit of these reflections, three quartets, Op. 41, was a matter of time, and as it happened, they were completed in less than two months.[1] They were followed by a Piano Quintet, Op. 44, a Piano Quartet, Op. 47, and a Piano Trio. The last Schumann eventually judged to be of questionable integrity, and the movements were cut down and published as *Fantasiestücke*, Op. 88, a title already used for a set of piano miniatures.

So far variety of instrumental texture had spiced Schumann's

---

[1] The dates are shown in the 'household book':
  1842
  1 April   Constantly quartets. Studied Mozart.
  28 April Quartets by Beethoven.
  6 May   Studied quartets by Haydn.
  2 June   Quartet essays.
  4 June   Quartet in A minor begun.
And then successive entries tell of the composition of the three works—Nos. 1 and 2 simultaneously—until on 22 July Schumann could joyfully record the completion of No. 3. On 8 April he had written to Breitkopf asking to be sent 'the scores of all the Mozart and Beethoven quartets', and on the 20th wrote again, enquiring anxiously whether the first letter had gone astray. Specific Beethovenian models can be traced here and there in Op. 41, e.g. Beethoven's Op. 18, No. 5, near the end of Op. 41, No. 1.—*Ed.*

invention in these three years and kept it at a high stage of concoc-
tion. A dramatic cantata, *Paradise and the Peri*, followed, and, after
Schumann's move to Dresden, a bout of fugue. Then came another
symphony, No. 2 in C. In the following year, 1847, Schumann
returned to chamber music, this time with two piano trios, in D
minor and F, Opp. 63 and 80. The opera *Genoveva* accounted in the
main for the historic and disturbing year 1848. In the following year
appeared four of the miscellaneous sets for string or wind instrument
and piano (Opp. 70, 73, 94, 102). In 1850 what was substantially
Schumann's last symphony, No. 3 in E flat, was finished and in 1851
the earlier symphony eventually issued as No. 4 in D minor was
revised. In the latter year appeared the two Sonatas for violin and
piano, Opp. 105 and 121, separated by a third Piano Trio, in G minor,
Op. 110, and in addition the *Märchenbilder* for viola and piano,
Op. 113. These were Schumann's last chamber work commitments,
except for a third Violin Sonata in A minor, consisting of an intermezzo and finale contributed to a composite violin sonata by Dietrich,
Brahms and himself and the movements,[1] still unpublished, which he
proposed to substitute for those by his two friends (1853). Thus after
the Quartets and Quintet of the fruitful year 1842, Schumann's
chamber work may be conveniently summarized as the two Trios of
1847, the miscellaneous group of 1849, and the Violin Sonatas and
Trio of 1851.

In this way Schumann's quartet output started somewhat as
Beethoven's had done—with a set of quartets on top of a very considerable piano output—but after that it stopped, while Beethoven
went on to the masterly Razumovsky set, a document in personal
expression which did not play a less integral part in Beethoven's
artistic life because it was succeeded, much later, by the unprecedented
developments of the six Quartets, Opp. 127–131. Like Schumann,
Brahms wrote only three quartets, but at a period of maturing
powers in the chamber music line, and while his string quartet
writing has an uncertain touch, his more contrapuntal manner of
thought naturally stretched itself in four real parts. His Quartet in
A minor is particularly satisfying as a whole. For Schumann the
quartet was a stimulating novelty, not an essential thread, and once
tried it gleamed no more in his mind. For the rest, he was content
with various piano combinations. In the Piano Quintet Schumann
claims historical priority in a distinguished group which includes the

---

[1] Ziemlich langsam, 3/4, and Lebhaft, 3/8, dated 1 November 1853, and
preserved in the Library of the Paris Conservatoire.

names of Brahms, Franck and Dvořák. In the Piano Quartet he constitutes an important link between Mozart and Brahms. In the trios he added somewhat to the repertory of the Viennese School. The violin-piano duet, by which Beethoven and more especially Brahms and Franck honoured their art, was adopted by Schumann at a late date in his development, when his powers were far from increasing.

There is no epic story or deepening intimacy about Schumann's chamber-music development. It began fairly well and it went on hither and thither from time to time. Negatively, it entailed a certain emancipation from the literary fancy and stanza-like structure which had informed both the song-cycles and not a few of the major piano works, including the F sharp minor Sonata; an emancipation, too, from the cultivated vagueness of piano harmony and counterpoint, 'con pedale', under the spreading shadows of which all transitions and clashes of register, key and mood may be appreciably dimmed into easy agreement. This release is obvious in the case of the quartets, and it is equally applicable to the string groups of the works for piano and strings. Positively, the chamber music involved the realization, in so far as it suited the composer's thought, of the complete polyphony and antiphony of the string quartet, or the partial polyphony of string groups over against the piano, in place of the piano's blend of clear-cut melody and sonorous sequence, or of the orchestra's rough and ready assembly of wood and brass in conjunction with the strings, in Schumann's case an often questionable assembly aesthetically.

Structurally, a certain impression of formality reaches the listener after the many touches of the curious and impromptu in the piano music, songs, the Piano Concerto and the symphonies, especially the Fourth. Of the ten major works which eventually accumulated, all but the A minor Violin Sonata contain four movements. The first of these invariably is or contains an allegro in a clearly disposed sonata form. The next two movements are of the scherzo and the lyrical or grave andante type, the scherzo receiving precedence in three quartets, one trio and one sonata. The scherzo is of the mercurial 3/8 or 2/4 type—as opposed to the more articulate unevenness of 3/4—in all works except the Piano Quartet and the Trio in F, where it is in the normal 3/4. Its key is placed in a near or identical relation to the main key except in the flatward scherzos of the Quartet and Trio in F. A plain ternary structure prevails, with an interlude in a contrasting key and a da capo. In the Quartet in A major the scherzo is a variation-movement, and in the Piano Quartet the scherzo movement contains two interludes. The slow movement is mainly in one mood (ternary or variations); only in the A major Quartet does it achieve full sonata form. Its key usually borders on the tonic, on one side or the other; in the Quartet and Trio in F the slow movements have remoter key-centres on the flat side, with scherzos of like tendency in the minor. The finales are in expanded sonata structure except for the broader ternary course in the Quartet in A and the G minor Trio. There is thus a constant resort to the developed and the plainer classical structures and a corresponding avoidance of remote keys in a given movement, the 'cyclic' disturbances of themes from previous movements, and general asymmetry, as rhetorical factors. The expression lies mainly in the association and development of themes, not in any originality of context. The one striking exception, the F major allegro of the first movement of the A minor Quartet, tonic only in the introduction (echoed later in the adagio in F) is a curiosity of thought, not a revolution. In size and general scope the Piano Quintet and Quartet and the Trio in D minor are conspicuously beyond the rest, especially the Piano Quintet, but the string quartets have a consistency of their own which no combination or antiphony of piano and strings can show.

General expectations having been roughly summarized, we may turn to individual works, in the order of writing, except that it will be convenient to consider the Trio in G minor with the other trios rather than with the violin sonatas, and to survey together the miscellaneous works for piano and another instrument.

The Quartet in A minor, Op. 41, No. 1, begins, as has been said, with an odd ambiguity of key, an introductory andante of thirty-three bars in A minor[1]—of which the last four bars were originally intended to be the introduction to No. 2—followed by a normal allegro in F. The sequent scherzo in A minor (with intermezzo in C) appears to restore the balance or even to constitute a fulfilment of the first movement, making the allegro in F a 'romantic' digression. But the third movement, an adagio in F, only confirms the bitonality. The finale duly casts its weight in favour of A minor, transformed to A major at the end. The duplicity of key-centre may not trouble

---

[1] The entries in the 'household book' show that the Andante espressivo introductions to Nos. 1 and 3 of Op. 41 were afterthoughts; the later addition of such introductions and brief postludes was entirely characteristic of Schumann's method of work. The seven bars of introduction to Op. 41, No. 3, were originally eight; on the other hand the four bars, 13–16, in No. 1 were originally six; Schumann sometimes sought for, instead of avoiding, squareness of phrase-structure.—*Ed.*

the casual listener but it is a factor to be reckoned with in the long run, since the musical structure is based on the classical principles of a definite key-centre in each movement (normally) and inferentially of one for the whole work. The introduction is also distinguished from the allegro it precedes by being polyphonic in impression and initially canonic. In the allegro the main texture is that of a single line, harmonically coloured. The recurrence of 8-bar periods serves to draw attention to the harmonic tones, such as the glance at A minor in the repetition of the first phrase (bars 44–5), and the rising sequence in G flat, A flat, and B flat in a phrase which evokes the return of the first phrase with rather more intense harmony and a slight fugato bridge-passage to the second subject. It is unnecessary to quote these changing shades in print. They can be readily heard in performance, and the successive suggestions of the subdominant minor (bar 67) and so forth are not worth even the student's precise attention since they never materialize beyond a single chord. The main impression is of an expanding tunefulness, which none can miss. A more subtle point is the development from the third phrase (bars 50–1) (Ex. 39), now

Ex.39

rendered staccato, of a vague second-subject group, in which constant key-change (C, D minor, B minor, E minor and G before gravitating to C) is an integral feature. The same phrase, aided by the G major sequence (bars 125–6), instigates a more orthodox development of 100 bars, almost as long as the whole exposition and ranging from A flat major to B minor on the one hand and A flat minor on the other. It is rather surprising that in the restatement the composer is content to bring back the first phrase again, subdominant minor and all, and to repeat the second subject 'in toto', a fifth lower than before, forgetting that the development of Ex. 39 has been so markedly extended in the middle of the movement that a return to the first bout amounts to withdrawal rather than confirmation. The experienced listener will find this restatement a lengthy proceeding. The coda is a brief recollection of the opening phrase, more lingering than before. The whole texture is apt for strings.

The scherzo is a straightforward 6/8 skirmish in the 'Wild Rider' style. The main section of the scherzo, a sequence of three rigid

8-bar phrases in ABA formation, returns after a more wayward gallop. A stanza-like intermezzo tune, in a legato chromatic style but in precise 8–bar measures, provides a sentimental contrast in a reiterative manner, after which the complete return of the ABA scherzo presumes somewhat on the interest of the much recurring first phrase. The adagio in F thrice pursues one main theme in conjunction with a short secondary phrase, intensified by key (B flat minor) and the reverberation of a florid figure in the inner strings. The theme is on common ground with the unforgettable melody of the adagio of the Ninth Symphony, and may therefore be quoted with Beethoven's, reduced to the same key for ease of comparison (Ex. 40). The curve of Schumann's melody can well stand that

Ex.40
a) Schumann
Adagio

b) Beethoven
Adagio molto

searching comparison. A viola quarter-beat figure, somewhat tiresomely syncopated throughout, at once measures the sostenuto quality of the violin melody at the first and last occurrences. At the second and shorter stage the traditional 'aching' string of the violoncello, the A, bears the burden against bowed and plucked harmony. The suggestion of A minor (bar 9) and similar relationships palls in repetition and the historically minded listener, for whom a good precedent is of some concern, misses the miraculous interludes (in the mediant and submediant major or kindred keys) from which the main theme could have emerged, as from a remote sphere. Yet the melodic quality is sensitive.

The finale is a vigorous, impulsive presto in a developed structure, sonata-form in type though not in detail. It suffers (more than the first movement does) from the similarity between the opening | d : d | s : | of the first subject and the like plain ascents or descents which characterize the second subject, here appearing unequivocally in C and formally restated in F. (The general recurrence throughout the exposition of the bustling thirds of bar 3 in itself makes for consistency of style rather than confusion of content, like the similar

figure in the finale of Mozart's G minor Symphony (K. 550); but
in the context this adds to the indistinctness of the second subject.)
The further fusion of the ascent of the first subject with the plainer
corroborative detail of the second (bars 65–6), throughout the
development, may seem to show that for the composer they are one
and the same theme (see Ex. 41); but except in a canonic inversion
'at zero', ascent and descent defy amalgamation; it must be one or
the other of these opposites, and the composer should have chosen

Ex.41

one and kept to it. Once the fusion is established by the entire
development, the return to the descending second subject (with
which the restatement begins) is awkward; and when in bar 210 the
amalgamated theme reappears with dominantward harmony and is
answered at once by the assertion of the tonic in the restatement of
the first subject in its original detail (bar 218), the intellectual impression is of a simple pun hopelessly misplaced near the climax of the
movement: 'Old Gaunt indeed, and gaunt in being antiquated.'
Once more it may be recalled that when Beethoven 'irons out' a
theme, as in the codas of the first movements of the First and Fourth
Symphonies, he never returns to the original detail, as Schumann
does here. Also anticipation at bar 210 spoils the close entries of the
ironed-out theme from bar 246 onwards. This may seem carping
criticism, but the partial assonance is a constant vexation to the
alert ear. It must be allowed that in letting two intonations of a
common rhythmic formula to proceed in parallel and then, projected
along the same line, make a third, the composer was courting confusion, and should really have confined the *three* to his sketch-books.
However, the amalgamation is finally celebrated in the major, into
which the movement glides with Beethovenish naïveté, with the
bustling thirds in earnest attendance, keying up to F sharp minor

before the German augmented sixth gives the signal for a cheerful exit.[1] Structurally—that is, in the matter of impressing the listener by rich relationships on the scale of successive movements—this Quartet confirms a lack of thematic distinctness in second subject which the composer had already shown (perhaps deliberately) in his D minor Symphony, as well as in the earlier F sharp minor Sonata. In the Quartet in F Schumann, it appears, is concerned to recover the traditional balance of interest as between first and second subject, alike in the first and in the last movements. The opening subject, the curve of which in bars 2–3 owes something to the third and fourth bars of Beethoven's Violin Sonata in the same key, Op. 24, is less tuneful than that of the previous Quartet but it has more buoyancy. It lends itself to polyphonic treatment, as its immediate repetition shows (bar 35) in contrast to that of the A minor. The development confirms this possibility. The dominant-tonic background also adapts itself to almost any context where cadence is required. Again the undulating thirds of the viola are suggestive. The second subject has at least two clear features: the rising diminished seventh developed in descending sequence in A and E minor (rejoinder to a previous subdominant tendency), and the falling fifth phrase announced canonically by pairs of instruments. An arpeggio offshoot of the rising interval, now an octave, is developed imitatively and in sequence, and this with the original sequence soon takes the development as far as a half cadence in A minor, from which a rhetorical or romantic turn of mind (call it what you will)[2] finds F major and

[1] The sketch of Op. 41, No. 1, shows numerous instances of Schumann's habit of leaving specified numbers of empty bars at certain structural points; his sense of large-scale rhythm demanded *something* of a certain length at those points; precisely *what* was left for later decision. Even when the lacuna was filled with imitative work, as in the first movement of Op. 41, No. 1, bars 61–4 of the development, the actual music generally fitted very nearly into the previously specified number of bars. Similar empty spaces were left for a different reason (simple time-saving) in the finale of this Quartet—originally intended as a rondo—for the recurrences of the principal subject; the rondo-theme, beginning with the familiar tag that opens the finale of the *Jupiter* Symphony, is referred to once in the definitive form of the movement. The octave descent heard in various forms in the course of the movement also originated in the rondo theme.—*Ed.*

[2] The sketch shows here how Schumann, like Beethoven, sometimes sought to disperse the congestion caused by too many direct references to a theme, in distinction from certain modern composers who pride themselves on making every detail thematic; the last eight bars of the development began as in Ex. 42.—*Ed.*

Ex. 42

return. This restatement is serene and imperturbable (again the repetition of the first subject is left unaltered) but is not spoilt by previous over-development. An extension of the rhetorical return provides a coda to this compact movement. Rooted in F, it calls for contrast, and this an andante in A flat supplies. The rhythm, key and general absorption of the movement seem to echo the andante of Beethoven's Quartet in E flat, Op. 127. After what proves to be an introduction of two eight-bar phrases a theme of like measure and content is announced in a syncopated rhythm. Harmonically the beginning of the second half in E, with an enharmonic change from D sharp to E flat, is a striking transition and return, and it remains to hear how it can be made interesting and not cloying in repetition. Four variations follow. In the first a plain rhythm emerges, qualified by flowing quavers. In the second an elaborate chromatic line of semiquavers, countered by plain arpeggios later, supplies coloratura treatment. In the third, shorter but molto più lento, an oscillating chordal figure is noticeable; the first half does not modulate to E flat, as before, but remains in the tonic, leaving E flat to become D sharp, as usual, but more abruptly. The fourth variation, poco più vivace, also short, assumes gallantry. The return of the introduction, da capo, ushers in a short coda based on the second variation. The texture is a contrapuntally rich polyphony, varied by harmonic sequences. That first striking modulation to E has become a rather tiresome and mechanical enharmonic change by the last variation.

A scherzo in C minor, again a presto, 6/8,[1] dispenses reflection. It is, however, very ineffective. The extended arpeggios across the strings and back, on which the scherzo proper mainly depends rhythmically, are pianistic, not violinistic, and the tonic, dominant and diminished seventh chords which make up the essential harmonic basis do not form a chain of compelling sonorities. Incidentally the structure of the scherzo (A BA BA') is not quite satisfactory. The first and second parts end in E flat, and only the third reaches the tonic. The brusque and offhand conclusion in the tonic via the Neapolitan sixth chord, a matter of eight bars, does not balance the corresponding *sixteen* bars which led back to E flat; a more pronounced or more prolonged rejoinder is required. The trio in the major which forms the usual interlude is incredibly trite; the restatement of the initial phrase at the end confirms (or dispels) any doubts which the listener may have in the matter. Nor does the

---

[1] But as the sketch shows, originally written out in 3/4 time, and Ländler-like in character.—*Ed.*

mingling of the trio and scherzo material in a wistful major make a good postscript to the restatement of the scherzo. The finale[1] starts with one of those subjects which violinists describe as scratchy. The second subject, too, is scrappy and survives a slight development in various keys later but scarcely a formal restatement. For development the composer relies mainly on two impromptu themes, one a trochaic phrase in B flat minor, the other a banal scalewise phrase of four bars introduced, animato, by the violoncello. There is nothing wrong with scales in their right place, as Bach's fugal episodes show in innumerable examples, but when they are exposed too much to the main attention they sound merely funny. The Quartet does not, then, fulfil the promise of the first movement.

The Quartet in A major begins, andante,[2] with a questioning chord, the sixth being added to the triad, and this is the mainspring of the first subject of the allegro which follows; the chord and the fall of melody concerned materialize further in a short development. Falling fifths also feature in the formal 8-bar melody of the second subject. It must be admitted that after the dance which the piano leads us, in a certain sonata, by the same token of a falling interval of the added-sixth chord—a dance now gracious, now abandoned to the fit of the moment—Schumann's consistently affectionate treatment seems far too precious. I refer to Beethoven's E flat Piano Sonata, Op. 31, No. 3 (first movement); and the same brusque treatment of falling fifths may be observed in the finale of Elgar's Violin Concerto. In either case the technical distinction is that the recurrent intonation is absorbed in a much wider rhythm—in Beethoven's case in a definite rhythmic figure from the start—so that the repeated falls become mere consistencies, not integral elements. Schumann *bases* several rhythmical phrases on the chosen sonority (and a mechanical 4-bar period) and it soon wears thin. A similar weakness attends the rising-fifth motive of Parry's *War and Peace*, as it is treated. It is interesting to contrast Wagner's reservation of recurrent falling fifths, in *The Ring*, for (1) the fixed malignant brooding of Mime and the Nibelungs, (2) the ineffectual aspirations of Gutrune, (3) the simple, absorbed happiness of Brünnhilde when she awakens to find Siegfried. The diagnosis of the inherent weakness

---

[1] Like that of No. 1, it was intended in the first place to be a rondo but the definitive form of the theme is here much closer to the original form. The two-bar 'curtain' in front of the theme proper is reversed in direction, but the semiquaver moto perpetuo itself has only been made more piquant by chromatic appoggiaturas and tightened up by a couple of four-bar cuts.—*Ed.*

[2] Cf. footnote on p. 142.

of this movement has taken many words, but it seems worth while establishing, from the comparisons made, that the mere pursuit of an interval or relished sonority is not necessarily weak or inexpressive. It all depends on context.

After this allegro molto moderato, a movement of the scherzo type is inevitable. The assai agitato in question, in the relative minor, displays a syncopated rhythm in three 16-bar periods, emphasized by repetition of the first and of the remainder, and also by certain changes of tonality in the second and third. From this theme four variations are derived with reasonable resource and developed with a firm climax of tone, from which the music relaxes to a quiet coda in the major, freshened by striking changes from F sharp to E flat and back. There is more dialogue and variety of texture in this movement than in most of Schumann's chamber music. It is balanced by an adagio in D in what may be called free sonata-form. The first subject is in the style of Beethoven's most sustained and conjunct instrumental melodies,[1] coloured with chromatic touches and unusually early modulations, harmonically in the manner of *Träumerei*, Op. 15, No. 7. The second subject is more an episode of contrast than a complementary statement of the mood of the whole movement, but it shows audible connection with the rising phrase of the first subject. Its tonality is peculiar, ranging from E flat major to C sharp minor. However, the elusive relationship of first and second subject is confirmed in complete restatement a fourth higher (i.e. one degree on the flat side of the foregoing) and straightened out in the return of the first subject and a subtle hint of the second in the tonic. The finale is a loose-limbed movement in which, nevertheless, a certain order may be observed at further hearings. Its broadly ternary shape may be indicated as follows:

Phrase 1.	*a*	*b*	*a*	*c*	*a*
Keys	A to D	A to E	Back to A	F sharp minor	Back to A
			2. *d*		
			F		
3. *a*	*b*	*a*	*c*	*a*	
F	C to G	G to C	A minor to	E	
		d			
		Coda E to A			

[1] The original forms of bars 2 and 6 of the melody (Ex. 43, *a* and *b*) are worth comparing with the final version.—*Ed.*

Ex. 43

It will be noticed by most listeners that the restatement is decidedly on the flat side of A major. (The relaxation of key can be perceived by any listener, and the mention of the key-centres involved is merely a precise statement of the aural impressions received.) This is balanced equally obviously by the reappearance of d, the middle episode (entitled Quasi trio in the score) in the dominant. An almost Schubertian tumult marks a long coda. The added sixth (root, the subdominant) is the starting point of the main subject throughout, and it may briefly be said that it never fails to provide the same question and answer in any key whatever, leaving an impression of inattentiveness to the previous repetitions of what, after all, is no new discord. This is a well-organized ballet-movement rather than a finale.

In the Piano Quintet in E flat, Op. 44, Schumann was a good deal happier than in the Quartets. Familiar with the piano's general capacity for clear-cut melodic phrase, ringing chords and more solvent decorative harmony, he was able to call on the strings for melodic imitation and relief, supplementary harmony or counterpoint of varying thickness, and occasionally for a general amplification in the more sustained or vibrant tones which distinguish the strings. The resultant polyphony is surprisingly successful, although there are barely half a dozen bars in the whole Quintet in which the piano is not playing. The pianistic activity, in fact, leaves the strings freer for those answering phrases and supporting sounds of single instruments or groups, which are missing in the Quartets. Above all, the return to the piano called into existence more vivid and durable intonations, some capable of considerable development in varying contexts of key and instrumentation. The general burden of each movement is particularly clear, although the structure is in each case not a simple relationship or confined to a single mood. The first movement begins with a rousing, upward-stretching theme (Ex. 45, a), which is also capable of more intimate expression, as soon appears, with key centres oscillating between C flat major and E flat minor. On a nod from the piano, which has already assumed the position of master of ceremonies after the opening tutti, the strings announce the second subject in the orthodox key, propelled by piano harmony in a consistent syncopation. The main phrase, delivered by the violoncello, is jejune, its inversion, with which the viola answers, not much better, and the resulting sequence still less striking. Yet when all this is restated, the addition of the violin parts makes considerable difference (Ex. 44). In the development the diminution of the third and fourth bars of the first subject, over a tonic pedal aided by the rising intonation of the first bar, forms a *point d'appui* for rhythmic periods of mainly 4 bars in a variety of 'flat' keys (Ex. 45, *b*). They range from A flat minor down to G flat minor and back to E flat minor. From this point it only needs a firm period with F (dominant

Ex. 44

of the dominant) in the bass to pull the key-centre up to the 'north' side, relaxed to 8 bars on the basis of B flat, culminating in a tense chromatic sequence, further tightened with chromatic counterpoint

Ex. 45

(Ex. 45, *c*). Schumann had not studied Beethoven for nothing, and his mastery of detail over this monothematic, almost monotonous development makes it a stronger continuation of the exposition than most of his developments. The restatement, on the other hand, is surprisingly literal, the pitch subsiding to one a fifth lower, leading to the second subject, in the tonic, at the earliest possible moment, and no salient detail being changed. In my judgement the pronounced flatward direction of the tonality in the development calls for some sharpward gesture between first and second subject (cf. the *Jupiter* Symphony, finale, and the *Eroica*, first movement, for such gestures, without any such urgency as the Schumann Quintet provides). It is a small point but may explain a certain feeling here of complacency, from which the best restatements, however formal, are free. The coda extends the resumed first subject just enough, by means of fresh development of the third bar, to bring the main rhythm to a firm, insistently plagal conclusion. The combination of rhythmic interest and harmonic colour is deft and natural (Ex. 45, *d*).

In no way deterred by the formal cut of this movement, in which the joins of the balancing pieces sewn together are little concealed by any contrapuntal weave of string and piano tone, Schumann casts his slow movement in a plain, almost cut-and-dried sonata rondo in the relative minor key. The main subject is a sort of march in three balanced phrases. Unlike the *March against the Philistines*, this is at least apt for the symmetrical movement of the feet, but the tempo (two beats in a bar) lies between that of a normal march and that of a funeral march, and its temperamental sequences would not sound well if they were played in strict time. There is a nice shortening of the middle phrase by a bar. The first episode effectively displaces the march by a completely harmonic rhythm, amplified by different components in the piano and inner strings : a serene and yet nervous major. The second episode sinks down to F minor (the subdominant) for its somewhat artificial agitation, in which the diminished seventh chord is overworked. The key-centre remains unrestored when the march returns (an effect already anticipated in the third phrase of its original occurrence), and Agitation continues to shake her head in the outside strings and piano rhythm. The return of the nervous first episode in F major is therefore more consonant in its context than at first. Did Schumann mean it to be? In the final return of the march the opening phrase is reshaped to be, if anything, on the flat side of F minor, softening the point of the modulations of the resumed original patterns (B flat minor and F minor; F minor and C minor), which resolves on C major. These coincidences of key, and the again flatward trend, are irritating to a listener with a sense of the total effect. This is not a subtle point: with such square phrasing, the key-centres are exposed to the ear the whole time. With so much of Eusebius one needs Florestan with a beaker more of the more bracing North, of the unblushing supertonic. The excursions in the tonic and subdominant major at the appearances of the first episode are somehow not enough, with the weight of the second on the other side. This is a problem which haply performers may solve or conceal by imported vigour or by understatement of the subdominant here and there. There is certainly a provocative relationship of centres of melodic interest, aggravated by tendencies in the first movement: all the more provocative if they are unconscious. We may contrast, once more, the superior balance of an almost equally flatward main movement, the scherzo of Beethoven's Fifth Symphony, salted by the move to G minor and purified by the unequivocal and diatonic seizure of C major (and G) for the middle section.

When it is noticed, then, that the scherzo, a creation of plain, soaring vigour in 6/8, drops to G flat major and A flat minor respectively for its two interludes, a certain wilfulness (or deafness) forces itself on the attention. The salient phrase of the first interlude is also not reassuring. The second (in 2/4) is stronger stuff, and by means of the enharmonic connection between C flat-A flat and B–G sharp rises to E major, and reaches F sharp minor later, but the texture (pairs of strings in octaves, punctuated by piano or string chords) is scratchy. The burden of the scherzo (a little reinforced by extra strings at the beginning of its last return) is thus no light one to carry off with élan. A short coda does something to ensure poise.

It is thus with something like relief that the sensitive listener discovers the finale to be a sonata rondo distinguished by constant irregularities of key from the start (and those all on the sharp side), plastic episodes artfully approached from the main rhythm, and a vigorously expanding coda that achieves dramatic finality by a singular blend of fugal rhetoric, recurring afterthought and cyclic reverberations from the first movement (Ex. 46). The main subject leads off in G minor ('north' side) before finding E flat. Its next two returns are in B minor (a long distance north of E flat) and in G sharp minor, still further. These bear the same relation to their preceding context, the G major of the first episode and the E in which the second episode, indebted to the first but with its own

L

melodic assets, begins. Having thus arrived pat on its cue, the key of the second return is almost bound to move along; it goes across to B, its relative major, and then drops enharmonically south to B flat minor, in the shadow of which (B flat being the dominant of the main key) the tonic is readily gained for the first episode. This brings in the main subject once more a third higher (G minor), thus

Ex.46

returning naturally and compulsively to the initial key, not by some sort of hangover. The key-indicator arrives by natural processes at E flat, but Schumann, much more form-conscious than usual, enlivens this return with a brisk unison of the full ensemble and a new questioning sequence, pricked out with syncopation on the piano. Thus freshly stimulated, the listener is prepared to hear the main subject in a dashing fugato, with double invertible counterpoint in various keys (the kind of thing which Bach did without thinking, but in which Schumann expressed himself more seriously or at least consciously, as his prelude here seems to show). The second episode now establishes its connection with the main subject, in richer texture, the tune in octaves on the piano balanced by viola and violin. This, rhetorically prolonged, serves to prepare the ear for a further and more decisive structural coup. It proves to be more fugue, and no fudge this time but a full exposition of the first subject of the Quintet with a derivative of the subject of the finale as counter-subject (Ex. 46, *d*). For the rest, however, Schumann falls back on the questioning syncopated sequence to enhance the vivacity of the occasion and arouse greater attention to a climax of considerable power and final sweep. Thus by invoking alert listening from the start, he conditions the mind for a variegated procession of principal and subordinate material, and coda to match, and fulfils expectations. Incidentally the fugal bouts give the strings opportunity for distinguishing their textures. On the whole, then, the finale reintegrates a work which is beginning to fall into too formal patterns, and to betray an unacceptable bias towards key-colour of flatward tendency. It does this by means of monotonous but strong rhythmic phrases, capable of carrying all the key-variation and fugue which it has to support.

A string trio is in one sense the hardest string combination to write for. It has neither the ready fullness of a quartet or quintet nor the frank and imaginatively stimulating austerity of two instruments. A 'piano' quartet is at a corresponding disadvantage when it comes to combining the piano with the string ensemble, whether antiphonally or in harmony. In turning, then, from a quintet to a quartet, Schumann was asking for trouble. His solution of the problem, in his Op. 47, shows resource. For the first subject of the allegro he chooses a theme, compounded of what may vulgarly be termed a *Finlandia* phrase, amenable to pianistic delivery with string amplification, and of a decorative figure for piano only. The first phrase reappears as a string cantabile later, the reverse of *Finlandia*. In the second subject piano and strings, each in plain octaves, are in canon at first. Later the pianist's right hand and the violin maintain the canon, and the left hand, supported by violoncello bass and viola reiterations, supplies the harmony. At other times one or two strings maintain the melodic line in unison or in imitation, the piano accompanies, and vague string counterpoint or harmony fills odd gaps. In the finale a contrapuntal texture harmonizes each string part and a piano line, or both in octaves. In the scherzo, on the other hand, any attempt of the piano and violoncello to keep in unison in a plain bustling figure is not likely to be effective. The violoncello is surely a nuisance there. Again, the main tune of the andante is well enough in the hands of the violoncello and violin, plainly accompanied by the piano, or (as in the restatement) of the viola accompanied by violin coloratura descant and a rather more vibrant piano figure; but the light chug of the other strings on the third beat in the first instance is tiresome, and in the second episode of the finale the literal amplification of self-contained two-part harmony by the string trio in the 160th and following bars is vexatiously superfluous and dull. Indeed, throughout the Quartet there is no question of the strings being anything but adjuncts of the piano materially. There are scarcely ten bars without piano: there are two in the opening sostenuto, repeated later; one in the second trio of the scherzo, also repeated; one at the end of the andante and three (viola lead) at the beginning of the finale—virtually seven in all. Schumann's insensitiveness to the thump of the hammers, with strings at his command, seems odd.

The structure of each movement is straightforward. The first movement is an unmistakable sonata-form pattern, with the first subject introduced at first by a sostenuto sequence of string chords which impressively returns at the end of the exposition, as if to begin the conventional repeat, but actually to give the key a brutal twist into D minor for the ensuing allegro development; after which there can be no return to the plain, undeviating absorption of the sostenuto, and instead restatement blazons forth a fervent fortissimo, with harmony sustained by repetition, on top of a throbbing dominant minor ninth. The opening of the second subject in G minor and C minor, relative to the dominant and tonic on which the remaining exposition and restatement are respectively based, effectively tempers the warm sentiment of the first subject with a breath of more bracing air. The tonality of the development wanders as far as D sharp minor in bar 175. Finally we reach the solemn unison that brought back the sostenuto. And then? A new theme in the strings in faster tempo, agitatedly and confusingly accompanied by strings and piano: a gesture paralleled in the allegro of the First Symphony, and in my estimate a rather extravagant and emotional one. It is emotional by its analogy with songs like *Er, der Herrlichste von allen* and also because the underlying feeling is less that of a conclusion or after-thought, compelled or evoked by the context, than of an artificial lyricism, which must needs devise new matter and, having quickly exhausted it, wear down a stage further the already overworked *Finlandia* theme. Listeners who succumb to the violoncellist's poignant cantabile on the A string will not suffer from such misgivings. All the same, there is a lack of necessity about the coda, which no performance can quite conceal.

In the next movement the scherzo proper has a good idea but nevertheless sounds scrubby. As in the First Symphony (and in No. 2 in C which followed this chamber-music year) there are two interludes. The first has a plain but effective contrapuntal texture of two main parts, coloured by passing harmony, punctuated by references to the scherzo. In the second, in the relative major, similar references to the scherzo form, rather oddly, a contrasting section to a sequence (for those who attend to the metre at the point at which it begins) of uniformly syncopated chords. The scherzo returns unabashed, and the first interlude glides in for a moment. Are Florestan and Eusebius at it again? There seems to be some extra-musical motive to account for the intrusion or confusion, in the absence of which the second interlude seems to draw too much on the scherzo to justify its already superfluous appearance.

The simple ternary design of the andante (in the dominant key) suffers from no such overlapping. The main theme is a piece of straightforward, aspiring violoncello cantabile, in which the descending sequence is a little obvious. The interlude adumbrates a new rhythm and a change of key-centre to G flat. Violin and piano in turn illuminate with loving, if not amorous, descant the return of the main theme as it appears on the viola, and on violin with viola. The latter incident happily avoids the descending sevenths, besides bracing the key in the direction of the dominant, which the composer answers by bringing the violoncello back against an undistinguished piano ripple, over a tonic pedal. And so to what? Again a new phrase. This time it is a short pensive intonation, delivered contrapuntally and unobtrusively and then melting into delicate scale-figures, in thirds or tenths, in graceful contrary motion towards the cadential point desired.

However, the new phrase proves to be the salient curve, B flat, E flat, C, of the main subject of the vivace finale, rhythmically balanced by a miniature cascade of falling eddies of sound, a third apart. The eddies make fugue, or at least fugued music, and the upward stretch to the submediant is handy for passing gestures of punctuation and integration. The violoncello starts off an episode when the main subject is finished. It begins in the relative minor, but soon reaches the dominant key, thus suggesting the growth of a sonata rondo. A chromatic decorative figure, founded on the new dominant seventh, keeps the rhythm demurely going. According to convention the main theme would now be expected, but all that is heard of this is a suggestion, after the manner of the epilogue of the previous movement, leading to the real theme. This is compressed into two bars and imitated at one beat's interval in a stimulating variety of keys, from E minor to C flat (assisted by the decorative figure of the first episode) and then by a dominant pedal to the tonic (E flat) for four bars of punctuation, not full restatement, since a fugal exposition does not admit of this. Thus, although the development of the theme immediately after the first episode has seemed to be the normal course in a sonata-form type of procedure, the key-centre is no sooner steadied for recapitulation than the music sinks to the subdominant for the second episode. This is a graceful piece of flowing and partly chromatic polyphony, in primarily two parts, and at the same time in four balanced phrases. This middle section is an odd blend, then, of the development and the avoidance of the main theme, but on the whole we may regard it as stages of recurrence and digression in a sonata-rondo pattern. As in other sonata-rondos (e.g. Beethoven's Piano Concerto, Op. 58, finale) the first episode recurs before the main subject returns again. It duly reaches the tonic after a false start in C minor. The main theme returns and expands almost exactly as it did previously, with close imitation and key-range from A minor to F flat—a fifth below the previous development—thus re-establishing its integrity after the episodes. This time the gesture of punctuation is naturally heightened and prolonged by rhythmic and sequential devices and the final mark is not a full stop but a colon (dominant seventh). On the other side is a brief piece of double fugue, compounded of a suggestion of what I have called 'the salient curve', and of the previous fugue subject, re-accented and extended; riveting bowed and hammered sound, until the hammer prevails. The violoncello affects episode for a moment in order that it shall be swept aside by a general rush to a conclusive stamping of the main beats. This coda was presumably suggested by that of the Quintet, but since it relies on a much-worked theme, not on a reverberant appeal from the first movement, it inevitably reaches its goal much more perfunctorily and bluntly. It is nevertheless satisfactory in its context, much more so than the end of the first movement.

In his Trios Schumann naturally treated the strings more than ever as complementary to the piano. The first, the D minor, Op. 63, is far the longest and breaks new ground. The first movement has a definite integrity of mood and is well equipped with keyboard and string material for the sonata form (Ex. 47). The development is extensive and inclined to be diffuse. The phrases Ex. 47, $a2$ and b (canon in bass at the octave) are recalled, at first in rather odd conjunction, and the diminished seventh of $a3$ (bar 1, *) is useful for modulating in a circular hither and thither. The new theme x thus appears after considerable palaver in F, the key in which the exposition naturally ended. It then sinks through B flat to D flat,

surrounded by *a2* and *b*, the latter worked up to a reasonably com-
pulsive dominant pedal, on the basis of which the characteristic
diminished interval of *a1* formulates a cadence after the manner of the
reprise in the first movement of the Piano Concerto. The difference

Ex.47

is that in the Concerto the salient phrase is that of an impromptu
ornamental suspension, soon forgotten in the return of the main
theme. Here the return of *a1*, discreetly neglected throughout the
development, is considerably diminished in force by its anticipation
eight bars earlier in D minor itself. In the restatement *b* is put into
D major, compensating for the usual flatward trends in the development. When D minor has reasserted itself, *x* restores the major but
at once slips into B flat, from which the Neapolitan sixth (E flat) is
an easy target, and so to a passionate D minor finish. It may be
remarked that the piano is playing throughout, always with the
lion's share in its mouth.[1]

[1] Two earlier versions (Exs. 48, *a* and *b*) of bars 13 et seq., in the sketches, show
the gradual evolution of this passage from the original tame repetition of bar 3,
and an awkward caesura, to the definitive form reached in a third sketch. Some
13 bars later the sketch shows as a single line a melody of which only the first four
notes were retained in this position, in the right-hand piano part, the continuation
being transferred to the 'cello. Like a number of other Schumann movements, this
opening allegro of Op. 63 sprang from—or rather, perhaps, was 'controlled' by—
an idea which never appears in its original form: in this case the fragment quoted

Ex.48

The second movement is a simple-minded scherzo in F, with a weak trio in the same key,[1] marked by constant imitation at the octave in a chromatic style, and a slight and graceful coda. A scherzo in the relaxed key of the relative major is surely a confusion of impressions. The slow movement that follows is, indeed, in the dominant minor. But it consists of a violin theme of the *Träumerei* type interspersed in a clear-cut ternary plan with a very conventional agitato in, I regret to say, F major. Like the A minor slow movement of the D minor Symphony, the movement ends with a half cadence in D minor, leading to the next movement, here a long finale in the major. This finale, capricious rather than the 'fiery' of the main expression mark, makes play out of modulation from the start. After twenty bars the first subject touches F sharp minor and then F, and the second subject moves from B minor to C sharp minor via F sharp minor and A. These sequences make more impression than the melodic material. The square-toed opening theme is distinctly limp, as its recurrence during the second subject, in the bass, where it is much more suited, indicates. The development sinks to F, but pulls up to E minor and G for further instalments of the second and then of the first subject. The third bar of the latter is taken up in close canon, with effective inversions and an urgent antiphony of piano and strings, which culminates in formal restatement, with the piano now doubled by violin (for better or worse). The key is pushed north at first (C sharp minor and C) but then settles down to the second subject a fifth lower than before. A tightening pulse and odd rhythmic sallies produce a good final blaze, in a small and glowing salon.

The Trio in F, Op. 80, is one of Schumann's best chamber works. The movements are well and memorably contrasted, and their con-

as Ex. 49. Its influence may be felt from the beginning of the movement and is perceptible in the otherwise rather puzzling passage for strings ponticello and piano una corda (Ex. 47, *x*), though it does not appear even partially clearly until after this. The subtleties of Schumann's thematic workmanship can easily escape attention.—*Ed.*

[1] This trio gave Schumann a great deal of trouble. For one thing he experimented with a transition from scherzo to trio. And he wished to give the opening of the trio a much tighter imitative texture than he ever managed to achieve; some of the successive stages of his struggle with recalcitrant material are shown in Ex. 50. (The quavers at the beginning of *a* show one of the attempts at dovetailing with the scherzo proper.) Exs. 50, *a* and *b* were later marked 'Trio II', suggesting that Schumann afterwards thought of using these earlier versions after all for a second trio in accordance with his frequent practice; Boetticher sees in them 'strong similarities to the chief ideas of the third movement' which was certainly composed last. (The first draft of Op. 63 had no slow movement.)—*Ed.*

struction is satisfying on the whole. The first movement has good material, homogeneous and yet not too dependent on a particular melodic curve (Ex. 51). The resort to a new theme (*c*) for the opening of the development is surprisingly effective; *b2* makes a good canon by inversion, and *c* in the minor provides suspense before restatement. The latter is suggested by a sudden and solitary entry of *a* in an unusual setting, adjusted at once to the original. Surely this is too unitary to be an integral anticipation? There was a

Ex.49

Ex.50

similar incident in the finale of the A minor Quartet. The coda is
effectively based on an accelerating c.[1] The slow movement is in D
flat.[2] The main mood is Schumann at his most contemplative, but
an initial strophe of eight bars can be felt as the kernel of this lyrical

Ex.51.

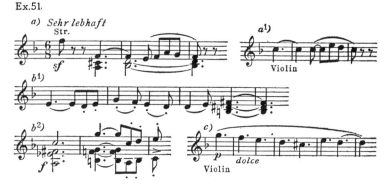

expression. A long and wayward middle section, with many changes
of key, serves to heighten this melodic experience when it is represented. The recurrence of the main strophe in the dominant in
the middle of the movement tightens the structure somewhat, but
this return interrupts the musical thought without striking the 'home'
note, and it is not the kind of theme to be introduced pat like a rondo
theme. Either this should have been in the tonic, making a brief
but firm recapitulation, or it should have been in a distant key, or
(best of all) it should have been omitted and the middle section
shortened. The theme makes a clear impression at the outset in its
mannered style and one formal recollection is quite enough. The

---

[1] The 20-bar passage, beginning with a crescendo, just before the appearance of
the second subject of the first movement, fills a gap for which 18 blank bars had
been left in the first draft. And the sketches show a number of abandoned experiments in contrapuntal device; the second subject several times appears in stretto
and three or four passages near the end of the movement were originally in
canon. The sketches for the development show several points of interest. The
sequential imitations beginning at bar 164 are considerably condensed from their
first form; the more sustained passage (beginning at bar 175) is compounded of
two quite different ideas (Ex. 52, a and b); and the passage on the rising scale
(beginning at bar 208) appears first as a bare harmonic skeleton in minims, thus
standing revealed as the mere ingenious curiosity it is.—*Ed.*

[2] It originally began with a section that was completely scrapped but is worth
reproducing as an example, presumably, of Schumann's improvisation at the
piano (Ex. 53). Three other sketches were made before the definitive form emerged
—characteristically by way of the imitative passage, originally marked 'E major',
at the first change of key-signature. The one feature common to all the sketches
and to the final form is the long melodic descent.—*Ed.*

Ex.52

a) (sic!)

b)

Ex. 53

etc.

balancing movement is a moderato type of scherzo in B flat minor
(the relative minor of D flat) originally marked allegretto. The

main movement is founded on a syncopated figure delivered by the piano with the violoncello or violin in canon throughout, a somewhat wearisome relationship of whose limitations the formal restatement does little or nothing to conceal: but the movement has character.[1] The finale proceeds from one of those flowing queries of which Florestan is so fond,[2] supplemented by a breezy descending motive which is also prominent in the second subject. The movement expands concisely into sonata-form. The combination of the two elements of the first subject (bars 3 and 5), in close antiphony which verges on counterpoint, leads up to a new minatory theme in D minor with a close canon which is not overworked and is replaced by the initial theme (bar 3) in counterpoint with the new one. From this the restatement emerges easily, nicely suspended at first by means of a rhetorical halt. A further flow of the opening rhythm, the middle theme with its frown smoothed over, and the second subject, make a ready coda. It is brought to a head by some arresting discords on a tonic pedal. This finale is a successful rejoinder to the lively opening movement, rounding off the Trio with unusual spontaneity.

The Trio in G minor, Op. 110, is of noticeably loose construction after the first movement, the remaining movements being all broadly ternary without as much inner compulsion as is necessary to bind separate sections in a total impression. In the first movement the main themes show a palpably emotional tone of a romantic type. The first subject (Ex. 54, *a*) sweeps nervously up and down over a tonic

Ex. 54

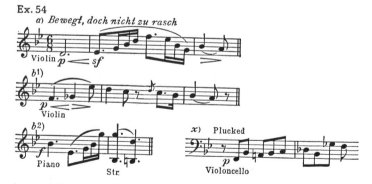

a) *Bewegt, doch nicht zu rasch*

---

[1] Its middle section originally consisted of a smooth, hymn-like passage, akin to Ex. 52, *a*, of which traces remain in the coda.—*Ed.*

[2] Now divided between the pianist's right-hand and the 'cello, it is noted on one stave in the sketch—thus appearing more obviously as a continuous thought; but there is a fermata on the B flat in bar 6, and a rest; the caesura was afterwards obliterated and the music continued differently.—*Ed.*

pedal and is then urged on by various chromatic sequences in which the diminished seventh is prominent; the second (relative major) (Ex. 54, b^1) begins with a more conventional ascent from G flat to the upper E flat and down the scale by discreetly gradual stages, and then uses the rhythmic figure of the first subject to approach a fresh chordal sequence (Ex. 54, b^2). The brief development takes the second subject into F minor and B flat minor (both on the flat side of the main key) and from there works back, chiefly by means of a new and persistent staccato theme (Ex. 54, x), plucked on the strings. Once more the point of restatement is considerably blunted by its anticipation (with the violoncello plucking away at the previous theme) four bars earlier towards the end of a dominant pedal which continues in the restatement, producing an equivocal effect. A definite restatement on a dominant pedal would have made sense, or a suggestion on the same basis, followed by the theme in itself—on a tonic pedal; but two right turns do not lead forward. The second subject returns in the tonic major, and the use of one main rhythmic feature in both subjects leaves the finish a technical problem which Schumann solves by a quicker tempo, close imitation, and a new and epilogal theme on the piano, fading out into a hint of the pizzicato figure and so home in the tonic major. The listener, incidentally, is spared the tempting return of the plucked theme, pursued ad nauseam to a vanishing point that should have been reached several bars earlier.[1] The slow movement, in E flat, proceeds by way of a simple-minded rising-sixth melody in 12/8, definitely precious in its stress of diminished fourths and similar features (Ex. 56). A more or less conventional outburst of faster, more strenuous music in 9/8 follows; the restatement dwells

Ex. 56   *Ziemlich langsam*

[1] This Trio was, exceptionally, sketched in score: a practice Schumann adopted only towards the end of his career. The draft of the opening contains a curious interpolation, enclosed in brackets: a theme (Ex. 55) easily recognizable as the embryo of Ex. 54, b. And there are the usual traces of foundered canons and fugues. Ex. 54, x was first noted down marginally in a rather different form and tested for all kinds of stretti.—*Ed.*

Ex. 55

lovingly on the first four bars of the movement, with repeated sequences which cannot be described as inventive.[1] A scherzo movement in 2/4 (in C minor) banishes idle affection in an arpeggio theme which strays into D flat as easily as the tonic. The insoluble F sharp, too, in the first bar nicely catches the attention (as a scarcely resolved chromatic accented passing note) and it reappears as a provocative appoggiatura in bars 29–30. There are two interludes, a syncopated figure with gracious chromatic chords in major and a jaunty trochaic theme in A flat, which almost evokes a Sullivan patter song and certainly persists in one track too long. The key-explorations of the arpeggio theme wear rather thin in fully triplicate presentation. The finale (originally marked 'mässig', 'moderato'), in the tonic major as in the D minor Trio, is weak and scrappy. The opening outburst of strength and humour may be accepted, though scarcely as a major theme in the finale of a Trio so far serious in tone.[2] The second theme, in D, suggests a desultory second subject, but it is displaced by a queer sort of ballad theme, in a heroic rhythm, in G minor, not unlike *The Two Grenadiers*. Elements from the first subject pick up this histrionic theme and thus link it with the restatement of the main subject,[3] but this does not qualify the bluntness of the ballad's original appearance. The final swirling dance is vivacious in detail and the desultory theme is carried into it without being given time to be desultory. So it is, after all, the second subject of what might be termed an unbalanced sonata-form structure, with an episode in the centre in lieu of development. (Something like the middle section of the piano *Fantasie* in C also makes an appearance.) Nevertheless, this disorderly movement is not the convincing voice of insouciance but that of a confused mind. The fact is that a sonata in the minor has its difficulties. If the first movement cuts below the surface the finale has to go deeper, which argues an unusual concentration of basic mood, or to assume in the main a more perfunctory air. Perfunctory minor

[1] The dying fall at the end of the slow movement was at first prolonged by two additional bars (Ex. 57).—*Ed.*

Ex. 57

[2] The sketch shows that this theme, too, was tried out fugally.—*Ed.*

[3] In the sketch this 'ballad theme' was prolonged; its abrupt termination by the unexpected return of first-subject elements at bar 26 of the G minor section was a fortunate afterthought.—*Ed.*

is difficult to devise; it so easily becomes a contradiction of strain and relaxation. But perfunctory major does not make a movement, and it always arouses the suspicion of technical 'escape' in the wary listener. Schumann seems to be innocent of all this; or else he was tired. It is dangerous, however, to start arguing that this Trio was written when his faculties showed signs of decline and therefore shows evidence of deterioration. The proof of music is in the hearing, not in psychological conjectures.

Comment on the minor mode of the two Sonatas for piano and violin, composed in the same year as the G minor Trio, should similarly avoid unwarranted inferences on the composer's increasing depression. All that may be said is that these three works all resort to the strain of the disharmony of the minor scale, as an underlying stratum of expression, and that they exhibit certain inhibitions of positive vigour, of which the listener becomes conscious when he considers these works in the aggregate; more conscious, for example, than he is of the minor-key character of the particularly expressive fugues in E flat, F, B flat and B minor in the first book of *The Well-tempered Clavier*, or even of Beethoven's *Coriolan* and Fifth Symphony. There is, indeed, no notable analogy for so many exclusively minor works of pure music in a short creative period; but we may be content to observe that Schumann here (and after the noticeably minor gravitations of the *Études symphoniques*, the sonatas for piano and the Piano Concerto) shows signs of specializing exclusively in that choice of mode which led Bach, at a certain stage and after a considerable leaning to the minor in the earlier organ fugues, through various works to a new advance in expression, with a manifest cumulative effect which the contemporary major works (1722) do not show.

It may be noticed, however, that in both Schumann's Violin Sonatas the violin part favours the lower strings; each first movement, for example, has fewer than twenty bars which go above A above the treble clef. Contrariwise, the aptness of the violin for melody and melodic phrases in the upper register, in antiphony with the piano, is singularly neglected. With this unyielding address of hammer and bow in conjunction, the stress of mood is a considerably more salient feature than it might have been.

The Sonata in A minor, Op. 125, is in three movements, the finale incorporating a scherzo element in a developed structure. The first subject is characteristic: it shows an opposition of 6/8 and 3/4 metres of which the ear easily tires. (The quick abandonment of a similar counter-stress in the widow's song in *Elijah* exhibits Mendelssohn's more adroit craftsmanship.) There is a supplementary phrase (bar 27) of a somewhat trite nature, and the second subject is negligible apart from key. In the development the two elements of the first subject and a new version of the opening two bars in a more pronounced rhythm, begun by the piano in the bass, provide the main material in a series of oscillating key-assertions. The restatement adds little to the exposition except for the inevitable delivery of the second subject in the tonic major. A slight attempt at bravura marks the coda. The allegretto sequel, in F, has a wayward refrain and two episodes. The first of these, in F minor, gives the violinist a brief chance for showing his cantabile; the second is a perfunctory bustle in D minor. In the finale violin and piano skirmish a good deal in thirds, sixths and canons at one bar's interval; the second subject, based on a light phrase, is in F, the key whose association with A minor was forced on our attention in the A minor Quartet, and now, coming after the allegretto, betrays itself as a perverse mannerism. The development relies mainly on new matter, partly in E major, and thus the formal restatement is rather more significant than in the first movement. A final skirmish concludes a monotonous but by no means gloomy movement and so establishes a certain classical symmetry with the first movement.

The D minor Sonata is nearly twice as long and has more substance. After beginning with pointed deliberation, the first movement settles down to a developed structure. The first subject (Ex. 58, *a*) is of a contrapuntal nature. The broad DAFD of the violin, anticipated in the introduction in a jerky triple metre, is interwoven with cross-rhythm in the piano, all at a low pitch. This cross-rhythm persists in the second subject, in which two elements may be distinguished, the rising diminished fifth phrases of uncertain tonality in the violin, and the piano response which moves into the relative major (Ex. 58, b^1 and b^2). All these motives are developed, now separately, now in close contrapuntal or melodic association. An early descending off-beat phrase on the piano, which now decorates the resolution of an augmented sixth, and a rising sixth phrase suggested by the first subject and at first essentially syncopated (Ex. 58, c^1 and c^2), aid the musical expansion; and the arpeggio of the first subject is also treated in diminution and in canon, the latter placed a beat early with harmonic results which reverberate later without a canon. The key meanwhile falls to C minor, rises to E minor, sinks back to C minor, and recovers C minor from D flat—the usual

flatward tendency—and this harping on the leading-note minor will
be remembered by alert ears when the finale is heard. The upshot
is that the restatement is far more necessary when it occurs, enriched
by the complexity of associations which have just been maintained.
The second subject duly reaches the tonic major, leaving the composer the opportunity of reasserting D minor by the token of the

Ex. 58

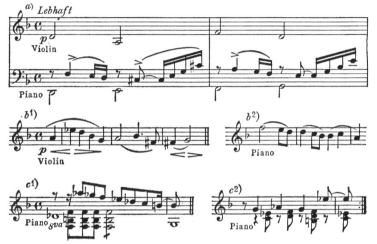

first subject in the jerky manner (but not the metre) of the introduction, with sweeping and accelerating impromptu phrases in response.

The second movement is a scherzo in type: a 6/8 in B minor. The
main section has a plain impulsive motive, suggestive of Brahms to
modern ears; there are two interludes, a two-strand episode (violin
in 2/4 with piano bass) in F sharp minor, and another in the tonic
and in a positive 2/4. A moment's diversion in the direction of C
introduces the return of the scherzo. The next movement has a
tranquillo theme, plucked on the fiddle, of distinct charm. This is in
triple metre in G. There are two variations, an interlude in E minor,
which transforms the scherzo into 9/8 (written as 9/16), a third
variation with flowing pianistic arpeggios in a facile style and no
alteration of the original harmonic sequence, and a brief coda. After
the straightforward scherzo the harmonic uneventfulness of this
slow movement is surprising. The finale is considerable. The first
subject has three distinct elements, the first two of which round off
the second subject (Ex. 59). The troubled first-subject opening
(difficult to make resonant on the fiddle) naturally flows over into

M

the development, not least in C minor; a^3 contributes, and a^1 and a^2 (bass) are treated in constant antiphony, eventually reaching E flat minor, from the dominant of which the return to D minor is easy. The restatement of the second subject in B flat adds slightly to the flatward tilt. It is counterbalanced, also slightly, by a coda in D major, in which every primary phrase finally recurs in a brusque

Ex. 59

synthesis (b, a^2, a^1, a^3, a^1). The sonata may be criticized for this and that weakness, but it shows no decline of invention. Rather, as the last considerable work of pure music, it hints at a special creative effort.[1]

These ten full-scale chamber works show a certain struggle for developed expression, and for one listener a notable lack of progress after the Quintet, but they fill the respective repertoires with music of a definite stature and reasonably characteristic style.

It remains to survey the miscellaneous suites and separate pieces for strings or wind and piano, the soloists including viola, violoncello, oboe, clarinet, and horn. Apart from the horn piece, there are five suites of mainly short movements, whose tonality and ordered contrast imply a musical connexion, not just an accidental aptness for the same instrumental group. The four *Fantasiestücke* for piano, violin, and violoncello, Op. 88, are four movements of which the second is an awkwardly framed scherzo, the third a short wistful reverie for the

---

[1] The sketches for Op. 121 throw further light on Schumann's methods of work. The original development section of the first movement, for instance, was afterwards rejected in its entirety but Schumann salvaged from it a (there) new theme which he ultimately made the second subject of the movement (Ex. 58, b^1); the very act of composition with Schumann often generated new and better ideas. As so often, he tried in vain to work this theme, or modifications of it, in canon. Two passages in the third movement illustrate, by comparison with the final versions, his efforts to eliminate the straggling and the fussy, to achieve classical cleanness and

two strings in a canonic style, and the last another awkward ternary structure in the original key. The slight *Romanze* in 6/8 which comes first rules out the possibility of a full-blown sonata structure, such as appears to have been in Schumann's mind when he originally planned this work. The *Humoreske* in F which follows this A minor *Romanze*

simplicity of outline: the passage leading back to the first theme (Ex. 60: note the two sharps in the key-signature) and a passage in the final section itself (Ex. 61). On the back of the sketches for the finale of Op. 121 appears a trial of the main theme in inversion. More important is the evidence of the sketches on the relationships between finale and first movement. The original coda of the first movement was based on a new theme worked in very tight canon (Ex. 62): this was abandoned in favour of the present quite different lyrical idea. But the other one was not discarded altogether; it was introduced in the finale in an altered form capable of being worked in less strenuous stretto (cf. bars 7–9 and 29–30 after the double bar). Finally, the left-hand piano-part at the end of the finale was to have clinched the musical argument with a major transformation (Ex. 63) of the main theme of the first movement (Ex. 58, *a*): another instance of Schumann's ultimate preference in certain cases for veiled or altogether concealed, instead of open, thematic connexion.—*Ed.*

Ex. 60

Ex. 61

Ex. 62

etc.

Ex. 63

has an insistent but light-hearted main section, a two-piece interlude whose incongruity is provocative, and a da capo. The *Duet* (No. 3) has something of Mendelssohn's neatness of expression, along with Schumann's brooding harmonies. The *Finale* has a commonplace march-theme, suitable for a parade of chocolate soldiers, and another interlude. A brief da capo is absorbed in an unconvincing and extended major conclusion. The four movements are neither consecutive in feeling nor complementary. They remain a series of mainly extended pieces, none of them of overwhelming interest.

The three *Fantasiestücke* (originally *Soiréestücke*) for clarinet and piano, Op. 73, begin with a thoughtful, symmetrical piece in A minor. The other two are each in A major, and present a formal interlude in a plain da capo process with coda. The tautology of key precludes any balance, and the material is not of a kind to conceal its plain mould, though the last piece is the more interesting. The dialogue of clarinet and piano, accompanied by piano, is reasonably effective. The three *Romanzen* for oboe and piano, Op. 94, are similar in texture and structure. The first, in A minor, is the best, partly because it is ternary without being positively sectional. The second, in A major, has a middle section in the relative minor, which dips a good deal into the oboe's bottom register in a suspiciously casual manner; it is on the naïve side and 'offers no new material for the critic'. The third returns to A minor and a certain affinity with the opening, making a better sequence than the clarinet pieces. It is in a somewhat rhapsodic mood, and for interlude there is a brief stanza which begins in F, the key into which Schumann is so much too prone to drop from A minor. The coda exploits (or happens on) the oboe's low register. The suite, if suite it is, is of the slightest order. It sounds better in my judgement when the wind part is played on the more sympathetic clarinet.

Of the two suites for a stringed instrument and piano the five *Stücke im Volkston* for violoncello and piano, Op. 102, are once again grouped round A minor. The first, marked 'Mit Humor', is jaunty, with an arpeggio-esque interlude in F. The second is a melody in F, mainly on a tonic pedal, spaced out into two stanzas by a short phrase in F minor between them. The third piece, wistful in three stages of minor, major, and minor-major, is the most distinctive of the set. The stalwart mood of No. 4 in D is well contrasted with a suggestive middle section which centres on F sharp minor. An impetuous closing movement, with an interlude of wavering tonality, is far the most conclusive finale of these various suites. Of the four *Märchen-bilder* for viola and piano, Op. 113, in which D is the key centre, the first, in the minor, displays distinctive contrasted phrases in viola and piano which happily combine in restatement. The second piece, in F, has a strenuous rhythm which is well maintained and relieved by two different episodes in a florid style. No. 3 returns to D minor in true bravura manner, with a slight but well-placed interlude in B major. The last movement stabilizes D major in a slow, melancholy piece which is presumably intended to dispel the restless spirit of the minor movements. It may be doubted whether its melodic line has any positive quality. The four *Märchenerzählungen* for clarinet, viola, and piano, Op. 132, begin and end in B flat. In the first the viola announces an agitated theme of some character, aided by the early shifting of the tonality towards G minor. The second piece is a vigorous sketch in G minor with a pleasant middle section in E flat in which clarinet and viola move endearingly in thirds. In the tranquil sequel, in G major, the clarinet delivers the 'tune' in true cantabile style. The finale is a somewhat capricious movement, in which the main phrase recalls the opening of the Piano Concerto, arpeggio figures are noticeable in the clarinet and viola, and an absorbed interlude in G flat supplies poise to the dominant wayward-ness. This suite is neglected by the combination which invariably turns to Mozart. Nevertheless it is something of a relief to go from these somewhat routine suites to the *Adagio and Allegro* for horn and piano, Op. 70, in A flat. The adagio, originally entitled *Romanze*, has a reasonably cantabile tune, and the allegro presents an impulsive ternary paragraph at two stages, separated by a quieter passage in B which recalls the adagio. There are alternatives for violoncello, violin, or oboe in place of horn, but in capable lips the horn is the best, with the violoncello coming rather near.

In 1853 Schumann added a piano part to the six Bach sonatas for violin solo[1]—virtually a continuo part. At most points he has simply added pianistic body to the implied harmony. He has not disturbed the harmonic texture or added new contrapuntal strands, and in so doing he has shown discrimination and a careful study of Bach's text. One or two amplifications are surprising: at the last quaver of the third and fifth bars of Sonata No. 6 in E, Schumann has amplified a *passing* chord of F sharp with B (inverted pedal) by a sharp dominant chord on the piano, thus altering what was originally tonic harmony (E, B, G sharp, B on the beat) to tonic challenged by

[1] Also to the six violoncello sonatas, though these have never been published.

dominant off the beat: a slight disturbance of the steady tonic centre
upon which the movement opens in preludial style. In the C major
andante of the third sonata, similarly, Schumann supplies a startling
F sharp in the bass to a passing D C chord, on the last quaver beat,
and incidentally spoils by anticipation the F sharp in the violin two
bars later. In general Schumann's chording usefully explains the
harmony implied to listeners who might otherwise be far less aware
of it. This is not to say that Bach's solitary part needs this continuum.
In some chamber works Bach is incredibly utilitarian, in defiance of
the instrumental texture he selects or at least consents to; but on the
violin Bach is himself.

In conclusion, something may be said here about the original
version of the *Andante and Variations*, for two pianos, Op. 46. As
Mrs. Dale has explained,[1] this includes parts for two violoncelli
and horn, with correspondingly less in the piano parts, and the later
version also shows considerable omission and abbreviation of the
essential music, apart from the omission of the string and wind parts.
The differences may be tabulated as follows. (I shall use the term
'now' to refer to the later version for two pianos only, since it is far
the commoner experience.)

(*a*) Six bars' introduction, in which sequential suspensions (on subdominant, dominant), are noticeable. Now omitted.

(*b*) Variation 5—B flat minor; più lento:[2]

First half: horn plays rhythmic theme, now in piano 2. Violoncello 1 plays 'second', now the alto in piano 2.

Second half: horn as before for four bars, with piano 1 in canon
two beats later. Then theme in piano 2, an octave lower than
now, with horn in canon at the higher octave.

(*c*) Then comes a section, Un poco più lento, of 17 bars. The
violoncelli in harmony are answered antiphonally by piano 1 or 2.
The main phrase is suggestive of the motto-theme of the *Frauenliebe und -leben* cycle, but has been implied by the introductory
bars of the Andante. This section leads into Variation 6 (animato).
It is now omitted, presumably as interrupting the main measure
too much.

(*d*) Variation 7 (in E flat):

First half: horn plays the solo-notes now played by piano 2.
B flat octave in second-time bar, now D flat. Second half: Bar 1.
Violoncello plays the octave figure now in piano 1.

---

[1] See p. 68.

[2] In the first four variations the accompanying instruments play only a minor role.

Bar 2. No descending figure.

Bar 4. Horn plays descending figure.

Bar 5. Violoncello plays descending *fifth*, now an octave.

Bar 6. No figure.

Bar 8. Horn plays a descending fifth, now the octave in piano 2.

(*e*) At the end of Variation 8, instead of proceeding to the recapitulation of the tune, the bass is forced from F to F sharp, evoking 6 extra bars, now omitted.

(*f*) This leads to a 'doppio movimento', an extended diversion of 144 bars in 2/4. A brusque tonic-dominant phrase is prominent. The key is G minor in the first part; in the second it moves towards B flat. This diversion is now cut out.

(*g*) At the very end, after the suspended diminished seventh, there are four bars' conclusion, now extended to eleven.

CHAPTER V

THE ORCHESTRAL MUSIC

By MOSCO CARNER

To call Schumann one of the Cinderellas among the important nineteenth-century symphonists may seem severe. Yet what are the facts? Though much more firmly established than Bruckner's and Mahler's, his symphonies—to say nothing of the rest of his orchestral music—enjoy far less popularity than those of Schubert, Mendelssohn, Brahms, and Tchaikovsky. To the public at large he is the composer of delightful piano miniatures, of the Piano Concerto, and the Piano Quintet. In the sphere of the *Lied* we greet him as one of Schubert's few great successors—an eloquent and inspired singer of the bliss and sorrow of romantic love. Yet Schumann the symphonist and orchestral writer takes a back seat in our esteem. In the programmes of orchestral concerts his symphonies and overtures make but rare appearances, for the simple truth is that their lack of brilliance and generally ineffective orchestration make it difficult for conductors to earn kudos with them. 'Schumann we cannot and will not play' was Steinbach's curt reply when invited to London in 1902 to conduct a series of concerts with the celebrated Meiningen Orchestra. And Weingartner considered the symphonies far more effective if played as piano duets.[1] It might be argued that the likes and dislikes of conductors and orchestras are often an uncertain guide to the intrinsic qualities of an orchestral work. Yet even the unbiassed cannot help boggling at the clumsiness and unevenness of Schumann's symphonic technique, his frequent lack of orchestral sense and insight into the mechanics of an orchestra.

Yet despite such weaknesses the symphonies contain some of his most inspired music, and it is no exaggeration to say that without them the literature of nineteenth-century orchestral music would be greatly the poorer. We do not value them for their classical attributes but for the romantic spirit that keeps breaking in. Schumann's deliberate turn from the romantic miniature of his early period to the larger and stricter forms of the classical symphony and chamber music—thus forcing upon himself a change of approach,

[1] *Die Sinfonie nach Beethoven.* Stuttgart, 1901.

style, and technique—could not altogether stifle his romantic Muse. In fact, it is in those very movements in which the Romantic overcomes the neophyte to classicism that he made his individual contribution to the history of the nineteenth-century symphony. About the sincerity and nobility of his symphonic utterances there can be no doubt. And compared with Mendelssohn's, as for patent reasons they must be, the Schumann symphonies are far more original in thought, more adventurous in their formal novelties, at once more inward and powerful, issuing as they do from a greater depth of feeling. True, they have nothing of Mendelssohn's brilliance, polished elegance, and savoir-faire—much to their detriment in the concert hall. Yet Schumann was emotionally the richer personality, possessed by an elemental, and at times demoniac, urge which was lacking in the genius of his involuntary rival. It is perhaps for that very reason that Schumann, unlike Mendelssohn, was unable to find the formula by means of which to integrate the classical heritage with his own brand of romanticism. This battle between two opposing ideals was not peculiar to Schumann only; it had to be fought out by every romantic symphonist. But in his case it was less likely to resolve itself because underneath, as it were, went on another battle, the fight to reconcile the limitations of his genius with the self-imposed demand for an extension of its creative range. It is here that the chief problem of Schumann as a symphonic writer lies.

By nature a lyrical miniaturist, his self-chosen domain was first the short self-contained piano piece and song. In both these media Schumann was able to create undisputed masterpieces. There is nothing of the 'petit maitre' about his diminutive works. In fact, had he died in 1841, posterity would have acclaimed him along with Chopin as a great master in the small forms. Yet, unlike Chopin, he had the ambition 'to fight his way through to the larger forms', as a much lesser figure—Grieg—said of himself. (However, Grieg was wise enough not to persist in this endeavour.) These 'larger forms' included, in Schumann's case, not only symphony and chamber music but also opera and oratorio. It is of course difficult to say whether this aspiration to conquer the whole vast field of musical composition originated in a veiled desire to emulate his foremost models, Beethoven and Schubert, or resulted from a genuine instinctive urge. The fact is that this expansion to new regions proved too great a test for a composer of Schumann's particular genius. It can be no coincidence that with a very few exceptions the music after 1841—the year when he seriously embarked on composition other than piano works and songs—shows a decline, though a very gradual one, in spontaneity, freshness, originality, and inventive distinction. It would appear that the necessity to face and solve formal problems of a new order tended to sap his power of inspiration. The special problem that confronted Schumann in his symphonies was two-fold. First, how to deal with the sonata-form in the single movement, and secondly, how to create an inner unity between the four movements? Not that he had not come across this problem before 1841, as witness the abortive G minor Symphony of 1832, and the Piano Sonatas in F sharp minor and G minor. And we know how inadequate they are from the point of view of formal treatment.[1] I shall not expatiate on the general technical handicap of a composer who up to his eighteenth year was much more interested in literature and writing, and for years was only an amateur musician, albeit a highly gifted one, who, to all intents and purposes, acquired the knowledge of his craft by self-tuition. The technique that served him well in the congenial media of short piano pieces and songs was certainly not sufficient to make symphonic writing an easy task. And what he himself first thought of the sonata-form may be gathered from his dictum in 1839 that 'isolated beautiful examples of it will certainly still be written now and then—and have been written already—but it seems that this form has run its life-course'. Yet two years later he made a complete volte-face and concentrated for a time almost exclusively upon works in sonata-form.

How did he handle it in his symphonies? His first handicap here was his inability to invent true symphonic themes, themes capable of development and further growth. One of the virtues of his small-scale works was the short epigrammatic theme. With a few exceptions, he applied the same method to his symphonic first and last movements, the testing-places of the true symphonist. Even so, superior technique, as Brahms has shown, could have made something of such unsymphonic static ideas. Yet development from within is very rare with Schumann. Like Schubert's, his normal way of filling the large canvas is by repetition and sequence of square-cut patterns, and, in the development sections, by transposition of large blocks wholesale. This is not to say there are no attempts at real working-out, as in the Second and Third Symphonies, but Schumann's instinctive tendency was towards mere juxtaposition of mosaics: the formal style of his piano pieces. When he suddenly reverts to true development, one gets the impression that he resorted

[1] On the Sonatas, see pp. 42–4; on the G minor Symphony, see p. 187 et seq.

to it chiefly because 'thematic work' was the way of the classics. One feels much the same kind of formalism in his cumulative use of canon and imitation—a favourite device long before his more intense Bach studies of 1845 (e.g. in the first movement of the early G minor Symphony).[1] In short, there is much to show that in his symphonic writing Schumann often paid mere lip-service to the masters of the past. Another weakness (which he also shares with Schubert) is his clinging too long to the same rhythm, thus adding to his melodic unwieldiness. This seems all the more surprising in a composer who was so much given to rhythmic experiment as Schumann. Yet once he has hit upon a fresh rhythmic pattern, he is inclined to do it to death.

This brings us to another, related, feature. It is Schumann's tendency to build up a whole movement from a single-pattern theme, to swamp it with a melodic-rhythmic ostinato, the most characteristic example of which is the first movement of the D minor Symphony. It is psychologically interesting to note that it is usually in movements or single pieces of a curiously restless, one might almost say, demoniac, character that Schumann resorts to this toccata-like treatment.[2] It has much in common with his device of retaining the same accompaniment figure throughout a whole song. True, such technique makes for thematic unity, yet in a symphonic movement, with its greater length and more complex texture, the advantage is bought at the price of melodic and rhythmic monotony. Schumann was no Beethoven to bring off such a monothematic tour de force as the Viennese master did in the first movement of the Fifth and the outer movements of the Seventh Symphonies. Moreover, thematic unity by itself does not create that higher form of coherence which results from the ability to think in a sustained and consistent manner. With the exception of the first movement of the *Rhenish*, there is nowhere in the Schumann symphonies a wide sweep of ideas, a continuous growth from within. Even the extraordinary thematic economy of the first movement of the D minor Symphony does not succeed in creating an organic whole, nor do the various thematic cross-references between its four movements make for an inner

[1] Cf. his remark in one of his early letters that 'it is most extraordinary how I write almost everything in canon, and then only afterwards detect the imitations and often find inversions, rhythms in contrary motion', &c.

[2] Piano Trio in G minor, Op. 110, first movement; Violin Sonata in A minor, Op. 105, first and third movements; Violin Sonata in D minor, Op. 121, first and fourth movements; *Concert sans Orchestre*, Op. 14, finale; *Fantasiestücke*, Op. 12, *In der Nacht* and *Traumeswirren*; and *Kreisleriana*, Op. 16, Nos. 1 and 7.

unity. One cannot dismiss the impression that in his, at times obsessional, preoccupation with the monothematic device, Schumann consciously attempted by a purely technical means to achieve the inner coherence which was not inherent in the fabric of his symphonic thought.

Now on turning from the single sonata-movement to the symphonic form as a whole we shall not be surprised to find other symptoms of Schumann's structural weakness. The supreme criterion of a symphony since Beethoven is whether it presents a whole in the sense that a central idea informs *all* the movements and makes them appear as inseparable parts of the musical organism. Herein lies the crux of the symphonic form, classic, romantic or modern. Barring the Second Symphony, Schumann never fully obtained an organic unity between movements, a unity by which a movement is felt to be the corollary of the preceding one. To repeat: a born miniaturist, his primary, instinctive way of musical thinking was in terms of small, static, self-contained, and independent mood-pictures.

And here we come to another important factor. Schumann appears to have needed the stimulus of poetic ideas and literary images to bring his imagination to the boil, and this was bound to have a decisive bearing on the way he conceived of formal coherence. Take his cycles of piano works and songs. What holds them together is less inner, musical, unity than the intellectual link provided by a literary programme. In other words, his cycles represent a succession of musical tableaux whose progress and purpose are chiefly determined by extra-musical thoughts and such general aesthetic considerations as contrast and formal balance. In his symphonies Schumann still clings to the tableau manner. Here too we find a more or less loose succession of romantic mood-pictures and character pieces, only with the difference that the adoption of the symphonic form forced upon him greater formal discipline and a more sustained manner of thinking. Up to a point Schumann gradually acquired both; yet something of the loose, casual character of a suite remains. Hence the difficulty of forming a unified picture of a Schumann symphony. Like Mendelssohn's symphonies, Schumann's are at bottom romantic *Spielmusik*—music in which the capricious play of romantic fancies and moods dominates over a more abstract, more intrinsically musical, central thought. The whole is less than its parts.

Only once, when under the impact of a terrifying personal

experience, the spectre of madness was before him—and a very real spectre, as it later turned out—did Schumann abandon his *Spielmusik* conception and, stepping out of his romantic dream-world, make a real-life experience his symphonic 'theme'. This was in the Second Symphony, his only symphony with something of Beethoven's 'moral character'. Hence its greater *inner* unity and the feeling that the four movements flow from one central idea and in their sequence illustrate the peripeteia of a psychological drama. Yet Schumann achieved this higher symphonic aim at a considerable cost, for, with the exception of its adagio, musically the C major Symphony does not rise above mediocrity. The thought suggests itself that once Schumann tried to detach himself from literary programmes and poetic fancies and looked into his inner self for inspiration, his creative powers sagged, producing but laboured, aesthetically disappointing music. But of that more later.

That literary subjects, poetic images, and nature impressions played upon his fancy, Schumann admitted both explicitly and by implication in his various writings, notably his long essay (1835) on the *Symphonie fantastique*.[1] Yet while most of his piano pieces have titles, in his symphonic music he was much more reticent, fearing no doubt that an open admission of the presence of a programmatic background would be likely to detract from the absolute, purely musical significance. As he said in the essay on the Berlioz work, 'If the eye is once directed to a certain point, the ear can no longer judge independently'. Hence the subsequent suppression of the titles which he originally intended for each of the four movements of the B flat Symphony and two movements of the Third. Yet for all his circumspection there is sufficient internal evidence to suggest a programmatic origin for his symphonies. It is this very intrusion of poetic ideas that gives Schumann's symphonic work its special place in the history of the post-Beethovenian symphony. He opened to the symphony a world of Romantic imagery and lyricism which was at once new and personal. It was a world both truly German and truly Schumannesque, created from the fantasies of Jean Paul and E. T. A. Hoffmann, the magic of the German fairy-tales,

---

[1] Cf. his *Gesammelte Schriften über Musik und Musiker*; also his letter to Clara, of 13 April 1838: 'I am affected by everything that goes on in the world and think it all over in my own way, politics, literature and people, and then I long to express my feelings and find an outlet for them in music. That is why my compositions are sometimes difficult to understand, because they are connected with distant interests; and sometimes striking, because everything extraordinary that happens impresses me and impels me to express it in music.'

the old-world atmosphere of ancient Rhenish cities, and from the intimacy and hidden poetry of Schumann's domestic hearth.[1] Who but the romantic Schumann could have written a *Spring* Symphony or thought of such things as the romanza and the slow introduction to the finale of the D minor Symphony, and the 'Cathedral' movement of the Third? Yet there was little in Schumann of Schubert's romanticism which was naïve, mystical, cosmic. Schumann fed his mind on the *rational* element of German literature. His was the romanticism of the rising German middle-class, the German burgher with his solid education and his genuine love of *Kultur*. Consciously or unconsciously, Schumann departed from that universality of audience at which the Viennese classics aimed. In his symphonies he no longer addressed himself to a European élite, the public of Haydn, Mozart, and Beethoven, but to a public with the same national and social background as his own. This has often been described in a derogatory sense as the bourgeois element in Schumann's artistic make-up. Yet while it is true that it sometimes produced music of an innocuous, homely, Philistine nature, it was on the other hand responsible for the wonderful inwardness and *Versponnenheit* of many of his mood-pictures. In fact such introspective, non-classical movements as his andantes and scherzi were Schumann's most personal contribution to the post-Beethovenian symphony; they are symphonically extended character-pieces.

Yet while for obvious reasons more felicitous in the simple form of such movements, the inspired Romantic in Schumann is by no means absent from the formally stricter, more complex and more 'classical' outer movements of his symphonies. In particular, the slow introductions turn into inspired mood-pictures: idyllic in the First Symphony, sombre, dream-like and solemn in the Fourth, tormenting and restless in the Second. (It is significant that the first movement of the Third, Schumann's most 'classical' movement, dispenses with a romantic preamble.) In form these introductions all present the same picture: two parts, the first more static, lyrical, the second, more dynamic and mostly containing a tempo acceleration to the ensuing allegro. Another characteristic is that without exception these introductions contain some of the chief material of the allegro. (Schumann thus made a principle of what

[1] I find it difficult to square this with the fact that Schumann's music enjoys such marked popularity in, of all countries, France. It is, by the way, the same world in which the Mahler of the first four symphonies and of the early songs felt very much at home.

Haydn and Schubert did only occasionally.) This thematic integration is carried a long step further when other movements as well derive some of their ideas from the opening introduction, as in the Second Symphony and, most strikingly, the Fourth. It seems more than probable that Schumann's love of thematic germ-cells, mottos, and the monothematic device in general was nurtured by such precedents as Beethoven's C minor Symphony, Schubert's *Wandererphantasie* and Berlioz's *Symphonie fantastique*. In fact, there is an unmistakable echo of Berlioz's idée fixe in the Schumann symphonies which so far seems to have escaped notice. In three out of the four, Schumann introduces the same characteristic figure of three notes rising step-wise to the major third.[1] The manner of its use suggests a special programmatic significance for the composer. With one exception, it is always scored for the brass and the three notes are to be played with an accent. I venture to suggest that Schumann associated with it a signal or call, perhaps a kind of 'sursum corda', for that is the effect it creates. And its reiterated appearance in works so different in character points to its being a 'fixed idea' in the literal sense of the term.[2]

So much for Schumann's borrowings from immediate forerunners. More important, however, is the fact that in his D minor and C major Symphonies he foreshadows diverse techniques in the more advanced use of mottos and theme-relations: Liszt's theme-transformation, Wagner's leitmotive, Tchaikovsky's motto, and Franck's 'idée cyclique'.[3] And strange as it may seem, there is an intrinsic affinity between Schumann's 'thematic reservoir' (e.g. the introductions to the Second and Fourth Symphonies) and the basic tone-row of twelve-note music. *Mutatis mutandis*, he might have said with Schönberg, 'I was always occupied with the aim to base the structure of my music consciously on a unifying idea which produced . . . all the other ideas'.[4] For all his structural weaknesses, Schumann was a pathfinder in the means of achieving formal-thematic compression and thus forms an important link between

---

[1] Cf. motto-theme of the First (Ex. 69, *a*, figure *x*), chorale-theme of the slow introduction to the finale of the Fourth (Ex, 90, *a*, figure *c*), and scherzo and adagio of the Second (Ex. 107, *a*, figure *x*).

[2] Careful analysis might discover it in other works.

[3] It is as well to recall the fact that the root of all these nineteeth-century devices is the 'reminiscence' of the eighteenth-century opéra comique, also found occasionally in the music of an earlier period.

[4] See Schönberg's letter to Nicolas Slonimsky, published in the latter's *Music since 1900*. Compare also pp. 159 (footnote) and 281.

Beethoven and the 'intensive' instrumental writers of a much later period.

If this is perhaps the most striking positive feature of Schumann's symphonic technique, there are others equally characteristic. I would mention in the first place his predilection for melodic surprises which he springs on us in the form of fresh tunes—introducing them, as often as not, into the development section and, notably, the coda. His inclusion in his scherzo movements of two contrasting trios is of this order.[1] Schumann was a born melodist; a glance through his piano and song cycles proves it beyond doubt. Yet while such loose succession of melodies was for obvious reasons banished from the sonata-form, Schumann would not altogether restrict himself here to two main themes, and used the formally more fluid sections for smuggling in fresh ideas. Some may have originated in poetic intentions such as the Beethoven quotation in the finale of the C major Symphony, and the unexpected lyrical parenthesis in the coda of the first movement of the B flat. Others again serve the purpose of providing new material for a second development, or lyrical contrast, or to crown a movement with a final apotheosis, as in the *Overture, Scherzo und Finale*. Here again Schumann foreshadows what was to become a characteristic feature of the late nineteenth-century symphony.

To complete this list of novelties, mention must be made of a characteristic device by which Schumann achieves harmonic surprise. This is the statement of a theme, usually the second subject, in what I would call harmonic inversion. Instead of introducing it at once in the expected key, he starts his theme in a related one[2] to lead it subsequently to its home key. This inversion has a two-fold effect: it momentarily obscures the tonality, and if such harmonic duality is maintained for a longer stretch, the impression is created that Schumann's exposition and recapitulation are laid out on three different harmonic planes. Beethoven has it sometimes but only on a small scale,[3] with Schubert we find it more frequently and extensively, yet Schumann's reiterated use of it makes it a fingerprint of his harmonic style.

[1] Cf. his First and Second Symphonies, and the coda of the scherzo of the *Rhenish*.

[2] Usually the supertonic or upper mediant, occasionally the relative major or minor.

[3] See the recapitulation of the first movement of the *Waldstein* Sonata, Op. 53, second subject first in A, then in C.

A few general words about his scoring have already been said at
the outset. It forms a sorry chapter in the critical evaluation of his
orchestral works. Brilliant, colourful, varied—in short, imaginative
—scoring has a way of covering up, or at any rate detracting from,
structural weaknesses. Striking cases in point are the Tchaikovsky
symphonies; Tchaikovsky's formal defects are much the same as
Schumann's, yet as *orchestral music* the Russian's symphonies are
singularly effective. Had Schumann been endowed with a better
grasp of the orchestral mechanics and with a more sensitive ear for
the blending and balancing of instrumental colours, his Cinderella
rôle as an orchestral composer might have been less marked. For
his symphonies are tuneful and generally lively in rhythm. It might
be argued that the specific character of his orchestral music is such
as *not* to demand a dazzling garb.[1] And this could be supported by
a reference to Brahms's orchestra. Whatever one may think of
Brahms as an orchestrator, it is indisputable that his orchestral style
is part of his musical thought and thus serves the purpose of his
symphonic utterances admirably. To a certain extent this is also true
of Schumann. On the other hand there is ample evidence that his
orchestral technique *was* deficient, leading him into such well-nigh
incredible blunders as the revision of the D minor Symphony. Not
that Schumann was congenitally unable to think in orchestral terms,
as is frequently stated. But, with a few startling exceptions, he
failed to make the orchestra an eloquent, flexible instrument of his
thought. As early as 1832, while working on his youthful G minor
Symphony, he confessed to putting in 'often yellow instead of blue'
and considered orchestration an art 'so difficult that it'll take long
years' study to give one certainty and self-control'. The bane of
Schumann's orchestra is its thickness and heaviness, caused by superfluous doublings, notably of the inner parts, and the preponderant,
injudicious use of the brass for inner pedals and mere rhythmic
accentuation. In addition, the woodwind are often employed in
registers where they do not 'speak' readily. Though the handling of
the strings shows greater experience, Schumann often scores a
melody for the first violins only, so that they have to contend single-
handed against a heavy accompaniment. Nor does he allow his
orchestra to 'breathe' sufficiently, using the various instrumental
groups for too long a stretch. The frequent result is unrelieved

[1] Even his writing for the piano, the medium from which he started and which
remained most congenial to him, is not brilliant; consider his limited use of the
high and low registers and the crowding of the texture by thematic inner parts.

N

thickness of texture and murky opaque colour.[1] The puzzling thing is that at times Schumann would score with a delicacy, economy, and sensitiveness to colour and balance that make one almost wonder if such passages are by the same pen which put in 'yellow instead of blue'. And it is interesting to find that it is largely in the slow movements that Schumann shows himself inspired and imaginative in handling the orchestral palette.

À propos of Schumann's revisions in the Fourth Symphony, Tovey makes the interesting suggestion that it was the composer's inadequacy as a conductor that induced him to make 'all entries fool-proof by doubling them and filling up the rests', a possible but not plausible explanation resting on the assumption that if one group of instruments missed Schumann's cue, the other would not. Yet it must be presumed that even in Schumann's times professional orchestral players could be relied upon to count their bars and come in on their entries. Nor does Tovey's suggestion explain why Schumann's scoring was at times as good as it was. The striking discrepancy in one and the same work between good and bad scoring seems to argue a more fundamental reason than incompetence and lack of practical experience. It is true that Schumann had no particular knack for the orchestra and often appears to have conceived his orchestral music in terms of the piano, which would partly explain the doublings and the massiveness of texture. Yet I venture to suggest that the marked unevenness of his orchestral writing may have had something to do with his mental illness, the first outward symptoms of which date back to 1834, if not before. We know that intermittently it affected his auricular sense, and it may be that during these periods it also affected the clarity of the inner sound-picture of the music Schumann happened to be writing at the time. It is conceivable that its projection into concrete orchestral terms carried with it the mark of such disturbances—a hypothesis which of course would need substantiation on the part of a psychiatrist conversant with Schumann's pathological history, but for all we know it may account for the disconcerting inequality of his orchestral style.

We may now examine the symphonies separately and more closely, although no minute analysis is attempted but rather a detailed discussion by way of substantiation of, and enlargement upon, the points already made.

[1] It is for this reason that Weingartner and Mahler revised the orchestration of the four symphonies. A specimen of the latter's revision will be found in Ex. 114. For a detailed account of Mahler's rescoring, see the present writer's essay in his book *Of Men and Music* (London, 1942).

Schumann's very first symphonic essay is the unpublished Symphony in G minor written at the age of twenty-two (1832–3).[1] Its first movement, at any rate, already shows Schumann's finger-prints. There is no mistaking the *Sturm und Drang* of the young composer, manifesting itself in a restless drive and a feeling of almost Promethean strength. The Beethoven of the first allegro of the *Eroica* evidently stood godfather to this movement. Its spaciousness and a development section of considerable length point in that direction. There are also some more tangible parallels: the 3/4 time-signature, the opening with its tutti crash, the heroic character of the first half of the main subject, the syncopated accompaniment (Ex. 64), and the martial bridge-theme with its quaver counter-

Ex. 64

point (Ex. 65). Nor was Beethoven's remarkable transition to the reprise lost on the young composer; yet while Beethoven's was a harmonic surprise, Schumann's is thematic. After the development has petered out in a whole-bar silence, the first subject is anticipated in adagio tempo, tutti and forte—the surprise being all

[1] A copy of the MS. of the first two movements was kindly placed at my disposal by the Editor, through the good offices of Dr. Eismann, the present Director of the Schumann Museum at Zwickau.

Ex. 65

the more effective for the almost complete absence of first-subject material from the preceding development. (We shall see that such dramatic passages, shortly before or at the entry of the reprise, were to become a characteristic feature of Schumann's mature style.) Truly Schumannesque are the soaring, 'springing' opening of the first subject (Ex. 64) and the romantic yearning of the second (Ex. 66), and, alas, the weakness of the development.

Ex. 66

It has no sense of direction, modulates aimlessly, and shows an almost obsessional use of imitation and stretto, not to mention the inadequacy of the orchestration. It is significant that this early movement should attract by its ideas and fail in its structure—a discrepancy which, though in diminishing degree, we shall notice throughout the whole of Schumann's symphonic output.

This first movement was performed three times: at Zwickau on 18 November 1832, at Schneeberg in the revised form just described on 12 February 1833, and in Leipzig on 29 April of the same year. At Schneeberg Schumann heard Beethoven's Seventh Symphony which obviously influenced the second movement of his own work.[1] The choice of key for this second movement is odd: relative minor of the dominant, that is to say B minor. But Schumann made the same choice for the scherzo (third movement) of his first mature symphony.

[1] His variations on the allegretto from the Seventh Symphony (cf. p. 23) date from later in the same year.

This 'Andantino quasi allegretto', all too clearly modelled on Beethoven's allegretto (Ex. 67), opens with a wood-wind fanfare which recurs later in the movement where its sequential repetition

Ex. 67

emphasizes that it is the origin of a theme (molto più vivace) in the *Marche des Davidsbündler* of *Carnaval*, and the parallel to Beethoven's A major melody duly makes its appearance on flute and clarinet (Ex. 68). A novel feature of one of the two drafts of the movement is a middle section, marked 'Intermezzo quasi scherzo': an allegro assai in 6/8 time, for which Beethoven's first movement clearly sat as the

Ex. 68

model; at the end its pace is slowed to that of the andantino which then returns with different scoring (at first pizzicato). The figuration of this final section is specially pianistic but the whole movement leaves the impression of a weak piano-piece feebly orchestrated. The D major scherzo and the (largely fugal) finale of the Symphony exist only in incomplete sketches; part of the fugue was incorporated in the Impromptu, Op. 5.[1]

Nine years were to pass before Schumann made another, and this time incomparably more successful, attempt at a symphony. The Symphony in B flat, Op. 38, actually numbered 1, was sketched in the astoundingly short space of four days (23–26 January 1841). 'Born in a fiery hour', its composition caused the composer great happiness, 'but entirely exhausted me. Think of it', he writes to the critic E. F. Wenzel in January 1841, 'a whole symphony, and what's more, a *Spring* Symphony—I can't believe myself that it's finished. But I have not scored it yet'. The orchestration was completed by 20 February, and the first performance took place at Leipzig Gewandhaus on 31 March, with Mendelssohn conducting. What interests us in the above letter, is Schumann's hint at the poetic idea that inspired the work. He later amplified it in a letter to Spohr, (November 1842), saying that he wrote it 'in that spring urge which comes afresh over everyone, even the oldest'. Though denying descriptive intentions, he admits that 'the period in which it was written influenced its character and partly made it what it is'. The allusion is to his own love spring, the happiest and most blissful period in his life. In 1840, the year of his marriage, it had found its lyrical expression in a veritable flood of inspired songs, and now it provided the incentive for his first serious symphonic essay. It is thus not difficult to read into the impetuosity, the fervour and general high spirits of the work, the expression of bliss and contentment that possessed the young romantic husband of Clara.

Yet in addition to his general 'programme', Schumann has given us some more details of the meaning of certain sections. In a letter to W. Taubert, a Berlin conductor (January 1843), he exhorts Taubert to 'try to inspire the orchestra with some of the spring longing which chiefly possessed me when I wrote the symphony in February 1841. At the very beginning I should like the trumpets to sound as if from on high, like a call to awaken. In what follows of the

---

[1] See p. 22. The sketches for the scherzo and finale, and the different versions of the first two movements, have been described in detail by Professor Abraham in *The Musical Quarterly* (January 1951).

introduction there might be a suggestion of the growing green of everything, even of a butterfly flying up, and in the following allegro of the gradual assembling of all that belongs to spring. . . . Concerning the last movement, I only want to tell you that I think of it as Spring's Farewell'.[1] Yet, as I have already pointed out, Schumann was always anxious to destroy the suspicion that he had allowed himself to be directly inspired by a programme, and he hastens to add that 'these are fancies that came to me *after* the completion of the work'. Equally, his original intention of giving each movement an explanatory title—'Spring's Awakening' for the first, 'Evening' for the larghetto, 'Merry Playmates' for the scherzo, and 'Spring's Farewell' for the finale—may have been an afterthought. That the titles were abandoned before publication was probably due to his desire not to detract from the supposedly 'absolute' character of the music and thus stress his new 'classical' approach. Yet the very fact that he could think of titles and give epistolary explanations *while* writing the music leaves no doubt about the play of poetic ideas upon his creative fancy. Moreover, we have Clara's word for it[2] that the 'first impulse' for the *Spring* Symphony came from a 'spring poem', identified by Jansen in his book, *Die Davidsbündler*, as one of Adolf Böttger's then fashionable *Frühlings- und Liebesmelodien*, of which the last line directly inspired the motto-call of the symphony.[3] Yet, oddly enough, the poem referred to by Jansen shows nothing, except its last line, to connect it with the mood of the Symphony. On the

[1] The affinity between Schumann and Mahler, to which reference has already been made, may be seen from the partial identity of this programme with the ideas that Mahler attempted to suggest in his Third Symphony.

[2] Cf. Litzmann, *Clara Schumann*, Vol. II, p, 27.

[3] Du Geist der Wolke, trüb' und schwer
Fliegst drohend über Land und Meer.

Dein grauer Schleier deckt im Nu
Des Himmels klares Auge zu.

Dein Nebel wallt herauf von fern
Und Nacht verhüllt der Liebe Stern:

Du Geist der Wolke, trüb' und feucht
Was hast du all' mein Glück verscheucht!

Was rufst du Thränen ins Gesicht,
Und Schatten in der Seele Licht!

O wende, wende deinen Lauf,—
Im Thale blüht der Frühling auf.

contrary, it expresses a dark depressive feeling of which there is not
the slightest hint in the music. This sent me back to the rest of
Böttger's verses where I lighted upon a poem that completely tallies
with Schumann's description given to Taubert of the first movement
(see above), and whose sentiment and verbal imagery are wholly
in tune with what the movement suggests.[1] I suspect that this
second poem was Schumann's real incentive and that the last line
of the first poem provided him with only the motto whose verbal
image and iambic metre struck his fancy.

The Symphony opens with a slow introduction which in Schubertian fashion falls into two sections, each with its own material. The
very opening on horns and trumpets, following the metre of the last
line of Böttger's poem (Ex. 69, a), the 'call from on high', is more
than a mere motto.[2] For in addition to its literal quotation (first and
last movements), it generates the first subject of the ensuing allegro
(Ex. 69, b) and seems to have been responsible for the markedly
upward tendency (both stepwise and in leaps) of the main themes of

[1] Der Frühling wirkt auf Thal und Halde
Aus Blum' und Gras sein buntes Tuch,
Und gibt dem Vögelchen im Walde
Der Blätter grünes Notenbuch.

In meiner Brust erweckt er wieder
Erstorbne Lust, glückselge Pein,
Und wirft mir eine Hand voll Lieder,
Des Lenzes Melodien, hinein.

Und diese Lieder ohne Noten,
Musik der Seel' im starren Wort,
Send ich zu dir als Liebesbothen,
Zu ihrem neuen Frühling, fort.

Nimm, was der Mai mir zugeflüstert
Von Lieb' und Herzensharmonie—
Und wo sich meine Seele düstert,
Verkläre deine lichtre sie!

[2] Its original version was scored for horns only and began a major third lower,
as in the opening of the allegro. Still using 'natural' horns, Schumann overlooked
the fact that thus the two stopped notes G and A, if blown forte, as he demanded,
would produce an ugly, almost grotesque sound—which was what happened at
the first rehearsal under Mendelssohn—as if the instruments 'had a bad cold in
the head' (letter to Mendelssohn, October 1845). Yet, in 1853, when sending a
copy of the published score to the Dutch composer and conductor, J. J. H. Verhulst,
Schumann expressed his regret at having had to alter the pitch of the motto. As
by that time valve instruments were already in common use—Schumann employing them himself in other works—it is all the more puzzling that he did not restore
the original version; this was done by Verhulst and, later, Mahler.

the other movements.[1] It is perhaps no coincidence that, like Schumann's motto, the germ-motive of Schubert's Ninth Symphony is also characterized by the rising third, and on its very first statement appears in a similar scoring (horns). Did not Schumann say that hearing Schubert's work made him 'tingle to be at work on a symphony'? Beethoven, too, seems to be echoed in the slow introduction: in the dramatic string runs and the majestic tutti crashes (bars 8–14). Similarly, the general texture of its second section with its sustained wood-wind chords and the triplet figuration on the strings (bars 25 et seq.), is strongly reminiscent of part of the slow introduction of the *Fidelio* Overture. None the less the Schumannesque touch is not to be missed in such things as the 'butterfly' suggestion of the woodwind (bars 19–24),[2] certain harmonic progressions, and the characteristic accelerando to the allegro.[3]

The first subject (Ex. 69, *b*) derived, as was said, from the

Ex. 69

---

[1] It is interesting to note that the majority of the allegro themes of Schumann's instrumental and vocal works show a tendency to soar. The same feature is to be found in the melodic styles of Richard Strauss and Elgar—perhaps a clue to the psychological make-up of these composers.

[2] The importance of 'butterfly' images in Schumann is worth investigation. He was delighted when a friend discovered a butterfly in the first movement of the G minor Symphony: 'Becher's thought at the transition to G: Lo! There the butterfly flies away! High, high in the air—is very poetic' (Boetticher: *Robert Schumann: Einführung in Persönlichkeit und Werk*, p. 319). The reference is to Ex. 65, or rather to the parallel passage in the recapitulation; the similarity to *Papillons*, No. 1, also deliberately quoted in *Florestan* of *Carnaval*, will not have escaped the reader.—*Ed.*

[3] In the letter to Taubert, quoted above, Schumann wishes the più vivace section at once to be taken considerably faster than the preceding tempo so as to lead imperceptibly to the Allegro molto vivace. Too literal an observance of this demand, coupled with the printed 'poco a poco accelerando' involves the risk of arriving at the Allegro at a speed in excess of ♩ 120, which is Schumann's own metronome marking. This is one of the many instances in Schumann's works where his demand for tempo acceleration must be interpreted most judiciously lest the speed of the new section should become so fast as to impair a clear and intelligible articulation of the music.

opening 'spring call' is anything but a symphonic theme; rather is it
in the nature of quick-march tune. Yet despite its self-contained
epigrammatic character, its rhythmic impetus is so strong as inevitably to propel the music forward—another reminder of the Schubert's
Ninth, notably the finale.[1] Equally Schubertian is the sudden and,
owing to the impetus, unexpected entry of the lyrical second subject
(Ex. 70). Like the Viennese master, Schumann does not *modulate* to

Ex. 70

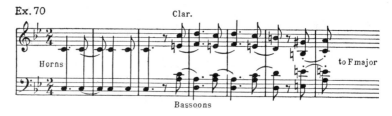

the new key, but 'bumps' into it by means of a one-note pivot
(C on the horns). The new key is A minor instead of the orthodox F
major which, however, asserts itself in the second part of the theme—
a typical instance of Schumann's characteristic predilection for what
I have called harmonic inversion. The theme itself might have come
from a Schumann song. Its square build would fit to perfection a
four-line stanza, such as the composer delighted in setting. Also the
melodic line and intimacy of expression suggest the atmosphere of
the romantic *Lied*. The impression of a parenthesis or unrelated
episode, already created by the manner of its introduction, is further
strengthened by the fact that Schumann makes no use of it in the
development. In other words, it is a *tune* rather than a second *subject*
and thus has no real symphonic significance, charming though it is.
It is quickly submerged in the bustle of the development-like codetta,
not to reappear again until the recapitulation.

The development section strikes an uneven balance between true
thematic work and mere transposition of the first-subject matter. As
this sort of mixed technique is typical of most of Schumann's
developments, it will be as well to study it here more closely, at the
risk of boring the reader with a tedious analysis. Schumann begins
promisingly enough (Ex. 71). The first two bars of the main theme
are repeated in sequence a third higher, all in the tonic key (strings).
This is answered by motive *x* in 'broken work' (flute—oboe—second

[1] According to the composer, the call on the third and fourth horns solo (bars
54–55) should be played as loudly as possible. In the first sketch this short passage
was scored for the first and second trombones.

violin—viola), plus a variant of the 'spring' motto (clarinets and bassoons); at the same time Schumann modulates to C major, in which key the previous pattern is repeated. This is immediately followed up with a new melodic idea (woodwind) of a sustained nature, a counterpoint that contrasts well with the restless sequences below (strings).

Ex. 71

Not content with that, Schumann also resorts to the contrapuntal device of a stretto (Ex. 72) between the clarinets and the upper strings (with rhythmic diminution of the new theme on the strings) while, below, the ostinato sequences of the first subject continue their bustle. After this excursion into the contrapuntal domain Schumann becomes homophonic again, and in a crescendo we reach what at first seems the climax of the development—the entry of the complete

Ex. 72

first subject in D major, forte. This is the 'classical' Schumann at his best—real thematic work, variety of keys, and texture—all concentrated and with a clear sense of direction. Yet what follows is a disappointment. On reaching the climax, the listener might well get the impression of a pseudo-reprise à la Haydn, and thus expect a short dénouement to lead to the recapitulation. If so he would not be reckoning with Schumann's formalism and awkwardness in handling sonata-form: his irritating habit of padding by unnecessary repetitions. And this is done here on a generous scale. For from bar 202 onwards, no fewer than the first 44 bars of the development are now repeated in another key (starting on F major), to which, into the bargain, is tacked the codetta of the exposition, though extended and made more significant by canonic imitations of a scale-variant of the first subject. In other words, about two-thirds of the development consists of going over the same ground, with no 'argument' of any further interest. Add the composer's faithful adherence for most of the time to the same rhythmic pattern ♩ |♩ |♩ (Tovey's 'Walrus and Carpenter' metre) plus the almost ubiquitous short-winded two-bar phrasing, and the weakness of Schumann's symphonic treatment begins to stare one in the face. Yet, oddly enough, providing Schumann's energetic tempo is maintained in performance, the strong youthful impetus of the music somehow manages to carry the listener successfully over the shallows and reefs of the composer's technique.

Turning to the recapitulation, we find that for all his formalism Schumann avoided a mere repetition of the exposition. Instead of beginning again with the first subject which had been ridden to death in the development, he opens with the 'spring' call from the slow introduction, and by scoring it for the full orchestra achieves the effect of a dramatic apotheosis of the motto.[1] The apt way in which he introduces it makes it at once the final climax of the development and beginning of the recapitulation.[2] There is also a rhythmical subtlety worth noting: though the tempo is that of the allegro, through the augmentation of the original crotchets to minims (♩= 66 now becoming ♩=60) Schumann achieves the broad majestic effect of the very opening—one of the many instances of this predilection for rhythmical experiments. Another irregular feature of the recapitulation is the parenthetical introduction in the coda of a new lyrical theme (bar 438 et seq.)—a burning, yearning song-tune whose general 'feel' recalls the atmosphere of *Frauenliebe und -leben* written

[1] Cf. the similar treatment of the same point in the youthful G minor Symphony.

[2] The integration, in the shape of an apotheosis, of the slow introduction with the main movement proper, had already been anticipated by Schubert in his First Symphony and, most remarkably, his Ninth.

a year before the symphony (Ex. 73). As another reminder of that song cycle is to come presently, we cannot go far wrong in ascribing this unexpected interpolation—which incidentally introduces a much needed relief from the prevalent dotted rhythm—to some poetic idea associated with Clara.

With the larghetto ('Evening'), a romantic mood-picture wistful

Ex. 73

and ruminating, we enter Schumann's true world. Its natural flow, its succinct form, the richness of its texture and instrumental colour make it the outstanding movement of the symphony. It takes the form of a rondo with two related episodes and a coda. The rondo theme[1] is pure lyricism and a poetic significance may be read into the fact that the cadential phrase (Ex. 74, *a*) is almost identical with the vocal phrase 'heller, heller nur empor' (Ex. 74, *b*) in the first song of

Ex. 74

the *Frauenliebe und -leben* cycle. Yet the continuous growth of the melody to twenty-four bars, avoiding metrical caesurae, is truly instrumental and in the best symphonic manner. Remarkable in this movement is the rich texture, somewhat reminiscent of that of the largo of Beethoven's Second Symphony and a good illustration of Schumann's use of the Viennese classical *obligates Akkompagnement*. Schumann went here perhaps a little too far, the writing, notably for the strings, being ornate and arabesque to an almost bewildering extent. As for the scoring, while it is not free from unnecessary doublings, there are a number of passages of marked beauty, such as the different scoring of the rondo theme on each of its three appearances, and the almost impressionistic effect (bar 41, et

[1] Joan Chissell, in her excellent *Schumann* (London, 1948), goes so far as to relate the three ascending notes of the second bar to the motto of the first movement.

seq.) produced by the combination of plucked first violins and basses, the low murmur of the second violins and violas, and the syncopated chords on the woodwind, through which maze the rondo theme winds its way on the cellos, cantabile. Yet the master-stroke comes in the last part of the coda: the three trombones, silent up to now, unexpectedly intone *pp* what seems at first a last reminiscence of the larghetto theme, but turns out to be a chorale-like anticipation of the playful scherzo. The mysterious, one is tempted to say Brucknerian, effect of this trombone passage, followed by a 'farewell' on strings and woodwind, is a high-light in Schumann's orchestral writing.

The scherzo, in Beethovenian tempo (molto vivace), follows without break. The key is D minor, but in Schumann's characteristic inversion it opens in the subdominant, in fact hoaxing us into the belief that G minor is to be the tonic key of the movement. It is a wholly delightful movement. Even without Schumann's original clue to its meaning, the playfully obstinate scherzo theme, with its wilful leaps upwards and the remonstrating cadential figure,[1] and (in the second part of the scherzo) the innocent charm of the lyrical waltz, suggest pictures such as we find portrayed in the *Kinderscenen*. The formal novelty of the scherzo lies in its having two trios, thus approximating to a rondo with two episodes. The idea may have presented itself to Schumann as a variant of Beethoven's procedure in the Fourth and Seventh Symphonies, where the second repeat of the trio is obligatory; or it may have been a romantic copying of the eighteenth-century minuet with two 'alternativos'. Moreover, a scherzo with two trios different in character well accorded with Schumann's thinking in terms of tableaux. Indeed, the scherzo of the *Spring* Symphony is at bottom a set of three character pieces, only more organic and closer in form than those we find in his various piano cycles.

Of the two trios, the first in D major is by far the better. Its charm lies in the playful bandying-about of a rhythmic figure[2] and the transparent pen-point orchestration. Attention must also be drawn

[1] Emphatic trochaic and dactylic phrase-endings (♩ ♩ |♩ ; ♩♩♩|♩) seem a characteristic feature of those Schumann themes which are of an energetic character and in fast triple-time: cf. the scherzo of the Fourth Symphony, first subject of the first movement from the *Rhenish*, Nos. 6 and 10 of *Papillons*, *Grillen* from the *Fantasiestücke*, &c., &c.

[2] Anxious lest the figure ♪ | ♩. ♪ ♪ should become indistinct on the strings, Schumann suggested playing it as though it had no slur, the whole passage 'to be extremely delicate and light' (letter to Taubert, January 1843).

to its 2/4 time, at that period unusual for a symphonic trio,[1] though here again Beethoven provided a precedent with the trios in the scherzi of the *Pastoral* and the Ninth. Trio II (in the subdominant, B flat) makes much play with a scale figure in canon, yet it is a much less original piece—a pale reflection of some Beethoven scherzo. The true Schumann returns in the coda: a mosaic of short reminiscences, with nostalgic melismata on the woodwind and a gay presto to follow in which the composer's characteristic syncopations between strings and woodwind seem to suggest a children's 'catch me if you can'. The scoring here—note, for instance, the amusing solo D on the drum near the end—is another instance to confound the over-severe critic of Schumann's orchestral technique.[2]

According to Schumann, the finale is to be thought of as 'Spring's Farewell' ('for this reason I do not wish it to be taken too frivolously'). If so, it is singularly free from any feeling of melancholy or wistfulness which the title would lead one to expect. On the contrary, its prevalent note of high spirits and exuberance might equally suggest 'Summer's Advent', or any other seasonal rejoicing. The only passage evocative of a 'Farewell' is the short cadenza before the recapitulation, with its nostalgic Wagnerian horn-arpeggios rising to a dominant ninth. The emotional key-note of the finale is struck at the very opening—an intrada in Schumann's characteristic soaring manner, which anticipates the second subject (Ex. 75, *b*). As in

Ex. 75

the first movement, the first subject is anything but symphonic, being one of those single-pattern themes which we so often find in his piano-writing—a graceful arabesque with little thematic and

[1] See also the finale of the *Papillons* in which the 'Grossvatertanz' in 3/4 is followed by a galop.

[2] With its abrupt tempo change and sudden halts, this coda proved a pitfall for Schumann's orchestra (letter to Taubert, 1843) as it still does today.

rhythmic contrast.[1] In compensation, the second subject is of complex build, and in several keys. First comes an idea whose close contrast suggests a lively dialogue between Eusebius and Florestan
(Ex. 75, *a* and *b*), *a* deriving from the finale of the *Kreisleriana*, and
b from the intrada theme. Starting in G minor, the pattern is
repeated in D minor, when suddenly the first subject breaks in to
lead to F major, the 'true' second-subject key, and to a variant of *b*.
In bar 74 we finally reach what might be called the core of the second
subject (Ex. 75, *c*), a song-like theme immediately repeated by the
full orchestra in triumphant fashion. There is certainly no lack here
of thematic, harmonic, and rhythmic contrast. In fact, the changes
occur with the swiftness of a kaleidoscope, which is another way of
saying that mere juxtaposition takes here the place of organic growth.
However, Schumann attempts to introduce some inner coherence,
as may be seen from the way in which the lyrical core of the
second subject is foreshadowed by the intrada theme. This
anticipation is as characteristic as is the harmonic inversion of the
second subject creating a Schubertian three-key exposition (first
subject in B flat major, second subject modulating from G minor to
F major).

Yet the development is, surprisingly, as concentrated and economi-
cally handled as Schumann was capable of at this stage. If in the
corresponding section of the first movement he exclusively concentrated on the first subject, here he puts only the second subject
through its paces. Of interesting details, I may mention the mysterious opening with its sudden Beethovenian shifts of harmony, the
dramatic announcement of the 'spring call' on the trombones (bars
116–17), and the swiftness of modulation through no fewer than eight
keys, the pivot-notes of the bass-line (bars 116–49) hinting at a whole-
tone scale (D flat-E flat-F-G-A-B-C sharp-E flat-F). A novel and
extremely poetic touch is the conclusion of this lively section in a
quiet nostalgic cadenza which may have suggested to Mendelssohn
the idea of letting the development culminate in the soloist's cadenza
in the first movement of his Violin Concerto (1844). The recapitulation is more or less identical with the exposition. At 'poco a
poco accelerando' we seem to be making for a second development
which introduces an inversion of the motto on the second trombone

---

[1] It closely resembles an episode in the rondo finale of the String Quartet in A,
Op. 41, No. 3, written a year after the *Spring* Symphony; it also pays homage to
Mendelssohn's String Octet, Op. 20, for its striking similarity to the second
subject of Mendelssohn's first movement cannot be mere coincidence.

and first horn (bars 302–10), but it soon assumes true coda character and concludes the movement on a note of youthful exuberance. The next fruit of Schumann's most 'symphonic' year was the Overture, Scherzo und Finale, Op. 52, written between 12 April and 8 May 1841 and dedicated to the Dutch composer and conductor Verhulst. Originally the composer intended to call it 'Suite', then Second Symphony with its present designation as sub-title, and next 'Symphonette': probably because 'the whole has a light, pleasant character. I wrote it in a most joyous mood' (letter to Hofmeister, November 1842). But he ultimately abandoned any reference to the work's symphonic character. He appears to have thought of this work in terms of its original title, 'Suite', for he told Hofmeister that 'what distinguishes it from a symphony is that the several movements could be played separately'. Also the absence of a slow movement may have been responsible for dropping the 'symphonic' appellation, though Schumann might have legitimately pointed to Beethoven's Eighth where the slow movement is replaced by an Allegretto scherzando. Yet in actual form and treatment Schumann's Op. 52 *is* a symphony. A certain degree of unity is achieved by thematic cross-reference and an overall feeling of good spirits. Yet in view of the fact that the first and last movements have a powerful, at times, heroic element in common, Schumann's 'light and pleasant character' can only apply to the Scherzo, which is the best of the three pieces.[1] Overture and Finale suffer from longueurs and the lack of significant thematic invention, though there is no lack of rhythmic life and drive in them. And for the student of Schumann's symphonic style they contain some interesting features.

The Overture (E major) is prefaced by a short, slow introduction in the minor which strikes a serious, if not tragic, note. The marked contrast within its main idea clearly points to some dramatic scene (Ex. 76): a tortuous, lamenting motive (reminiscent of the lyrical

Ex. 76

wood-wind figure from the slow introduction of the *Egmont* Overture) answered by a descending figure of heroic, Cherubinian,

---

[1] Yet, according to the 'Haushaltbuch' (entry of 29 April) this movement cost him some exertion ('Scherzo zur Ouvertüre gemacht, doch mit Anstrengung').—*Ed.*

o

character. Short though this introduction is, it has atmosphere and character; and, like that of the later overture, *Die Braut von Messina*, it is an example of Schumann's successful imitation of the classical tragico-heroic style—a style fundamentally alien to him. The ensuing allegro, however, hardly fulfils the expectation roused by its introduction. In fact, Schumann appears undecided as to what character the allegro should have.[1] In kaleidoscopic manner the moods change from the grace of the first subject[2] (Ex. 77) to the

Ex. 77

whimsicality of the second (Ex. 78), and the heroic character of some passages before the codetta and in other places. The result is a curious hybrid which fails to hold our attention for its whole length. Points of purely technical interest include the thematic use of the material of the slow introduction in various sections of the allegro;

Ex. 78

the insertion of a dramatic development between second subject and codetta which was presumably Schumann's reason for doing without a development proper in the orthodox place; and in the coda, the poetic reminiscence, in augmentation, of the first subject.

It would be worth hearing the whole work, if only for the Scherzo. For this is a wholly delightful movement, graceful in melody and rhythm, transparent in its orchestral texture, and whimsical in its modulation—music on which the fairies of Mendelssohn's *Midsummer Night's Dream* Overture appear to have cast their spell. In the character of a lively gigue, its theme is one of Schumann's characteristic rhythmical one-pattern ideas, and from it he builds up the whole movement. One would not be far wrong in looking to the

---

[1] According to Clara (Litzmann, Vol. II, p. 30) he spoke of it, when it was finished, as 'siren-like'.

[2] An offshoot from the polonaise theme of No. 5 of *Papillons*.

first movement of Beethoven's Seventh for the god-parent of this Scherzo, and a possible clue to its poetic meaning may be found in its striking rhythmic affinity with the song *Der Knabe mit dem Wunderhorn*, Op. 30, No. 1, the poem of which tells us about a youth who with his magic horn rides through the world seeking adventures wherever they may be found. As in the *Spring* Symphony, the trio is in 2/4 time, introducing a song-tune in Schumann's typical vein, charmingly scored as a dialogue between wood-wind and strings. The surprise of the coda is a pointed reminiscence (in diminution) of the first subject of the Overture.

The Finale (revised in 1845) is a movement of remarkably dynamic, powerful character.[1] It is not difficult to name the master to whom it pays unconscious homage; its relentless drive, its pronounced rhythmical character[2] and its formal spaciousness all reveal the indelible impression the Schubert of the Ninth left upon the mind of the young man to whom we owe the unearthing of that masterpiece. It is chiefly through its breathless speed ($\circ = 74$) and is rhythmical tour-de-force that this movement makes its impact. For, as in the Overture, the thematic invention lacks distinction and Schumann's padding of the development by rather aimless modulations, repetitions and transpositions, creates a feeling of tedium. Yet it would be unjust to leave it at that and not to point to some unusual and aesthetically satisfying features. One is the novelty of the first subject's exposition, which is in the form of a three-part fugato.[3] (Both Overture and Finale show a marked tendency to contrapuntal treatment.) Another is, in the second subject, the lyrical parenthesis —an impassioned Mendelssohnian passage whose intensity is

---

[1] An outward sign of this is the addition, ad lib., of the trombones which are absent from the two preceding movements.

[2] One is here reminded of the song *Aus alten Märchen* from the *Dichterliebe* which also shows a melodic resemblance to the first subject of this movement (see Ex. 79).

[3] It is perhaps worth pointing to the close resemblance between Ex. 79 and the theme of the *Préambule* from the *Carnaval*; such ascending lines are characteristic of Schumann's melodic style.

Ex. 79

effectively heightened by close imitations (Ex. 80). In passing I may also mention some structural extensions and enriching of the texture in the recapitulation. As usual it is in the coda that Schumann plays

Ex. 80

Strings

his trump card: a new, broad, chorale-like tune (Ex. 81) which provides the crowning climax to this dynamic movement. In retrospect

Ex. 81

we now see that the first subject (Ex. 79) was derived from the opening of the chorale—a subtle example of Schumann's endeavour to achieve thematic coherence.

May 1841 saw the completion of the Overture, Scherzo, and Finale, and already on 13 September, which was Clara's birthday, Schumann was able to present her with a new symphonic work. Originally styled 'Second Symphony' it received (together with Op. 52) its first performance at a Gewandhaus concert on 6 December. The reception was cool and the composer withdrew the score. However, ten years later he revised it—'completely re-orchestrated', as he wrote to Verhulst in May 1853, 'and certainly better and more effective than it was before'. This revised version, originally styled *Symphonistische Phantasie*, was subsequently published as Fourth Symphony in D minor, Op. 120. Apart from the orchestration, the revision affected the substance of the original version only in minor details; we may therefore

legitimately regard the D minor as Schumann's 'real' Second
Symphony for which reason it will now be discussed before the
chronologically later Second and Third Symphonies.

It is Schumann's most 'romantic' and eloquent symphony, and of
the four the most frequently performed. Though technically, on the
whole, inferior to the two later symphonies, it contains at once some
of his most characteristic and felicitous ideas, and holds the listener's
attention by its truly Schumannesque mixture of daemonic restlessness (first and third movements), romantic nostalgia (introduction
and Romanza), majestic sombreness (introduction to the finale),
and youthful exuberance (finale). That Schumann later thought
of naming the work 'Symphonic Fantasy' is an indication of
its true character. And of details pointing to an interplay of poetic
images there are plenty; yet contrary to his general habit of making
revealing remarks to his friends on the programme of his works, the
composer was in this case singularly reticent. The Fourth is not only
an outstanding example among the German romantic symphonies,
but for its period unique in the consistency with which Schumann
pursues his favourite idea of deriving most of the thematic material
from a few germinal ideas. Let us consider this point first.

The ideas in question are all contained in the slow introduction to
the first movement (Ex. 82): the brooding step-wise melody at the
very opening (*a*),[1] the semiquaver figure on the first violins (*b*),

Ex. 82

and above it the chord punctuation on the wind (*c*). Now looking
through the four movements we find that in the first movement, *b*
provides the first-subject matter, and *b* and *c* a new theme for the
development (bars 121 et seq.); in the Romanza, *a* occurs in the first
section, and a scale-variant of it provides the theme for the D major
middle section; in the scherzo, the main theme on the strings represents an inversion of *a* punctuated by *c* on the wind, while the trio
is built upon the above scale variant of *a*; and lastly in the finale,
the slow introduction makes use of both *b* and *c*, the latter growing
into a hymn-like tune on the brass, and in the following allegro the

[1] A similar idea opens the C major Symphony.

first subject derives from *b* and *c*. (Some minor cross-references will be mentioned later.) The technique employed here varies between mere quotation (Romanza), theme transformation (scherzo and finale) and organic growth (first movement, and introduction to finale). The Fourth thus illustrates on the largest scale Schumann's tendency to thematic homogeneity. The significance of this feature for monothematic devices of a later period has already been referred to. Yet to repeat: thematic unity does not *ipso facto* create emotional unity between the movements of a symphony. This, it would appear, results only if the 'symphonic' experience is strong and profound enough to affect the character of the music as a *whole*. For all his endeavour to create such unity by *technical* means, Schumann fails because it does not seem to lie in the primary conception of the work. Again the composer of mosaics, of musical tableaux, is very much in evidence.[1] Listening to the Fourth is like gazing at a one-man exhibition of pictures, in which the subjects seem only very generally and loosely related, each canvas having an intrinsic beauty of its own.

As for the form of the introduction, it shows Schumann's customary division into a more static section and a transition to the allegro (bars 1–22: 22–29). It is this first section that at once engages our interest. For here is pure Schumann: first a solitary call of the whole orchestra on A, forte, as if sounding the signal that we are about to enter the magic world of a fairy-tale.[2] Then starting *pp*, a continuous swelling begins, gradually surging up to a climax (bar 18), and quickly receding again. We are reminded of Schubert with whom this feature of what one might call 'tidal waves', enters the symphony for the first time (Unfinished and Ninth). It is an expression of that romantic yearning for the indefinable and ineffable, which on a much larger and more imposing scale was to become the hallmark of Bruckner's symphonies.

The ensuing allegro might well have been inscribed with Goethe's 'Meine Ruh' ist hin' (as was the second of Schumann's Intermezzi, Op. 4), for its prevalent note is daemonic restlessness. The whole movement is dominated by the first subject matter, an agitated single-pattern theme (Ex. 83, *a*), fragments of which turn up now here, now there, like will o' the wisps—an impression heightened by Schumann's frequent use of imitations and 'broken work'. There

[1] This was forcibly brought home to me at a concert where I happened to conduct Haydn's *Oxford* Symphony in G and Schumann's Fourth in the same programme: the Haydn seemed to me much more of a piece than the Schumann.

[2] This call later opens the development of the allegro.

is no lyrical second subject, the necessary contrast (as in the early classical symphonies) being purely harmonic: the modulation to F, the relative major of the tonic key (bar 51 et seq.). Thus this exposition is the most characteristic symphonic example of

Ex. 83

Schumann's monothematic construction. He apparently realized that this was a perilous thing in a symphonic movement, where, owing to the large dimensions, melodic and rhythmic monotony was bound to result. That may have been at the back of his mind when he introduced new ideas into the development section.[1] These are, first, a mysterious motive on the trombones (bars 104 et seq.) (Ex.

Ex. 84

84). (The general texture of the passage reminds one of Schubert's magic trombone passages in the exposition of the first movement of the Ninth.) Next comes a march-like theme (Ex. 85) deriving from

Ex. 85

Ex. 82, c; and finally we arrive at what we have so far been missing in the allegro, a truly lyrical theme (Ex. 86). It is as if the composer wished to compensate us for the absence of a lyrical contrast in the exposition. Note its true Schumannesque stamp: the shapely curve and song-like expansive quality of the melodic line, the square build fitting some verse stanza as a glove fits the hand, and the harmonic

---

[1] Precedents may be found in the first movements of Beethoven's Third Symphony and Violin Concerto, although the appearance there of new themes is due to other reasons.

inversion whereby the tonic (D minor) is preceded by its relative major (F), which relation continues, albeit transposed to other keys, at some of the later entries of the theme. True, the purist might well call such kaleidoscopic succession of new ideas unsymphonic. Yet Schumann's idea may have been from the first to write a 'symphonic fantasy' where formal freedom and a loose, almost improvisatory sequence of themes would not be amiss. Moreover, there is no

Ex. 86

F major ——————————————— D minor

denying the element of surprise that is created for the listener's ear by such a method, notably at the first entry of the lovely lyrical theme. Yet no reference to any intended fantasy character can justify Schumann's way of continuing this development. For what follows (bars 167–240) is merely a transposition, a minor third higher, and thus into the region of the sharp keys, of all that we have heard before. It is the same disconcerting habit that we have already encountered in the first movement of the *Spring* Symphony, and shall come across again in the subsequent works. And, as in the allegro of the B flat Symphony, the development section covers the greater part of the whole movement. This fact, combined with his obsessional use of the ubiquitous first and only subject, must have induced Schumann to omit the recapitulation completely. The fantasy-like character of the movement is thus further stressed, the development overflowing the formal boundaries and breaking straight into the coda (letter M). But before doing so, it introduces (at letter L) a variant of Ex. 82, *b* and *c*, which is to form the first subject of the finale. Similarly, the coda (in D major) already contains in the bass (8 bars after N) the theme of the coda of the finale—both passages being particularly good illustrations of Schumann's play with thematic cross-references. Another feature of the coda is the restatement of the lyrical theme in terms of a climactic apotheosis.

With the second movement, following without the formal break, we come to one of the gems of Schumann's orchestral music. What the nocturne was to Chopin, the romanza was to Schumann—a form most congenial to his particular genius. Its simple scheme A–B–A, its formal shortness, its demand for simple song-like melodies, and its traditional association with a romantically poetic content: all this made a strong appeal to a composer of Schumann's cast of mind.

Hence his markedly frequent use of that form. And the very inclusion of a romanza in a symphonic work is yet another pointer to the fantasy-character of the Fourth. It is only fifty-three bars long, an intermezzo rather than a full-grown symphonic andante: a feature repeated in the third movement of the *Rhenish*. Its provenance from the composer's short character-pieces is evident. Its simplicity and the perfect harmony between means and end are almost Mozartian. Here everything is in its right place. And what could be simpler yet more expressive than the opening oboe solo, accompanied by the guitar effect of the plucked strings? A troubadour singing to his mistress? A 'once upon a time'? We do not know and are left guessing at the poetic image behind this suggestive passage. Yet unless we assume an inner programme, the continuation with, or rather juxtaposition of, Ex. 82, *a*, from the introduction appears musically abrupt and arbitrary. As if to justify this unexpected quotation Schumann makes it an organic part of the movement by deriving from it the theme of the D major middle section (Ex. 87).

Ex. 87

I cannot leave this piece without mentioning some details of its superb scoring. The opening theme, for instance, bears every trace of having been spontaneously conceived in terms of the oboe's characteristic genius. And here for once, the octave doubling by the celli is not a miscalculation, but a subtle touch softening the reedy tone of the oboe and giving the whole passage a mellow 'brown' tinge. Of the guitar effect in the accompaniment, I have already spoken.[1] The imaginative touch of the middle section is the introduction of a violin solo, weaving tender arabesques round the tutti of the strings (Ex. 87). Note also the judicious use of the bassoons and trombones, and, at the end the impressionistic effect of the short run on the flute.

[1] The accompaniment might have gained in lightness if Schumann had not thought fit to add the clarinets and bassoons. They can easily mar the delicate pizzicato effect unless, as I have found out from practical experience, they are toned down to a pianissimo.

Equally felicitous in invention and treatment is the scherzo—restless, turbulent, with Beethovenian accents in its early part, and pastoral, waltz-like in its later course (after letter Q). Remarkable, too, is the abundance of canonical imitations: one of the many instances confirming Schumann's statement on the way in which he often conceived his themes.[1] As was already said, the theme of the scherzo (Ex. 88) represents an inverted variant of Ex. 82, *a*, (strings)

punctuated by the chordal figures of Ex. 82, *c* (wind). Similarly, the trio in B flat uses previous material, its theme (Ex. 89) being taken from the opening of the D major middle section of the Romanza—with the ornamentation of the solo violin now in the first violins,

tutti. Thus it is related to the opening (Ex. 82, *a*) of the slow introduction to the Symphony. In other words, scherzo and trio derive from the same thematic source. The trio shows an interesting and rather unusual instance of cross-phrasing in that the *rhythmic* beginning of each phrase does not coincide with the *melodic* beginning, so that the impression is created that the tune is limping behind its bass, or the bass running ahead of the tune[2]—a rhythmic trick that introduces a fascinating element of excitement into the smooth flow of the melody. It only remains to add that, like Beethoven in the Fourth and Seventh Symphonies, Schumann makes the repeat of the trio after the return of the scherzo obligatory. A most beautiful piece of writing is the gradual fading-away of the coda into the mysterious opening of the finale.[3] This is transition in the true sense of the word, continuous, smooth, and imperceptible, whereas Schumann's links by means of pauses between the preceding movements are mechanical

---

[1] See p. 179 (footnote 1).

[2] Compare also the coda of the scherzo of the *Spring* Symphony (see p. 199).

[3] Beethoven's wonderful transition in the Fifth, from the scherzo to the finale, may well have served Schumann as a model.

—a mere reduction of the interval the conductor would allow for a normal break between movements.

The introduction to the finale belongs to the most inspired pages of Schumann's orchestral writing. The mystery of its string opening, the solemn chorale of the brass, and the ecstatic fanfare of the woodwind: all seem to suggest the atmosphere of some religious ceremony. Whatever the image behind it, this music, so prophetic of Bruckner, must have been written in a flash of glowing inspiration, the *Einfall* of a true romantic genius. And, technically speaking, one does not know which to admire more, Schumann's thematic ingenuity or his orchestral imagination. The material derives, as was said, from Ex. 82, *b* and *c* in the slow introduction to the first movement. Yet that fact in itself is less important than the new use Schumann makes of his old ideas, notably the organic expansion of Ex. 82 *c* into a chorale-like melody with a climactic Phrygian cadence (Ex. 90, *a*).

Ex. 90

But is this introduction[1] really a preparation for what Schumann has to say in the following allegro? In my view, it is not. I fail to see any close emotional link between the two sections. For the allegro is in an exuberant care-free mood, storming along in Schumann's youthful, spontaneous vein, which seems to be worlds away from the mood conjured up by the introduction. The latter is a self-contained mood-picture, apparently written for its own sake and with little bearing on what is to follow it—once again an illustration of Schumann's conception in terms of contrasting, loosely connected tableaux.

The allegro is a brilliant rousing piece of music. Vital rhythmic

[1] Its formal function is to provide a modulation from B flat, the key of the preceding trio, to the dominant of D major, the tonic of the allegro.

energy and felicitous melodic invention combine to make it perhaps the most effective of Schumann's symphonic finales. There is a perfect fusion of continuous rhythmic impulse with lyrical ideas. Here is Schumann's kaleidoscope again, but the changes and surprises (notably in the development and coda) occur with such swiftness that we are given no time to reflect on whether it is all truly symphonic. As I have already pointed out, the first subject (Ex. 91) takes up a

Ex. 91

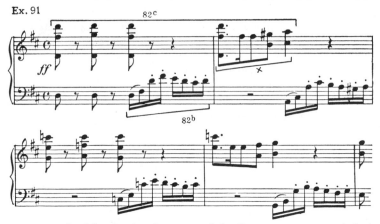

pattern evolved in the development of the first movement, and thus derives from Ex. 82, *b* and *c*. (The figure 82 *b* was added as an afterthought in the final version, evidently to make the link with the first movement closer than in the original, shown as Ex. 92. Yet, as this

Ex. 92

is the only place in the finale where *b* occurs, its use seems mechanical —a mere rubber-stamping.) The character of the first subject is that of an impetuous march and is well contrasted with the lyrical episode that follows it (Ex. 93). Note the joyous octave leaps of the melody and the urgency of the obstinate semiquaver figure in the accompaniment into which the horns break with their resounding signal.

Ex. 93

The whole passage brims over with the impatience of happy youth. Structurally, it forms the bridge to the second subject (Ex. 94),

Ex. 94

another lyrical theme of a quieter and sweeter character, with characteristic feminine endings, and figure x relating it to the first subject. Like the bridge, the codetta introduces yet another idea (Ex. 95): runs on the strings whose opening notes are punctuated by the brass in such a way as to appear to form a counter-motive.

Ex. 95

The similarity between the codetta and a passage from the development of the first movement (starting at letter K) should not be overlooked as one more link between the two movements. The development, introduced by an unusual 'swell' motive, is short and concentrated. After first making sequential use of figure x from the first subject, Schumann provides yet another melodic surprise with the sudden breaking-in of a vigorous hymn-like tune on the horns (bars 104 et seq.) (Ex. 96).

But he had surreptitiously hinted at it already at the beginning of the development as the insignificant-looking bass to figure *x* (bars 85

Ex. 96

et seq.). The horn theme is followed by a new combination of the 'swell' with the bridge theme (Ex. 93). It all passes very swiftly, and before we know where we are, Schumann has already led us into the recapitulation. It begins with the second subject, the obvious reason for the omission of the first being (as in the first movement of the *Spring*) its constant use in the development. The coda, opening with the 'swell', suggests another development; instead, Schumann introduces yet another fresh theme, or rather motive, and at 'Schneller' we have what at first appears a fresh idea which really comes from the coda of the first movement (bars 337 et seq.). Treated in invertible counterpoint, it subsequently leads to a reminiscence of Ex. 93, and a brilliant presto rounds off this exhilarating movement in which no fewer than seven different tunes have made their appearance.

A discussion of the Fourth Symphony would be incomplete without closer reference to its original version of 1841.[1] I do not propose to attempt a minute comparison between the two works—which would serve no useful purpose here—but will confine myself to such differences as are of structural importance, or give some indication of the workings of Schumann's mind. To start with, except for the link between scherzo and finale, the original version was not continuous, and the first movement had no repeat of the exposition. Nor were the thematic links within and between the first and last movements as close as they are now. For instance, the original transition from the introduction to the first movement did not contain the anticipation of the first subject. Instead of Ex. 82, *b*, the strings doubled the wind figure, Ex. 82, *c*, and then the lower strings led by way of a four-bar chromatic scale perfunctorily to the allegro. Similarly, the first subject of the finale

---

[1] It was not until 1891, half a century after it had been written, that Brahms, not without objections on Clara Schumann's part, arranged for a publication of the original version which is not included in the Breitkopf and Härtel Edition of Schumann's collected works.

did not at first contain the 'rubber stamp' of Ex. 82, *b*, and was melodically and harmonically slightly different (Ex. 92). On the other hand, in the first version the introduction hinted (in bars 4–5) at the 'sursum corda' motive with which the chorale of the finale introduction opens; and the lyrical theme (Ex. 86) in the development of the first movement was originally set against the first subject (violas, poco marcato) to give it a legitimate parent, as it were. Such thematic counterpoint was likely to detract attention from the new theme and thus impair the element of melodic surprise, which was evidently Schumann's reason for scrapping it and replacing it by arpeggios (second violins) which only hint at the original idea. Yet it was a pity that Schumann thought fit to simplify the effective contrapuntal writing of a passage from the scherzo (Ex. 97), deleting

Ex. 97

both the rousing horn-calls (before Q) and the thematic imitation on clarinets and bassoons (after Q). A clear improvement, however, is, in the present introduction to the finale, the extension of the chorale theme from eight to ten bars, the melody gaining thereby in shape and emphasis (Ex. 90, *a* and *b*). Similarly, the opening call at the very beginning of the symphony is now made to last a beat longer, which allows more time for a gradual f ⃕ pp.

Another group of alterations, concerning notation and tempo, were presumably prompted by the experience gained at the first performance. The allegro of the first movement was originally notated as shown in Ex. 83, *b*. In a fast tempo it is more practical to have longer rhythmical units, i.e. to get a longer phrase into the bar,

which may explain Schumann's subsequent change of the former
♪ to the present ♪, two bars of the original now corresponding to
one bar of the final version. (It is also more comfortable to beat.)

A similar alteration occurs in the allegro of the finale which was
originally notated in 2/4 time (see Ex. 92). As for tempo indications,
Schumann made three kinds of changes. First, he added metronome
figures to each movement. Secondly, in what was probably a con-
cession to patriotic feeling, he substituted for the original Italian
indications, German markings,[1] which on the whole demand slower
tempi than was the case in the original version. Thus the 'Andante
con moto' of the opening and the 'Andante' of the Romanza
became 'Ziemlich langsam', and the 'Allegro di molto' of the first
movement and the 'presto' of the scherzo turn to 'Lebhaft'. And
lastly, the original version contains a number of tempo indications
which Schumann subsequently dropped. They will not interest the
general reader, but may be useful to conductors.[2]

If Schumann had confined himself to the alterations mentioned,
his statement to Verhulst that the symphony was 'certainly better
and more effective than before' would have been fully justified, for
they constitute a definite improvement on the original. Unfortunately, he thought of improving the orchestration as well, chiefly
that of the first and last movements and therein blundered beyond
comprehension. The original scoring while not without blemishes
had the merit of being in comparison clearer, more economical and
better balanced. By the time Schumann undertook the revision, he
had heard and written a great deal of orchestral music, and gained
some practical experience from his work, albeit short-lived, with the
Düsseldorf Orchestra. Unless this revision was made during a period
in which his mental condition was particularly disturbed, it will
remain a mystery why with such experience he should have so spoiled
what to all intents and purposes was a reasonably good score. The
second version abounds in superfluous doublings and in clumsy
changes of the spacing and lay-out of the texture. A listener
ignorant of the facts might well get the impression that, so far as the
scoring goes, the 1841 version is the later and more mature of the two.
The publication of the 1841 version has put us into the position of

[1] Cf. Wagner's *Über das Dirigieren.*

[2] First movement, 14th bar after E: 'animato'; scherzo, 17th bar after Q: 'un
poco più lento', with 'a tempo' at the following crescendo; coda of scherzo: 'rit
sempre', instead of 'poco ritenuto'; finale, letter U, 'più vivace'; 13th bar after Y,
'poco rit', with 'a tempo' at the entry of the second subject; 4th bar after Aa,
'stringendo sin al presto', the presto starting 8 bars before Bb.

being able to make the best of both worlds: to take advantage of its better scoring and adopt it for the later version which from the point of view of shape and structure is to be preferred. This 'third' version would have the indisputable merit of authenticity and would at the same time obviate the makeshift choice between Mahler's revision or Weingartner's or, for that matter, making one's own—a temptation to which many a conductor, including the present writer, has yielded.

It would be useless here to go into details in order to show the orchestral differences of the two versions. For a profitable study of such things the reader would need both scores at his elbow. Yet to give a rough idea of Schumann's perpetrations, I have quoted two examples from the 1841 version (Ex. 98, *a* and *b*) which should be

Ex. 98ª

Allegro di molto – (1st movement, opening of *Allegro*)

P

Ex. 98ᵇ

Finale   (entry of 2nd subject)

compared with the corresponding passages in the revised work. It may be added that Schumann made no alterations in the Romanza, and in the scherzo only minor ones.[1]

Schumann's spontaneous and sudden symphonic urge that marked the year 1841 petered out in a Symphony III in C minor which, although 'pretty well finished' ('ziemlich ganz fertig') by 26 September, was never completed.[2] He now began the conquest of other

[1] Cf. p. 215.
[2] The openings of the sketches of the four movements are given by Boetticher (*Robert Schumann: Einführung in Persönlichkeit und Werk*, pp. 568 and 570). That of the scherzo identifies it—though Boetticher has failed to notice this—with the Scherzo in *Bunte Blätter* (cf. p. 67). The openings of first movement, adagio and rondo finale are shown in Ex. 99, *a, b,* and *c.—Ed.*

Ex. 99

fields (chamber music and oratorio) and it was not until the end of 1845 that he returned to symphonic composition. The first sketch of the Second Symphony in C major, Op. 61, was made between 12 and 18 December, and the work completed in the autumn of the following year, receiving its first performance under Mendelssohn at the Leipzig Gewandhaus on 5 November 1846. To explain its peculiar character and special significance, let us recall a few biographical facts. Since 1843 Schumann's mental health had shown serious symptoms of deterioration and a severe crisis occurred in 1845. Recovery from depressive suicidal moods was slow and it was in a state of both mental and physical exhaustion that the Second Symphony was begun. 'I might indeed say', he wrote to Dr. Otten, 'it was the resistance of the spirit that was here at work and helped me to combat my condition. The first movement is full of this struggle and in its character it is capricious and refractory.' And three years after its completion, he sometimes fears that 'my semi-invalid state can be divined from the music. I began to feel more myself again when I wrote the last movement and was certainly better when I finished the whole work'—a work 'so stamped with melancholy' and reminding him of 'dark days'. As we have already said, here for once, Schumann allows the work to grow from one central idea—the fear of and struggle against the spectre of madness. This profound emotional experience lends inner unity to the movements and creates the feeling of a dramatic development from the 'struggle' of the first movement to the 'victory' of the finale. In other words, it is the Schumann symphony which comes nearest to Beethoven's symphonic conception.

Though the product of an intensely subjective experience, in style and treatment it is Schumann's most classical symphony and completely free from the romantic fancies, fairy-tales and pastoral images that form the programmes of his other *Spielmusik* symphonies. Its ultimate significance is that of a symphonic confession such as characterizes the symphonies of Beethoven, Brahms, Bruckner and Mahler. In that it stands worlds apart from the rest of his symphonic output. The tragedy is that, for all the higher intellectual thoughts that went into its making, aesthetically it is a poor work. As has already been suggested, once Schumann turned from literary programmes and poetic imagery to real experience and sought his inspiration in that, his imagination lost freshness, spontaneity, and originality. Moreover, Schumann was no heroic figure; emotionally a feminine type, he must have found the subject of which he wished to treat in the Second Symphony, fundamentally uncongenial and beyond his powers. That his mental state at the time was an important factor in contributing to the pathetic failure of this work, is not to be gainsaid. Laborious, dull, often mediocre in thematic invention, plodding, and repetitive in argument, the C major Symphony has now fallen into almost complete neglect. All the same, it has a number of interesting and characteristic features to show—features pointing to greater technical maturity—and it contains in the adagio a movement that would well justify occasional performances of the whole work.

As in the previous symphonies, Schumann resorts here to the device of thematic cross-reference between the movements, and anticipation of a number of thematic ideas in the opening slow introduction—more so than in the *Spring* Symphony, but with less consistency and in a more disguised fashion than in the Fourth. Like the *Spring*, the Second Symphony contains a motto theme (Ex. 100, *a*). First announced in the slow introduction, it recurs in

Ex. 100

the allegro and finale, and is also hinted at in the brass part of the scherzo, notably its coda. In melodic shape and scoring (brass) it is prophetic of Bruckner's powerful chorale themes and presumably symbolizes what the composer described as 'the resistance of the spirit'. The clear-cut and diatonic character of this 'resistance' theme is well contrasted by a counter-theme on the strings (Ex. 100, *b*)—a drawn-out, creeping melody, tortuous and brooding, which restlessly winds its way up and down, and shows a—for Schumann—unusually continuous, seamless structure of fourteen bars. There is a certain resemblance to the opening theme of the slow introduction to the D minor Symphony, and its programmatic significance may readily be found in Schumann's reference to his 'dark days'. From it derives a subsidiary theme (Ex. 101), which in turn generates another idea

Ex. 101

(Ex. 102) of a more lively and growingly aggressive and martial character which heralds the first subject of the allegro (Ex. 103). Thus the most characteristic feature of this introduction[1] is its continuous, imperceptible growth, both thematically and in its inner

Ex.102   *espressivo*

drama. If not as marked as in the introduction to the D minor Symphony, the ebb and flow lend the music a typically romantic, Schumannesque feeling.

The first subject of the allegro (Ex. 103), derived, as we have seen,

Ex. 103

from *x* in Ex. 102, has a pronouncedly heroic character; note its dotted rhythm, and the jagged line caused by the aggressively rising intervals;[2] unfortunately, its effect is impaired by Schumann's obstinate clinging to an unvaried rhythmic pattern. Like the first subject, the bridge passage and the second subject (Ex. 104, *a* and *b*)

Ex.104

refer back to the slow introduction, the former to Ex. 101, the latter in a more general way to Ex. 100, *b*. In the second subject, with its characteristic chromaticism and its restless movement of line, the dark mood of the opening of the slow introduction is once more hinted at.[3] And the complete lack of lyrical quality does nothing to lighten it. In passing, I may point again to Schumann's device of

[1] It also shows Schumann's typical division into two sections, the second of which, marked 'un poco più vivace', represents the transition to the allegro.

[2] Schumann's reference to his symphony as 'somewhat armoured' ('etwas geharnischt') is borne out by this theme and its later development.

[3] The close resemblance of this theme to the main theme of the second movement of the Piano Concerto, which was completed shortly before Schumann began the Second Symphony, is striking. A comparison shows the profound effect of chromaticism in changing the expressive character of a melody.

harmonic inversion, the theme first appearing in E flat, and only later in the orthodox dominant, G, thus creating a three-key exposition. The codetta is thematic, using fragments from the 'dark days' theme of the introduction, and the first subject.

In the development the suggestion of an inner struggle, of warring elements, is particularly marked. Schumann throws all his forces, gathered in introduction and exposition, into the battle. There is hardly a strand in the texture that is not thematic. One is inevitably reminded of Brahms, for Schumann weaves every thematic scrap into this development, and while he cannot get away from sequences and transpositions, the seams are better covered up than in any of his previous developments. Yet what we miss is a clear sense of direction. Now this motive appears, now that, and the total effect remains (once again) mosaic-like. However one cannot dismiss the notion that this device may have been used intentionally here to suggest 'a mad flight of ideas' which would fit in with the avowed programme of the music. The trouble is that, if such was Schumann's intention, its musical suggestion is aesthetically unconvincing. The best part of the development is the transition to the recapitulation (commencing on bar 216)—an extended pedal on the dominant which leads most effectively to the dramatic entry of the recapitulation—such entries being a fairly characteristic feature of Schumann's symphonic writing.[1] As for the recapitulation, except for certain formal extensions and a more massive orchestration, with a great deal of brass reinforcement (notably by emphatic note-reiterations in triplets) it is an orthodox repeat of the exposition. The development-like coda, into which horns and trumpets thunder the 'resistance' motto, clinches the impression of conflict and defiance.

It is difficult to say exactly what prompted Schumann to reverse the traditional order of movements and, after the allegro, continue with a scherzo, as he does here and in the *Rhenish*. He may have possibly felt that the mood which inspired the first movement was so agitated that it could not readily be followed up by a slow movement. The allegro seemed to demand—as in Beethoven's Ninth—a continuation in a related emotional key. And indeed, the following scherzo with its nervous restlessness, its continuous drive and agitation is a corollary of the things said in the preceding movement. And it is perhaps no coincidence that, like Beethoven's scherzo, Schumann's continues in the key of the allegro (C major). This daemonic piece

[1] Cf. the first movement of the *Spring* Symphony, the finale of the Second, and the outside movements of the Third.

has much in common with the first movement of the Fourth Symphony, and, like it, shows monothematic construction. Thus the scherzo proper is dominated by an aggressive motive (Ex. 105) whose thrust-like opening *x* derives, significantly, from a figure frequently occurring in the tortuous string theme of the slow introduction (Ex. 100, *b*), the same figure that in a variant pervades the second subject of the first movement. And in a more disguised form

Ex. 105   *x*

x enters the texture of the two trios of the scherzo. An old acquaintance, Schumann's 'fixed idea' of the three rising notes also makes its appearance here (bars 27–28). Not only its melodic character, but the constant flux of the harmonic progressions and the resulting obfuscation of clear tonality indicate the mood that informs the scherzo proper. Its two trios are in the keys of G and C respectively. The first introduces some rhythmic and melodic contrast, but is a mediocre piece adopting a homely, playful attitude that is completely out of tune with the character of the scherzo proper. Trio II strikes a more serious note. Its lovely song-tune, imbued with gentle nostalgia is the first lyrical idea that we have so far encountered in this symphony. Its subsequent fugal treatment, with a counter-subject derived from the scherzo, figure *x*, clearly echoes Schumann's study of Bach in 1845,[1] the year in which the Second Symphony was begun. Nor must we overlook the masterly skill with which Schumann leads from the trio back to the scherzo (bar 282, et seq.)—fragments of the trio melody (woodwind) being dovetailed with figure *x* of the main movement (strings). The reappearance in the coda of the 'resistance' motto (in fragments) has already been mentioned.

The outstanding movement of the symphony is the adagio—a supremely beautiful, inspired and well-shaped piece of music. Like the Romanza from the D minor Symphony, it belongs to Schumann's most proper domain—a mood-picture in which his romantic melancholy finds poignant expression. Indicative of Schumann's maturity is the fact that the romantic urge so strong in the Romanza, here is controlled and subjected to a classical discipline: consider the shape of the themes, the form, the texture and the consistency with which Schumann sustains one mood throughout the entire movement. Here at last the battle of the allegro and the daemonic drive of the scherzo

[1] See pp. 45–6.

make room for a more inward and reflective mood. Yet the comparative tranquillity of this movement is by no means free from the
shadows and painful accents of the 'dark days'. Take its sombre key
of C minor and the lament of its main theme with its expressive wide
intervals and the appoggiaturas on falling sevenths (Ex. 106, *a*).[1]
Something of the Bach of the cantatas and the lyrical arias of the
Passions lies here. On the other hand the feeling of pathos caused by
the falling and rising intervals (bars 5–9) is not unrelated to the
sentiment which Schumann expressed at the climax of *Die alten,
bösen Lieder* from the *Dichterliebe*, where at the words 'denn solchem

Ex. 106

grossen Sarge gebührt ein grosses Grab' the voice moves in a similar
line (Ex. 106, *b*). I have already had occasion to draw attention to the
markedly continuous nature of certain themes of this symphony.
The main theme of the adagio is another instance—an originally
eight-bar phrase organically extended to nineteen bars.

Similarly, the formal treatment of the movement deserves special
attention, for it is another instance of Schumann's persistent endeavour to introduce new features into the classical scheme. While the
form of the adagio is the traditional A–B–A[1], the novelty lies in the expansion and enrichment of this basic scheme through elements from
the sonata and variation. Let us look at it more closely. Section A
extends to bar 62 (letter O), B is represented by the following twelve
bars, and A[1] reaches to bar 118 with an epilogue of reminiscences
added. What seems disproportionate in this scheme is the shortness
of the middle section B. The reason for that will be seen in a moment.
Section A itself is tripartite. First Aa (bars 1–19), containing the
main theme of the movement and modulating from C minor to its
relative major E flat. The middle section Ab (bars 20–35) has two

---

[1] Ex. 106, *a*, also shows the weaker original form of the melody.—*Ed.*

new ideas: the first (Ex. 107, *a*) marked by mysterious horn signals (note the octave leaps, echoing Schubert's famous horn passages from the Unfinished and Ninth, and the 'sursum corda' figure, bar 3, on the trumpet and upper woodwind), the second (Ex. 107, *b*)

Ex. 107

characterized by chromaticism and a restless flux of harmonies. Figure *x* clearly derives from the tortuous theme (Ex 100, *b*) of the slow introduction. This section modulates from E flat to B flat. Now if we look at A¹ (bar 74 et seq.), we find this middle section transposed to C major. In other words, Schumann treats Ab like a second subject in sonata-form, bringing it back to the tonic major in the recapitulation. We may, therefore, call the first section A the exposition with the orthodox two subjects, and A¹ the recapitulation. Yet what of Aa¹? Instead of a mere repeat of Aa, Schumann introduces what looks like a set of three short variations on the main theme, the first variation (bars 36–47) marked by canonic imitations, while the second (bars 48–55) and third (bars 56–62) are of a more decorative nature.[1] Thus we arrive on E flat at the main middle section B (bars 62–74). Having expanded A to such an extent, and introduced sufficient contrast of melody, key and texture, Schumann apparently did not feel the need for a full-fledged middle section and, instead, confined himself to a short transition to A¹. Yet he lends this section significance by treating it as a fugato, with the fugal subject derived from the horn-arpeggio of the so-called exposition (bars 21–22) and so giving it the appearance of a development.[2] This is followed by a shortened repeat of A in the manner of a sonata-form recapitulation with, as I have said, the second theme in the tonic major. Such uncommon fusion of different elements leaves no doubt as to the degree of constructive ingenuity and imagination of which the 'symphonic'

[1] In the 'yearning appoggiaturas' of oboe and clarinet in bars 57–59, Schumann seems to have reached the idiom of *Tristan* at the period of *Tannhäuser.—Ed.*

[2] The short fugato in the allegretto of Beethoven's Seventh Symphony—Schumann's possible model—fulfils the same function.

Schumann was at times capable. It is matched by the richness of the texture; the enlivening of its subsidiary strands by thematic part-writing, which can stand comparison with the best classical examples. As for the scoring, its delicate, chamber-music effect and the varied, at times concertante, treatment of the woodwind again confirm the puzzling fact that slow movements were apt to kindle Schumann's orchestral imagination.[1]

Schumann's statement that while composing the finale he began to feel more himself is fully borne out by the general character of the movement. Its impetuous vigour seems to testify to the composer's recovery of his good spirits, not to mention the note of joyful relief and even victory that mark its latter part. The parallel with Beethoven's Fifth, to which we have already alluded, is also to be seen in a formal detail: like Beethoven with his scherzo reminiscence in the last movement, so Schumann, by using part of the main theme of the Adagio for the second subject of the finale, seems to wish to remind us of the spectre that haunted him in his 'dark days'. For the rest, the movement owes more to Schubert than Beethoven. Glancing through it, one is struck by its dynamic, powerful character, and as, with the finale of Schubert's Ninth, it gives the impression of being propelled by an irresistible force that carries the music along in a headlong rush. With its six-hundred odd bars, it is the largest of Schumann's symphonic finales. Yet Schumann lacked the Viennese master's breadth and sweep of ideas, nor have the thematic ideas sufficient distinction to justify such length. There is a great deal of movement without real progress. Yet to dismiss this finale out-of-hand would be unjust, for despite its weaknesses it does constitute the dénouement of the drama of the Second Symphony—a 'victory over dark powers', and is thus a psychologically true conclusion of the whole work. In addition, it has some novel formal features worth considering.

The very opening is significant in this respect.[2] The four-bar intrada is not a mere flourish, but anticipates in the ascending minim

---

[1] See, for instance, the bassoon solo (bars 9–15)—'the melancholy bassoon' as the composer described it, the writing for which caused him 'particular pleasure'.

[2] The sketch shows an attempt at a connecting passage from adagio to finale (Ex. 108).—*Ed.*

Ex. 108

figure a theme which does not occur until the coda. (As the reader will remember, the same thing happens in the finale of the *Overture, Scherzo, and Finale.*) Another cross-reference has already been mentioned—the derivation of the second subject (Ex. 109) from the main

Ex. 109

theme of the preceding adagio (Ex. 106), while its crotchet continuation seems to point to the 'dark days' theme of the slow introduction (Ex. 100, *b*). The adagio also provides the arpeggio motive (woodwind and horns, bars 46–63) for the bridge between the first and second subjects. In passing, we may note the considerable length of the first subject, its harmonic inversion and its Schubertian march-rhythm tediously reiterated throughout this theme (Ex. 110).[1] A

Ex. 110

noteworthy formal feature is the omission of the development from its orthodox place between exposition and recapitulation. What Schumann does, is to telescope development and reprise into one section (beginning at bar 105), indulging at the same time his favourite device of mosaic structure in which the motto of the first movement makes several entries. The restlessness of the melodic and harmonic changes, and the broken, fragmentary nature of the texture, suggest a temporary return to the mood that informed the development of the first movement. Similarly, the conclusion of this development-cum-recapitulation on the key of C minor must be interpreted in that sense.

Yet if the finale was to signify, as the composer implied, the ultimate triumph of 'the resistance of the spirit' over dark forces, it could not end on such a sombre and unhappy note. Hence the addition of a considerable coda—it forms nearly half of the whole movement—in which the composer is seen labouring to work the music up to a victorious ending. He first makes a false start, as it were. The first half of the coda, separated from the second half by a silent bar (bar 393) does not quite succeed in bringing about a sufficiently strong change of mood. So Schumann begins again and

---

[1] Its start echoes the opening of Mendelssohn's *Italian* Symphony.

it is not until shortly before the entry of the 'resistance' motto (bar 481) that an optimistic mood begins to assert itself and leads the movement to its triumphant conclusion. Like most of Schumann's codas, this, too, is not without one or two surprises in the shape of a new idea and programmatic cross-references. The new idea here is a song-tune already previously hinted at in the main body of the movement (Ex. 111, *a*). We remember similar things in the codas of

Ex. 111

(quoted from a later entry)   Nimm sie hin denn, die se Lie-der

the other symphonies, when we suspected some programmatic intention behind this device. Here suspicion becomes certainty, for the tune contains in its opening a pointed reference to the song *Nimm sie hin denn, diese Lieder* from Beethoven's cycle *An die ferne Geliebte*[1] (Ex. 111, *b*), already quoted in the first movement of the piano *Fantasie*, Op. 17.[2] But why the allusion here? In the last song of the Beethoven cycle the lover offers his music to the 'distant beloved' as a token of his devotion and hopes for reunion with her. The allusion to Clara in the *Fantasie* is unmistakable. Did Schumann, now in the finale of his Symphony, perhaps intend a similar message to her? He may have felt separated, this time not by geographical distance and Wieck's interference, but a sense of spiritual separation: a separation which he may have thought to exist between his wife and himself, caused by his mental state when writing the Symphony. The added significance which Schumann attached to this new tune may also be seen from the fact that, contrary to his usual practice, he no longer treats it as a mere lyrical episode or reserves it for a final apotheosis,[3] but makes it the subject of an extended coda-development. That disturbing thoughts from the past still haunted Schumann's mind in the finale, is further evidenced by the unexpected re-appearance of one of the 'dark days' themes from the slow introduction (Ex. 101) at bar 453 et seq. (woodwind), and this impression is enhanced by the dramatic intrusion of the 'resistance' motto (brass) and the conflict of cross-rhythms (3/2 against 2/2).

[1] An allusion to this Beethoven song also occurs in the andante of Mendelssohn's *Hymn of Praise*.

[2] See footnote on p. 45.

[3] Cf. the coda of the first movement of the *Spring* Symphony, the last movement of the Fourth, and Finale of the *Overture, Scherzo and Finale*.

If, with the exception of the adagio, the Second Symphony shows a deterioration in the overall quality of its thematic invention and thus, perhaps, indicates a decline of Schumann's creative powers, no such thought suggests itself in considering his last Symphony in E flat, Op. 97. Completed at Düsseldorf on 9 December 1850, it was first performed there under the composer's baton on 6 February of the following year. During the gap of four years which separates it from the C major, the composer's mental health showed signs, albeit deceptive ones, of a definite improvement. Moreover, the change of environment, the healthy and happy atmosphere of the Rhineland coupled with the contentment caused by his Düsseldorf appointment (September 1850) must have combined to make the Third Symphony what it is: a work brimming over with robustness and joy of life. It is as if the very genius of the Rhenish country and its people had been caught up in it, and had helped the composer to assert once more a youthful optimism. True, in its melodic invention, it no longer has the spontaneous freshness and distinction of the First and Fourth Symphonies, but it excels them in craftsmanship, and, in the first and last movements, in its powerful grandiose conception. In fact, the first movement, in its key, time-signature, certain formal and thematic details, and its general feeling, has some kinship with the opening allegro of the *Eroica*. As for the so-called 'Cathedral' movement, it stands unique in the history of the nineteenth-century symphony. Thus, the *Rhenish* marks technically and emotionally an advance in the composer's symphonic style—a style which, judging from the last movement of the *Overture, Scherzo, and Finale* and the Second Symphony, tended more and more to the heroic grand manner. Whether this was the result of an attitude adopted only in later years or a trait inherent in Schumann's musical personality from the beginning, is difficult to decide. The Schumann we like to think of is certainly the one who wrote the *Spring* Symphony and the first version of the D minor, yet we cannot withhold our admiration from the man who wrote the Second and the *Rhenish* and thus showed that he could discipline himself in a style that seemed fundamentally uncongenial to his genius.

Another question is whether the *Rhenish* forms an emotional whole to the same extent as the Second Symphony. The first and last movements certainly belong to the same sphere, though the finale shows a certain tailing-off in significant invention and technical treatment. What unites them is a powerful open-air feeling that at times reaches elemental grandeur. At a pinch we can still relate the rusticity of the scherzo and the mysterious nature-mood of the trio to the idea that inspired the two outer movements. Yet it is difficult to see how the two inner movements fit into such company. The A flat movement is a pretty, gently nostalgic piece in Schumann's domestic vein. Nor does the solemn ecclesiastical majesty of the fourth movement stand in any emotional relation to the rumbustiousness of the finale. It is no intrinsic *introduction* to the finale, as has often been suggested. In other words, the two inner movements are in the nature of tableaux loosely inserted. This has, of course, no bearing on their purely musical merits. In fact the 'Cathedral' movement surpasses in its suggestive power the rest of the Symphony. Yet, as in the *Pastoral*, Schumann's model for the *Rhenish*, we have to remind ourselves of the programmatic background of the work in order to perceive its unity. Without this crutch, the *Rhenish* is a five-movement symphonic suite rather than a symphony.

As if the composer could no longer contain his pent-up energies, he discards the slow introduction for the first time in his symphonies and plunges into the first subject, a theme remarkable for its vigour and length (Ex. 112, *a*).[1] But for its exemplary structure it might have come from the pen of the young man who wrote *Carnaval* and the

Ex. 112

Davidsbündlertänze. Youthful exuberance radiates from the soaring wide intervals and the lilt of its waltz rhythm, to which an irresistible swing is imparted by Schumann's characteristic syncopation. Out of this theme grows the first-subject matter extending to ninety bars (up to letter B). It is Schumann's longest, yet most organic symphonic subject. The phrases grow out of one another in a continuous unforced manner, without a trace of the usual cobbling. Though of a piece, this (for Schumann) enormous first subject shows three sections A–B–A¹, the middle section (bars 21–56) introducing an aggressive Beethovenian figure[2] (Ex. 112, *b*) to be used as the

---

[1] Its echo may still be heard in the first movement of Brahms's Third Symphony.

[2] Cf. *Eroica*, first movement, bars 60–64.

main propelling agent of the movement. In tune with the remarkable
continuity of this section, is the smoothly gliding transition (via four
anticipatory bars) to the main theme of the second subject (Ex. 113).
Like the first, it has an A–B–A¹ structure and declares its descent

Ex. 113

from the first-subject matter by the drooping fourths and the
brusqueness of its middle section. Yet its predominant character is
lyrical—a gently flowing line imbued with true Schumannesque
yearning, a 'Valse sentimentale' after the sturdy 'Walzer' of the first
subject. Characteristic also is Schumann's change from the bright
'loud' E flat tonality to the mellow 'quiet' G minor in which unorthodox key the second subject as a whole is cast.[1] With the extended
codetta firmly establishing the orthodox dominant, we get a large-
scale example of a romantic three-key exposition.

In the development we find similar continuity and organic growth.
There is no haphazard flight of ideas, but a clear plan devoid of padding and tedious repetitions. The impression of the composer's being
at a loss how to go on, so disconcerting in his previous developments,
is here almost completely absent. (Why 'almost' will be seen in a
moment.) Schumann had obviously reflected how best to order the
sequence of development patterns. For there are four different
sections, smoothly run into one another. The first reaches from the
double-bar to letter H,[2] and in the main deals with both the 'aggressive' figure of the first subject (Ex. 112, b) and the lyrical second subject now enriched by imitations. Next comes the section (letter H
to K) which works exclusively on the first subject. It is here that the
only flaw occurs, for Schumann relapsing into his old habit repeats
a whole passage (H to I) a fourth lower (I to K).[3] The third section
(K to L) refers to both first and second subjects, and is followed by
a remarkable transition to the recapitulation: resting for a long
stretch on the dominant pedal, it intrigues the ear with deceptive
anticipations of what is to come most dramatically at letter N—the
entry *fff* of the first subject with the four horns thundering out its

[1] The middle section reverts for a moment to the orthodox key of the dominant
(B flat).
[2] There is no repeat of the exposition, the transition to the development being
effected by an abrupt Beethovenian shift from B flat to G.
[3] Cf. developments of the first movements of the First and Fourth Symphonies.

opening figure in unison. A magnificent climax this—growing from within and welding the end of the development with the beginning of the recapitulation.[1] This is, incidentally, one of the passages where Mahler greatly improved on Schumann's rather inept scoring. A comparison of Ex. 114 with the original shows the gain in clarity which Mahler achieved with a few deft strokes: (1) the thematic line (first violins, violas, 'cellos and basses) becomes more prominent and is given a sharper definition by the augmentation of Schumann's fussy semiquavers and the reinforcement on the second violins; (2) the texture is considerably lightened by the elimination of the trumpets and timpani, which are reserved for an effective entry on the climax at letter N, by the introduction of rests in the horn parts, and by the reduction of doublings in the middle parts.

In the recapitulation Schumann shortens the first subject by cutting out its middle section (Ex. 112, *b*) yet retains harmonic dualism

Ex. 114

[1] A subtle harmonic detail here is Schumann's avoidance of the expected dominant-tonic progression. Shortly before N, he shifts from the dominant pedal via C minor to the German sixth on E flat which the ear is at first inclined to interpret as the dominant harmony of E major (Ex. 114). Thus the resolution on to the six-four chord on B flat comes as a harmonic surprise. Altogether the passage is admirable for its harmonic fluidity.

Q

by casting the second subject in C minor. The coda with its
prominent brass writing reaffirms the powerful dynamic element of
the movement.[1]

As in the Second Symphony, the allegro is followed by a scherzo
(C major), though a scherzo only in name. For its heavy, leisurely
gait (Sehr mässig) in three beats to the bar with tenuto punctuations
on the second and third beats (brass and upper strings), and the
common-chord arpeggio of its theme proclaim it a true Teutonic
cousin of the Austrian 'Ländler'. 'Morning on the Rhine' was its,
subsequently suppressed, title, and if the scherzo suggests a rustic
scene, the mysterious remote feeling that pervades the trio (A minor)
may have had something to do with impressions evoked by the
atmosphere of medieval Rhenish castles. The interesting formal
feature of this movement is its extension through elements from
sonata-form, an experiment already made by Beethoven and, more
especially, Mendelssohn.[2] Schumann introduces a development with
material from both scherzo and trio as though the latter took the

---

[1] It is strange, in view of its general character, that Schumann should have
abstained from using the trombones in this movement. They are not introduced
until the fourth and fifth movements.

[2] Cf. the scherzo of Beethoven's Ninth Symphony and Mendelssohn's Octet,
Scottish Symphony, and *Midsummer Night's Dream* music.

place of a second subject. He also extends the scherzo proper by the addition of what has the deceptive look of a variation,[1] and finally, there is a true coda with Schumann's favourite surprise in the form of a new melodic idea. Of attractive details in the trio may be mentioned the protracted pedal on the unusual mediant note (C in A minor) on which the whole of the trio rests, partly contributing to its mysterious effect. Further, the enlivening of its texture by the mercurial figure from the scherzo extension, and the morendo at the very end. Lastly, there is some lovely four-part horn-writing in the trio, cheek by jowl with some of Schumann's most insensitive scoring (e.g. in the scherzo extension, the woodwind doublings which completely obliterate the effect of the light airy string staccato).

The first of the two slow movements (A flat) is an intermezzo in no way related to what has come before and what is to come after. Schumann turns here to the homely world of the *Kinderscenen*. It is a pleasant piece and in its shortness (54 bars) another example of the intimate symphonic miniature such as we find in the Romanza of the Fourth Symphony, but with themes more classically cut and a richer texture reminiscent of the C minor andante from the Second Symphony. Its form is A–B–A, A consisting of three ideas, while B (bars 18/34) is treated in Schumann's development-by-transposition manner. The whole movement is an excellent study in the composer's art of mosaic, the short themes being made to fit one another like so many pieces of a jig-saw puzzle. There is some felicitous woodwind writing, especially for clarinets and bassoons, yet, as so often, also clumsy doublings and reinforcements, tending to thicken and coarsen the colour of the strings.

The fourth and most outstanding movement of the work originally bore the inscription 'In the manner of an accompaniment to a solemn ceremony', the ceremony being the elevation to the Cardinalate of Archbishop Geissel of Cologne on 30 September 1850, at which the composer was present. It is Schumann's greatest suggestive mood-picture. A listener ignorant of its programme could not help associating the music with some profound religious experience. Indeed, its awe-inspiring Gothic effect, its hierarchic grandeur and, toward the end, its ecstasy—all bear witness to the spell the solemn occasion must have exercised upon the composer's impressionable mind. Whether, in view of certain works by Mozart and Beethoven, one would agree with Tovey who declares it 'one of the finest

[1] Its sedulous semiquaver motive is used again in the third movement of the Violin Sonata in A minor, Op. 105.

examples of ecclesiastical polyphony since Bach' is doubtful.[1] Yet there is no denying that for Schumann such sustained polyphonic writing is most remarkable, perhaps the ripest flower of his intense study of Bach. The technique employed is that of free, yet close imitation in four parts. Certain features such as the polyphonic writing for the brass[2] and the slow rhythmic pulse (3/2 and 4/2) are reminiscent of seventeenth-century church music. But the scoring in general, the harmonies, the E flat minor tonality, and the surge of the music—similar to the 'tidal waves' of the slow introductions in the Fourth (finale) and Second Symphonies—are clearly romantic. The tortuous outline of the main theme (Ex. 115) reminds one of

Ex. 115

those symbolic 'Crucifixus' themes of Bach and the older polyphonists. A variant of its opening, in diminution (*x*), tacked on in the sixth bar, is subsequently used as the main counterpoint to the theme. Though the music is continuous, generating its own form, three sections may be discerned, each with its own time-signature (4/4, 3/2, 4/2), and a coda. Among interesting features we may mention the rhythmic variations of the theme and the deceptive effect of a tempo acceleration produced by the fact that from the 3/2 time onwards the counterpoint figure *x* moves at double the previous speed ($\int$ = previous $\int$) while the theme, due to its augmentation, seems to continue at its original slow rate.[3] The entry of the coda is marked by a sudden change from E flat minor to B major and from polyphony to simple homophony; the ecstatic outburst into a fanfare-like arpeggio on the combined wind recalls the jubilation at the end of the slow introduction to the finale of the Fourth Symphony.

To turn from this movement to the finale is like stepping from the sombre atmosphere of a medieval cathedral into the sunshine and bustle of life outside. It was probably some such reaction that drew

[1] *Essays in Musical Analysis*, Vol. II.

[2] Note the significant addition of the trombones.

[3] Cf. the same effect at the entry, in augmentation, of the motto in the recapitulation of the first movement of the *Spring* Symphony.

forth from Schumann's pen a movement of such lively and joyful character. Yet neither in thematic invention nor in treatment can it quite compare with the rest of the symphony. One is here reminded of Schubert's weak finales, and like Schubert, Schumann manages to hold óur interest by his impetus and vigorous drive rather than by distinction of ideas and structure. As in the first movement, the dimensions are large. The first subject comprises forty-seven bars and consists of a kaleidoscopic arrangement of three ideas (Ex. 116),

Ex. 116

a reminding one of the song *Aus alten Märchen* from the *Dichterliebe*, and *c* referring back to Ex. 115, *x*, in the previous movement. The general character is that of an energetic quick-march in Schumann's favourite dactyls. It is difficult to speak of a second subject proper, since the whole exposition, including the codetta, is built from the opening theme—though there is a hint at one in the brass fanfare, Ex. 117. The development is strictly thematic, perhaps too self-consciously so. There is no 'inner' development, such as Schumann

Ex. 117

achieved in the first movement—more an assembling of patterns than organic growth of ideas. At letter D a new theme is introduced which clearly derives from the fanfare, Ex. 117, and marks the beginning of the transition to the recapitulation. Its dramatic crescendo to the climax of the first subject's entry[1] is similar to that in the corresponding section of the first movement. After the recapitulation, with a shortened first subject, the coda provides the real climax of the whole movement. It is as if Schumann meant to

---

[1] It is here that the trombones enter for the first time in this movement.

pass some of his powerful themes in a last quick review: first a new combination of first subject and the fanfare, then (letter L) an emphatic reference to the 'Cathedral' theme, soon followed by an allusion to the first subject of the first movement (bars 287, et seq.) which culminates at 'Schneller' in the fanfare from the development section. A potpourri coda rather than a symphonic conclusion, it is none the less effective in its elemental drive and feeling of grandeur.

Schumann's turn, after his symphonic swan-song, to the programmatic concert overture seems to have been largely due to his preoccupation in the immediately preceding years with opera and incidental music. In fact his first concert overture *Die Braut von Messina*, Op. 100 (1850), written immediately after the E flat Symphony, owes its origin to Richard Pohl who had been responsible for the connecting text in *Manfred*, and had now sent him an opera libretto based on Schiller's play. Schumann, however, was continually wavering between acceptance and refusal of 'this interesting subject'. In the event he refused, arguing that 'such well-known subjects are always risky. Ah! If Schiller hadn't written that play, I would have jumped at it', as he wrote to Pohl[1] (19 January 1851). Already, two or three weeks earlier, after several readings of the play itself, he had summed up his impressions in an overture: 'short and more of the theatre than a concert-overture, clear and simple in invention'. It is, however, not so very short nor does the theatrical element obtrude. In fact, of the four independent overtures, it is the most suitable for the concert hall. It shows concentration, has clearcut themes and the symphonic treatment is of as high an order as Schumann was able to attain. In short, style and technique make it Schumann's most 'classical' overture. That it was an adopted style, does not seem to have affected the quality. I have already[2] mentioned Schumann's gift of successfully assimilating the grand heroic manner of Beethoven and Cherubini. In *Die Braut von Messina* this gift is turned to best account. For Schumann manages to impregnate the music with a, for him, rare sense of sustained, tense drama and tragic conflict. (The very choice of C minor—an obvious allusion to the 'heroic' Beethoven—is significant.) And he achieves this by avoiding a description of particular incidents of the play, concentrating upon its general atmosphere and the characterization of its

---

[1] Seeing that he had tackled Byron and Goethe, Schumann's respect for Schiller seems puzzling; the real reason was fairly obviously his feeling that Pohl's libretto was unworthy of Schiller.

[2] See p. 202.

protagonists. Schiller modelled his tragedy on the ancient Greek
drama—an inexorable curse imposed by the gods upon Messina's
ruling dynasty and resulting in incest, patricide and suicide. Thus
the *agens* of the play is the curse, and with a dramatic insight un-
suspected in a composer of his type, Schumann fastens upon the
Schillerian curse and symbolizes it in a leitmotive that in one form
or another pervades the whole overture.[1] It opens the slow introduction most dramatically (Ex. 118): a figure brutal, threatening, and

Ex. 118

strangely un-Schumannesque. It might have readily fitted into the
realistic style of some late ninteenth-century opera.

In the allegro (Sehr lebhaft) Schumann appears to have aimed at
a portrayal of the main dramatis personae: the two ideas constituting
the first subject (Ex. 119, *a* and *b*)[2] presumably stand for the two

Ex. 119

[1] Cf. the use of leitmotives in *Genoveva* (see p. 278).

[2] The sketch shows a different form of the main theme, in the usual careless
notation (if Boetticher is to be trusted) (Ex. 120) and tried out fugally in the
margin. Traces of this earlier form remain in the development, soon after the
passage quoted as Ex. 121.—*Ed.*

Ex. 120

Ex.121

Violas col Fag. I

hostile brothers, while Beatrice the Bride seems to be suggested by the expressive sweep of the second subject scored for Schumann's favourite clarinet and bassoon (Ex. 119, *c*). In the short development, attention may be drawn to the contrapuntal combination of four different thematic ideas (Ex. 121) and the excellent transition to the recapitulation by means of the 'curse'. motive.[1] The agitated coda concludes in C minor, thus symbolizing the tragic end of Schiller's drama. Why Schumann's public remained unimpressed by so dramatic a piece is difficult to account for, unless it preferred the more romantic style of his *Genoveva* and *Manfred* overtures, works less accomplished in craftsmanship than *Die Braut von Messina*, but certainly truer Schumann.

[1] The transition is much feebler in the sketch (see Ex. 122), which also shows a much more laboured version of the 'Im Tempo' leading to the final 'Più mosso' (Ex. 123).—*Ed.*

Ex. 122

Ex. 123

With the rest of his concert overtures we may be brief. None reaches the quality of *Die Braut von Messina*. They sadly illustrate the composer's gradual decline to dull mediocrity and perfunctory writing, though occasional flashes of his former genius are not absent. In *Julius Caesar*, Op. 128 (1851), an overture to the Shakespeare play, the inspired classicism of the previous work deteriorates to rather shallow academicism. In the key of the *Egmont* Overture, it opens with a first subject—there is no introduction—that looks promising enough in its suggestion of majesty and heroic grandeur (Ex. 124).[1]

Ex. 124

Yet with the second subject which is not much more than an insignificant arabesque, the music begins to sag and though the development is strictly thematic (as always in Schumann's later style) one cannot help feeling that he is losing his grip and sense of direction, and the grandiose apotheosis of the coda is but a momentary attempt to impart some afflatus to a work that is rightly forgotten.

On a relatively higher level stands *Hermann und Dorothea* (1851), dedicated to 'his dear Clara' and posthumously published as Op. 136. Goethe's verse-idyll had long figured in Schumann's plans as a subject for a concert-oratorio—no doubt on account of its homely quiet atmosphere and the intimate charm of its love-story. Nothing came of it, nor of the suggestion subsequently made by Moritz Horn, the librettist of *Der Rose Pilgerfahrt*, to adapt Goethe's poem as a *Singspiel*. Yet as with Schiller's play, these plans proved not altogether abortive, in the event resulting in an overture 'written with much pleasure in a few hours'. A feature of the work is the programmatic use of the Marseillaise—the fourth time Schumann had resorted to the French tune.[2] Its presence here is explained by the fact that, as we learn from a footnote to the score, the first scene of the *Singspiel* was to have shown the departure of soldiers of the

---

[1] According to Boetticher (*Robert Schumann: Einführung in Persönlichkeit und Werk*, p. 550), it originated *in the major*, but otherwise in its present form, as the end of the song *Jung Volkers Lied*, Op. 125, No. 4, composed a week or two earlier. —*Ed.*

[2] The other works being the *Faschingsschwank aus Wien, Die beiden Grenadiere*, and the March, Op. 76, No. 4.

French Republic.[1] It must be supposed that the *Singspiel* contained certain sad and dramatic incidents absent from Goethe's idyll, for there is an atmosphere of wistfulness and also of conflict in the overture. Its key is B minor and the opening idea (Ex. 125) of the first subject—of which the second part is formed by the

Ex. 125

Marseillaise—has something in common with the sombre winding theme of the slow introduction to the Fourth Symphony. Note also the dark colour of the scoring. It is possible that the opening verses of the Goethe poem suggested this mood. For Goethe makes Hermann's father speak of the 'sad procession of poor refugees' and 'the misery of decent people fleeing' from their country.[2] The trouble with the work as a whole is that Schumann could apparently not make up his mind whether to follow a tragic or idyllic course, and for all its good craftsmanship—such as the skilful weaving-in of the Marseillaise—and the general facility of its writing, the music lacks physiognomy.

There is more character in the *Festouvertüre mit Gesang über das Rheinweinlied, Bekränzt mit Laub*, Op. 123, written to celebrate the Lower Rhine Festival at Düsseldorf in the spring of 1853. Here Schumann successfully hits off the note of hilarious conviviality and popular rejoicing, though the material itself has little distinction. Yet the work has an interesting formal feature combining, as it does, an instrumental overture (in sonata-form) with a choral coda. The melody of the 'Rheinwein' song is anticipated in a somewhat Handelian slow introduction and snatches of it recur in the subsequent allegro. After an orthodox recapitulation,[3] a tenor solo leads, in much the same way as the baritone solo in the Ninth Symphony, to the choral section (mixed chorus) which introduces the rousing

[1] Gerald Abraham ('On a Dull Overture by Schumann', *Monthly Musical Record*, December 1946) puts forward the interesting suggestion that the work was really Schumann's 'democratic' reaction to the coup d'état of 2 December 1851, by which Louis Napoleon overthrew the Second Republic.

[2] Yet the original tempo-marking was 'lebhaft' ('lively') which would have given the theme a flavour of defiance rather than of sadness.—*Ed.*

[3] The connecting words are by Wolfgang Müller.

drinking song 'Bekränzt mit Laub'.[1] Its effect is cumulative, thanks to Schumann's triple repetition in *f–p–ff*.

It is perhaps idle to speculate on the course Schumann's career as a symphonic composer might have taken, had his life not been so tragically cut short. All the same one cannot help wondering whether symphonic writing would have been a feature of his later years. The facts of his actual career seem to speak against it. With Schumann each genre of composition had its peak period when he produced in spates, after which his interest appeared to turn to another field. Thus symphonic composition was concentrated into the short space of roughly one year—1841—during which he wrote three symphonies if we include the *Overture, Scherzo and Finale*. And, significantly, he produced his best in the *Spring* and D minor Symphonies. The two other symphonies were composed in the ensuing ten years, at intervals of four and six years. With another composer no special significance might attach to that, but with Schumann it seems to argue that after 1841 symphonic writing became a more or less casual activity. Moreover, the lengthening of the interval between the writing of his last two symphonies would suggest an increasing lack of interest in this form. It may be that the composing of concert overtures was a kind of substitute, though a meagre one, for full-fledged symphonies. Yet it would appear that in his late period Schumann's real interest tended to works for voice (or voices) and orchestra, a medium in which he could now combine his inborn disposition for vocal writing with the experience and knowledge gained from his orchestral writing. For all we know, another symphony or two might have come from his pen if his life had been prolonged. Yet it seems to me more likely that Schumann's *Rhenish* would have been his symphonic swan-song even if Providence had decreed for him a normal span of life.

[1] Perhaps an old favourite of Schumann's; at the age of thirteen he had played Ries's variations on the melody at a concert at the Zwickau Lyceum.—*Ed.*

CHAPTER VI

THE WORKS FOR SOLO INSTRUMENT AND ORCHESTRA

By MAURICE LINDSAY

MOST of Schumann's works for solo instrument and orchestra were written during that feverish burst of creative activity which preceded the end of his active life. The Pianoforte Concerto does not belong to the main group, for it was composed during the height of his powers, and contains some of his most imaginative and powerful writing. Apart from youthful essays which have not survived,[1] his only other works in this category are the *Introduction and Allegro appassionato* for pianoforte and orchestra, Violoncello Concerto, the Violin Concerto, a *Concert Allegro* for pianoforte and orchestra, the *Fantasie* for violin and orchestra, and the *Concertstück* for four horns and orchestra.

Of these later works, only the first two are fit to rank with the best of Schumann's earlier music. The Violoncello Concerto used to be neglected because, like so much of Schumann's string writing, it is ungrateful to play and only in comparatively recent years have the advances made in the technique of stringed-instrument playing rendered this objection invalid. The *Fantasie* for violin and the later *Concert Allegro* for pianoforte are rarely heard outside Germany, yet although they are not Schumann at his most poetic, they undoubtedly deserve an occasional hearing. The Violin Concerto is in a peculiar position, as I shall show in due course. The Press publicity bestowed upon it in advance of the first public performance in 1938, gave rise to ridiculous expectations. When these were disappointed, the Concerto sank from sight again under an equally undeserved weight of outright condemnation. The *Concertstück* for four horns, described by Tovey as 'an impossible piece', is rarely heard for the obvious reason that it is not often possible to produce four solo horn players. The neglect of the *Introduction and Allegro appassionato* is less easy to understand, for it is full of fresh poetic touches, and worthy of a higher rôle than that of a 'trying-out' piece for advanced students in those musical institutions fortunate enough to be able to run efficient concerto classes.

[1] See list of works, p. 309.

However much its sister works may languish unplayed, the Pianoforte Concerto suffers from the reverse complaint. It has grown steadily in popularity since those early days when Clara Schumann had to present her husband's music in small doses because of its supposed difficulty and relative unpopularity. Now, it shares with the Grieg Concerto and the Tchaikovsky B flat minor the doubtful honour of being one of the three most over-played works of its kind. The trouble with an over-played work is not so much that it cannot stand up to repeated hearings (in this respect Schumann wears infinitely better than Grieg) as that it becomes a vehicle for every pianist who can struggle through its technical difficulties to overlay with his or her personal (and usually idiotic) idiosyncrasies. It is a sign of its greatness that none of the countless bad or mediocre performances of Schumann's Piano Concerto which we hear, can prevent its deeply-felt poetical romanticism moving us when it is really well played.

In one respect at least, Schumann's works for solo instrument and orchestra are amongst his most satisfactory productions for relatively large forces. They do not suffer to the same extent from those defects of orchestration which affect, in varying degrees, his four symphonies. In the concertos and concert pieces, he is mainly concerned with the question of balancing the utterances of his solo instrument with the full body of orchestral tone, or with component parts of that tone. Because of this, he usually evades the problem of satisfactorily contrasting woodwind and strings so that the weaker instruments' individuality should not be gruffly trodden upon. No doubt because of his intense feeling for the pianoforte, an instrument which stands out against almost any early nineteenth-century combination of orchestral sound, the three works for solo piano and orchestra are the most striking in this respect. In the Violoncello Concerto the orchestra has necessarily to play a subdued part and remain rather quiet in colour because of the low register of the solo instrument. By the time Schumann came to his last major work, the Violin Concerto, his grip had begun to slacken, and there are moments when the orchestra merely plods along, dragging heavy footsteps after each other. Nevertheless, although he still uses the woodwind relatively sparingly, this Concerto offers more instances of their appearance, unfettered by heavy string duplication than do most of the purely orchestral works. There are, in fact, moments in the Violin and Violoncello Concertos which suggest very strongly that Schumann's feeling for horns and woodwind was becoming more acute, possibly as a result of his practical, though rather unhappy, intimate contacts with the orchestra at Düsseldorf. The Concerto for pianoforte and orchestra, Op. 54, dedicated to Ferdinand Hiller and first performed by Clara Schumann in 1846, is undoubtedly the finest of Schumann's works in the medium. From the first opening crash of the orchestra, to the last sustained chord, its fabric is well-knit, its lyricism has breadth and dignity, and it shows Schumann completely the master of a difficult large-scale form. It abounds in poetic ideas of a high imaginative order, yet it makes use of most of the technical pianistic developments which were considered advanced in Schumann's day. The first movement was composed in 1841, and existed by itself as a fantasia for pianoforte and orchestra for four years. This sporadic method of composition was quite characteristic of Schumann in his earlier days, and whatever its disadvantages might be in theory, in practice his instinct usually led him to strengthen and broaden his first design when he eventually expanded it. His instinct was certainly not wrong either in his G minor Piano Sonata, another major work whose movements were separated by a number of years, or in this Concerto. Schumann could rarely contain himself within the classical sonata-form, nor even within the much loosened forms of the later Beethoven. As if to show quite clearly that it intends to assert itself in a very unclassical way, after the opening orchestral chord, the piano utters a bold, defiant introduction before it gives place to the orchestral statement of the first subject (bars 4–11). This restless, yearning little tune, square-cut in the favourite Schumann manner, is given out by the woodwind, and here at once is an example of an effective orchestral touch, for it contrasts plaintively with the solo instrument's restatement of the theme immediately afterwards. A transitional theme (bars 119–21) containing the germ phrase for much of the later development leads to the second subject, derived very clearly from the first. The movement evolves within a large-scale loose sonata form,[1] although the orchestra contents itself with sharp outbursts of assertion, and does not attempt at any time a ritornello in which all the themes are stated. The development begins at bar 152, where the key suddenly changes to A flat, the tempo from common time to six four, and solo instrument and orchestra bandy about in tenderly affectionate fashion a variant of the first subject. This sort of interruption with a sudden, tender phrase was one of the happiest

[1] Perfectly comprehensible if one considers the key-scheme and disregards the virtual identity of the themes of first and second 'subjects'.—*Ed.*

of Schumann's touches. Sometimes, as Dr. Carner has shown in the previous chapter, he does it with a completely new theme which rises out of the memory of all that has gone before, as in the closing bars of the first movement of the *Spring* Symphony (No. 1 in B flat); sometimes, as in this work, a subtle transformation is wrought in the material which has been under discussion. This period of repose is shattered by the excited insistence of the piano as it argues with the orchestra over its opening introductory assertion. This, in turn, gives place to some impassioned dialogue based on the first subject. The more or less orthodox recapitulation culminates in a passage marked 'cadenza', which is really rather a written-out improvisation entirely lacking the element of display; indeed its pace is just twice as slow as the rest of the movement. A final allegro molto in 2/4 time is based on a fresh transformation of the initial main theme.

As a work on its own, the first movement would no doubt have been well enough able to stand on its feet, for it is rich in thematic material, and imaginative in the use to which the material is put. Yet in its final place against the movements which follow, it gains in perspective to an astonishing degree. The Intermezzo is in Schumann's most lovable and gentle manner. A sustained, aspiring, manly sort of tune (bars 29–44), which moves around the key of C major contrasts with the questioning playfulness of the first theme (bars 1–87), and leads back to it. By way of a coda, orchestra and piano toss its rhythm carefully to and fro until clarinets and bassoons suddenly recollect the first few notes of the first subject of the previous movement. The piano answers them with a passage of diminished sevenths resolved in A major; they repeat the suggestion in the minor and the piano tumbles down its diminished sevenths again, this time resolving them in the minor too. The third time the winds are joined by the oboes, asserting A major, and the piano rushes up the A major scale, and swings away into the finale, allegro vivace. This is surely one of the loveliest links in all concerto literature.

The finale abounds in delicious themes, excited and exciting. The first subject jumps gaily around in Schumann's most energetic manner. The second is unusual because of its curious cross-rhythm. This is countered with flowing quavers on the piano which, in bar after bar of restless arpeggiated movement, varies its counter-measure to the second subject. The development opens with a new bold striding theme (bar 391), which is developed at some length. The recapitulation, when it does come (bar 497), is lengthy, full, and varied, and as if to show us that there is quite a lot which is new under the sun, the piano suddenly runs away with another pregnant theme at the beginning of the coda (bar 771), made longer because of the development this latest arrival is subjected to.

One of the outstanding points about this great Concerto is that with all his rich profusion of highly original thematic material, Schumann at the height of his powers lets little of it go past without making it yield a great deal. This is in strong contrast to his Violin Concerto which falls down not so much because of its poorer themes, but in this matter of development. The masterly use to which Schumann turns his material, both here and in other major works, surely gives the lie to Wagner's cynical under-estimation of Schumann's considerable power of handling extended forms.

Schumann's next essay for solo instrument and orchestra was the *Introduction and Allegro appassionato* for pianoforte and orchestra. It was composed in the spring of 1849, while he and Clara were sheltering at Kreischa from the political disturbances in Dresden. This *Concertstück*, as he called it, is an attractive work in Schumann's most inspired vein, overflowing with original themes and personal imaginative touches. Yet from its unlucky first performance in Leipzig in 1850 when it was coldly received—Clara Schumann was not at the top of her form, it seems, and played badly—it has been over-shadowed by its greater brother, the Concerto. The piano gives out its first theme in G major over an arpeggiated background, and it is commented upon by the orchestra and developed until the tutti restatement, which ends the introduction, leads into the link with the following Allegro appassionato. There is a slightly Mendels-sohnian flavour about this theme (Ex. 126), perhaps explained by the

Ex. 126

fact that Schumann had been grief-stricken on hearing the news of his friend's death earlier in the year; the same may be said of the angry march-like subject in E minor which orchestra and solo instrument announce between them; but the treatment they receive is entirely Schumannesque. A brief excursion into C major lets the piano announce a tender theme which leads back to E minor and a new, strong subject, the first few notes of which are rhythmically based on a phrase from the theme of the Introduction, and play an

R

important part in the development of the material later on. Out of this grows yet another theme, this time on the dominant of C. The second group contains four new themes, and the inventive manner in which these are woven into the texture during the unfolding of the development, over which fragments of the theme from the Introduction hover amongst the wind instruments as if to give still further cohesion to this well-knit piece of writing, is masterly. When the recapitulation comes, the most important theme of the second-subject group reappears not in E, as might have been expected, but in G, the key of the Introduction, thus giving a further feeling of formal unity. The coda occupies itself mainly with a new theme running along in quaver triplets, a rhythm which plays so large a part in this work and is in fact one of the most characteristic ingredients of the Schumann idiom. This work might well provide a second item for pianists when they are appearing with an orchestra; it would be a welcome change from the inevitable Chopin group. It deserves every bit as much attention as is at present given to the more favoured Concerto.

The same can be said, with rather less force, of the *Concert Allegro with Introduction*, Op. 134, for pianoforte and orchestra. This was one of the batch of works composed with great rapidity by Schumann during the middle of 1853. On 18 September, Clara's birthday, the score, together with those of other newly completed works, was laid upon the new piano which was a present from her husband. Clara wrote in her diary: 'Perhaps it sounds presumptuous to say so, but is it not true that I am the happiest woman on earth?' The work seems to have been dedicated in the first place to Clara herself; the arrival of the young Brahms from Hamburg on 30 September, arousing the warmest enthusiasm in both the Schumanns, was no doubt responsible for the dedication as it now stands, to the younger composer. After a short, dramatic introduction in D minor, during which the piano gives out in slow triple time a theme that appears again in changed guise in the main section of the piece, orchestra and solo instrument gather energy for the plunge in a characteristic sort of 'Shall we?' 'Yes, let's' dialogue passage, hovering around the dominant, with a gradual hastening of the tempo. The first subject (Ex. 127) is a loud, indirect assertion of

Ex. 127

the home key (D minor) and there is no mistaking the energy of the music right from the start. It leads into another theme (Ex. 128) in which the solo instrument strengthens the general assertiveness, and

Ex. 128

then into a transition tutti, no less aggressive. The figure which first appeared in the short introduction reappears here and leads rather unexpectedly into the second subject in the relative major (Ex. 129). This subject plays a considerable part in the development, which follows after another march-like outburst by the orchestra.

Ex. 129

When the recapitulation comes, the figure from the introduction leads us this time into D major for the second subject, and for the cadenza and coda which follow. In the coda, the piano breaks into a headlong gallop, and the work ends with a vigorous flourish of energy. In the *Concert Allegro*, much of the subtlety of development which characterizes the two earlier works for pianoforte and orchestra is lacking. The thematic material is less generously supplied and is less exciting. A sort of static feeling creeps into many of Schumann's themes during the last months of his creative life. It is, indeed, almost as if many of them were manufactured automatically from habit. The second subject (Ex. 129) is a case in point; its slight similarity to the haunting, tragic second subject of the first movement of the Violin Concerto (Ex. 133) may be noted in passing. Even so, the *Concert Allegro* by no means deserves the total neglect which has overtaken it. Technically, the pianoforte part is less difficult than is usual with Schumann's writing.

In order to consider the three works for pianoforte and orchestra together, I have passed over the *Concertstück* for four horns and orchestra. It dates from the spring of 1849, the year of the Dresden riots and of the *Introduction and Allegro appassionato* for pianoforte and orchestra. To his usual orchestra Schumann adds a piccolo and three trombones. It is an extended work, in three movements which are played without a break. The first movement, in F major and marked 'lebhaft', opens with two brisk chords from the full orchestra, and a fanfare-like phrase on the four solo horns (two valve instruments, two natural), containing a triplet rhythm of which considerable play is made throughout (Ex. 130). The orchestra hints at the

Ex. 130

4 Horns in F

first subject which, however, is actually given out by the horns. The movement is in loose sonata form, although there is no great amount of development, possibly because of the limitations imposed by the nature of the solo instruments. A great deal of the thematic material, in which the work is rich enough, is handled by the horns, and only discoursed upon in the orchestral tuttis. The Romance is a short movement based on two song-like themes, the second of which appears over a running bass sustained by the 'cellos, and is one of Schumann's loveliest melodies (Ex. 131). A restatement of this first theme leads to the finale, marked 'sehr lebhaft', in D minor. The second subject is merely a modification of the first. A characteristic Schumann rhythm ♫♩♫ | ♪♫ gives this movement its sense of determined drive. It abounds in good episodic themes, and quite a lot of contrast is drawn between the peculiar tone-quality of the horns and the large orchestra. Schumann uses his solo instruments in a most un-hornlike way, by all previous standards, but none the less effectively. Two things weigh against this *Concertstück*: the difficulty of the horn parts and the ineptness of the scoring. Anyone who takes delight in telling us that Schumann could not handle a large orchestra will find ample evidence to support his contention here, though not in the other concertos or concert-pieces. The scoring is thick, the woodwind entries being almost always overlaid with a heavy covering of string tone.

The Violoncello Concerto, Op. 129, was composed in 1850, soon after the Schumanns had moved to Düsseldorf. No doubt contact with an orchestra which contained some fine instrumentalists opened Schumann's mind to the possibilities of writing concertos for stringed instruments. At any rate, in this fine, terse work, he showed himself keenly aware of the violoncello's qualities and limitations

and the scoring, which could so easily have become gruff and over-
whelmed the low-pitched solo instrument, is extremely imaginative
and skilful. The work is in three interlinked movements played without a break. There is no vain show of virtuosic passage-work of any

Ex. 131 (Violin and Viola parts omitted)

4 Horns in F

Cellos I
Cellos II

pizz.

pizz.

sort, and after three opening chords from the orchestra, the 'cello
enters with the first subject proper, in A minor, a broad flowing
theme of great dignity and nobility. The orchestra does not comment
upon this theme, but enters with a new, excited theme of its own,
still in the tonic. The second group is ushered in with a tender little
figure on the solo instrument, a figure which plays an important part

in the development. The development itself is concerned very largely with a triplet figure derived from the comment by the solo instrument on one of the themes in the second group. During the course of the development, the first theme suddenly makes its reappearance on the solo instrument in F sharp minor, a touch of heightened colour which is most effective. This gives way to a further outburst of the triplet figure, gravitating back to the home tonic and a normal recapitulation. The brisk tutti coda, in which the triplet figure again asserts itself, is suddenly interrupted when the solo instrument enters with four recitative-like bars which change the key to F major and the tempo to 'langsam'. A long, sustained song-like melody of great beauty makes up the slow movement. There is an exquisite moment when the 'cello breaks into a passage of double-stopping; the effect is as pulse-quickening as the entry of the sudden new 'striving' themes in so many of the earlier works. The wood-wind bring this lovely reverie to an end by alluding to the first subject of the first movement, and the solo instrument breaks into troubled recitative, leading to the extremely hale and hearty finale—'Browningesque', as Tovey called it. This method of transition was, as we have seen, a favourite one with Schumann. The feeling of spiritual unity which it tends to give plays no little part in creating the illusion of a more integrated structural unity than does, in fact, exist.

The finale is the least successful movement of the Concerto from the point of view of the soloist for great play is made with the lower reaches of the instrument. Much emphasis is laid on the contrast in mood between the bluff first subject and the tender, pleading second subject. The cadenza, which is lightly accompanied by the orchestra, is considered unsatisfactory by some soloists, and one by Jacobi is sometimes substituted. This must necessarily violate Schumann's text to some extent, and the desire of the virtuoso to show himself and his instrument to more dazzling advantage cannot be admitted to be valid in the case of an accompanied cadenza such as this (if at any time). Tovey felt unhappy about Schumann's cadenza—and also about Jacobi's; he confessed to a hankering to write one himself, but never did. The greatest 'cellists of our day have had no difficulty in making this whole work, cadenza and all, seem extraordinarily fine and effective.

The *Fantasie* for violin with orchestra, Op. 131, composed in 1853 for Joseph Joachim, is a short, compact work. Its serene, almost classical feeling must have made it very congenial to Joachim who, according to Clara Schumann, interpretated it 'magnificently' at the first public performance. In none of Schumann's works for solo instrument and orchestra does the orchestra ever present or gather up the thematic material in the tutti sections, as in classical concertos or those of Brahms. Nowhere is the orchestra so subordinated to the solo instrument, however, as in this *Fantasie*. In the short introduction, the orchestra gives out a rather wandering theme which reappears in the development of the main movement. The violin enters with a dramatic arabesque, and indulges in florid passage-work while the orchestra leads round to the first subject as the pace quickens. This is announced by the solo violin, in A minor, as is the key-hovering second subject. The orchestra bursts out with a march-like theme to herald the development, which is short and much less ingenious than the parallel sections of Schumann at the height of his powers. The recapitulation brings with it no surprises. While there is undoubtedly an awkwardness about the solo part which must have made the work seem ungrateful when it appeared (although it is child's play to the modern virtuoso), enough is made of the violin's natural resources to suggest that Joachim perhaps had a hand in revising it, as he had the solo part of the Violin Concerto. As with the *Concert Allegro*, Op. 134, the thematic material is less plentifully dispensed, and there is an absence of that spontaneity which so delights in the earlier works.

Last of all, we come to the Violin Concerto, of which the manuscript is dated 21 September to 3 October 1853. It is the most ambitious of a group of works turned out at an amazing rate during the fateful autumn of that year. In a letter to his friend Strackerjan, dated 28 October 1853, Schumann gives the list of his recently composed works as '. . . an Overture to *Faust*, . . . the final stone to a large group of scenes from *Faust*; a *Concert Allegro* for piano and orchestra; three *Sonatas for the Young*; a cycle of four-hand dances for piano called *Kinderball*; Concerto for violin and orchestra; a *Fantasie* for same. . . .' It is hardly surprising that most of them bore signs of having been written in considerable haste, and but cursorily revised. Indications of Schumann's approaching breakdown, leading to the Rhine tragedy, became apparent during the last two months of the year. The Violin Concerto is thus his last major work. In the entry in her diary for 7 October, Clara Schumann notes that her husband 'has completed a highly interesting Violin Concerto . . . he has played parts of it to me. I should not dare to pass a final opinion of the work until I have

heard it once again'. It has several times been suggested that the
work was never really completed, but in his diary entry of 1 October,
the composer himself records that the 'concerto for violin is finished'
and on 3 October that the Concerto was 'completely orchestrated'.
Had Schumann retained his health, there would no doubt have been
further revision. A copy of the score was sent to Joachim with a
note dated 13 October asking him to return it 'as quickly as possible,
so that the band parts may be copied'. Joachim hailed the work
enthusiastically. It was not until after Schumann's death that either
Joachim or Clara Schumann appears to have been dissatisfied with it.
On 27 November 1857, Clara Schumann wrote to Joachim asking
him if he would consider rewriting the last movement. The month
before, Joachim had complained to her that in the last movement,
there were some 'dreadful passages for the violin'. Almost certainly
about this time, Joachim ran through the work at a Gewandhaus
rehearsal in Leipzig, and Clara Schumann was present, for in March
1858 she reminds him by letter: 'Be careful: don't forget how
unwillingly the musicians played Robert's Concerto.'

Nothing more was heard of the work until Joachim's biographer,
Moser, enquired about it by letter in 1898. On 5 August Joachim
replied, explaining that the work was never published because 'it is
not equal in rank with so many of his [Schumann's] glorious creations'. Thereafter he supplies a commentary on the merits and
shortcomings of the work, a commentary singularly penetrating and
corresponding more or less with the views of the more responsible
critics when the work was at last performed in 1938. Schumann's
daughter, Eugenie, supplied the final links in the history of this work
in an article translated by herself into English printed in *The Times*
on 15 January 1938. (It had originally appeared in a Swiss periodical.)
She wrote, 'never shall I forget the moment in our home at Frank-
furt-on-Main when my mother came in to see us and said, with deep
but suppressed emotion visible on her face, I have just settled with
Joachim and Johannes [Brahms] that the Concerto is not to be
published, not now or at any other time. We are quite agreed on the
subject'. Joachim left the manuscript to his son, Johannes, who sold
it to the Prussian State Library in Berlin. In 1937 it was edited by
Georg Schünemann and published by Schott and Sons, and although
Eugenie Schumann sought to prevent its performance, she found that
she could at best delay the event until after her death and contented
herself with the dignified protest from which I have quoted.

There are enough happy touches in the Concerto to justify its retaining an occasional place in the violinist's concerto repertoire, now that it is available. The 'dreadful passages' have been smoothed out, presumably by the editor. Schumann himself made several alterations, but in some cases replaced a passage impossible to play by one only just physically possible but still hopelessly ineffective. Schumann comes nearer the classical concerto exposition in this concerto than in any of the others, for both the first and second subjects are stated by the orchestra before the violin makes its entry.

The first movement begins with a strong, dramatic theme (Ex. 132)[1] full of urgent passion. But Schumann's bent was always for

Ex. 132

the lyrical rather than the dramatic, and he rarely worked his really dramatic themes such as this through anything like their fullest implications. Before very long, it gives way to the second subject in F major (Ex. 133), which for six bars hovers over its dominant before the new tonic is established harmonically. A brief repetition of the

Ex. 133

first subject ends the exposition, and the solo instrument takes up the material, weaving on to it figurations which sometimes sound a little forced. It is in the passages of double-stopped figuration that Schumann seems to have perpetrated most of his technical errors in violin-writing. The development does not make use of material which to the Schumann of earlier days would have been full of possibilities. A slackening of grip gradually becomes apparent, and it is only partly compensated for by the violin's sudden rich outburst

[1] Related to other D minor opening themes, before and after—Wagner's *Faust Overture*, Bruckner's *Third Symphony*—all perhaps descended from Beethoven's Ninth.—*Ed.*

with the second subject on the G string. Brass and woodwind play a more prominent and individual part in this work than in many more closely-knit earlier masterpieces, mainly in the matter of echoing comment. The recapitulation is normal, the cadenza brief, as in the Violoncello Concerto (a reflection, perhaps, of Schumann's increasing dislike of display) and the coda contains a charming little phrase which, in the days of the Piano Concerto, would have been bandied about happily.

The second movement opens with a figure on the 'cellos, oddly akin to the twelfth of Elgar's *Enigma* Variations. There is a curious affinity of spirit between the second subject of the first movement (Ex. 133) and the main theme of this movement (Ex. 134), sung by

Ex.134 *ausdrucksvoll*

the solo instrument. It is the theme which haunted Schumann's mind,[1] and which he imagined that spirits had dictated to him during the early days of his collapse in February 1854. It is a lovely melody, at times interwoven with the first 'cello tune, and brought through a beautiful modulatory sequence as the movement draws towards the 'alla polacca' finale (not, by the way, so marked on the score). The first subject of the finale and a later phrase which plays a prominent part in the movement are both reminiscent of the haunting second subject of the first movement. The home key is D major. Much play is made with an impudent little woodwind phrase which appears and reappears almost too often. With this loosely constructed movement containing almost nothing in the way of development other than stretches of rather static orchestral comment upon the matter the solo instrument has expounded, the work comes to a strainedly cheerful end.

In his concertos and other works for solo instrument and orchestra, Schumann solved none of the architectural problems set by Beethoven and resolved by Brahms. Schumann was content to employ a looser relationship between solo instrument and orchestra than the classics had done, and formal considerations were in any case never greatly his concern. But he has left at least two major works in this category—the Piano and the 'Cello Concertos—at least

---

[1] On its appearances elsewhere in his work, see p. 71.

one smaller masterpiece of the same rank, the *Introduction and Allegro appassionato,* and four other works, three of which are well worth an occasional performance. His two major concertos repudiate the sneers of those who tell us that he could not write on a large scale. At his best, he stands where he wished to place himself—at the side of Schubert; in his Piano and 'Cello concertos he is certainly at his best.

CHAPTER VII

THE DRAMATIC MUSIC

By GERALD ABRAHAM

IT seems at first sight rather heavily ironical to devote a chapter to Schumann's music for the theatre; it consists of an opera that has never held the stage more than precariously, incidental music to a play that the author never intended for the stage, and a collection of settings from a play which Schumann himself regarded primarily as a species of oratorio. Yet these three works—*Genoveva*, the *Manfred* music, and the *Scenen aus Goethes 'Faust'*—contain some of Schumann's finest music and *Genoveva* has the peculiar interest of rivalling the Wagner of the same period, the Wagner of *Lohengrin*, in the use of the device specially associated with the younger man: the 'characteristic themes', derived from the older device of thematic reminiscence, which were soon to develop into the symphonic leitmotive. The three works also form a natural group—apart from the literary relationship of Byron's poem to Goethe's. But for a few numbers of *Faust* (Part III, Nos. 1, 2, and 3 and perhaps a first attempt at No. 7, written in 1844, and the overture, added in 1853), they were all written during the period 1847–50: *Genoveva* and two versions of the final chorus of *Faust* during 1847–8, the *Manfred* music and Part III, Nos. 4, 5, and 6, of *Faust* in 1848, Part I of *Faust*, with No. 4 of Part II, in 1849, and the rest of *Faust* (Part II, Nos. 5 and 6[1]), in 1850. Collectively, then, they represent the best part of Schumann's last creative period and provide an excellent field for the study of his last-period style, a style that puzzled his contemporaries —to many of whom it seemed ultra-modern—and has gone on puzzling critics who expect a composer to develop in a straight line or 'logically'. The later, in some respects more classical, Schumann is admittedly less attractive than the early lyrical Schumann; his work sometimes lacks the warm, exuberant vitality of that written by his younger self; but there is no evidence of any real decline in his powers, no reason to attribute the change of style to the shadow of

[1] Parts I and II of the *Scenen aus 'Faust'* are numbered consecutively in the score, Part III is numbered separately, and the overture is excluded from the numbering.

approaching insanity. (If we wish to look for marks of mental instability in Schumann's music, we shall find them equally in his earliest work.) The somewhat crabbed themes, and consequently crabbed harmonies, that are among the characteristics of late Schumann must be attributed not to oncoming insanity but to the eminently sane influence of Johann Sebastian Bach.

Just as the kernel of Schumann's early style is measured lyrical melody based on the four-line stanza of poetry, the kernel of his later style is the fugue-theme. Schumann worked at fugue intermittently almost throughout his creative career, from 1830 onward; one of his note-books of about 1836–8 is entirely devoted to what he calls 'Fugengeschichten'; he even began to compile a *Lehrbuch der Fugenkomposition* based on Marpurg and Cherubini;[1] and during the 1840's these studies were intensified. Their obvious fruits, such as the six organ Fugues on BACH, Op. 60, and the piano Fugues, Op. 72, are known to all,[2] but it is their less obvious fruits that are most important. Boetticher, as a result of exhaustive study of the sketches, was able to assert[3] that 'a great number of his themes and motives [of the mature period] originated in failed essays in fugue'. A typical instance is the second subject of the *Manfred* overture (Ex. 135), which sprang from a fugue-subject (Ex. 136) that

Ex.135 ($\unicode{x2669}$ = 144)

Ex.136

Schumann actually embodied complete, in a slightly altered form and non-fugally, in the development section of the overture. It is easy to see how the first three notes with their diminished fifth drop, always a perfect fourth in the overture, generated by the characteristic devices of fugue—inversion and so on—the whole of Ex. 135, which

[1] Schumann's more independent contributions to this projected text-book, with a thematic catalogue of nearly seventy of Schumann's unpublished fugues from the 'Fugengeschichten' and other note-books, are printed as appendices to Boetticher's *Robert Schumann : Einführung in Persönlichkeit und Werk.*

[2] Cf. pp. 72–7.

[3] Op. cit., p. 572. All references to Schumann's sketches in this chapter are based on Boetticher's work.

might well be a strand in a fugal texture (cf. the fourth Fugue on
BACH). And one can see how in the overture it also generated, for
instance, a typical romantic-chivalrous continuation in the manner
of Weber (at the beginning of the F sharp minor passage marked 'Mit
grosser Kraft'); the sketches also show (cf. Ex. 137) that a passage

Ex. 137

70 bars earlier, which one would have hesitated to connect with this,
is in fact its earlier form: likewise a continuation of Ex. 135, *a*. Even
the very unusual key of the overture—E flat minor—relates it to
another magnificently gloomy orchestral piece written under the
shadow of Bach, the 'Cologne Cathedral' movement of the E flat
Symphony of two years later. But it is worth noting how easily these
angular baroque figures fit into the romantic idiom of the 1840's.
Not only can Ex. 135, *a*, run without any incongruity into a Weberian
pendant; Ex. 135, *b*, which evidently characterizes the brooding
Manfred, is not at all unlike the theme with which Wagner a few
years earlier had characterized the brooding of Manfred's literary
prototype in *Eine Faust Ouvertüre*.

It was undoubtedly the character of Manfred himself that fascinated Schumann; Wasielewski was almost certainly right in supposing
that Schumann, like other Romantics of the period, secretly regarded
himself as a counterpart of Byron's hero. He had read the poem in
youth. One of his earlier diaries, the so-called *Hottentottiana*, records
on 26 March 1829: '*Manfred von Byron—schrecklich!*' The impression was not weakened in later years for Wasielewski has recorded
the curious incident at Düsseldorf, that is, in 1850 or later,
of his emotional collapse while reading the poem. 'I have never
before devoted myself to a composition with such love and such
exertion of my powers as to *Manfred*', he said in conversation. A
subject that has been so long, perhaps unconsciously, maturing in
a man's mind is likely to be exceptionally fine when it at last takes
artistic shape; it is not surprising that the *Manfred* overture turned
out a masterpiece: a superb orchestral character-study. It is no
flawless masterpiece. It begins with one of Schumann's most celebrated miscalculations: three syncopated chords before any regular
beat has been established. (The intention is perfectly clear to the
eye; it is never fulfilled to the ear.) Much of the texture and figuration is evidently pianistic in origin; the scoring is often thick, with

Schumann's familiar unnecessary doublings. But the thick texture matters less in such an intentionally gloomy piece and there are even some fine strokes in the scoring, such as the *pp* and *ppp* trumpet chords in the coda. The device, borrowed from Berlioz, of basing the first subject of the allegro—'In passionate tempo', as Schumann marks it—on the material of the slow introduction has never been more effectively employed than here.

It must be confessed that the remainder of the *Manfred* music equals the overture in neither power nor profundity. It consists of fifteen numbers which Schumann intended to be used for a stage-performance of the play in an adaptation by himself of the translation by 'Posgaru' (Karl Adolf Suckow);[1]

Act I:

    1—Song of the Spirits: 'Mortal to thy bidding bowed' (alto), 'In the blue depth of the waters' (soprano), 'Where the roots of the Andes' (bass), a couplet telescoping the speeches of Byron's Sixth and Seventh Spirits (tenor), 'Earth, ocean, air' (quartet).

    2—Melodrama accompanying Manfred's 'O God! if it be thus'.

    3—The Incantation ('When the moon is on the wane') (four basses).

    4—Cor anglais solo accompanying Manfred's 'Hark! the note' and so on, and his dialogue with the Chamois Hunter.

Act II:

    5—Entracte.

    6—Adjuration to the Witch of the Alps. Melodrama accompanying 'I will call her. . . . Beautiful Spirit! with thy hair of light', &c.

    7—Hymn of the Spirits of Arimanes: 'Hail to our Master!' (chorus).

    8—Four-bar chorus, 'Prostrate thyself, and thy condemned clay'.

    9—Two bars of choral outcry, 'Crush the worm! Tear him in pieces!'; E flat minor chord on Arimanes' 'Yea'.

    10—Melodrama accompanying the summoning of Astarte: 'Shadow! or Spirit!'

    11—Melodrama accompanying Manfred's address to the shade of Astarte: 'Hear me, hear me.'

Act III:

    12—Melodrama accompanying Manfred's 'There is a calm upon me'.

    13—Melodrama accompanying Manfred's farewell to the sun: 'Glorious Orb!'

[1] *Byrons Manfred. Einleitung, Übersetzung u. Anmerkungen von Posgaru*, Breslau, 1839. Schumann altered very little, despite the statement in his letter to Härtel of 21 April 1853; he reduced the number of spirits in the first scene from seven to four, made cuts and transposed a few scenes.

14—Melodrama accompanying the scene with the Abbot and the Demon, beginning with the Abbot's 'Nothing'.

15—Chorus behind the scenes, 'Requiem aeternam', accompanying the final dialogue between Manfred and the Abbot ('Alas! how pale thou art').

It will be noticed that melodrama predominates. Schumann must himself have been satisfied with his essays in this not very satisfactory form for he returned to it in 1849 with a setting of Hebbel's *Schön Hedwig* and in 1852 with settings of the same poet's *Ballade vom Haideknaben*[1] and Shelley's *The Fugitives*, all three with piano,[2] though in none of these piano melodramas does he repeat the experiment in the last three numbers of *Manfred* of actual notating some or all of the speech-rhythm. *Schön Hedwig*, at the words 'Ein zartes Mägdlein tritt heran und füllt ihm den Pokal', brings an almost note-for-note quotation of the opening of No. 11 of the *Manfred* music, while No. 3 in turn begins with a striking reminiscence of the theme of the *Études symphoniques*.

There is a certain amount of thematic relationship between the several parts of *Manfred*. Ex. 135, *b*, from the overture is quoted twice: when Astarte's shade vanishes and when Manfred dies; possibly Schumann associated it with the idea of Manfred's remorse. The Hymn of the Spirits of Arimanes is played crescendo and fortissimo by the orchestra on Manfred's exit at the end of Act II (end of No. 11). One little motive that recurs several times (two bars before the end of the overture, end of No. 5, beginning of No. 6, beginning of No. 9, beginning of No. 10) seems to have no particular dramatic significance and is perhaps nothing more than a temporary and unconscious melodic obsession, though it certainly helps—like the tendency to gravitate toward the keys of B minor and E flat major and minor—to give the whole music a sense of inter-relationship.

The sinuous melody that accompanies the summoning of Astarte is typical late Schumann; we may perhaps regard it as a softened, more lyrical form of the angular baroque type of melody to which he was turning more and more. But *Manfred* also contains specimens

[1] Afterwards orchestrated by Tchaikovsky. This is the 'ballad by Schumann' which I was temporarily unable to identify (see p. 251 of *Tchaikovsky: a Symposium*) and which Herbert Weinstock describes as 'Arrangement for voice and orchestra of *Eternal Sleep* (ballad)'; the Russian title really means 'The Prophetic Dream'.

[2] See also p. 112.

of the earlier type of Schumannian lyricism (cf. No. 11); No. 12
shows complete fusion of the two types. But the most surprising
feature of the other *Manfred* numbers is the handling of the orchestra.
Manfred's address to the Witch of the Alps, in particular, is quite
outstanding—almost unique in Schumann for the lightness and
imaginativeness of the scoring (see Ex. 138 for the passage at the

Ex. 138

words 'in thy calm clear brow, Wherein is glass'd serenity of soul',
with the little percussive touches on the harp, the first violins muted,
the lower strings reduced to two violas and two 'cellos). The unaccompanied cor anglais solo, No. 4, alternately slow and fast, may

S

owe something to the 'Scène aux champs' of Berlioz's *Symphonie fantastique* but may well, in turn, have helped to suggest the shepherd's pipe in *Tristan.* Finally it is perhaps worth mentioning that the sketches reveal Schumann's original intention to continue No. 12 for another seven bars to a more emphatic—and more commonplace—cadence (Ex. 139), and that the last number was to have had a

Ex.139

similar short orchestral epilogue (Ex. 140) that was even included in the full score (in the Berlin Staatsbibliothek) but afterwards crossed out.

The *Scenes from 'Faust'* should not properly be considered as a

Ex. 140

'work', a unity. They were composed, as we have seen, at different times and perhaps with different ends in view. According to Wasielewski, Schumann had at one time contemplated writing a *Faust* opera; soon after his first essay—the last scene—he asked Eduard Krüger: 'What do you think of the idea of treating the whole material as an *oratorio*? Is it not bold and beautiful?'; and again after the composition of his Parts I and II he asserted that in writing them he had 'thought mainly that they perhaps could serve for concert-programmes, since there are hardly any such compositions for soloists and chorus on a small scale'. He was opposed to the performance of all the *Faust* music 'in succession on the one evening': 'at the most it might be done only as a curiosity'. We can regard it merely as a series of 'essays in composing *Faust*'.

The overture, written last, again shows Schumann under the influence of Bach, more specifically of the great Chaconne in the same key which, with other unaccompanied Bach for violin and for 'cello, he had 'harmonized' a few months before. The element of romanticized baroque figuration and harmony, with its grinding appoggiatura and changing-note clashes, is much more obvious in the *Faust* overture than in that to *Manfred*.[1] It is significant that Schumann had once written of 'the by no means to be rejected idea of opening a *Faust* drama with a fugue, the most deeply thoughtful form of music', and characteristic that there is nevertheless little contrapuntal texture in the overture; it is only that nineteenth-century form and texture are here enriched by types of theme and figuration and harmonic method drawn from the early eighteenth century. The fusion may be concisely illustrated by quotation of the second subject (Ex. 141); the baroque semiquaver figure here seems

Ex. 141

to have obsessed Schumann during the composition of *Faust* for it appears also in I. 1 on the bassoon at the appearance of Mephistopheles, in I. 2 to suggest the organ in the cathedral, throughout the

---

[1] The piano-piece *Verrufene Stelle*, No. 4 of the *Waldscenen*, Op. 82, shows a similar application of baroque material to romantic ends. Cf. also Dr. Carner's remark on p. 236.

accompaniment to III. 2 (solo of Pater Ecstaticus), and at one
passage in the earlier printed version of the final 'Chorus mysticus'.
The first sketches for the overture (dated 15 August 1853) show it
also at the *opening* (Ex. 142); there is a relic of this at bars 9–10 of the

Ex. 142

final version. A later sketch for the opening of the overture is nearer
its present form but is still in 3/4 instead of 4/4 time (Ex. 143).

Of the rest of the *Faust* music, the six numbers that make up
Schumann's Parts I and II may almost be regarded as fragments
from an unwritten opera based directly on Goethe's text. For

Ex. 143

although Schumann made fairly drastic cuts and took one or two
trifling liberties he was generally faithful to his poet. The first
number is typical. Schumann takes the latter part of Goethe's
'garden' scene, beginning with Faust's 'Du kanntest mich, o kleiner
Engel, wieder' and sets it just as it stands down to 'eine Wonne zu
fühlen, die ewig sein muss!', inserting a not absolutely necessary
'doch' in one of Gretchen's lines, cutting Faust's exclamation, 'Du
holdes Himmelsangesicht!' and making him cry 'Süss Liebchen!'
twice instead of once; he then cuts to the following 'summer-house'
scene, beginning with Mephistopheles' 'Es ist wohl Zeit, zu scheiden'
and ending with Gretchen's 'Auf baldig Wiedersehn!'—in which
line he takes it upon himself to correct her grammar. The words are
set in a free arioso style, quite different from the balanced lyrical
melody of the earlier Schumann; only after Gretchen's play with the
flower, 'He loves me—loves me not'—subtly and touchingly handled
—does Faust break into a warmer melody corresponding to his
heightened emotion. This scene may not be great music but it displays a by no means contemptible dramatic technique. This, as
Ernest Newman pointed out many years ago,[1] is really Goethe's

[1] 'Faust in Music' in *Musical Studies* (London, 1905).

Gretchen. And her protrait is truthfully filled in and its shades deepened in the two next numbers, 'Ach neige, du Schmerzensreiche', and the cathedral scene—its opening a sort of study for the fourth movement of the E flat Symphony—with the Evil Spirit and the choir chanting the 'Dies irae'.

Part II begins with the opening of Goethe's Part II and challenges comparison with the famous 'scene on the banks of the Elbe' in Berlioz's *Damnation*; despite the real charm of Schumann's orchestration (Ex. 144) it hardly bears that comparison. The setting of 'Des Lebens Pulse schlagen' is undistinguished, but the portrait of Faust—and again it is really Goethe's Faust—begins to emerge in No. 5, the scene with the four grey women (characterized by a motive which recurs not only throughout their music but in the orchestra just after Faust's words 'Nun ist die Luft von solchem Spuk so voll, dass niemand weiss, wie er ihn meiden soll' and is perhaps intentionally incorporated in his voice-part a little earlier at 'Das war ich sonst' though that particular form occurs elsewhere). The fine D flat passage 'Ich bin nur durch die Welt gerannt' recalls the Schumann of the best songs, Faust's monologue after his blinding rather the Wagner of nearly the same period, the Wagner of *Tannhäuser*. The death-scene, too, is painted with grim power; even the diminished-seventh harmony—a typical dramatic convention of the period—when the Lemurs seize Faust's body, is hardened by emphasized passing-notes; the wonderful hushed moment when the chorus in a suddenly remote key echo the words of Mephistopheles, 'Steht still! Sie schweigt wie Mitternacht. Der Zeiger fällt', is unforgettable.

All in all, one may say that these first two parts show surprising dramatic power for a composer whose natural inclination was not at all to the dramatic. Like Tchaikovsky, another intensely subjective composer, Schumann could project himself only into fictitious characters that already resembled himself or for whom he felt intense pity; thus he could succeed unexpectedly with Manfred and Faust and Gretchen. In the Third Part he was almost completely released from the obligation to think dramatically. It has really no place in a study of Schumann's dramatic music, but for the sake of completeness in this cursory study of the *Faust* music it is worth pointing out such beauties as the passage 'so ist es die allmächtige Liebe, die alles bildet, alles hegt!' (very close to mature Wagner in technique and feeling) in No. 3, the whole solo of Dr. Marianus (No. 5), and the thoughtful beauty of the choral writing generally, which offsets much of the squareness of the structure. Both printed versions of the final

Ex. 144

'Chorus mysticus' ('Alles Vergängliche ist nur ein Gleichniss') are very fine. The opening, common to both, is on a theme of two dropping fifths that constantly recurs in Schumann's music from the

opening of the Impromptus, Op. 5 onward (cf. the first trio of the
Piano Quintet). There is naturally plenty of scope for imitation and
fugue in this great choral epilogue and it is noteworthy that the
sketches show the fugal origin and testing of themes not so used
ultimately; for instance the last theme (at letter F: 'zieht uns hinan')
of the earlier version began as Ex. 145 which could not possibly have
fitted these words.

Ex: 145

There remains for consideration Schumann's most important
dramatic work, the opera *Genoveva*. It was not quite his first
operatic venture. As early as 1840 he had contemplated an opera on
Byron's *Corsair*; in 1844 he negotiated with Oswald Marbach for a
libretto on that subject and actually began the composition; the
Berlin State Library possesses the manuscript of an opening 'Chorus
of Corsairs' in D minor, 'Auf den Wellen' (obviously based on 'O'er
the glad waters') and a fragment of an aria for Conrad (probably
based on 'Ay! at set of sun' in the seventh stanza), which I have not
been able to examine. Indeed from 1840 onward Schumann dwelt
from time to time on a number of possible opera-subjects, the one
that attracted him most—after *The Corsair*—being E. T. A.
Hoffmann's *Doge und Dogaressa* from the second part of the
Serapionsbrüder.[1] The search was ended by the discovery in 1847 of
Hebbel's tragedy, published four years earlier but still unperformed.
Unfortunately Schumann did not base his libretto directly and
solely on Hebbel; he wished to combine with it elements from Tieck's
drama of nearly half a century earlier, *Leben und Tod der heiligen
Genoveva*, the very play that had exasperated Hebbel to write *his*
version. After the painter-poet Robert Reinick had made two unsuccessful attempts to fuse the two plays into a libretto, and after Hebbel
himself had declined to collaborate,[2] Schumann himself worked on
Reinick's second draft both before and during the composition of
the music; Reinick declined to accept responsibility for the result and
the libretto was finally published as 'after Tieck and F. Hebbel'.

 The action of Hebbel's play may be summarized as follows:

[1] For full details of Schumann's search for an opera-subject see Wasielewski's
Robert Schumann (Leipzig, fourth edition, 1906), pp. 378–82.

[2] Though in later years he prepared two different 'stage-versions' of his play,
with drastic cuts.

Act I: The Pfalzgraf Siegfried is off to fight the Moors, leaving his steward Golo as guardian of his wife Genoveva and his castle. At the moment of parting Genoveva faints in the arms of Golo who secretly adores her; Siegfried departs; Golo kisses his unconscious mistress.— Fearing the consequences of his passion Golo 'tests' Providence by risking his life on the battlements.

Act II: Golo is safe; he is reproached for his foolhardiness by his adoring old nurse Katharina, and by Genoveva. Golo begs the latter to 'consecrate' his sword; she consecrates it to 'the defence of helpless womanhood'. She goes to the chapel to pray for Siegfried.—Jew-baiting scene inessential to the plot.

Act III: Katharina's wicked old sister Margareta appears, pretending to be a pilgrim. She detects Golo's love for Genoveva; Katharina agrees to shelter her in the castle.—Genoveva's room: a knight, Tristan, brings a letter from Siegfried and tells a long story of his own captivity. When he has gone, Golo 'tests' Providence again by asking Genoveva whether a man knowing himself to be on the verge of a terrible crime should commit suicide. She refuses to answer and Golo bursts forth with a declaration of his passion; she is saved by the entrance of Katharina.—Servants' hall: Margareta and Golo induce the faithful but simple-witted Drago to hide in Genoveva's room 'to prove her innocent of a scandalous accusation'; they then induce the other servants to break into the room; Drago is found and stabbed. Golo orders Genoveva to be imprisoned as an adultress.

Act IV: Two scenes showing how Golo has offered Genoveva freedom and the clearance of her name for the price of 'a kiss'.—Margareta's room in Strassburg: enter Golo, who has told the returning Siegfried the lie about Genoveva's guilt Siegfried comes to see 'the truth' in Margareta's magic mirror, which actually shows him love-scenes between Genoveva and Drago. He orders Golo to take his sword and signet-ring, go home and kill both Genoveva and the child she has borne while in captivity. When both men have gone, Drago's ghost appears to Margareta foretelling the punishment that awaits her in seven years' time when she herself will have to reveal the truth to Siegfried.

Act V: The dungeon: Golo, who cannot bring himself to do the deed personally, brings two servants Balthasar and Hans and orders them to take mother and child to a wood and kill them.—The wood: the two servants are also unwilling murderers and they give the sword, Siegfried's sword, to the idiot Klaus who has followed them. Klaus, God's instrument, promptly kills Hans and would kill Balthasar too but for Genoveva's intervention; she persuades Balthasar to allow her to escape with the child and hide in the depth of the forest. Golo, who has come to see the murder, meets Balthasar, quarrels with him and stabs him to death. Siegfried enters with another servant, Kaspar, who brings news of Katharina's suicide—evidently from remorse at her share in the plot. Siegfried, seeing that Golo is near collapse, tells him compassionately to go out into the world for a time and try to forget all these bloody scenes; on his return he shall be Siegfried's heir. He goes. Golo can bear his guilt no more; he will blind himself and Kaspar shall bind him naked to a tree and leave him to the wild beasts. But Kaspar kills him at once with Siegfried's sword.

In 1851—that is, not till after the first performance of Schumann's opera—Hebbel, on the suggestion of Holtei, added a 'Nachspiel' showing the finding of Genoveva and her son by Siegfried, the revelation of the truth and the reconciliation. But all that was inessential to his plan. His central figure is Golo; and his play, with all its exaggerated romantic horror and evil magic, is a psychological study of the overthrow of a not altogether ignoble character by passion. The earlier play by Tieck, on the other hand, keeps closer to the old legend; the central figure is Genoveva. Tieck's play is not divided into acts; indeed he can never have contemplated a stage-production; it wanders discursively, includes a number of lyrical poems (Schumann borrowed the idea of Golo's musical proclivities from Tieck), and introduces Charles Martel, the Moorish king, and other subsidiary historical characters, with battle-scenes and much else that is inessential to the plot. It would serve no useful purpose to summarize the action but a number of points are worth noting.

Tieck introduces a hymn for Siegfried's departing troops; Schumann adopted the idea for his opening scene but used other words. Similarly the roystering chorus of the vassals in the second act of the opera is closely imitated, but not actually borrowed, from Tieck. When Golo frankly declares his passion, Tieck makes Genoveva cry 'Hinweg! gottloser, ehrvergessner Mann!', which in the libretto is sharpened to 'Zurück, zurück, ehrloser Bastard!', an insult which helps to explain Golo's revengefulness. Tieck introduces the character of Hidulfus, Bishop of Treves, who appears in the opening and closing scenes of the opera. He also shows Siegfried's finding of Genoveva and her child, and the words of the duet 'O lass es ruh'n Dein Aug' auf mir!' are a curious patchwork of phrases from Tieck, some of them slightly altered, interwoven with Reinick's or Schumann's own.

There is similar patchwork with Hebbel's words at other points in the opera: Margareta's 'Ich sah ein Kind im Traum' and the apparition of Drago's ghost, both in the finale of Act III, and Genoveva's dialogues with Golo and the murderers in Act IV. Sometimes only a single phrase is borrowed, out of its original context, sometimes a longer passage; words are cut or changed, syllables inserted, not always for an obvious reason. One change may have been due to prudery or to fear of the censorship: in 'Ich sah ein Kind im Traum' Hebbel's Margareta for a moment regrets her murder of her child because if she had grown up a beauty a wooer might have come knocking at the door, such a one 'who brings money by night' ('der das Geld bringt bei der Nacht'); in the libretto this becomes one 'who brings good-fortune in a night' ('der das Glück bringt über Nacht'). Both in such verbal details and in general outline the libretto owes far more to Hebbel than to Tieck. Only Hebbel is condensed and compressed, with loss of subtlety and motivation (particularly in the part of Golo); Katharina and Margareta are fused into a single character, Kaspar's name is transferred to Hebbel's Hans, and the idiot Klaus is replaced by a mute, but not apparently imbecile, Angelo. The action of the opera, then, is as follows:

Act I: Bishop Hidulfus (baritone) despatches the Christian warriors; Golo (tenor) regrets that he is not accompanying them. Siegfried (baritone) takes farewell of Genoveva (soprano) and his retainers. Genoveva faints in the arms of Golo, who kisses her. This is observed by Margareta (mezzo-soprano), who proceeds to play on Golo's feelings.

Act II: Genoveva mourns Siegfried's absence; the revelling servants are getting out of hand. Golo comes to comfort her; they sing a duet at the end of which he declares his passion. Repulsed, he swears revenge; meeting Drago (bass), he suddenly has the idea of the plot—and hides him in the room. Margareta tells Golo she will intercept Siegfried on his way home and poison him.—The servants break into Genoveva's room, seize her and kill Drago.

Act III: A condensed form of Hebbel's Act IV, the scenes of the magic mirror (which in the opera Siegfried smashes with his sword) and Drago's ghost.

Act IV: The forest: Genoveva and child led by Balthasar (bass), Caspar (baritone) and Angelo (mute). Golo has one last interview with her (Hebbel's dungeon scene transferred) and leaves her to the murderers. Caspar loses his nerve and runs away; Angelo seizes his sword and attacks Balthasar; hunters and retainers are seen; Genoveva faints as Siegfried appears, led by the repentant Margareta. Reconciliation; joyful return to the castle where Hidulfus blesses them.

This hotch-potch of ill-motivated actions by stock figures of melodrama, lacking both the charm of the old legend and the psychological interest of Hebbel's play, was little calculated to inspire genuinely dramatic music; but if we try to see it, as Schumann did, through the lens of Hebbel we shall at least understand what he was aiming at. The overture in particular is, so to speak, pure Hebbel—as appears from the entries in Schumann's 'Haushaltbuch'[1]:

1 April 1847: Hebbel's *Genoveva*. Overture thoughts and decision on this text.
2 April 1847: *Genoveva* thoughts and cheerful mood.
4 April 1847: Early at Reinick's and agreement on *Genoveva*.
5 April 1847: 1st sketch of *Genoveva* overture completed—Joy.

The later entries for April contain a number of references to the libretto—one of them coupled with the phrase 'A German warrior', apparently a reference to Siegfried; a rough scenario seems to have been sketched as early as April 8. But musically Schumann was occupied with the final scene of *Faust*, the C major Symphony, the D minor Trio;[2] it was not till 26 December that he orchestrated the overture and began the composition of the opera itself.

The *Genoveva* overture, then, has some claim to be considered as an independent composition, worked out in essentials eight months before Schumann began the rest of the music: the same reversal of the usual order as in *Manfred*, but here much more striking. As an orchestral character-study, it is inferior to the *Manfred* overture— but to that alone in Schumann's orchestral music. The slow introduction seems to have been influenced by the corresponding passage in Beethoven's E flat String Quartet, Op. 74; it is, as we shall see in a moment, based on two figures (on first violins in bar 3 and on 'cellos in bar 4) associated with the guilt-laden figure of Golo. The transition to the 'Leidenschaftlich bewegt' allegro gave Schumann some trouble; three earlier attempts at the end of the 'Langsam' passage are shown in Ex. 146. But what are we to make of this 'passionately moved' allegro in which such a prominent part is played by the 'cello figure quoted in the last bars of Ex. 146, *a*, *b* and *c*, which is of course none other than the 'baroque figure' we have already noticed in *Faust*.[3] It is customary to associate the first allegro subject with Genoveva and her sufferings, the second subject on the

---

[1] See Boetticher's *Robert Schumann in seinen Schriften und Briefen*, p. 423.

[2] Of which the finale is echoed at the opening of the duet, 'So wenig Monden', in Act I.

[3] See p. 267; cf. also the end of Act III of *Genoveva* when Margareta rushes out, enveloped in flames, and bar 11 of the accompaniment to Genoveva's prayer, 'O Du, der über Alle wacht'.

horns with Siegfried; but while it is true that there are allusions to Genoveva's music—or, rather, Genoveva's music alludes to the first subject of the overture (cf. bars 10–11 with her 'drohende Gründe' and 'gönnt eine Weile Ruhe der Müden', at the beginning of Act IV, bars 35–8—themselves closely related to the 'baroque' figure—with what Hermann Abert[1] regarded as her leitmotive), this music is

Ex. 146

quite different in general character from the 'Genoveva' music of the opera. It seems far more likely that the whole allegro, indeed the whole overture, is a musical study of Hebbel's Golo, that if Genoveva entered into Schumann's conception at this point it was only as the temptation tormenting Golo's mind, that the fresh horn-theme with its dolce woodwind answer represents not Siegfried but Golo's recollections of lost innocence. What seems to be the final triumph of the principal 'Golo' theme, *fff*, tutti—which appears to have given the cue for the beginning of the opening chorus of the opera—is inexplicable, like the parallel final exit, in triumphant major, of the unrepentant and unpunished Golo in Act IV. (Schumann's correspondence with Julius Rietz shows that he at one time thought of introducing Golo's dead body on the stage near the end of the opera, but the idea was abandoned.)

The opera itself is a very typical German romantic opera of the second quarter of the nineteenth century, not only in subject and incidents, but in its musical conventions. Schumann certainly had a very high opinion of *Euryanthe*, an opera with certain parallel dramatic situations; an entry in the 'Haushaltbuch' for this very

[1] His article 'Robert Schumann's *Genoveva*' in the *Zeitschrift der Internationalen Musikgesellschaft* (XI, No. 9, 1910) first drew attention to Schumann's use of characteristic themes.

period (23 September 1847) records an evening's enthusiasm over Weber's masterpiece. He may well have been specifically influenced by *Tannhäuser*, notably in one of the subsidiary 'Golo' themes (bar 4 of the overture). But, as with certain harmonic features that suggest contemporary or even later Wagner (for instance, the opening of Act IV), the similarities of musical handling spring from a common local and period style. The music still falls into 'numbers' but the texture is really continuous, though (unlike Wagner) Schumann disregards unity of key; the finale of Act I, for instance, begins in A minor and ends in B major; the opera itself begins with an overture in C but ends in E major. The recitative is always accompanied and usually inclines to arioso; in some notes 'On Opera Composition'[1] probably made at this period Schumann wrote '*Recitative*: It must not be omitted. The listener is rested, as are singers and orchestra.[2] The accompaniment is to be strengthened with wood and brass only at extraordinary passages; otherwise strings suffice. The usual cadences of tonic after dominant are not to be used too often'; but except on the last point his practice did not accord with his theory.

One of the most interesting features of this operatic style, the one afterwards developed so vigorously by Wagner that he was long popularly credited with its invention, was the free use of thematic reminiscence mainly to make dramatic points but also to some extent for the purpose of characterization. Schubert in *Fierrabras* and Weber in *Euryanthe*, a quarter of a century earlier than *Genoveva*, had employed characteristic themes, simple and transformed, and the Wagner of *Tannhäuser* had surpassed them only in broad theatrical effectiveness; it was only later that he was to arrive at the full symphonic treatment of characteristic themes. And it is only in theatrical effectiveness that Schumann's use of such themes is inferior to Wagner's at the same period.

Consider the musical characterization of Golo. Even the beautiful aria near the beginning of Act I, in which he prays for peace of mind, is music in which *Schumann* speaks (as in any of his songs with piano). But, as Abert pointed out, Schumann tried to give his musical character 'inner unity' by association with two or three definite motives of which the most important is that constantly

---

[1] Published for the first time in *Robert Schumann in seinen Schriften und Briefen*, p. 432.

[2] A complete change from the view, expressed a few months earlier in a letter to Franz Brendel (20 February 1847) that the absence of recitatives in *Das Paradies und die Peri* represented 'a real formal progress'.

heard in the overture but first *definitely* associated with him at the beginning of the finale of Act I, when Margareta sarcastically remarks on his gallantry toward Genoveva (Ex. 147); in that more

Ex. 147

Sich' da   welch' fei   ner   Rit - ters · mann!

extended form it dominates the entire finale and, on piccolos and clarinets, punctuates the servants' drinking chorus at the beginning of Act II at the words 'ist der Knappe Herr im Haus'. The motive itself (*a*) recurs a number of times in his duet a little later with Genoveva—also in her part—and, modified, at the beginning of his duet with Drago. The full form of Ex. 147 is heard again when Golo asks Margareta, 'Und hörtest Du, wie sie mich nannte?' ('Didst thou hear what she called me?') but here again the effect is confused by a half-reference two bars earlier in Margareta's part. In any case, these isolated fleeting references to a not particularly striking theme, indefinite in expression, are bound to pass unnoticed by the ordinary opera-goer; they were unnoticed even by students of the score until Abert drew attention to them in 1910. The same criticism must be levelled at most of Schumann's other recurrent themes. The motive heard in bars 4 and 6 of the overture is an exception; in the opera it appears first when Golo calls Genoveva an 'enchantress', again after 'ehrloser Bastard', yet again when he approaches her for the last time in the wood; it is specifically the theme of his hatred of her, and we are constantly reminded of it again when the would-be murderers are trying to tear her from the Cross. More subtle again, though underlined by the harmony, is the theme of (one supposes) Satanic influence, first heard in the orchestra near the end of Golo's aria in Act I, given a specific verbal context ('Would that I could retrace this dreadful way!') in the scene with Siegfried at Strassburg (Ex. 148), recurring a number of times later in the same scene,

Ex. 148

Ich möch   te zu   rück   den   grau · si - gen   Weg,

in the orchestra, sung by the invisible choruses at the end of the mirror scene, and heard again persistently during part of the scene with Drago's ghost. Yet another 'Golo' theme, of less importance, is played several times during Siegfried's reading of the false letter and again during Margareta's sleep (beginning of finale of Act III). Genoveva herself is dramatically so passive and featureless that, so far as music is concerned, she may be said to exist adequately in her various beautiful monologues. But Schumann has also tried, not very successfully, to give her musical character sharper definition by a specific theme in variant forms, including an ironical version by Margareta. It springs from such a typically Schumannesque motive (cf. the 'Innig' section of the piano *Humoreske*, Op. 20, on the one hand and the familiar figure of Exs. 141, 142 and 146 on the other) that one wonders whether its first appearance, at her words 'Der dich mir gab' in her first duet with her husband, may not be accidental. It first comes to the fore quite unmistakably in the finale of Act I, where at first it alternates with Ex. 147 and rivals it in thematic importance; it is again associated with Ex. 147 in the drinking chorus of Act II (rhythmically transformed at 'Stosst an und trinket aus') and in the dialogue between Margareta and Golo after Drago has been concealed in the bedroom. This version is heard again, in both voice and orchestra, just before the first unveiling of the mirror, its connection with Genoveva being made absolutely clear by association for the third time—once before in the finale of Act I, once in the drinking chorus—with the verbal phrase 'Fürwahr, ein schönes Weib des Küssens werth!' ('Forsooth, a pretty woman worth a kiss'). Another passage evolved from the beginning of this theme is played just before Genoveva's prayer in Act II, and again in the the finale when she appeals to Heaven for protection against the mob of servants; in the latter instance it is at once picked up, as if in mockery, in a variant of the ironical form by both voices and orchestra ('Wir müssen ihn finden'). Her prayer itself, 'O Du, der über Alles wacht', is dominated by what we may call a 'purer' form of the 'Genoveva' motive.

Again, these subtleties are bound to be lost on the average operagoer. But before we condemn them finally on that account, we must ask ourselves whether Schumann ever intended them to be noticed as such, whether they are not features of a composition-technique fundamentally different from Wagner's in a point where the two seem to have a great deal in common. Except where Schumann writes direct reminiscences for a dramatic purpose, as in the case of 'Fürwahr, ein schönes Weib des Küssens werth!', he may have wished to produce nothing more than a *sense* of consistency in musical characterization, not an obvious consistency, just as Beethoven would often disguise in a finished work relationships that the sketches show to have been definitely thematic.[1] In the act of instrumental composition, Schumann sometimes noted on the margin of his music-paper a sort of 'master-thought' as if to keep his mind in the right track[2] and the sketches for *Genoveva* actually show, noted beside the recitative No. 4 in Act I, a 'Siegfried' theme (Ex. 149, *a*) which is never once heard in the opera but which can be *felt* as an influence on a great deal of the music associated with him; one instance, the opening of his song 'Bald blick' ich dich wieder mein Heimathschloss' is quoted as Ex. 149, *b*. Similarly in the finale of Act III the music

Ex. 149

```
Bald  blick' ich  dich wie-der  mein    Hei    mat-schloss
```

to which Margareta sings 'Was bebst du, Feiger! Denke d'ran, wie Dich die Gräfin höhnte!' can hardly have been intended as a direct allusion to the Countess's theme, registering on the hearer's consciousness; it is no more than an impression of the 'master-thought' that is going to be firmly re-stamped twenty bars or so later.

The musical characterization of Margareta herself has often been adversely criticized—perhaps a little unjustly. Critics have observed only the lyrical simplicity of her 'Du lässt die arme Frau allein' without feeling its insinuating hypocrisy. The Schubertian charm of the music accompanying the first scene in her mirror has also been misunderstood; after all, as Siegfried remarks, the mirror itself pictures 'nichts zu schelten'. The opening of that finale, Margareta's account of her gruesome dream, and its close, the scene of the flaming mirror, bear comparison with the romantic horrors of Marschner and the Wagner of the *Holländer* respectively.

Nevertheless, with all its musical interest and real beauties and passages of dramatic power, *Genoveva* has grave weaknesses of which the unimaginative, unplastic, block-chordal treatment of the chorus is one of the worst.[3] The only even moderately interesting choral

[1] See Paul Mies, *Beethoven's Sketches* (English translation, Oxford University Press, 1929), pp. 114–122.
[2] Cf. pp. 159 (footnote) and 183.
[3] Cf. p. 284.

T

passage is that in the last Act where the 12/8 'May' chorus of Siegfried, Genoveva and their followers, dying away, is interwoven with
the ever-louder strains of the church chorus recalled from the
beginning of Act I. The already mentioned notes 'On Opera
Composition' include an entry on 'Treatment of the chorus':

> The choruses are to be kept as easy as possible. Unison of tenors and
> basses with octave-doubling in alto and soprano has the most powerful
> effect. The pure four-part with obbligato lay-out of the voices is suitable
> only in its place. The chorus must always show power and vigour. High
> tessitura is to be avoided in all parts.

Here again Schumann was not faithful to his preconceived principles,
though he began by fidelity in his opening chorale where, of all
places, four-part harmony would have been suitable; but his fear of
giving the chorus anything difficult led him to write for it music far
more square and conventional than the choral episodes of *Tannhäuser*
and *Lohengrin*.

Lack of confidence betrayed Schumann at more than one point
in his creative career. His correspondence with Julius Rietz, musical
director of the Leipzig opera, where *Genoveva* was ultimately produced in 1850, reveals his lack of confidence not only in matters of
theatrical effectiveness, but also in purely musical matters. Would
it not be better to write the violins an octave higher in a certain
passage in the overture, to drop the trombones altogether at the end
of the overture? Might not the drums, after Golo's final exit, 'easily
produce a comic effect'? And then there is the passage after Golo
has kissed the unconscious Genoveva:

> The first violins now have it on the G string. But it's not yet right.
> As if Golo's good genius turned from him, *that* is how it must sound.
> Help me! Perhaps on a wind-instrument! But which? for the clarinet
> directly after must be taken into account. . . .

Rietz's suggestion was to double the melody an octave lower on the
'cellos 'and from there onward with the first oboe as well; the deep
B of course sounds very well on the oboe'. On that point Schumann
took his own decision, which was (characteristically) to double the
G-string melody on the first clarinet; on others—such as the handling of the trombones at the end of the overture—he accepted Rietz's
advice. But the vivid idea of a dramatic subtlety ('as if Golo's genius
turned from him') and the failure to convey it musically are typical
of *Genoveva* as a whole.

CHAPTER VIII

THE CHORAL WORKS

By JOHN HORTON

IT would have been somewhat surprising if Schumann, with his decided literary bent, had remained untouched by the vogue of the romantic cantata, based on idealised medieval, oriental, or supernatural themes, and represented by a long line of works such as Marschner's *Klänge aus Osten*, Mendelssohn's *Die erste Walpurgisnacht*, Félicien David's *Le Désert*, and Gade's *Comala*. The genre remained in favour throughout the nineteenth century, with the cantatas of Elgar among its latest and most familiar representatives. To this prolific and nowadays rather outmoded family belongs the first of Schumann's larger choral works, and the one that not only gained widest popularity but also gave its composer the most personal satisfaction. He described it as 'an oratorio, but for cheerful people, and not for an oratory.' *Das Paradies und die Peri*, Op. 50, was composed at Leipzig between February and June, 1843, and was given a series of performances under the composer's direction in Leipzig and Dresden during December of the same year. It is a setting for soloists, chorus, and orchestra, of part of Thomas Moore's *Lalla Rookh*, as translated into German[1] by Schumann's friend Emil Flechsig, with some additional verses inserted to provide scope for quasi-dramatic treatment. As in several of his later works of this type, Schumann uses solo voices partly to carry on the narration, partly to represent characters in the story. It must be admitted at once that in *Paradise and the Peri*, and also in its successors, Schumann's writing for the solo voice and the orchestra is generally superior in skill and imagination to his handling of the chorus. His considerable experience in song-writing ensures variety, grace, and expressive declamation almost everywhere in the numerous and lengthy solo passages; in some of the Peri's music, indeed, the

---

[1] Those who are without first-hand acquaintance with *Lalla Rookh* may be relieved to know that Moore's verse is not quite as bad as the English retranslation of *Paradise and the Peri* suggests. It is true that Moore made the Peri exclaim, in the moment of her triumph: 'Oh! am I not happy? I am, I am——' but he did not eclipse this distinguished line with the one that is made to follow it in the English vocal score: 'For ever, Oh joy, my work it is done'.

boldness of the vocal line approaches that of Wagnerian music-drama (Ex. 150). From the orchestral aspect, *Paradise and the Peri* offers many felicities of scoring, including the suave polyphony of the introduction to Part I, the silvery splash and ripple of the Nile waters

Ex.150

auch ein Blatt, auf wel - chem rein das Sie - gel

prangt von Sa - lo - mo;

(Ex. 151), and the bizarre alternating string and wind chords[1] heard during the narration of the Peri's wanderings in plague-stricken Egypt (Ex. 152). On the other hand, whether from inexperience or timidity (the timidity of an unsure and uncomfortable choral conductor) Schumann rarely succeeds in producing effective and interesting part-writing for massed voices. His staple resources are a safe and dull homophonic plodding (as in the choruses that close the first and third parts of *Paradise and the Peri*), parallel movement in octaves and unisons, with the orchestra keeping things going, or, worst of all, series of trite imitative entries that fail to develop into a genuine polyphonic texture. But there are happy exceptions: the chorus of lamentation in Part I, for example, with its poignant overlapping thirds (Ex. 153), the song of the Nile spirits already referred to, the lovely elegiac chorus at the end of Part II, and the song of the Houris that opens Part III (Ex. 154). This last example is noteworthy for its delicate oriental colouring, and also as an illustration of the general truth that Schumann writes better for a chorus composed either of women or of men than he does for mixed voices. The Houris' chorus, that of the Nile Spirits, and the battle song of the followers of Mahound in Part I, are all interpolations into the original text of the poem. Their introduction may doubtless be objected to on dramatic grounds but, providing as they do welcome opportunities for exotic colour and some variation of musical texture, they must be held to justify themselves. Schumann certainly found them stimulating to his imagination, and therefore to his technique.

---

[1] Which probably suggested to Mussorgsky the opening of the coronation scene in *Boris Godunov*. *Paradise and the Peri* was well known to the Balakirev circle and Balakirev performed excerpts from it at his concerts in 1863 and 1864.—*Ed.*

Ex. 151

Ex. 152

Spitta's criticism of *Paradise and the Peri* as containing 'too much music' is not unjust. Although the composer has been at such pains to bring out the dramatic points of the story, his melodic and harmonic riches are lavished equally on narrative, descriptive, and

Ex. 153

reflective passages, so that the total effect, combined with what now seems an intolerably sentimental poem, is cloying and monotonous. Yet it was this very wealth of picturesque detail, fluent melody,

Ex. 154

highly original harmony, and vivid orchestration that attracted Schumann's contemporaries, and that still make it one of the most characteristic expressions of his musical personality. It is unlikely that *Paradise and the Peri* will ever return to the choral society repertory; but it should be given at least an occasional 'token' performance.

Apart from the romantic cantata, of which more must be said presently, the chief incentive to Schumann's experiments with choral forms was the rise of choral unions in mid-nineteenth-century Germany, and the parallel growth of male-voice societies or *Liedertafeln*. Both owed their origin largely to K. F. C. Fasch, who founded the Berlin Singakademie in 1790. Under Zelter, his successor, the Singakademie played a notable part in the revival of great choral music of earlier centuries, including Palestrina's and Bach's. In 1809 Zelter formed the male members of the choir into the first 'Liedertafel', and from that time the male voice choir movement spread throughout Germany, allied itself with political tendencies during the revolutionary period 1830–48, and sponsored songfestivals in the larger towns.

Schumann came into contact with the movement in his Leipzig days. A letter to his friend Keferstein, dated 19 February 1840, describes his excitement over his new-found interest in songwriting: 'I am at present writing nothing but music for the voice, on both a large and a small scale, besides quartets for male voices'. In 1848 he took over from Hiller the conductorship of the Dresden male voice choir. This was the year in which the drums and tramplings of the approaching Prussian hegemony began to force themselves upon the ears of Europe, and it is significant that Schumann should have composed, a few months earlier, the *Gesänge* ('Songs of War and Freedom'), Op. 62, for male voices, the three long suppressed 'revolutionary songs' for male voices in 1848, and the pugnacious fifth number of the *Jagdlieder*, Op. 137, in 1849. The *Ritornelle*, Op. 65, written about the same time, have greater intrinsic interest. They are settings of short motto-like verses by Friedrich Rückert, and each is treated in some variety of canonic form—a device that often stimulated Schumann to provide musicianly solutions to his self-imposed problems. These attractive minatures range from the convivial to the religious; the last of the set, *In Meeres Mitten*, is a grave little piece that might be inscribed 'Homage to J. S. Bach', so full of expressive power are its final bars (Ex. 155).[1] The *Ritornelle*, brief as they are, exceed in artistic value the more ambitious motet for male voices, *Verzweifle nicht im Schmerzenstal*, Op. 93, also to words by Rückert. It was written in 1849 for

[1] There is another setting for female voices of the same words, with an additional verse, in Op. 69.

unaccompanied singing and orchestrated three years later. The difficulties of bringing off an 8-part composition on this scale for male voice choir are severe; among them is the problem of securing harmonic variety within a compass of two and a half octaves, and Schumann here falls into the trap of writing unvocal chromatic progressions in

Ex. 155

close position—as in the passage beginning 'die Wolke droht'. A curious point in the opening of the work is a reminiscence of the slow movement of the Piano Concerto. The *Jagdlieder* ('Hunting Songs'), Op. 137, with their optional accompaniment for natural and valve horns, reflect a popular musical fashion of the period (Mendelssohn's *Huntsman's Farewell*, Op. 50, No. 2, is another example); their relationship with the *Waldscenen* for piano, Op. 82, has been referred to in an earlier chapter.[1]

Schumann gave up the Dresden *Liedertafel* after about a year, its good-humoured but insensitive heartiness being too much for his temperament. He continued to conduct a mixed voice choral society he had founded, and to write for the women's section of it some charming part-songs. The *Romanzen,* Op. 69 and Op. 91, show that some at least of the ladies of the choir were highly skilled. Op. 69, No. 5 (*Meerfey*) is laid out for an ensemble of solo voices in a manner resembling chamber music for strings (Ex. 156). Slighter in texture

Ex. 156

is *Der Bleicherin Nachtlied* (Op. 91, No. 11), an essay in 'volkstümlich' style. In 1850 Schumann again succeeded Hiller, this time at Düsseldorf, where choral singing had long flourished. But the Düsseldorf choir, though glad enough at the outset to welcome as

[1] See p. 90.

conductor a man of Schumann's distinction, soon found him quite ineffective on the rostrum. His directions in rehearsal were inadequate, and when given at all were hard to hear and understand. A decline in the standard of public performance soon became evident, and after a series of disagreeable incidents it was agreed that Schumann should conduct only his own works, leaving others to a deputy. He lacked all sympathy for the amateur choralist, who had then as now his limitations as well as his loyalties, and there is little doubt that mutual distrust between conductor and choir is reflected in the hesitant character of most of Schumann's choral writing.

While in Düsseldorf Schumann composed a quantity of part-songs with piano accompaniment—true a cappella singing being still rarely practised by amateurs at this period—and several works on a larger scale. *Der Rose Pilgerfahrt*, Op. 112, has incurred much derision from the sentimental nature of the text, a poem by Moritz Horn. Sentimentality, however, is a quality one must be prepared to accept in generous measure in dealing with mid-nineteenth century German literature and music, and Schumann's cantata is not without its musical qualities. One sometimes forgets that in the nationalist movements of the time German-speaking peoples had their share, and that Schumann can be as distinctively German as Smetana is Czech or Glinka Russian. The whole of this score is steeped in Teutonic folk-music. And not only the cast of the melodies themselves, but also their treatment, is typical. Nothing could be more naïvely ingenious, for example, than the canonic working of the opening tune in *The Pilgrimage of the Rose* (Ex. 157) or the beginning of Part II, with its 'gemütlich' picture of the miller's dwelling (Ex.

158); or the woodland scenes, where a male voice chorus accompanied by four horns and bass trombone recalls the *Jagdlieder*, Op. 137. The chorus of sprites at the close of Part I proves that Schumann could write fairy music as dainty as Mendelssohn's (Ex. 159). The

Ex. 159

dirge (No. 8) makes effective use of soloist and chorus in the manner
of the first scene of Gluck's *Orphée*.

The first bars of *Der Königssohn*, Op. 116, a setting of a ballad by
Uhland, are impressive in their romantic 'Balladtone' (Ex. 160) and

Ex.160

give promise that is hardly fulfilled by succeeding pages, though the
storm-music and the chorus that depicts the taming of the wild
horse are animated and picturesque. Schumann goes again to
Uhland for the text of *Des Sängers Fluch*, Op. 139. The poem, as
remodelled by Richard Pohl, provides opportunities for complete
self-contained solo numbers, among the best of which are the
Provençal Song the young minstrel sings to the Queen (Ex. 161),

Ex.161

and the old harper's ballad with its sombre scoring (Ex. 162). The male-voice hymn in praise of the Fatherland is an interesting topical touch. But the best music is to be found in the Epilogue, where the narrator tells how the old minstrel, bearing away the body

Ex. 162

of his young companion, turns back to lay a curse upon the King and his household. In dramatic power, orchestral colour, and above all harmonic originality this is one of the most remarkable passages in all Schumann's works (Ex. 163). Yet another ballad by Uhland, *Das Glück von Edenhall*, was set as a cantata, Op. 143. The weird legend, familiar to us in Longfellow's translation, demands and

Ex. 163

a) Nach und nach schneller

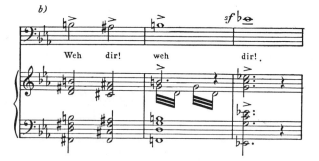

receives vigorous, forthright treatment with no musical feature calling for special comment.

Vom Pagen und der Königstochter, Op. 140, is based on four ballads by Emanuel Geibel. Schumann turns to good account the occasions provided for picturesque music. He uses the chorus sparingly but on the whole effectively, as in the hunting scene in the first ballad, the dance around the runic stone in the third, and the ball-scene in the fourth, where the waltz-rhythm is broken momentarily as the Princess thinks of her lost Page (Ex. 164). Here again

Ex. 164

there is some attractive scoring, especially in the fairy music and the passage depicting the Merman blowing on his conch-shell (Ex. 165).

To Schumann's Düsseldorf period belong his two attempts to supply music for the Catholic festival services that were a feature of the life of the town. The Mass in E flat, Op. 147, is, in spite of the

composer's efforts to achieve modernity of effect, an unconvincing
work. Not once does Schumann achieve the sonority of vocal
polyphony suggested instrumentally two years earlier in the *Rhenish
Symphony*. The academic note-spinning to which he subdues his

Ex. 165

lyrical imagination never comes to life, and even in the more freely-
conceived episodes, like the Offertorium, he shows less than his
usual spontaneity. Here and there are the germs of promising ideas,
for example the bold opening of the Dies Irae (Ex. 166), which

Ex. 166

wither almost as soon as they have sprung up. The Requiem, Op.
148, regarded by the composer as a more personal work than the
Mass, is no more distinguished for vigour or originality. The earlier
Adventlied, Op. 71 (text by Rückert) shows the composer more at
home in a type of work influenced by the church cantatas of Bach,
and giving evidence of a sense of the Lutheran tradition in some
striking chorale-like passages (Ex. 167). The *Neujahrslied*, Op. 144,
(text again by Rückert) is more secular in tone, but ends with the
chorale 'Nun danket alle Gott'. A large orchestra, including four
trombones, is used, and there are some good touches of scoring,

such as the flicker of violins, violas, and flutes over rapid cello scales and sustained oboe notes at the words 'In dunkelen Zügen, in flammender Glut'. The *Rheinweinlied* Overture, though partly choral, belongs properly to the orchestral music and has been dealt with in a previous chapter.[1] *Beim Abschied zu singen,* a setting of a

Ex. 167

poem by Feuchtersleben, dates from the Dresden days; it is both brief and simple, and the accompaniment for wind-band doubling the voices indicates that it was destined for outdoor performance.

Finally, two choral works stand somewhat apart from those already

Ex. 168

---

[1] See p. 243.

brachten wir ihn her!

considered. One is the *Requiem for Mignon*, from *Wilhelm Meister*, Op. 98 *b*. Here the pathos of the verses has inspired Schumann to achieve a more than usually satisfying effect in the choral passages. The orchestra, which includes a harp, is also used with skill. Especially poignant are the sobbing violin passages in the accompaniment to 'Ach! wie ungern brachten wir ihr her!' (Ex. 168), and the march-like rhythm, suggestive of a cortege, that persists throughout that passage is treated in another way, with interlacing figures for oboe and bassoon, at the bass solo: 'Kinder, kehret in's Leben zurück!' (Ex. 169). The *Nachtlied*, Op. 108, is based on a short poem by

Ex. 169

Kin - der, kehret in's Le-ben zurück!

U

Hebbel; the three stanzas dictate a well-balanced musical scheme, and once again there is some admirable orchestral writing, as in the darkly-coloured introduction (Ex. 170) and at the words 'In den

Ex. 170

ewigen Fernen, Sage, was ist da erwacht?' (Ex. 171). Less fortunately conceived is the alternation of upper and lower voices at the

Ex. 171

word 'Schlaf!' (Ex. 172), an instrumental idea alien to choral style.

From what has been said in this chapter it will be realized that little can be offered in the way of praise for Schumann's choral works as such. But moments of beauty these works do contain, even though one comes upon them more often in the orchestral than the choral parts of the score. That Schumann found not only pleasure but also technical profit in writing them is suggested by his remark

in a letter to Reinecke: 'The best way of developing one's melodic sense is to write a great deal for the voice, and especially for independent chorus'.

CHRONOLOGY

1810. Born at Zwickau, Saxony, 8 June.
1817–20. At Dr. Döhner's private school.
1818. First music lessons.
1820–8. Pupil at the Lyceum.
1822. Setting of Psalm 150.
1826. Sister's suicide; father's death.
1827. Enthusiasm for Jean Paul; earliest songs.
1828–9. Goes to Leipzig University to study law; songs; piano waltzes and four-hand polonaises; meeting with Wieck and Clara.
1829. Begins piano study with Wieck; law studies at Heidelberg; holiday in Switzerland and Italy.
1830. Returns to Leipzig and abandons law; *Abegg* Variations.
1831. Studies composition with Heinrich Dorn; first literary publication ('Ein Werk II').
1832. Injury to hand; Symphony in G minor; *Papillons* in final form.
1834–44. Edits *Neue Zeitschrift für Musik*.
1834–5. Engagement to Ernestine von Fricken; *Carnaval*.
1836. Wieck forbids communication with Clara; *Fantasie*, Op. 17.
1837. Formal engagement to Clara in defiance of Wieck; *Davidsbündlertänze; Fantasiestücke*.
1838. *Kinderscenen: Kreisleriana: Novelletten*.
1838–9. Winter in Vienna (September–March); discovery of Schubert's C major Symphony.
1839. Beginning of legal proceedings against Wieck.
1840. Great number of songs composed; marriage to Clara, 12 September.
1841. Symphonies in B flat and D minor; first movement of Piano Concerto.
1842. String quartets; Piano Quintet and Quartet.
1843. Period of mental exhaustion; opening of Leipzig Conservatoire; *Das Paradies und die Peri*.
1844. Visit to Russia; nervous breakdown (August); removal to Dresden (December).
1845. Piano Concerto completed.
1846. Symphony in C.
1848. *Genoveva: Album für die Jugend*.
1849. Dresden rising; *Manfred*.
1850. Removal to Düsseldorf; Symphony in E flat; 'Cello Concerto.
1851. Violin Sonatas.
1852–3. Pressure to resign Düsseldorf post.
1853. Meeting with Brahms; Violin Concerto.
1854. Publication of *Gesammelte Schriften*; attempted suicide (27 February); removal to asylum at Endenich.
1856. Death at Endenich on 29 July.

BIBLIOGRAPHY

ABERT, HERMANN: *Robert Schumann* (Berlin, 1903).
—— 'Robert Schumann's "Genoveva" ' (in *Zeitschrift der Internationalen Musikgesellschaft*, Jg. XI, 1910).

ABRAHAM, GERALD: 'On a Dull Overture by Schumann' (*Hermann und Dorothea*) (in *Monthly Musical Record*, Vol. LXXVI, 1946).
—— 'Recent Research on Schumann' (in *Proceedings of the Royal Musical Association*, 1948–9).
—— 'Schumann's "Jugendsinfonie" in G minor' (in *Musical Quarterly*, Vol. XXXVII, 1951).
—— 'Schumann's Opp. II and III' (in *Monthly Musical Record*, Vol. LXXVI, 1946).
—— 'The Three Scores of Schumann's D minor Symphony' (in *Musical Times*, Vol. 81, 1940).

D'ALBERT, MARGUERITE: *Robert Schumann: son œuvre de piano* (Paris, 1904).

ALDRICH, RICHARD: 'Schumann' in Cobbett's *Cyclopedic Survey of Chamber Music* (London, 1930).

ALTMANN, GUSTAV: 'Über Robert Schumanns Krankheit' (in *Die Musik*, Jg. V, 1905–6).

ALTMANN, WILHELM: 'Vier Briefe Richard Wagners an Robert Schumann' (in *Die Musik*, Jg. IV, 1904–5).
—— 'Bisher unveröffentlichte Briefe Robert Schumanns' (in *Die Musik*, Jg. XV, 1922–23).

AMBROS, A. W.: 'Robert Schumanns Tage und Werke' (in *Culturhistorische Bilder aus der Gegenwart*, Leipzig, 1860).

BAGGE, S.: 'Schumann und seine Faustszenen' (in Waldersee's *Sammlung musikalischer Vorträge*, 1880).

BASCH, VICTOR: *La vie douloureuse de Schumann* (Paris, 1928; English version, *Schumann, a Life of Suffering*, New York, 1932).
—— *Schumann* (Paris, 1926).

BEAUFILS, M.: *Schumann* (Paris, 1932).

BECKER, MARTHA: 'Neue Briefe von Rob. Schumann an Karl Kossmaly' (in *Die Musik*, January 1942).

BEDFORD, HERBERT: *Robert Schumann: his life and work* (London, 1925).

BERG, ALBAN: 'Die musikalische Impotenz der "Neuen Ästhetik" Hans Pfitzners' (on Schumann's *Träumerei*) (in *Musikblätter des Anbruch*, Jg. II, Nos. 11–12, 1920; reprinted in *Alban Berg*, by Willi Reich, Vienna, 1937).

BIENENFELD, ELSA: 'Der Stammtafel der Familie Schumann' (in *Archiv für Rassen-und Gesellschaftsbiologie*, 1932).

BOETTICHER, WOLFGANG: 'Ein neuer Marsch von Robert Schumann' (in *Die Musik*, Jg. 33, 1941).

—— 'Robert Schumann an Seine Königlicher Majestät' (in *Die Musik*, Jg. 32, 1940).

—— *Robert Schumann: Einführung in Persönlichkeit und Werk* (Berlin, 1941).

—— 'Robert Schumann in seinen Beziehungen zu Johannes Brahms' (in *Die Musik*, Jg. 29, 1937).

—— *Robert Schumann in seinen Schriften und Briefen* (Berlin, 1942).

—— 'Zum neuen Marsch von Robert Schumann' (in *Die Musik*, Jg. 34, 1941).

BOUYER, R.: 'Schumann et la musique à programme' (in *Le Ménéstrel*, 1903).

BÜCKEN, E.: *R. Schumann* (Cologne, 1940).

—— *Musik des 19. Jahrhunderts bis zur Moderne* (Potsdam, 1929).

CALVOCORESSI, M. D.: *Schumann* (Paris, 1906).

CARNER, MOSCO: 'Mahler's Re-scoring of the Schumann Symphonies' (in *The Music Review*, Vol. II, 1941; reprinted in *Of Men and Music*, London, 1942).

CHALUPT, RENÉ: 'Schumann musicien poète' (in *La Revue musicale* 1935).

CHANTAVOINE, JEAN: 'La jeunesse de Schumann' (in *Musiciens et Poètes*, Paris, 1912).

CHÉVILLARD, CAMILLE: 'Schumann' (in *Le Courier Musical*, 1906).

CHISSELL, JOAN: *Schumann* (London, 1948).

COHEN, M.: *Studien zur Sonataform bei Robert Schumann* (Vienna thesis, 1928).

COLLING, A.: *La vie de Robert Schumann* (Paris, 1931).

DAHMS, WALTER: *Robert Schumann* (Berlin-Leipzig, 1916).

DAVIES, FANNY: 'Some Notes on the Interpretation of Schumann's Chamber Music' in *Cobbett's Cyclopedic Survey of Chamber Music* (London, 1930).

DIETRICH, ALBERT: 'Über Robert Schumanns Ende' (in *Die Grenzboten*, 1854).

DUVAL, R.: 'L' "Amour du poète" de Schumann-Heine' (in *Rivista musicale italiana*, Vol. VIII, 1901).

ENGEL, HANS: *Die Entwicklung des deutschen Klavierkonzerts von Mozart bis Liszt* (Leipzig, 1927).

ERLER, HERMANN: *Robert Schumanns Leben und Werke, aus seinen Briefen geschildert*, 2 vols. (Leipzig, 1887).

—— 'Zwei ungedruckte Briefe von Robert Schumann' (in *Die Musik*, Jg. II, 1903).

—— 'Ein ungedruckter Canon und sechs ungedruckte Haus- und Lebensregeln Robert Schumanns' (in *Die Musik*, Jg. V, 1905–6).

ERNST, GUSTAV: 'Der kranke Schumann' (in *Die Medizinische Welt*, 1929).

FELBER, RUDOLF: *Robert Schumanns Lieder* (Vienna thesis, 1919).

—— 'Schumann's Place in German Song' (in *Musical Quarterly*, Vol. XXVI, 1940).

FRIEDLÄNDER, MAX: 'Balladen-Fragmente von Robert Schumann' (in *Peters-Jahrbuch*, 1897).

—— *Textrevision bei Robert Schumanns Liedern* (Leipzig, N.D.).

FULLER-MAITLAND, J. A.: *Robert Schumann* (London, 1884).

—— *Schumann's Concerted Chamber Music* (London, 1929).

—— *Schumann's Pianoforte Works* (London, 1927).

GEIGER, BENNO: 'Phantasiestück von Schumann: eine Deutung' (in *Zeitschrift für Musik*, Vol. 98, 1902).

GEIRINGER, KARL: 'Ein unbekanntes Blatt aus Schumanns Endenicher. Zeit' (in *Anbruch*, 1935).

—— 'Ein unbekanntes Klavierwerk aus Schumanns Jugendzeit' (the Polonaises for piano duet) (in *Die Musik*, Jg. 25, 1933).

—— 'Le feuillet d'Endenich' (in *Revue musicale*, 1935).

—— 'Schumann in Wien' (in *Zeitschrift für Musik*, 1931).

GENSEL, J.: *Robert Schumanns Briefwechsel mit Henriette Voigt, geb. Kuntze* (extended offprint from *Die Grenzboten*, 1892).

GEORGII, WALTER: *Klaviermusik* (Berlin and Zürich, 1941).

GERTLER, WOLFGANG: *Robert Schumann in seinen frühen Klavierwerken* (Wolfenbüttel, 1931).

—— *R. Schumann: sein Leben in Bildern* (Leipzig, 1936).

GOLDENBERG, R.: *Der Klaviersatz bei Schumann* (Vienna thesis, 1931).

GOSLICH, SIEGFRIED: *Beiträge zur Geschichte der deutschen romantischen Oper* (Leipzig, 1937).

GURLITT, WILLIBALD: 'Robert Schumann in seinen Skizzen gegenüber Beethoven' (in *Kongressbericht der Beethoven-Zentenarfeier*, Vienna, 1927).

HADOW, W. H.: 'Robert Schumann and the Romantic Movement in Germany' (in *Studies in Modern Music*, first series, London, 1892).

HERNRIED, ROBERT: 'Four Unpublished Compositions by Robert Schumann' (in *Musical Quarterly*, Vol. XXVIII, 1942).

HEUBERGER, RICHARD: *Robert Schumanns 'Szenen aus Goethes "Faust"'* (Frankfurt, N.D.).

HIRSCHBERG, LEOPOLD: 'Merkwürdiges aus einem Schumann-Erstdruck' (in *Die Musik*, Jg. XXI, 1929).

HOHENEMSER, RICHARD: 'Formale Eigentümlichkeiten in Robert Schumanns Klaviermusik' (in *Sandberger-Festschrift*, Munich, 1918).

—— 'R. Schumann unter der Einfluss der Alten' (in *Die Musik*, Jg. IX, 1909–10).

HÜBNER, R.: 'Ein Brief Schumanns über seine Faustmusik' (in *Goethe quarterly*, Leipzig, 1936).

ISTEL, EDGAR: *Die Blütezeit der musikalischen Romantik in Deutschland* (Leipzig, 1909).

JACOBS, ROBERT L.: 'Schumann and Jean Paul' (in *Music and Letters*, Vol. XXX, 1949).

JANSEN, GUSTAV: *Briefe von Robert Schumann: Neue Folge* (Leipzig, 1886; English version, *The Life of Robert Schumann told in his Letters*, London, 1890; second, enlarged, edition, Leipzig, 1904).

—— 'Briefwechsel zwischen Robert Franz und Robert Schumann' (in *Die Musik*, Jg. VIII, 1908–9).

—— *Die Davidsbündler: Aus Robert Schumanns Sturm und Drang Periode* (Leipzig, 1883).

—— 'Aus Robert Schumanns Schulzeit' (in *Die Musik*, Jg. V, 1905–6).

—— 'Ein unbekannter Brief von Robert Schumann' (in *Die Musik*, Jg. V, 1905–6).

—— 'Schumann und Vesque von Pütlingen' (in *Die Grenzboten*, 1894).

JONAS, A.: *Das Skizzenbuch zu Schumanns Jugendalbum* (in *Zeitschrift für Musik*, 1931).

JOSS, F. W.: *Der Musikpädagoge Wieck und Schumann* (Dresden, 1902).

KALBECK, MAX: 'R. Schumann in Wien' (in *Wiener Allgemeine Zeitung*, 1880).

KAPP, JULIUS: 'Schumanns *Études Symphoniques*, Op. 13' (in *Die Musik*, Jg. IX, 1909–10).

KARSTEN, OTTO: *Die Instrumentation Schumanns* (Vienna thesis, 1922).

KERST, FRIEDRICH: *Schumann-Brevier* (Berlin, 1905).

KINSKY, G.: 'Ein unbekanntes Fantasiestück Schumanns' (in *Schweizerische Musikzeitung*, 1935).

KNAYER, C.: 'Robert Schumann als Meister der rhythmischen Verschiebungen' (in *Musikpädagogische Blätter*, Jg. 37, 1914).

—— 'Schumanns Klavierstil' (in *Neue Musikzeitung*, 1911).

KORTE, WERNER: *R. Schumann* (Potsdam, 1937).

KÖTZ, HANS: *Der Einfluss Jean Pauls auf Robert Schumann* (Weimar, 1933).

KREISIG, MARTIN: *Stammbaum der Familie Schumann* (Zwickau, 1931).

KRETZSCHMAR, HERMANN: 'Robert Schumann als Ästhetiker' (in *Peters-Jahrbuch*, 13, 1906, and *Gesammelte Aufsätze*, Leipzig, 1911).

LEIBBRANDT, WERNER: 'Der kranke Schumann' (in *Die Medizinische Welt*, 1924).

LEYN, GERHARD: 'Die moderne medizinische Bewertung des Leidens Robert Schumanns' (in *Stolberger Anzeiger*, 9 September 1933).

LISZT, FRANZ: 'Robert Schumann' (in *Gesammelte Werke*, Vol. IV, Leipzig, 1882).

LITZMANN, BERTHOLD: *Clara Schumann: ein Künstlerleben nach Tage-büchern und Briefen*. 3 vols. (Leipzig, 1902–8; abridged English version, 2 vols., London, 1913).

LÜBKE, G. VON: 'Schumann und die Programmusik' (in *Neue Musikzeitung*, 1906).

MÄCKLENBURG, ALBERT: 'Liszt in seinen Beziehungen zu R. Schumann' (in *Der Klavierlehrer*, Jg. 28, 1905).

—— 'R. Schumanns Erstlingswerke' (in *Musikpädagogische Blätter*, Jg. 39, 1916).

MACMASTER, HENRY: *La Folie de Robert Schumann* (Paris, 1928).

MAUCLAIR, CAMILLE: *Schumann* (Paris, 1906).

MEY, KURT: 'Über Robert Schumanns Krankheit' (in *Neue Musikzeitung*, 1910).

MEYER, KATHI: 'Schumanns Faustmusik' (in *Frankfurter Zeitung*, 10 March 1926).

MEYERSTEIN, E. W. H.: 'A Note on Schumann's Last Composition' (in *Music Survey*, No. 3, May 1948).

MIES, PAUL: 'Goethes Harfenspielergesang "Wer sich der Einsamkeit ergibt" in den Kompositionen Schuberts, Schumanns und Wolfs' (in *Zeitschrift für Ästhetik*, Vol. 16, 1921).

—— 'R. Schumanns "Rheinische" Kompositionen' (in *Halbmonatsschrift für Schulmusikpflege*, Jg. 24, 1929).

MINOTTI, GIOVANNI: 'Schumann: Fantasie C dur' (in *Die Geheimdoku-mente der Davidsbündler*, Leipzig, 1934).

—— *Die Enträtselung des Schumannschen Sphinx-Geheimnisses* (Leipzig, 1926).

—— 'Die Enträtselung des Schumannschen Abegg-Geheimnisses' (in *Zeitschrift für Musik*, 1927).

MÖBIUS, P. J.: *Über Robert Schumanns Krankheit* (Halle, 1906).

MORSELLI, E.: *La Pazzia di Roberto Schumann e la psicologia supernormale* (Rome, 1909).

NAGEL, WILLIBALD: *Die musikalische Bearbeitung der Genoveva-Legende* (Leipzig, 1889).

—— 'Schumann und wir' (in *Neue Zeitschrift für Musik*, 1906).

NIECKS, FREDERICK: *Robert Schumann: a supplementary and corrective biography* (London, 1925).

NINCK, MARTIN: *Schumann und die Romantik in der Musik* (Heidelberg, 1929).

NOREN-HERZBERG, G.: 'Robert Schumann als Musikschriftsteller' (in *Die Musik*, Jg. V, 1905–6).

NUSSBAUM, E.: *Der Streit um Robert Schumanns Krankheit* (Cologne medical thesis, 1923).

OEHM, FRANZ: *Das Stimmungslied Schumanns* (Leipzig thesis, 1919).

PASCAL, DR.: 'Les Maladies mentales de Robert Schumann' (in *Journal de Psychologie Normal et Pathologique*, March–April 1908)⁴

306 SCHUMANN

PATTERSON, ANNIE W.: *Schumann* (revised edition by Eric Blom, London, 1934).

PESSENLEHNER, R.: 'Robert Schumann und die *Neue Zeitschrift für Musik*' (in *Neue Zeitschrift für Musik*, Jg. 100, 1934).

PFORDTEN, H. VON DER: R. *Schumann* (Leipzig, 1920).

PIERNÉ, GABRIEL, and WOOLLETT, HENRY: 'Schumann' (in 'Histoire de l'Orchestration' in Lavignac's *Encyclopédie de la Musique*, Part 2, Vol. IV, Paris, 1929).

PITROU, ROBERT: *La vie intérieure de Robert Schumann* (Paris, 1925).

POHL, RICHARD: 'Erinnerungen an R. Schumann' (in *Deutsche Revue*, 1878).

PUGNO, RAOUL: *Leçons écrites sur Schumann* (Paris, 1914).

PUTTMANN, MAX: 'Robert Schumann in seinen Klavierwerken' (in *Musikalisches Wochenblatt*, Jg. 41, 1910).

REDLICH, H. F.: 'Schumann Discoveries' (in *Monthly Musical Record*, Vol. 80, 1950).

—— 'Schumann Discoveries: a Postscript' (in *Monthly Musical Record*, Vols. 80–81, 1950–51).

REICH, WILLI: *Robert Schumann: Aus Kunst und Leben* (selected writings) (Basel, 1945).

REIMANN, HEINRICH: R. *Schumanns Leben und Werke* (Leipzig, 1887).

REINECKE, KARL: 'Über Robert Schumanns Krankheit' (in *Deutsche Revue*, 1896).

REISSMANN, AUGUST: R. *Schumann, sein Leben und seine Werke* (Leipzig, 1879; English version, *The Life of Schumann*, London, 1886).

RICHARTZ, DR.: 'Robert Schumanns Krankheit' (in *Kölnische Zeitung*, 15 August 1873 and *Signale für die Musikalische Welt*, 1873).

ROLLETT, HERMANN: 'Aus Robert Schumanns letzter Zeit' (in *Wiener musikalische Zeitung*, 1885–6).

ROSENWALD, H. H.: 'Die geschichtliche Bedeutung des Schumannschen Liedes' (in *Die Musik*, Jg. 24, 1932).

SCHAAFHAUSEN, ROBERT: 'Robert Schumanns Gehirn- und Gehörsorgane' (in *Korrespondenzblatt der Deutschen Anthropologischen Gesellschaft*, Jg. XVI, 1885).

SCHAUFFLER, ROBERT H.: *Florestan: the Life and Work of Robert Schumann* (New York, 1945).

SCHERING, ARNOLD: 'Robert Schumann als Tragiker' (in *Neue Zeitschrift für Musik*, 1901).

SCHMITZ, ARNOLD: 'Anfänge der Ästhetik R. Schumanns' (in *Zeitschrift für Musikwissenschaft*, Jg. 2, 1920).

—— 'Die ästhetischen Anschauungen R. Schumanns in ihren Beziehungen zur romantischen Literatur' (in *Zeitschrift für Musikwissenschaft*, Jg. 3, 1920–1).

—— 'Wie steht Schumann theoretisch zur Programmusik?' (in *Neue Musikzeitung*, Jg. 42, 1921).

SCHNAPP, F.: 'Robert Schumanns Plan zu einer Oper *Tristan und Isolde*' (in *Die Musik*, 1925).
—— *Heinrich Heine und Robert Schumann* (Hamburg-Berlin, 1924).

SCHNEIDER, LOUIS, and MARESCHAL MARCEL: *Schumann, sa vie et ses œuvres* (Paris, 1905).

SCHUMANN, ALFRED: *Der junge Schumann: Dichtungen und Briefe* (Leipzig, 1910).

SCHUMANN, CLARA: *Robert Schumanns Jugendbriefe* (Leipzig, 1885; English version, London, 1888).

SCHUMANN, EUGENIE: *Erinnerungen* (Stuttgart, 1927; English version, *Memoirs*, London, 1930).
—— *R. Schumann: Ein Lebensbild meines Vaters* (Leipzig, 1931).
—— 'The Diary of Robert and Clara Schumann' (excerpts quoted from the *Lebensbild*, in *Music and Letters*, Vol. XV, 1934).

SCHUMANN, FERDINAND: 'Ein unbekannter Jugendbrief von Robert Schuman' (in *Die Musik*, Jg. IX, 1909–1910).

SCHUMANN, ROBERT: *Erinnerungen an Felix Mendelssohn-Bartholdy* (Zwickau, 1947).
Gesammelte Schriften über Musik und Musiker. 4 vols. (Leipzig, 1854; fifth, critical edition in 2 vols. by M. Kreisig, Leipzig, 1914; English translation, 2 vols., London, 1877; new translation, selection in 1 vol., London, 1947).
(For letters see under Becker, Boetticher, Erler, Hübner, Jansen, Litzmann, Schumann (Alfred), Schumann (Clara), Schumann (Ferdinand), Straeten, Wasielewski, Weinhold).

SCHWARZ, WERNER: *Robert Schumann und die Variation* (Kassel, 1932).
—— *Schumann und die Sonatenform* (Königsberg thesis, 1932).

SCHWEIGER, M.: *Die Harmonik in den Klavierwerken Schumanns* (Vienna thesis, 1931).

SIMON, JAMES: 'R. Schumanns Klaviermusik' (in *Allgemeine Musikzeitung*, 1910).

SPITTA, PHILIPP: 'Schumann' in *Grove's Dictionary of Music and Musicians* (London, 1879).

STASOV, V. V.: *Liszt, Schumann i Berlioz v Rossii* (St. Petersburg, 1896).

STERNFELD, RICHARD: 'Einige Bemerkungen zum Schaffen Robert Schumanns' (in *Die Musik*, Jg. IX, 1909–1910).

STORCK, KARL: *Schumanns Briefe* (selection, 1896; English translation, *The Letters of Robert Schumann*, London, 1907).

STRAETEN, E. VAN DER: 'Mendelssohns and Schumanns Beziehungen zu J. H. Lübeck und J. J. H. Verhulst (unpublished letters) (in *Die Musik*, Jg. III, 1903–4).
—— 'Streiflichter auf Mendelssohns und Schumanns Beziehungen zu zeitgenössischen Musikern (in *Die Musik*, Jg. IV, 1904–5).

STRASSBURGER, DR.: 'Schumanns Krankheit' (in *Die Musik*, Jg. VI).

STRICH, FR.: '*Manfred* von Schumann' (in *Singer-Festgabe*, Tübingen, 1930).

TESSMER, HANS: *Robert Schumann* (Stuttgart, 1930).

TIERSOT, JULIEN: 'Robert Schumann et la Revolution de 1848' (in *Revue Musicale*, S.I.M., Vol. IX, 1913).

TORCHI, L.: 'R. Schumann e le sue *Scene tratte dal Faust di Goethe*' (in *Rivista musicale italiana*, Vol. II, 1895).

TOVEY, DONALD F.: Analyses of *Carnaval*, Introduction and Allegro Appassionato, *Overture, Scherzo and Finale*, Overture to *Manfred*, Piano Concerto, Symphonies No. 1, 3, and 4, Violoncello Concerto, Novellette, Op. 21, No. 8, and Piano Quintet (in *Essays in Musical Analysis*, 7 vols., London, 1935–44).

—— 'Schumann's Concerto for Four Horns and Orchestra' (in *The Music Review*, Vol. I, 1940).

VANSCA: 'R. Schumanns Einfluss auf die Entwicklung der Programmusik' (in *Die Musik*, Jg. VIII, 1909).

VALABREGA, CESARE: *Schumann* (Modena, 1934).

VIDOR, MARTHA: *Zur Begriffsbestimmung des musikalischen Charakterstückes* (Leipzig thesis, 1924).

WAGNER, KURT: *Robert Schumann als Schüler und Abiturient* (Zwickau, 1928).

WALDERSEE, PAUL GRAF: 'Über Schumanns *Manfred*' (in *Sammlung Musikalischer Vorträge*, 1880).

WASIELEWSKI, W. J. VON: *Robert Schumann: Eine Biographie* (Dresden, 1858; English translation, 1886; fourth, revised and greatly extended edition, Leipzig, 1906).

—— 'Robert Schumanns Herzenserlebnisse' (in *Deutsche Revue*, Jg. XXII, 1894).

—— *Schumanniana* (Bonn, 1884).

WEINGARTNER, FELIX: *Ratschläge für Aufführungen klassischer Symphonien* —Band II: *Schubert und Schumann* (Leipzig, 1919).

WEINHOLD, L.: 'Geschäftsbriefe von grossen Musikern' (introduces new Schumann letters) (in *Leipziger Jahrbuch*, Jg. 40, 1939).

WILCKE, G.: *Tonalität und Modulation im Streichquartett Mendelssohns und Schumanns* (Rostock thesis, 1933).

WINDSPERGER, LOTHAR: Skizzenbuch R. Schumanns zu dem 'Album für die Jugend' (introduction and notes to facsimile) (Mainz, 1924).

WOLFF, V. E.: *Robert Schumanns Lieder in ersten und späteren Fassungen* (Leipzig, 1914).

—— 'Robert Schumannns Lyrik' (in *Die Musik*, Jg. IX, 1909–1910).

WÖLFFLIN, EDUARD: 'Zur B-Dur Sinfonie von Robert Schumann' (in *Musikalisches Wochenblatt*, 1898).

WÖRNER, K. H.: *Robert Schumann* (Zürich, 1949).

WUSTMANN, GUSTAV: 'Zur Entstehungsgeschichte der Schumannischen *Zeitschrift für Musik*' (in *Zeitschrift der Internationalen Musikgesellschaft*, Jg. VIII, 1907).

CHRONOLOGICAL LIST OF COMPOSITIONS
(*with page references*)

ORCHESTRAL WORKS

Opus
No.

(7)   Symphony in G minor (1833): 22, 178-9, 185, 187-90, 193, 196.

38   Symphony No. 1 in B flat (1841): 139, 156, 181-4, 190-201, 203, 208, 210, 214, 221, 223, 229-30, 232, 236, 244, 248.

52   *Overture, Scherzo and Finale*[1] (1841; Finale revised 1845): 184, 201-4, 228-30, 244.

120   Symphony No. 4 in D minor (1841; completely revised 1851): 139-41, 146, 160, 179, 182-3, 185-6, 204-19, 221-2, 224, 230, 232, 235-6, 244.

None   Symphony in C minor (complete sketches; scherzo published as piano solo, Op. 99, No. 13) (1841): 67, 219.

61   Symphony No. 2 in C[2] (1846): 140, 156, 178, 180-4, 205, 220-30, 234-6, 276.

97   Symphony No. 3 in E flat (*Rhenish*) (1850): 140, 178-9, 181-2, 184, 198, 205, 209, 223, 230-8, 244, 262, 295.

100   Overture to Schiller's *Braut von Messina* (1851): 202, 238-42.

128   Overture to Shakespeare's *Julius Caesar* (1851): 242.

136   Overture to Goethe's *Hermann und Dorothea*[2] (1851): 242-3.

123   *Festouvertüre über das Rheinweinlied* (with chorus) (1853): 243-4, 296.

WORKS FOR SOLO INSTRUMENT WITH ORCHESTRA

None   Piano Concerto in F minor (unfinished) (1827).

None   Piano Concerto in F major (unfinished) (1830): 15.

None   Introduction, Paganini theme and sketches for four Variations, for piano (1830): 17, 34, 43.

None   Piano Concerto in D minor (unfinished) (1839).

54   Piano Concerto in A minor (first movement as *Fantasie*, 1841; remainder 1845): 67, 72, 139, 141, 159, 167, 173, 176, 222, 245-9, 258-9.

86   *Concertstück*, for four horns (1849): 245, 251-2.

92   *Concertstück* (Introduction and Allegro appassionato in G major), for piano (1849): 245, 249-51, 259.

129   'Cello Concerto in A minor (1850): 245-6, 252-4, 258-9.

131   *Fantasie* in C, for violin (1853): 245, 254-5.

134   Concert Allegro with Introduction, for piano (1853): 89, 245, 250-1, 255.

None   Violin Concerto in D minor (1853): 71, 245-6, 251, 255-8.

[1] Arranged for piano solo by the composer (1853).
[2] Arranged for piano duet by the composer.

CHAMBER MUSIC

Opus
(1) Piano Quartet in C minor (1829): 15, 49, 138-9.
None String Quartet (lost) (1838): 139.
None Openings of three string quartets (lost) (1839): 139.
41 Three String Quartets (1842)
  No. 1 in A minor[1]: 139-40, 142-6, 148, 162, 168.
  No. 2 in F major[1]: 51, 139-42, 146-8.
  No. 3 in A major: 139-42, 148-50, 200.
44 Piano Quintet in E flat (1842): 67, 92, 139-40, 142, 150-5, 158, 171, 176, 272.
47 Piano Quartet in E flat (1842): 67, 139, 141-2, 155.
None Piano Trio in A minor (material later used in Op. 88) (1843): 139.
None Andante and Variations for two pianos, two 'cellos and horn (original version of Op. 46; see Works for Two Pianos) (1843): 68-9, 174-5.
63 Piano Trio No. 1 in D minor (1847): 140, 142, 158-61, 166, 276.
80 Piano Trio No. 2 in F (1847): 140-2, 161-4.
70 Adagio and Allegro for horn and piano (1849): 140, 171, 173.
73 *Fantasiestücke* for clarinet and piano (1849): 140, 172.
94 *Drei Romanzen* for oboe and piano (1849): 140, 172.
102 *Fünf Stücke im Volkston* for 'cello and piano (1849): 140, 172.
88 *Fantasiestücke* for piano trio (1850): 58, 139, 171-2.
105 Violin Sonata No. 1 in A minor (1851): 140-1, 167-8, 179, 235.
110 Piano Trio No. 3 in G minor (1851): 140, 142, 164-7, 179.
113 *Märchenbilder* for viola and piano (1851): 140, 173.
121 Violin Sonata No. 2 in D minor (1851): 140, 167-70, 179.
None Violin Sonata No. 3 in A minor (1853): 140.
132 *Märchenerzählungen* for clarinet, viola and piano (1853): 173.
None *Fünf Romanzen* for 'cello and piano (1853).

WORKS FOR PIANO SOLO

None *Sechs Walzer* (afterwards used in *Papillons*) (1829-30): 33-4, 36.
7 Toccata (originally *Étude fantastique* in D, 1829; second version in C, (orig.6) 1832): 7, 42, 46, 67.
1 Theme on the name ABEGG with variations (originally for piano and orchestra) (1830): 13-15, 18-21, 35, 39, 50, 61, 63.
None Sonata in A flat (two movements only) (1830?): 42.
8 Allegro in B minor (1831): 15, 17, 34, 42-3, 46, 64-5.
None Variations on an Original Theme (Andante in G, 'Mit Gott') (1832): 17-19, 23.
None Prelude and Fugue (1832): 15.
2 *Papillons* (1832): 10, 13-15, 18, 21, 33-9, 41, 43, 48-50, 52, 61, 63, 77, 85, 193, 198-9, 202.
3 Studies after Capricci by Paganini (1832): 13, 15, 21, 28-33.
(orig. 2)

[1] Arranged for piano solo by the composer (1853).

Opus

4   Six Intermezzi (originally *Pièces fantastiques*) (1832): 7, 15, 17, 34,
(orig. 3) 48-50, 64, 99, 139, 206.

None *Burlesken* (one published as Op. 124, No. 12, the remainder lost or
       unidentifiable) (1832).

None *Phantasie satyrique* (*nach Henri Herz*) (unfinished) (1832).

(4)   Fandango (afterwards used in Op 11) (1832): 43, 66.

(5)   *Exercice fantastique* (1832).

None Sketches for a movement in B flat, a fugal piece in B flat minor, and
       a canonic piece in A (1832?).

None Fugue No. 3 (adapted in the G minor Symphony and as finale for
       Op. 5) (1832): 22.

5   Impromptus on a Theme by Clara Wieck (1835; new version omitting
(orig. 8) two variations but introducing a new one, 1850): 8, 13, 18, 21-3,
       25, 52, 73, 190, 272.

(10) *Scènes musicales* (variations on Schubert's *Sehnsuchtswalzer*) (1833):
       17, 23, 39-41.

None *Etüden in Form freier Variationen über ein Beethovensches Thema* (one
       published as Op. 124, No. 2) (1833): 17, 23-5, 40, 50, 188.

None Andante in F (1833).

10   Concert Studies on Caprices by Paganini (1833): 13, 17, 28-33, 40, 67.

None *Variations sur un Nocturne de Chopin* (1834): 17-18.

9   *Carnaval* (1835): 13, 15, 18, 24, 33-4, 39-41, 45, 48, 52-3, 57, 61, 63-4,
       70-1, 73, 76, 88-9, 92, 152, 189, 193, 203, 231.

11   Sonata No. 1 in F sharp minor (1835): 15, 42-3, 47, 49, 64, 66-7, 98,
       141, 146, 178.

None Sonata movement in B flat (1836).

17   *Fantasie* (1836, as *Obolen auf Beethovens Monument*; revised 1838):
(orig.12) 35, 43, 45, 47-8, 63-4, 66-7, 92, 166, 229.

13   *Études symphoniques* (1836; revised edition in 1852 as *Études en forme
       de variations*; five more variations published in Supp. Vol. of *Gesamt-
       ausgabe*; one completed variation still unpublished): 13, 15, 23-8,
       47, 62, 64, 66, 71-2, 91-2, 102, 167, 264.

14   *Concert sans orchestre* in F minor (1836, published without scherzi;
       revised edition with Scherzo II restored, as Sonata No. 3, in
       1853; Scherzo I published in Supp. Vol. of G.A.): 13, 27, 42, 44,
       47-8, 62, 66, 179.

None Sonata No. 4 in F minor (unfinished) (1833-37).

12   *Fantasiestücke* (1837; a ninth piece, without title, published in
       Schweizerische Musikzeitung, 1935): 15, 24, 48, 50-1, 53-5, 57-9,
       62, 64-6, 68, 76, 94, 111, 136, 179, 198.

6   *Davidsbündlertänze* (1837; revised edition in 1851 as *Die Davids-
       bündler*): 24, 33, 49-53, 56-7, 61, 63-4, 66, 86, 231.

None Five Short Pieces (Nos. 1, 4 and 5 unfinished) (1837-8).

15   *Kinderscenen* (1838): 5, 53-5, 58, 61, 65-6, 77, 79, 83, 117, 149, 160,
       198, 235.

16   *Kreisleriana* (1838): 33, 49, 52, 54-9, 63, 65-6, 76, 91, 179, 200.

18   *Arabeske* (1838): 55, 57, 59-62, 65.

21   *Novelletten* (1838): 33, 48, 53-9, 61-5, 88.

312   SCHUMANN

Opus

22   Sonata No. 2 in G minor (1838; original finale of 1835 published in
        Supp. Vol. of G.A.): 24, 33, 39-40, 42, 44, 47-9, 55, 63, 65, 98,
        178, 247.
19   *Blumenstück* (1839): 55, 57, 59-61.
20   *Humoreske* (1839): 55, 57, 59-66, 75-6, 280.
32   *Clavierstücke* (1838–9): 48-9, 55, 57, 59, 64.
23   *Nachtstücke* (1839): 45, 48, 55, 57, 61-2, 66, 74, 77.
28   *Drei Romanzen* (1839): 55-7, 59, 62.
None   Allegro in C minor (lost) (1839).
None   Scherzino (lost) (1839).
26   *Faschingsschwank aus Wien* (1840): 43, 45-8, 50, 55, 59, 62-4, 68, 74,
        92, 242.
None   Sonatina in B flat (unfinished) (1840).
72   Four Fugues (1845): 72-3, 76-7, 261.
124   *Albumblätter* (1832–45): 15, 23, 34, 41, 50-1, 53, 55-6, 58, 61, 63, 67-8,
        72, 75, 77, 82-3, 93.
68   *Album für die Jugend* (1848; four more pieces in both fascimile and
        transcription, and five in facsimile only, published 1924): 53, 72,
        79-84, 96.
76   Four Marches (1849): 89, 91-3, 96, 242.
82   *Waldscenen* (1849): 53, 71, 89-91, 95-6, 267, 289.
99   *Bunte Blätter* (1834–49): 25, 41, 50, 55-8, 67-8, 77, 92-4, 219.
111   *Fantasiestücke* (1851): 58, 89, 94-6.
118   *Drei Clavier-Sonaten für die Jugend* (1853): 69, 71, 73, 79, 81, 83-4,
        86, 255.
126   *Sieben Clavierstücke in Fughettenform* (1853): 72, 77-9, 83.
133   *Gesänge der Frühe* (1853): 61, 63, 70-1, 78.
None   *Thema mit Variationen* (1854): 71.
None   Canon on F. H. Himmel's song *An Alexis* (date unknown): 73, 75.
None   *Romanza* in F minor (unfinished) (date unknown).

WORKS FOR PIANO DUET

III   Eight Polonaises (1828): 14-15, 35-7, 45, 61, 84-8.
None   Variations on a Theme by Prince Louis Ferdinand (lost) (1828): 15.
None   Capriccio (unfinished) (c. 1832): 15.
66   *Bilder aus Osten* (1848): 84, 86-8.
85   *Zwölf vierhändige Clavierstücke* (1849): 79, 81, 83-7, 96.
109   *Ball-Scenen* (1851): 85-6, 88-9.
130   *Kinderball* (No. 3, 1850; remainder 1853): 39, 79, 84-6, 89, 255.

WORK FOR TWO PIANOS

46   Andante and Variations (see also under Chamber Music) (1843):
        68-9, 71, 95, 174.

OTHER KEYBOARD WORKS

Opus

56 Six Studies for pedal-piano (1845): 72-4.

58 Four Sketches for pedal-piano (1845): 72-4.

60 Fugues on the name BACH, for organ or pedal-piano (1845): 72-3, 75-7, 261-2.

None Piece in two movements, for harmonium (1849).

DRAMATIC WORKS

None Fragments of an opera, *Der Corsar* (Oswald Marbach, after Byron) (1844): 272.

81 Opera, *Genoveva* (composer, after Tieck and Hebbel) (1848): 79, 140, 239, 241, 260, 272-82.

115 Overture and incidental music to *Manfred* (Byron) (1848): 238, 241, 260-7, 276.

None Scenes (and overture[1]) from *Faust* (Goethe) (1844-53): 255, 260, 266-72, 276.

WORKS FOR CHORUS AND ORCHESTRA

(1) *Le psaume cent cinquantième. Oratorium composée pour Soprano e Alto, Pianoforte, Deux Violons, Deux Flutes, Deux Hautbois, Deux Trompetes, Viola, Cor, Fagott et Tympani* (1822).

(1, No. 3) Overture and *Chor von Landleuten* (1822).

None *Tragödie* (Heine) (basis of Op. 64, No. 3: see Songs) (1841).

50 *Das Paradies und die Peri* (Flechsig, after Thomas Moore), for soli, chorus and orchestra) (1843): 140, 278, 283-6.

84 *Beim Abschied zu singen* (Feuchtersleben), for chorus and wind (1847): 296.

71 *Adventlied* (Rückert), for soprano, chorus and orchestra (1848): 295.

93 Motet, *Verzweifle nicht* (see Works for Male Voices).

98b *Requiem für Mignon* (Goethe), for soli, chorus and orchestra (1849): 297.

108 *Nachtlied* (Hebbel), for chorus and orchestra (1849): 297-9.

144 *Neujahrslied* (Rückert), for chorus and orchestra (1850): 295.

112 *Der Rose Pilgerfahrt* (Moritz Horn), for soli, chorus and piano (afterwards orchestrated) (1851): 242, 290-1.

116 *Der Königssohn* (Uhland and Horn), for soli, chorus and orchestra (1851): 292.

139 *Des Sängers Fluch* (Uhland and Pohl), for soli, chorus and orchestra (1852): 292-3.

140 *Vom Pagen und der Königstochter* (Geibel), for soli, chorus and orchestra (1852): 294.

147 Mass, for chorus and orchestra (1852): 294-5.

148 Requiem, for chorus and orchestra (1852): 295.

143 *Das Glück von Edenhall* (Uhland and Hasenclever), for soli, chorus and orchestra) (1853): 293.

[1] Arranged for piano solo and piano duet by the composer (1853).

PART-SONGS

(a) for female voices

Opus
69   Romanzen—I (1849): 287, 289.
91   Romanzen—II (1849): 289.

(b) for male voices
33   Sechs Lieder (1840).
62   Drei Gesänge (1847): 287.
65   Ritornelle¹ (Rückert) (1847): 287.
None   Solfeggios (1847).
(65)   Three Part-Songs, with wind-band *ad lib.* (1848): 287.
93   Motet for double chorus, *Verzweifle nicht* (Rückert) (1849); *ad lib.*
            organ part orchestrated in 1852): 287-8.
137   Jagdlieder (Laube), with four horns *ad lib.* (1849): 90, 287-8, 291.
None   Am Anfange (date unknown).

(c) for mixed voices

None   Der deutsche Rhein (Becker), with solo voice and piano (1840).
55   Fünf Lieder (after Burns) (1846).
59   Vier Gesänge² (1846).
None   Solfeggios (1847).
67   Romanzen und Balladen—I (1849).
75   Romanzen und Balladen—II (1849).
141   Vier doppelchörige Gesänge (1849).
145 (orig. 102) Romanzen und Balladen—III (1849–51).
146 (orig. 107) Romanzen und Balladen—IV (1849–51).

SOLO SONGS WITH PIANO³

None   Verwandlung (E. Schulze) (1827).
None   Lied für XXX (composer) (1827).
II   Eleven Songs (1827-8): 43-4, 98, 100.
            1. *Sehnsucht* (Ekert); 2. *Die Weinende* (after Byron); 3, *Der Fischer*
            (Goethe); 4. *Kurzes Erwachen* (Kerner); 5. *An Anna* ('Lange harrt'
            ich') (Kerner); 6. *Gesanges Erwachen* (Kerner); 7. *An Anna* ('Nicht
            im Thale') (Kerner) (used in Op. 11, see Piano Works); 8. *Im
            Herbste* (Kerner) (used in Op. 22, see Piano Works); 9. *Hirtenknabe*
            (Ekert) (used in Op. 4, No. 4, see Piano Works); 10. *Erinnerung*
            (Jacobi); 11. Klage (Jacobi) (unfinished).
None   Maultreiberlied (1838).

¹ An eighth number belonging to Op. 65 was published in *Die Musik*, Jg. V.
² A fifth song intended for this set was published about 1929–30.
³ Chronological order has been modified in this section for the sake of easier
reference.

Opus
24   *Liederkreis* (Heine) (1840): 100-2, 104-6, 121, 123, 131.
     1. *Morgens steh' ich auf*; 2. *Es treibt mich hin.*; 3. *Ich wandelte unter den Bäumen*; 4. *Lieb' Liebchen*; 5. *Schöne Wiege meiner Leiden*; 6. *Warte, warte, wilder Schiffsmann*: 7. *Berg und Burgen schau'n herunter*; 8. *Anfangs wollt' ich fast verzagen*; 9. *Mit Myrthen und Rosen.*

25   *Myrthen* (1840): 100, 102-4, 110, 113, 119-23, 125-6, 131-2, 136.
     1. *Widmung* (Rückert); 2. *Freisinn* (Goethe); 3. *Der Nussbaum* (J.Mosen); *Jemand* (after Burns); 5. *Sitz' ich allein* (Goethe); 6. *Setze mir nicht* (Goethe); 7. *Die Lotosblume* (Heine); 8. *Talismane* (Goethe); 9. *Lied der Suleika* (Goethe); 10. *Die Hochländer-Witwe* (after Burns); 11. *Mutter! Mutter!* (Rückert); 12. *Lass mich ihm am Busen hängen* (Rückert); 13. *Hochländers Abschied* (after Burns); 14. *Hochländers Wiegenlied* (after Burns); 15. *Mein Herz ist schwer* (after Byron); 16. *Rätsel* (Catherine Fanshawe); 17. *Leis' rudern hin* (after Thomas Moore); 18. *Wenn durch die Piazza* (after Moore); 19. *Hauptmanns Weib* (after Burns); 20. *Weit, weit* (after Burns); 21. *Was will die einsame Träne* (Heine); 22. *Niemand* (after Burns); 23. *Im Westen* (after Burns); 24. *Du bist wie eine Blume* (Heine); 25. *Aus den östlichen Rosen* (Rückert); 26. *Zum Schluss* (Rückert).

27   *Lieder und Gesänge*—I (1840): 100, 103, 106, 113, 121, 124.
     1. *Sag' an, o lieber Vogel mein* (Hebbel); 2. *Dem roten Röslein gleicht mein Lieb* (after Burns); 3. *Was soll ich sagen?* (Chamisso); 4. *Jasminenstrauch* (Rückert); 5. *Nur ein lächelnder Blick* (Zimmermann).

30   *Drei Gedichte* (Geibel) (1840): 100, 102, 203.
     1. *Der Knabe mit dem Wunderhorn*: 2. *Der Page*; 3. *Der Hidalgo.*

31   *Drei Gesänge* (1840): 100, 110-12.
     1. *Die Löwenbraut* (Chamisso); 2. *Die Kartenlegerin* (after Béranger); 3. *Die rote Hanne* (after Béranger).

35   *Zwölf Gedichte* (Kerner) (1840): 100-3, 109, 113, 120-1, 124-7, 136.
     1. *Lust der Sturmnacht*; 2. *Stirb, Lieb' und Freud'*; 3. *Wanderlied*; 4. *Erstes Grün*; 5. *Sehnsucht nach der Waldgegend*; 6. *Auf das Trinkglas eines verstorbenen Freundes*; 7. *Wanderung*; 8. *Stille Liebe*; 9. *Frage*; 10 *Stille Tränen*; 11. *Wer machte dich so krank?*; 12. *Alte Laute.*

36   *Sechs Gedichte* (Reinick) (1840): 100, 102-3, 110, 121, 130-2.
     1. *Sonntags am Rhein*; 2. *Ständchen*; 3. *Nichts schöneres*; 4. *An den Sonnenschein*; 5. *Dichters Genesung*; 6. *Liebesbotschaft.*

37   *Gedichte aus 'Liebesfrühling'* (Rückert) (1841): 100, 103, 113, 123.
     1. *Der Himmel hat eine Träne geweint*; 2. *Er ist gekommen*;[1] 3. *O ihr Herren*: 4. *Liebst du um Schönheit*;[1] 5. *Ich hab' in mich gesogen*; 6. *Liebste, was kann denn uns scheiden*; 7. *Schön ist das Fest des Lenzes*; 8. *Flügel! um zu fliegen*; 9. *Rose, Meer und Sonne*; 10. *O Sonn', o Meer, o Rose*; 11. *Warum willst du andre fragen*;[1] 12. *So wahr die Sonne scheinet.*

39   *Liederkreis* (Eichendorff) (1840): 100-3, 109, 114, 119-23, 128, 130, 132, 136.
     1. *In der Fremde* ('Aus der Heimath'); 2. *Intermezzo*; 3. *Waldesgespräch*; 4. *Die Stille*; 5. *Mondnacht*; 6. *Schöne Fremde*; 7. *Auf einer Burg*; 8. *In der Fremde* ('Ich hör' die Bächlein'); 9. *Wehmut*; 10. *Zwielicht*; 11. *Im Walde*; 12. *Frühlingsnacht.*

---

[1] Nos. 2, 4 & 11 are by Clara Schumann.

Opus

40   *Fünf Lieder* (1840): 100, 102, 120.
        1. *Märzveilchen* (Hans Andersen); 2. *Muttertraum* (Andersen);
        3. *Der Soldat* (Andersen); 4. *Der Spielmann* (Andersen); 5. *Ver-
        ratene Liebe* (Chamisso).

42   *Frauenliebe und -leben* (Chamisso) (1840): 100-1, 103-5, 122-3, 156,
        174, 196-7.
        1. *Seit ich ihn gesehen*; 2. *Er, der Herrlichste von allen*; 3. *Ich kann's
        nicht fassen*; 4. *Du Ring an meinem Finger*; 5. *Helft mir, ihr Sch-
        western*. 6. *Süsser Freund, du blickest*; 7. *An meinem Herzen*; 8. *Nun
        hast du mir den ersten Schmerz getan*.

45   *Romanzen und Balladen*—I (1840): 100, 102, 110, 120.
        1. *Der Schatzgräber* (Eichendorff); 2. *Frühlingsfahrt* (Eichendorff);
        3. *Abends am Strand* (Heine).

48   *Dichterliebe* (Heine) (1840): 65, 100, 102, 105-8, 119-24, 129, 131,
        136, 203, 225, 237.
        1. *Im wunderschönen Monat Mai*; 2. *Aus meinen Tränen spriessen*; 3.
        Die Rose, die Lilie; 4. *Wenn ich in deine Augen seh'*; 5. *Ich will
        meine Seele tauchen*; 6. *Im Rhein, im heiligen Strome*; 7. *Ich grolle
        nicht*; 8. *Und wüssten's die Blumen*; 9. *Das ist ein Flöten und Geigen*;
        10. *Hör' ich das Liedchen klingen*; 11. *Ein Jüngling liebt ein Mädchen*;
        12. *Am leuchtenden Sommermorgen*; 13. *Ich hab' im Traum geweinet*;
        14. *Allnächtlich in Traume*; 15. *Aus alten Märchen winkt es*; 16. *Die
        alten, bösen Leider*.

49   *Romanzen und Balladen*—II (1840): 100, 110, 112, 121-2, 166, 242.
        1. *Die beiden Grenadiere* (Heine); 2. *Die feindlichen Brüder* (Heine);
        3. *Die Nonne* (Fröhlich).

None   *Ein Gedanke* (Ferrand) (1840).

None   *Nächtliche Heerschau* (Zedlitz) (unfinished) (1840).

None   *Der Reiter und der Bodensee* (Schwab) (unfinished) (1840).

51   *Lieder und Gesänge*—II.
        1. *Sehnsucht* (Geibel) (1840); 2. *Volksliedchen* (Rückert): 3. *Ich
        wand're nicht* (Christern) (1841); 4. *Auf dem Rhein* (Immermann)
        (1846); 5. *Liebeslied* (Goethe).

53   *Romanzen und Balladen*—III (1840): 100, 102, 110-12.
        1. *Blondels Lied* (Seidl); 2. *Loreley* (Wilhelmine Lorenz); 3. *Der
        arme Peter* (Heine).
        (a) *Der Hans und die Grete*: (b) *In meiner Brust*: (c) *Der arme
        Peter wankt vorbei*.

57   *Belsatzar* (Heine) (1840): 100, 110-12.

64   *Romanzen und Balladen*—IV: 109-11, 132, 134-6.
        1. *Die Soldatenbraut* (Mörike) (1847); 2. *Das verlassene Mägdelein*
        (Mörike) (1847); 3. *Tragödie*[1] (Heine) (1841):
        (a) *Entflieh mit mir*: (b) *Es fiel ein Reif*: (c) *Auf ihrem Grab* (duet).

77   *Lieder und Gesänge*—III: 102, 113-14, 124.
        1. *Der frohe Wandersmann*[2] (Eichendorff) (1840); 2. *Mein Garten*
        (Fallersleben) (1850); 3. *Geisternähe* (Halm) (1850); 4. *Stiller
        Vorwurf* (anon) (1840); 5. *Aufträge* (L'Égru) (1850).

None   *Der weisse Hirsch* (sketches) (1848).

                    [1] Originally (1841) for chorus and orchestra.
                    [2] Originally published as Op. 39, No. 1.

Opus

79 *Liederalbum für die Jugend* (1849): 110, 115, 117-18, 132-3, 136.
1. *Der Abendstern* (anon); 2. *Schmetterling* (anon); 3. *Frühlings-botschaft* (anon); 4. *Frühlingsgruss* (anon); 5. *Vom Schlaraffenland* (anon); 6. *Sonntag* (anon); 7. *Zigeunerliedchen* (Geibel); 8. *Des Knaben Berglied* (Uhland); 9. *Mailied* (duet *ad lib.*) (anon); 10. *Das Käuzlein* ('Des Knaben Wunderhorn'); 11. *Hinaus in's Freie!* (Fallersleben); 12. *Der Sandmann* (Kletke); 13. *Marienwürmchen* ('Des Knaben Wunderhorn'); 14. *Die Waise* (Fallersleben); 15. *Das Glück* (Hebbel); 16. *Weihnachtslied* (after Andersen); 17. *Die wandelnde Glocke* (Goethe); 18. *Frühlingslied* (duet) (Fallersleben); 19. *Frühlingsankunft* (Fallersleben); 20. *Die Schwalben* (duet) (anon); 21. *Kinderwacht* (anon); 22. *Des Sennen Abschied* (Schiller); 23. *Er ist's* (Mörike); 24. *Spinnelied* (trio *ad lib.*) (anon); 25. *Des Buben Schützenlied* (Schiller); 26. *Schneeglöckchen* (Rückert); 27. *Lied Lynceus des Türmers* (Goethe); 28. *Mignon* (Goethe) (identical with Op. 98a, No. 1).

83 *Drei Gesänge* (1850).
1. *Resignation* (anon); 2. *Die Blume der Ergebung* (Rückert); 3. *Der Einsiedler* (Eichendorff).

87 *Der Handschuh* (Schiller): 110, 112.

89 *Sechs Gesänge* (von der Neun) (1850): 113, 124.
1. *Es stürmet am Abendhimmel*; 2. *Heimliches Verschwinden*; 3. *Herbstlied*; 4. *Abschied vom Walde*; 5. *In's Freie*; 6. *Röselein, Röselein*.

90 *Sechs Gedichte* (Lenau) (1850): 103, 118, 122, 124, 131.
1. *Lied eines Schmiedes*; 2. *Meine Rose*; 3. *Kommen und Scheiden*; 4. *Die Sennin*; 5. *Einsamkeit*; 6. *Der schwere Abend*. Appendix: 'Requiem' (after Héloïse?).

95 *Drei Gesänge (aus den Hebräischen Gesängen Byrons)* (after Byron) (1849): 101, 103, 123.
1. *Die Tochter Jephthas*; 2. *An den Mond*; 3. *Dem Helden*.

96 *Lieder und Gesänge—IV* (1850): 101, 113, 120, 124.
1. *Nachtlied* (Goethe): 2. *Schneeglöckchen* (anon); 3. *Ihre Stimme* (Platen); 4. *Gesungen* (Neun); 5. *Himmel und Erde* (Neun).

98a *Lieder und Gesänge aus 'Wilhelm Meister'* (Goethe) (1849): 102, 110, 118, 132, 135.
1. *Kennst du das Land?* (identical with Op. 79, No. 28); 2. *Ballade des Harfners*; 3. *Nur wer die Sehnsucht kennt*; 4. *Wer nie sein Brot mit Tränen ass*; 5. *Heiss mich nicht reden*; 6. *Wer sich der Einsamkeit ergibt*; 7. *Singet nicht in Trauertönen*; 8. *An die Türen will ich schleichen*; 9. *So lasst mich scheinen*.

104 *Sieben Lieder* (Elisabeth Kulmann) (1851): 117-19.
1. *Mond, meiner Seele Liebling*; 2. *Viel Glück zur Reise*; 3. *Du nennst mich armes Mädchen*; 4. *Der Zeisig*; 5. *Reich' mir die Hand*; 6. *Die letzten Blumen starben*; 7. *Gekämpft hat meine Barke.*

107 *Sechs Gesänge*: 102, 109, 119, 121, 131, 136.
1. *Herzeleid* (Ullrich) (1851); 2. *Die Fensterscheibe* (Ullrich) (1851); 3. *Der Gärtner* (Mörike) (1852); 4. *Die Spinnerin* (Heyse) (1852); 5. *Im Wald* (Wolfgang Müller) (1851); 6. *Abendlied* (Kinkel) (1851).

117 *Vier Husarenlieder* (Lenau) (1851).
1. *Der Husar, trara!*; 2. *Der leidige Frieden*; 3. *Den grünen Zeigern*; 4. *Da liegt der Feinde gestreckte Schaar.*

Opus

None *Fruhlingsgrüsse* (Lenau) (1851).

119 *Drei Gedichte* (Pfarrius) (1851).
  1. *Die Hutte*; 2. *Warnung*; 3. *Der Bräutigam und die Birke.*

125 *Fünf heitere Gesänge*: 102, 242.
  1. *Frühlingslied* (Braun) (1850); 2. *Frühlingslust* ('Jungbrunnen'
  anthology) (1850); 3. *Die Meerfee* (Buddeus) (1850); 4. *Jung Volkers
  Lied* (Mörike)¹ (1851): 5. *Husarenabzug* (1851) (Candidus) (1850).

127 *Fünf Lieder und Gesänge*; 105.
  1. *Sängers Trost* (Kerner) (1840); 2. *Dein Angesicht* (Heine) (1840);²
  3. *Es leuchtet meine Liebe* (Heine) (1840);² 4. *Mein altes Ross*
  (Strachwitz) (1850); 5. *Schlusslied des Narren* ('When that I was')
  (after Shakespeare) (1840).

135 *Gedichte der Königin Maria Stuart* (trans. Vincke) (1852): 130.
  1. *Abschied von Frankreich*; 2. *Nach der Geburt ihres Sohnes*; 3. *An
  die Königin Elisabeth*; 4. *Abschied von der Welt*; 5. *Gebet.*

142 *Vier Gesänge* (1840): 105.
  1. *Trost im Gesang* (Kerner): 2. *Lehn' deine Wang* (Heine);² 3.
  Mädchen-Schwermut (anon); 4. *Mein Wagen rollet langsam* (Heine).²

None *Soldatenlied* (Fallersleben).

None *Die Ammenuhr.*

None *Das Schwert.*

None *Glocktürmers Töchterlein.*

None *Der Reitersmann.*

WORKS FOR VOCAL ENSEMBLE WITH PIANO

29 *Drei Gedichte* (Geibel) (1840).

34 Four Duets, for soprano and tenor (1840): 34, 114, 131.

43 *Drei zweistimmige Lieder³* (1840).

74 *Spanisches Liederspiel* (Geibel) (1849): 102, 115-17.

78 Four Duets, for soprano and tenor (1849): 114-15.

None *Sommerruh* (duet) (Schad) (1849).

101 *Minnespiel* (Rückert) (1849): 114, 120.

138 *Spanische Liebeslieder⁴* (Geibel) (1849): 115-7.

103 *Mädchenlieder*, for two female voices (E. Kulmann) (1851): 115.

None *Liedchen von Marie und Papa* (unacc. duet) (Marie Schumann) (1852).

114 Three Songs, for three female voices (1853).

None *Die Orange und Myrte* (composer) (S.A.T.B.) (1853).

¹ Originally intended as Op. 107, No. 4.
² Originally intended for Op. 48.
³ No. 1, *Wenn ich ein Vöglein war'*, afterwards used in the opera *Genoveva.*
⁴ Originally with piano duet; Schumann made a later version with piano solo.

MELODRAMAS

Opus
106   *Schön' Hedwig* (Hebbel) (1849): 110, 264.
122   *Zwei Balladen*; 110, 112, 264.
  1. *Ballade vom Haideknaben* (Hebbel) (1853); 2. *Die Flüchtlinge* (after Shelley) (1852).

PIANO ACCOMPANIMENTS TO WORKS BY OTHER COMPOSERS

None To Six Solo Violin Sonatas by Bach (1853): 173-4.
None To Six Solo 'Cello Sonatas by Bach (1853): 173.
None To Paganini's Violin Caprices (1853-5): 28.